W9-CCP-747

The current values in this book should be used only as a guide. They are not intended to set prices, which vary from one section of the country to another. Auction prices as well as dealer prices vary greatly and are affected by condition as well as demand. Neither the Author nor the Publisher assumes responsibility for any losses that might be incurred as a result of consulting this guide.

Additional copies of this book may be ordered from:

Collector Books
P.O. Box 3009
Paducah, KY 42001

@ $19.95. Add $2.00 for postage and handling.

Copyright: George W. Johnson, 1987
Values Updated 1990

This book or any part thereof may not be reproduced without the written consent of the Author and Publisher.

Printed in Singapore by Singapore National Printers Ltd through Four Colour Imports, Ltd.

DEDICATION

To Melissa, George C., Bryan
and
the child within us all.

ABOUT THE PICTURES IN THIS BOOK

Photographs are a necessity in a catalogue of this type. There are several things that the reader needs to keep in mind while enjoying them.

Although I have endeavored to photograph the best examples possible, the pieces shown do not always represent ornaments in good or fine condition. In that sense, they are not meant to be any type of standard for pricing.

Because there are no absolutes in the way an ornament was painted or decorated, those portrayed in the pictures are only typical examples.

Whenever possible, pre-war ornaments have been used in the photographs. However, believing the old adage that "a picture is worth a thousand words", I have occasionally used post-war pieces. Having been blown in the old molds, these will be exactly like their antique counterparts unless noted otherwise in the text.

Included in the photographs you will find a scale for judging the relative size of the piece. Some use a penny which is a known standard, but most use a one-inch scale. For a more exact listing of the ornament's size, see the text.

TABLE OF CONTENTS

ACKNOWLEDGMENTS

A book of this nature is only possible with a great deal of assistance and support from others. I would like to thank the following collectors who not only gave of their time and knowledge, but have also generously shared their collections with you, the reader.

David K. Chenault
Richard Christen
George Davignon
Mary Flegle
Pam and Norm Framberg
Harold and Doris Hensley
George W. and Jean Ann Johnson
Mollie Johnson
Daryl and Barbara Koppes
Bob and Diane Kubicki
Siegfried and Pat Kurtz
Marie Miller
Emmory and Geraldine Prior
Madeline Smith
and several anonymous collectors.

In a multitude of varying ways, the following people were also instrumental in bring about this book.

Bob and Sallie Connelly
Ron Harvey
John L. Hutchison
Doris and Roy Isaacs
George B. and Martha Johnson
George and Mollie Johnson
Bruce and Shari Knight
Warner and Ruby Lehman
Mary Steed-May
Maxine Trippy
James Wells' family
Rebecca White
Debra Witik
the people at the "Christmas Cottage in the Lane" and an extra special thank you to my wife, Jean Ann, who typed all the drafts and manuscripts for this book more times than I care to count.

Photography by George W. Johnson, Siegfried Kurtz and George B. Johnson

FOREWORD

In the past five years, there has been a tremendous rise of interest in antique Christmas ornaments and collectibles. It now seems that there are collectors everywhere. Ornaments are some of the most sought after items at antique shows and flea markets, and several nationwide auctions have been devoted exclusively to them. But unlike other areas of collectibles, there are few sources of information on this fast growing hobby. There are articles in the trade magazines and tabloids every year around Christmas that talk about the history, beauty and collectibility of these family treasures of yesterday. However, there are few books on the subject and one of these, *Alter Christbaumschmuck* by Eva Stille, is in German. Two other excellent books, *The Christmas Tree Book* by Phillip Snyder and *The Glass Christmas Ornament* by Rogers and Hawkins, have helped to fill this information gap. A fourth book by Margaret Schiffer, *Christmas Ornaments*, is a photographic collection of many fine ornaments.

Snyder's book is an excellent history of the development and use of ornaments down through the years. Rogers' and Hawkins' book began to catalogue and price the **glass** ornament. I hope you find this work to be a pleasing combination of both a history and a price catalogue for a wide variety of different types of ornaments.

First and foremost, this is a book by collectors and for collectors. Many people have had an opportunity to input ideas and comments. For this, I am grateful, and I feel it will make this book that much more helpful to other collectors. There are three main goals I hope to accomplish by writing this book: to catalogue, to inform and to give price guidance.

Some time ago, when I first read Phillip Snyder's book, I became very intrigued by his statement that:

"Today only a very large collection of old ornaments can give an idea of the seemingly limitless number of molds that were made between the 1880s and 1939. There is no way of knowing how many different designs there may have been, though five thousand might serve as a conservative estimate."

As a collector, I was very interesting in finding as many of these "five thousand" ornaments as I could. This search was aided by the fact that whenever two ornament collectors get together, they will usually find items in each other's collection that neither has seen before.

Therefore, I felt it would be very useful to have a catalogue of as many different ornaments as possible. Realizing this is quite an undertaking, I hope there will be subsequent volumes in which I can add to the list of known ornaments and provide photographs of them.

In this same idea, I hope to note whenever possible, the past and current use of given ornament molds. This will help the collector to determine some of the following information:

1. The ornament is "old" (prior to 1940) and has not been reblown or reproduced in the last forty years.

2. The ornament and mold are "old", but "newer" ones have been reblown in the mold since 1940.

3. The ornament and mold have both been created and used since 1940.

Of course, many collectors are interested in a wider variety of ornaments than just the glass type. Therefore, this book will also catalogue and price paper, wax, metal, and fabric ornaments, as well as lights and other miscellaneous Christmas collectibles.

A second goal is to use this work as a medium through which collectors can share information and ideas. By doing this, I hope to standardize some of the terms and concepts used by collectors.

Finally, I hope to establish a fair and reasonably accurate price guide that takes into account regional price variances, but is, nevertheless, based on the country as a whole.

It is my sincere wish that you, the reader, find this book both informative and enjoyable.

CHAPTER I

A HISTORY OF THE DECORATED CHRISTMAS TREE

In a book that deals mainly with the ornaments that decorated the trees of yesteryear, it is only natural that it should include a discussion of the decorated tree itself and how it has evolved and changed throughout its long history.

Because the tree has been the center of the Christmas celebration for several generations, many people might believe that it is a venerable old tradition. But in fact the popularity and widespread use of the tree as we know it dates back only about 100 years or so. In its fully developed state, the decorated tree is a young tradition indeed. However, its roots are deep and lost in the swirling mists of time, since they are the fusing together of many diverse traditions. The vision of a candle-lit, ornament-decked tree creates a warm tapestry in the mind. But following the thread of its history as it weaves in and out to create that picture is not an easy task.

The use of greenery and plants for celebration goes back thousands of years to the ancient Egyptians. Then, as today, evergreens were seen as a symbol of everlasting life and a promise of the rebirth of nature in the spring. Very early in man's history, we find that the evergreen was given a place of prominence in his religious celebrations. In the Bible, for example, we find the prophet Isaiah commenting: "The glory of Lebanon shall come unto thee, the Fir-tree, the Pine tree and the Box tree together, to beautify the place of my sanctuary."

Indeed most ancient religions have trees connected with them. In the Bible we find the Tree of Life, the Burning Bush, and the Tree of Knowledge, which was also called the Tree of Paradise. As we shall see later, this Paradise Tree will play a significant role in the development of the decorated Christmas tree.

In the Norse religion, the ash tree, Yggdrasill, was connected with the beginning and end of the world as well as all the important events in man's life.

The Druids held the oak to be sacred; the Romans, the fig tree; and, on the other side of the world, the Chinese revered the willow. In other religions such as those of the Hindus, Assyrians, Greeks, Teutons and Buddhists, the tree played an important and sacred role. Let us now look at the specific use of evergreens and winter religious celebrations that pre-date the Christian holiday by many centuries.

The Romans used holly, mistletoe, fir, pine trees, boxwood, pine cones, rosemary, laurel, yew and juniper in their celebration of Saturnalia. Celebrated throughout the ancient world from December 17 to 24, Saturnalia was a holiday dedicated to Saturn, the god of agriculture. Houses and buildings were decorated with flowers and greenery. There were torch light processions, lighted candles, and gift giving -- especially to the children. There was a general cessation of warfare and strife as feasting, merrymaking and brotherly love ruled supreme.

In Rome and northern Europe, the Kalends, or New Year celebration, was an extension of the Saturnalia. It is recorded by Libanius:

"People are not only generous themselves, but also towards their fellowmen . . . a stream of presents pours itself out on all that is connected with toil, and allow men to give themselves up to undisturbed enjoyment. From the minds of young people it removes two kinds of dread: the dread of the schoolmaster and the dread of the stern pedagogue . . . another great quality of the festival is that it teaches men not to hold too fast to their money, but to part with it and let it pass into other hands."

This sounds strikingly like our Christmas celebrations today, and it too was celebrated with the use of decorated evergreens.

In the Mithraic religion of the ancient world, December 25 was celebrated as the feast day or birth of the unconquerable sun. This same idea was observed as the winter solstice by most of the world's ancient cultures.

Narrowing down the thread of history and the use of evergreens, we find the most direct links with today's decorated tree and customs in northern Europe.

In the pre-Christian religions of northern Europe, the winter celebration was given the name of Yule, which referred to the sun as the wheel of the year. Its celebration lasted for twelve days, from about the 21st of December to the first of January, and holly, mistletoe, pine and ivy played important roles in its decoration and traditions.

Santa Claus and his elves also have their roots in northern Europe. Santa is linked to the Norse god Thor, who with his peaked cap and long beard lived in the cold northern regions of the world. To ancient men, elves, dwarves, fairies and other spirits seemed to abound at this time of year. It was felt that these nature spirits could become troublesome pranksters during the long winter when they had nothing to do. So they were welcomed, placated, and soon found their way into our Christmas legends. Thus we can see that it is no coincidence that Santa has elves and fairies working for him. Considering those Christmas customs which deal with spirits from the "other world", it is also no coincidence that Charles Dickens included three ghosts or spirits in his immortal *A Christmas Carol*. Indeed, the telling of ghost stories at Christmas was a popular evening pastime throughout the Victorian period. On the darker side, the winter of the year also brought the trolls, goblins, and malicious spirits into the home. However, it was believed that evergreens, light, cleanliness, joy and celebrations of love would drive them back into the cold winter's night. Bringing in evergreens and greenery at Yule, by which it was believed the gloom and evil spirits of the season would be dispelled, became such an important part of the celebration in northern Europe that it became known as bringing home Christmas.

We have seen now certain customs, including the use of evergreens, and even the late December holidays in which they were used, far pre-date the current Christian uses. Now let us examine how the customs of the pagan and Christian were fused into one.

These early pagan traditions and beliefs were displeasing to the first Christian missionaries into northern Europe. However, they were hard to dislodge. Therefore, in the year 598 A.D., Pope Gregory the Great issued a Papal Bull which stated that the priests should continue to use these old customs and beliefs, but turn them to the "Praise of God."

This idea of blending the old and new had an earlier precedent when about the year 320 A.D., Christmas was officially assigned to the 25th of December. Francis Weiser in *The Christmas Book* explains:

"The Church in Rome definitely assigned December 25 for the celebration of the birth of Christ. For a while, many Eastern churches continued to keep other dates, but toward the end of the fourth century, the Roman custom became universal. The church did not, of course, rule that we know the precise date of Christ's birth, but merely assigned a certain day in order to unify the celebration of a religious feast of such importance. The fact that December 25 was chosen does not seem to rest so much on historical findings as in the desire to replace the popular pagan celebration of the winter solstice by the festivities of a truly Christian holiday."

Under Pope Gregory's directive, old and new traditions began to merge into one. Holly, for example, a sacred greenery from the ancient world, was at first banned by the church. Later it was reintroduced with the explanation that it was the plant from which Christ's crown of thorns had been made. It was said that the berries were originally yellow but that his sacred blood stained them red forever. The white blossoms of its tree were said to symbolize his purity.

Rosemary is another example of the Christianization of old traditions. In the ancient world, it was an herb sacred to the sun; it was believed to encourage pleasant memories and make the old young again. Because the plant remains green during the European winter, it has long been used as greenery and its aromatic smell has long been associated with Christmas. Its use was sanctioned in a legend which relates that its once white flowers were turned blue when the Virgin Mary laid the baby Jesus' clothes on them to dry during the family's flight to Egypt.

Slowly the old beliefs and traditions that once centered around the rebirth of the sun at the winter solstice, were transferred to the new light of the world -- the Christ Child.

During the Middle Ages, many of the Christmas traditions as we know them today were formalized. Among these was the Christmas tree tradition. In the 13th century, there was a movement to humanize religion and to bring it to the people in terms they could understand. This resulted in many of our present Christmas stories, legends, carols and plays. Representative of this movement, St. Francis of Assisi started the tradition of a living manger scene on Christmas Eve in 1223.

We find the most direct link with today's Christmas tree in the Paradise Tree of the medieval passion plays that were an outgrowth of this humanizing movement. The Church had established December 24 as the feast day of Adam and Eve. To celebrate this and to communicate the Biblical message of our first parents to an illiterate populace, the clergy established what was known as a passion play. At first, these plays were performed only by the clergy and were strictly religious. However, as the popularity of these plays grew, so did their crowds. Eventually they were moved to the church yard and then the town square; and with each change, the secular influence became stronger. These plays were held on the major religious holidays, with the Paradise play being held at Christmas time. During the performance, the only prop on the stage was an evergreen tree hung with red apples. It represented the Tree of Knowledge, and the evergreen was chosen because of the old beliefs of immortality associated with it, plus the fact that it was the only tree still green at that time of year. Soon people began to copy the popular paradise tree and place one in their own homes. These early trees were hung with apples and communion wafers as their only decoration. The apple, representing the fruit of sin, remembered December 24 as the Feast of Adam and Eve. The wafer represented the Fruit of Redemption brought by Jesus Christ on the 25th. Soon this tree, which was already a delight to children, would have added to its decorations, cookies and cakes in the shape of Adam and Eve, angels, flowers and the star of Bethlehem.

Although the Paradise tree had its roots in a pagan past, it was the first Christianized use of the decorated tree. We will find, however, that even late into the Middle Ages, the blending of Christian and pagan aspects was still taking place. For example, we find community trees set up for Christmas celebrations recorded as early as 1444 in Stow's *Survey of London*:

"Against the feast of Christmas, every man's house as also their parish churches, were decked with holme (holly) ivy, bayes, and whatsoever the season of the year afforded to be green. The conduits and standards in the streets were likewise garnished; among the which I read that, in the year 1444, by tempest of thunder and lightning, towards the morning of Candlemas Day, at the Leadenhall in Cornhill, a standard of tree, being set up in the midst of the pavement (roadway) faste in the ground, nailed full of holme and ivy, for disport of Christmas to the people, was torne up and cast down by the malignant spirit (as was thought) and the stones of the pavement all about were cast in the streets, and into divers houses, so that the people were sore aghast at the great tempest."

In 1510 and 1514, records show that community trees were set up in Riga and Revel, cities that are now part of western Russia. After dancing around the decorated trees, members of a local merchants guild then set them on fire. Both these trees and the one in Leadenhall, England, certainly show that strong pagan influences still remained. They had not totally blended with the more Christianized idea of the Paradise tree.

In 1516, we find that a Christmas pageant held for England's Henry VIII included a golden tree atop a hill of piled stones. The tree was decoratd with roses and pomegranates. From the 16th century onward, we find increasing references to Christmas being celebrated with decorated trees. However, festivities with decorated trees were already a part of European folk customs.

During the Medieval period, the wassail-bob was a favorite tradition in Yorkshire and Westmoreland, England. Small trees were fashioned out of holly and other Christmas greens. They were then decorated with apples, oranges, ribbons, and small wax figures of the Virgin Mary and baby Jesus. When fully decorated, they were carried from house to house by yuletide carolers. Indeed, the use of decorated trees throughout the year was an age-old folk custom. In Germany, we find trees decorated with paper, ribbon and pretzels carried about on Fastnacht. This was accompanied by songs designed to usher in the summer. The may-pole itself is a descendant of decorated trees. The Palm Bushes of southern Germany and the forester's "topping out" tree are also examples of trees that were decorated and used in celebrations throughout the year.

In 1521, five years after Henry VIII's golden tree, we find the first mention of an outdoor decorated tree in the Alsace region of Germany. Considered to be the birthplace of the decorated tree as we know it, this region has been in dispute for centuries by Germany and France. Unfortunately, there is no description of the ornamentation of this tree.

Such outdoor community trees set up by guilds, churches, nobles, etc., have continued to be popular down to the present. However, the first description of an **indoor** decorated tree, the true grandfather of our present custom, comes from Strasbourg, Germany, in 1605.

"At Christmas fir trees are set up in the rooms at Strasbourg and hung with roses cut from paper of many colors, apples, wafers, spangle-gold, sugar, etc. It is customary to surround it with a square frame . . . and in front . . ."

Unfortunately the manuscript was damaged and the rest of the description is lost to us. However, it is interesting to note that this tree shows the custom in advanced stages. It has moved into individual homes and the ornaments are quite elaborate. Therefore the custom was certainly well established by this time. In cases such as this, it is important to remember that the date indicates the first time the custom was recorded and certainly not the first time it occurred. As further proof of the custom prior to the 17th century, we find in Ammerschwelr, again in the Alsace region, a 1561 forest ordinance which states:

". . . no Burgher (citizen) shall have for Christmas more than one bush of more than eight shoe's length."

This shows that there was enough popularity, even at this time, that the forest needed to be conserved and protected against the tradition of taking holiday greens and Christmas trees.

Down through the years, we find many such ordinances and forestry regulations, both in Europe and America, that were designed to protect the limited natural resources of the countryside. As a result of this conservation effort, several alternatives to using a cut tree developed over the years. While some were merely substitutes for the cut and decorated tree, others were traditions in their own right. With the passing of the years, most of these customs have eventually blended and woven themselves into our current Christmas tree traditions. As a means of conservation, some household "trees" were merely large branches or tops cut out of bigger trees. Other families recycled the same tree for many years. After it had dried and the needles were removed, the branches were covered with cotton held on with white or silver thread to give them a snow covered effect. This tree was then stored in the attic or barn and reused for several years.

In the Franken region of Germany, the cut branches of fruit trees were brought indoors on "Barbara Day" or St. Andrew's Day in late November. They were placed into buckets of water and coaxed into bloom by Christmas. This practice was inspired by the stories and legends which spoke of the blooming of flowers and trees on Christmas Day. Indeed the Christmas Thorn, a tree in Glastonbury, England, did just that for many centuries. Cuttings from this famous tree have been planted at the National Cathedral in Washington, D.C.

In the northern part of Germany, we find the tradition of the Christmas pyramid. These pyramid shaped frames were often decorated with small pine branches, candles, and cards or paper crosses with Bible verses or religious poems. Later, shelves were added to the pyramid, and in this manner toys, small gifts and nativity scenes could be included. When candles were added, the name Lichtstock was applied to the pyramid. It is commonly believed that the idea for the candle-lit tree, which is also pyramidal in shape, came from this candle-lit pyramid.

For many years, the tree and pyramid have existed side by side. Today, these pyramids, equipped with delicate carvings and moving parts that are turned by the heat of the candles, are just as popular as they were with those past generations.

In another early and curious custom of Austria and southern Germany, "crown trees" or the tops of evergreens, were hung upside down in corners or over the doorways. They were then decorated with gilded fruit and paper. Some were hung upright with an apple stuck on the sharpened trunk.

The yule tree is another early northern German custom which seems to be a close relative of the decorated tree. This was an undecorated tree that was placed in the yard, entrance way or in the house itself. They were often dug out and placed in a tub instead of cut. Thus replanted, they could continue to grow in the home throughout the winter. As with other greens, the yule tree was thought to dispel the gloom of winter and be a reminder of the rebirth of nature in the spring. Such trees were often considered the ancestral trees or the home to the farm's guardian spirit (brownies, elves, etc.) and were thus of extreme importance. In later years, such things would merely be considered good luck. Yule trees were sold as late as 1531 in a Strasbourg, Germany, marketplace.

During the late Victorian period, one of the first artificial trees was introduced. In years past, creative households had created "trees" out of such things as pine limbs and broom handles with holes bored in them. But the "feather tree" as they became known, were the first commercially produced artificial trees. Goose or turkey feathers which had been dyed green were wrapped onto wire "branches". These in turn were fastened by wire into slots in the "trunk" which was made from a large dowel rod. The whole tree was then inserted into a heavy wooden base. The feather tree was often decorated with red plaster berries or small candle holders, and later versions came with built in light sockets. A rarer white feather tree was also produced.

Customs such as these not only helped conserve trees, they also provided a broader base of traditions which have eventually enriched the history of the decorated tree.

From the late 1700s to the late 1800s, the decorated tree went through a period of phenomenal growth and acceptance both in Europe and America. Probably more than anything else that helped spread the Christmas tree custom during this early growing period were two commonly believed legends about St. Boniface and Martin Luther. Whether based on historical fact or imaginative fantasy, these stories Christianized the custom of the tree and seemed to put the church's stamp of approval on it. Daniel J. Foley in *The Christmas Tree* quotes these two influential stories:

"In the twilight of the Victorian era, Henry Van Dyke wrote *The First Christmas Tree*, which records one of the oldest legends relating to the origin of the Christmas tree. This charming narrative, although little read today, tells how St. Boniface, earlier known as Wynfred, brought Christianity to Germany. Like so many of the early missionaries who went into strange lands to preach the Gospel, his was a life of hardship and privations.

"His early work among the German people brought him recognition from Pope Gregory II, but he returned to his adopted country to find that the eldest son of the Chieftain Gundhar was to be sacrificed to the gods on Christmas Eve. A giant oak, sacred to their patron Thor, was to be the scene of the sacrifice. Boniface decided to destroy this pagan symbol in order to prove that the pagan deity was powerless. After one stroke with the axe, a wind toppled the mighty oak. The assembled throng was awed by what happened and asked Boniface for the word of God. Pointing to an evergreen which grew nearby he replied: 'This is the word, and this is the counsel. Not a drop of blood shall fall tonight, for this is the birth-night of the Saint Christ, Son of the All-Father and Savior of the world. This little tree, a young child of the forest, shall be a home tree tonight. It is the wood of peace, for your houses are built of fir. It is the sign of endless life, for its branches are ever green. See how it points toward Heaven! Let this be called the tree of the Christ-Child; gather about it, not in the wild woods but in your homes; there it will shelter no deeds of blood, but loving gifts and lights of kindness.'

"The wood of the fallen oak was used to build a little monastery and a church dedicated to Saint Peter. The fir tree was cut, taken to Gundhar's great hall, and set up for the observance of Christmas. This, according to the legend, was the first Christmas tree.

"Another greatly loved and widely told story about the origin of the Christmas tree refers to Martin Luther. It is related that after wandering about on Christmas Eve under a bright clear sky illuminated by countless stars, he returned home and set up a tree for his children. He lighted the little evergreen with numerous candles to impress his children with the true meaning of Christ, the Light of the World, who had so gloriously brightened the sky on that Christmas Eve. Since there is no documented record for this story, it has been relegated to the realm of tradition, but it could have happened. In fact, it might have transpired even though it was not recorded. Whatever the facts, the story lives on and gives color and meaning to the ever-growing garland of Christmas tree traditions."

Certain religious denominations embraced or accepted the decorated tree more readily than others, and indeed some even encouraged its use. The Episcopal, Moravian and Catholic Churches observed Christmas celebrations and many of its oldest customs. However, the most noteable was the Lutheran Church. Their acceptance was certainly enhanced by the already mentioned legend of Martin Luther and the first Christmas tree. Their congregations were quick to introduce the customs and traditions of Christmas wherever they migrated. In those areas and communities of Europe and America, where this denomination was prevalent, we find widespread acceptance and use of the decorated tree. Trees were often set up in both the Sunday school classrooms and the church itself, and many Christmas programs centered around them.

However, such celebrations were shunned by the Puritans, Methodists, Baptists, Quakers, Presbyterians, Mennonites and Amish as being frivolous and pagan. In fact, the New England Puritans had a law which fined anyone found celebrating Christmas in any way, five shillings. Indeed, members of their faith were expected to work even harder than usual on Christmas day. Even our beloved Christmas carols did not appear in many of these church hymnals until after the 1860s.

As we continue to follow the interwoven history of the decorated tree from the 16th to the 20th centuries, the frequency and quality of the descriptions increase. Therefore, it is probably best fo follow this recorded history in chronological order.

1444 - In this year, Stow's *Survey of London* describes a community tree. It is most likely related to the Yule tree custom, and was set up in the roadway of Leadenhall (quote previously given).

1510 - Riga, in Latvia, records show that members of a local merchants guild set up a tree decorated with paper roses in the town square. After dancing around it, the tree was burned.

1514 - In Reval, a city in Estonia, the same practice of decorating and burning the tree was observed.

1516 - During this Christmas season, a golden tree decorated with roses and pomegranates was set up for a Henry VIII court pageant.

1521 - A decorated community tree was set up in the German region of Alsace during this year.

1531 - "Yule" trees are recorded as being sold in the Strasbourg, a city in the Alsace region of Germany, marketplace. As with other yule trees, these were set up in the home but left undecorated as far as we can tell.

1561 - A forest ordinance in Ammerschwelr sets strict limits on the cutting of trees for Christmas.

1590 - Glassmaking begins in Lauscha, Germany, the future ornament capital of the world. However, at this time, their products were almost strictly utilitarian. In 1597, their first cooperative glass factory was built.

1597-1669 - Turkheim, a prosperous city in the upper Alsace region, was setting up a decorated tree in their guild hall during these years. The quartermaster bills show payments for apples, wafers, colored paper and thread used in decorating the guild hall's tree. Doubtless, it had started earlier and had become a custom by 1597.

1602 - The German writer, Balthasar Beck, in a type of travel log, describes the trees in his home town of Schlettstadt. The city, again the Alsace region which has been considered the birthplace of the Christmas tree, had fir bushes or trees decorated with light baked goods and apples.

1605 - For the Christmas season of 1605, we find the first record of a decorated indoor tree in Strasourg, Germany, (quoted previously).

1642 - By this year, the custom of the decorated tree was becoming so popular in Strasbourg that the minister Johann Konrad Dannhauer spoke against it, "Besides the trifles with which people celebrate the old Christmas time, more than with God's word, is the Christmas tree or fir tree, which one puts up in the house, and hangs it full of dolls and sugar."

1658 - The first mention of candles on a tree come from this year when the Countess of Orleans, Liselotte of Pfulz, had a candle-lit box tree as part of her childhood Christmas. However, it would not be until 1708 that it was recorded when the Countess wrote the description for one of her own daughters: "Tables are fixed up like altars and outfitted for each child with all sorts of things, such as new clothes, silver, dolls, sugar candy, and so forth. Boxwood trees are set on the tables, and a candle is fastened to each branch." The lighted tree seemed to have its birth and growth in the upper class circles while the rural area folk continued the tradition of the lighted Christmas pyramids.

1700s - During this century, the tree begins to move out of the guild halls and public places to become part of the home traditions. The popularity of the decorated tree began to increase especially in those areas of Germany where the Lutheran Church predominated. The Catholic and rural areas were slower to adopt the custom.

1737 - Records show that by this year, candle-lit trees, decorations and gifts were becoming popular in the German university city of Wittenburg. Karl Kissling remarks that a lady of his acquaintance had a small candle-lit tree for each of her children.

1740 - Candles, gilt nuts, sheep, dishes, dolls, fruit, cookies and figures of the Christ Child decorated a tree in Nassau.

1744 - *The Sorrows of Young Wether*, written by Goethe, describes a tree "with fruits and sweets lighted up with wax candles."

1747 - The Moravian Church in Bethlehem, Pennsylvania, set up a candle-lit pyramid covered with evergreens, apples and biblical verses.

1755 - Forestry laws passed in this year for Salsburg, Germany, forbade the cutting of small evergreens from the forest, thus indicating that the tree's increasing popularity was putting a strain on the natural resources of the area.

1757 - The decorated evergreen had become so popular in Strasbourg, Germany, that Johann Dannhauer in his book, *The Milk of the Catechism*, condemns them: "When comes the custom, I know not; it's child's play . . . Far better were it to point the children to the cedar tree - Jesus Christ."

1775-1781 - There are several legends involving the Hessian soldiers (German mercenaries) and Christmas trees during the time period of the American Revolution. Probably the most famous was the one which involved the battle of Trenton. Supposedly, George Washington surprised the German soldiers on Christmas 1776 while they were celebrating around a Christmas tree. There is no documentation to support the legend. However, it is very likely that the German troops did indeed bring this tradition with them from their homeland. They were from a region in Germany where the custom had been popular. It is also likely that they helped spread the custom to the American families with whom they were billeted during the war.

1795 - Eva Stille quotes the "Simplizanisch Calendar" of Nurnburg for this year as describing a decorated tree of that city: "First I want to describe to you a Christmas tree, the likes of which you have never seen in your life, and the wonder of it you can hardly imagine. You must know ahead of time, that we here in our area have the praiseworthy custom, every year shortly before Christmas to bring a variety of trees, such as cherry, apple, elder and others, into the house and put them in a pot or a support with water which then usually bloom at the time of Christmas, which no one can deny is a very beautiful sight.

"It stood in the middle of a corner of the room and its branches were so broad, that they covered almost half of the ceiling of the room and one stood under them as under summer leaves. In all of the branches hung all kinds of delicious confectionary and sweets such as angels, dolls, animals and the like, all out of sugar, which was very harmonious with the blossoms of the tree. There also hung gilded fruit of all kinds and in great quantities so that when one stood under the tree, it was like being in a larder; and it is just too bad that ham and bratwurst (of which I am a great connoisseur) and collared pork, ox feet, and roasted dove, did not also hang on it. In the middle of this 'warehouse' was the Holy spirit in its usual configuration, as a beautiful dove out of sugar, to the right hung the Christ Child, and to the left its mother, very pretty to look at and both out of sugar, so that I would have loved to eat them both, the Virgin Mary and her child, if it had been permitted. Finally the whole tree with all of its branches and fruit, was covered with a golden net that was artistically prepared from many thousands of gilded hazelnuts arranged on strings and decorated with garlands like a chandelier. Between all of these objects of value were lit an innumerable quantity of wax lights, like stars in the heavens, which was a splendid sight."

When full of gifts or edibles such as this example, the tree was also known as a sugar tree, gift tree, glutton tree, or raisin tree. Trees such as this belonged to the wealthy upper class and certainly were not common in the average home.

1798 - Samuel T. Coleridge sent a letter to an English friend describing the tree custom in northern Germany: "On the evening before Christmas Day, one of the parlours is lighted up by the children, into which the parents must not go; a great yew bough is fastened on the table at a little distance from the wall, a multitude of little tapers are fixed in the bough, but not so as to burn it till they are nearly consumed, and coloured paper, etc., hangs and flutters from the twigs. Under this bough the children lay out in great order the presents they mean for their parents, still concealing in their pockets what they intend for each other. Then the parents are introduced, and each presents his little gift; they then bring out the remainder one by one, from their pockets, and present them with kisses and embraces. Where I witnessed this scene there were eight or nine children, and the elder daughter and the mother wept aloud for joy and tenderness; and the tears ran down the face of the father, and he clasped all his children so tight to his breast, it seemed as if he did it to stifle the sob that was rising within it. I was very much affected. The shadow of the bough and its appendages on the wall, and the arching over on the ceiling, made a pretty picture."

1800-1850 - The tradition of a decorated tree was introduced and carried out by the Lutheran church in many German and Pennsylvania Dutch settlements. The number of accounts of its use in America and England steadily grew during these years. Like their German counterparts, early American trees were decorated with cookies, candles, fruits - both natural and gilded - and homemade paper items such as candy holders, cornucopias, and Jacob's ladders. The custom of the decorated tree spread the fastest in regions settled by German immigrants, Pennsylvania and Minnesota are good examples. The southern regions such as Virginia and the Carolinas carried on the traditional English customs of feasting and decorating with greenery. Puritan New England was slow to adopt any Christmas customs.

1804 - A tree was set up on the frontier at Fort Dearborn, Michigan, by a Captain Whistler.

1807 - Jerome Bonepart, King of Westphalia and Napoleon's brother, set up a tree decorated with property deeds which he handed out to his court favorites.

1811 - Charles Dickens was born. His later writings would help to popularize the tree and many other Christmas customs.

1819-1820 - A drawing in the Henry Francis du Pont Winterthur museum by J. L. Krimmel from this period shows a Philadelphia family gathered around a small decorated tree.

1819 - Dr. John Watking writes about the late 18th century Christmas celebrations of the English King George III and Queen Charlotte. Best remembered as being king during the American Revolution, George was a German by birth and celebrated Christmas with this custom of a decorated tree: "Sixty poor families had a substantial dinner given them; and in the evening the children of the principal families in the neighbourhood were invited to an entertainment at the Lodge. Here, among other amusing objects for the gratifications of the juvenile visitors, in the middle of the room stood an immense tub with a yew tree placed in it, from the branches of which hung bunches of sweetmeats, almonds, and raisins in papers, fruits, and toys, most tastefully arranged, and the whole illuminated by small wax candles."

1820s - During these years Lauschan glass blowers began blowing large glass balls, or kugels, for their own amusement. However, it would not be until 1848 that we find the first **recorded** order for them as Christmas ornaments.

1821 - On December 20, Matthew Zahm of Lancaster County, Pennsylvania, shows the first recorded cutting of Christmas trees in the United States: "Sally and our Thomas and William Hensel was out for Christmas trees, on the hill at Kendrick's Saw Mill."

1822 - On December 23, Clement Moore wrote his immortal "A Visit From St. Nicholas", later retitled "The Night Before Christmas". He had written it for his children and never intended it to be published, but it was printed the next year in the *Troy Sentinel*. Although it was printed and reprinted, it was not until 1844 that Moore was given credit for his poem. Interestingly enough, there is no decorated tree mentioned in the poem.

1825 - The December 10 edition of the *Saturday Evening Post* quotes " . . . trees visible through the windows (of Philadelphia), whose green boughs are laden with fruit, richer than the golden apples of the Hesperides, or the sparkling diamonds that clustered on the branches in the wonderful cave of Aladdin."

1832 - It is a popular belief that Prince Albert, Queen Victoria's husband, brought the custom of the decorated tree from his native Germany and set up the first royal tree in 1841. As we have already noted, both Henry VIII and George III had much earlier versions of the decorated tree. Furthermore, we find the tree was nothing new to Queen Victoria herself. A thirteen-year-old Victoria records in her diary a tree which was put up by her Aunt Sophia in 1832: "After dinner we went upstairs. Aunt Sophia came also. We went into the drawing-room near the dining room. There were two large round tables on which were placed the trees hung with lights and sugar ornaments. All the presents be-

ing placed around the tree. I had one table for myself and the Conroy family had the other together."

We also find the earliest reports of decorated trees in Boston, Massachusetts. Belonging to Charles Follen, it had been for many years considered the first tree set up in America. It was described in a penny pamphlet by Harriet Martineau in this manner: "I was present at the introduction into the new country of the spectacle of the German Christmas tree. My little friend Charley (Follen's son) and three companions had been long preparing for this pretty show. The cook had broken eggs carefully in the middle for some weeks past, that Charley might have the shells for cups; and these cups were gilded and coloured very prettily. We were all engaged in sticking on the last seven dozen of wax tapers, and in filling the gilded egg-cups and gay paper cornucopiae with comfits, lozenges, barley sugar. The tree was the top of a young fir, planted in a tub, which was ornamented with moss. Smart dolls and other whimsies glittered in the evergreen, and there was not a twig which had not something sparkling upon it.

"It really looked beautiful; the room seemed in a blaze, and the ornaments were so well hung on that no accident happened, except that one doll's petticoat caught fire. There was a sponge tied to the end of a stick to put out any supernumerary blaze, and no harm ensued. I mounted the steps behind the tree to see the effect of opening the doors. It was delightful. The children poured in, but in a moment every voice was hushed. Their faces were upturned to the blaze, all eyes wide open, all lips parted, all steps arrested. Nobody spoke, only Charley leaped for joy. The first symptom of recovery was the children's wandering around the tree. At last, a quick pair of eyes discovered that it bore something eatable, and from that moment the babble began again. I have little doubt the Christmas tree will become one of the more flourishing exotics of New England."

1836 - Alabama became the first state to make Christmas a legal holiday.

1838 - Arkansas and Louisiana became the second and third states to make Christmas a legal holiday.

1840s - During this period, the German village of Lauscha began making blown glass Christmas ornaments.

1840 - Phillip Snyder sites a community tree set up in York, Pennsylvania. It was advertised to the public in this manner: "Christmas Tree. For the amusement of the ladies and Gentlemen of York, and its vicinity, GOODRIDGE, will exhibit at his residence, in East Philadelphia Street, a CHRISTMAS TREE, the exhibition of which will commence on Christmas Eve, and continue, Sunday excepted, until New Year. Tickets to be had at his store."

1841 - England's Prince Albert set up an eight foot decorated tree at Windsor Castle for his son's first Christmas. Albert was from the Saxe-Coburg area of Germany, a region which was rich in the tree tradition. Seven years later, in 1848, the *Illustrated London News* printed a full page engraving of the tree and this description.

"On each tier, or branch, are arranged a dozen wax tapers. Pendent from the branches are elegant trays, baskets, bonbonnieres, and other receptacles for sweetmeats, of the most varied and expensive kind, and of all forms, colours, and degrees of beauty. Fancy cakes, gilt gingerbread and eggs filled with sweetmeats, are also suspended by variously-coloured ribbons from the branches.''

On top was a "Nurmburg" angel with arms outstretched and holding a small wreath in each hand.

As we have seen, this certainly was not the first English tree, but it was the one with the most impact. The time was right, and it caught the imagination of Englishmen of all social classes who then sought to emulate their beloved royal family. Two years later, in 1850, a slightly modified version of the *Illustrated London News'* engraving of the royal family at their tree appeared in America's *Godey's Lady's Book*. This caused much the same reaction as Americans too sought to follow the royal trend-setters.

1842 - In Williamsburg, Virginia, Charles Minnigerode, a teacher at the College of William and Mary, set up a decorated tree for Judge Nathaniel Tucker's family for the year's Christmas celebration. It was decorated with candles, nuts, popcorn and colored paper. They were so impressed that the judge set one up every year thereafter.

Also in this year, the *Kriss Kringle's Book* was published. It helped to popularize many customs.

1845 - The *Kringle's Christmas Tree* book was published. It helped to popularize not only the concept of Santa but also the fast-spreading custom of the decorated tree. The following is from the introduction of this book: "Fashions change, and of late Christmas Trees are becoming more common than in former times. The practice of hanging up stockings in the chimney corner for Kriss Krinkle to fill with toys, pretty books, bon-bons, etc., for good children, and rods for naughty children, is being superseded by that of placing a Christmas Tree on the table to await the annual visit of the worthy Santa Klaus. He has, with his usual good nature, accommodated himself to this change in the popular taste; and having desired a literary gentleman to prepare his favourite Christmas present in accordance with this state of things, the following volume is the result of the new arrangement, and all parents, guardians, uncles, aunts, and cousins, who are desirous to conform to the most approved fashion, will take care to hang one, two, or a dozen copies of the book on their Christmas Tree for 1847.''

Also during this year a painting by Carl A. Schwerdgeburth, of Martin Luther and his family around a candle-lit tree, gave new life to the Martin Luther and the first Christmas tree legend. As a result, the popularity of the tree grew, especially in Lutheran areas.

1846 - Reports of Christmas trees set up in Texas by German farmers. By the 1860s, decorated trees would be found throughout the West.

1847 - August Imgard set up the first tree in Wooster, Ohio.

1848 - The first record of commercially produced and sold glass ornaments was noted. "Six dozen of Christmas tree ornaments in three sizes,'' were ordered from a Lauchan glass blower. By 1889, ornament-making would become the city's chief business.

This year also saw large quantities of trees for sale in the Christmas markets of Philadelphia.

1850-1900 - During this time period, the tradition of the decorated tree, its roots firmly established in a venerable past, began its most rapid growth. During these years it became an almost universal custom in the western world. Popularized by English royalty and ladies magazines both in Europe and America, decorating the tree became a family tradition. During this same period,

the industrial revolution and the social desire for manufactured goods gave impetus to the birth and growth of the German ornament business.

1850 - A lighted and decorated tree was set up for the famous singer, Jenny Lind, while she visited Charleston, South Carolina. It was lit by tumbler-like fairy lamps.

Harriet B. Stowe, author of *Uncle Tom's Cabin*, gives this description of a tree in 1850: "Our Christmas tree was a fine spruce and when it sat on the table it touched the wall, and I made four gilt stars for the four top branches, and ma dressed a little doll like a fairy in white with gilt spangles & a gilt band around her head with a star on the end & gause (sic) wings spangled with gold. She was placed in the tree with her wand pointing to the presents on it & there was no end to the gilt apples and nuts etc.''

1851 - The first reported use of a decorated tree in an American church. It was set up by Reverend Henry Schwan, himself a German immigrant, in Cleveland, Ohio. His congregation was **not** pleased.

Also, Mark Carr began bringing large quantities of trees into New York City to sell at the Washington Market. This market grew so tremendously that by 1880, it was estimated that 200,000 trees were for sale in that one New York market alone.

1855 - Charles Dickens wrote *The Christmas Tree*, based on memories of his childhood trees. The following is a quote from it: "I have been looking on, this evening, at a merry company of children assembled round that pretty German toy, a Christmas Tree. The tree was planted in the middle of a great round table, and towered high above their little heads. It was brilliantly lighted by a multitude of little tapers; and everywhere sparkled and glittered with bright objects. There were rosy-cheeked dolls, hiding behind the green leaves; there were real watches (with moveable hands, at least, and an endless capacity of being wound up) dangling from innumerable twigs; there were French-polished tables, chairs, bedsteads, wardrobes and eight-day clocks, and various other articles of domestic furniture (wonderfully made, in tin, at Wolverhampton), perched among the boughs, as if in preparation for some fairy housekeeping; there were jolly, broad-faced little men, much more agreeable in appearance than many real men -- and no wonder, for their heads took off, and showed them to be full of sugar-plums; there were fiddles and drums; there were tambourines, books, work-boxes, paintboxes, sweetmeat-boxes, peep-show boxes, all kinds of boxes; there were trinkets for the elder girls, far brighter than any grown-up gold and jewels; there were baskets and pin-cushions in all devices; there were guns, swords, and banners; there were witches standing in enchanted rings of pasteboard, to tell fortunes; there were tee-totums, humming-tops, needle-holders; real fruit, made artificially dazzling with gold leaf; imitation apples, pears, and walnuts, crammed with surprises; in short, as a pretty child, before me, delightedly whispered to another pretty child, her bosom friend, 'There was everything, and more.' This motley collection of odd objects, clustering on the tree like magic fruit, and flashing back the bright looks directed towards it from every side -- some of the diamond-eyes admiring it were hardly on a level with the table, and a few were languishing in timid wonder on the bosoms of pretty mothers, aunts and nurses -- made a lively realization of the fancies of childhood; and set me thinking how all the trees that grow and all the things that come into existence on the earth, have their wild adornments at that well-remembered time."

1856 - The first decorated tree appeared in the White House, set up by President Franklin Pierce, and it became more or less a tradition thereafter.

1857 - Glass workers in Bohemia developed the silver-nitrate solution with which the inside of ornaments are given their mirror finish. This was used in beads which were popular clothing decorations of the period. This almost put the German glass workers in Lauscha out of business until Louis Greiner-Schlotfeger successfully duplicated the secret formula. By 1870 it was universally used in silvering ornaments.

1860 - A story by Lizzie McIntyre which appeared in *Godey's Lady's Book* gives the description of a tree of that year: "The square of green baize being tacked down, a large stone jar was placed in the middle of it, and in this the tree stood nobly erect. Damp sand was put around the stem till the large green tree stood firmly in place. A flounce of green chintz round the jar concealed its stony ugliness, and over the top, round the tree, was a soft cushion of moss. It was a large evergreen, reaching almost to the ceiling, for all the family presents were to be placed upon it. This finished, the process of dressing commenced. From a basket in the corner, Marion drew long strings of bright red holly berries, threaded like beads upon fine cord. These were festooned in graceful garlands from the boughs of the tree. While Marion was thus employed, Grace and the Doctor arranged the tiny tapers. This was a delicate task. Long pieces of fine wire were passed through the taper at the bottom, and these clasped over the stem of each branch, and twisted together underneath. Great care was taken that there should be clear space above each wick, that nothing might catch fire.

Strings of bright berries, small bouquets of paper flowers, strings of beads, tiny flags of gay ribbons, stars and shields of gilt paper, lace bags filled with colored candies, knots of bright ribbons, all homemade by Marion's and Grace's skillful fingers, made a brilliant show at a trifling cost, the basket seemed possessed of unheard-of capacities, to judge from the multitude and variety of articles the sisters drew from it.

Meantime, upon the wick of each little taper the Doctor rubbed with his finger a drop of alcohol to insure its lighting quickly. This was a process he trusted to no one else, for fear the spirit might fall upon some part of the tree not meant to catch fire. At last, all the contents of the basket were on the tree and then the more important presents were brought down from an upper room. There were many articles seemingly too clumsy for the tree, but Marion passed around them gay colored ribbons, till they formed a basket work and looped them over the branches until even Hester's workbox looked graceful. Dolls for each of the little girls were seated on the boughs, and a large cart for Eddie, with two horses prancing before it, drove gaily amongst the top branches, as if each steed possessed the wings of Pegasus. On the moss beneath the branches, Marion placed a set of wooden animals for Eddie, while from the top-most branch was suspended a gilded cage ready for the canary bird Dr. Gratley had purchased for the pet-loving Lizzie.

Various mysterious packages wrapped in paper and marked Grace, Marion, or Papa were put aside that all the delicious mystery of Christmas might be preserved. At length, all was ready, and carefully locking the doors, the trio went up to their respective rooms."

1863 - The first of the famous Thomas Nast cartoons appeared. This helped develope the jolly old Santa figure known in America today. He is distinctly different from the slender, old, and often sad-looking, Father Christmas, Weihnachtsman or St. Nicholas of Europe.

1864 - Neighborhood tree trims and "public trees" were a social function of this period. Neighborhood trees were often set up in Sunday schools, churches and other public buildings. They were used by the entire community and were sometimes even used for family gift exchanges.

"Public trees" were usually set up in private homes, but were open for viewing by the public for the cost of a modest admission fee.

1865 - *Demorest's Illustrated Monthly* encourages housewives to keep the spirit of Christmas by, among other things, having a tree: "Brighten your house, open your heart, hang wreaths and branches of evergreen upon the walls. Fill your children's stockings, and have a Christmas-tree for your friends and neighbors. Shut not your door in the face of Christ, but let him see your willingness at least acknowledge his existence and the influence of his birth, teachings, and character . . ." It also quotes "There is no holiday in the year which is thought of so much, or around which so many pleasant associations cling. Churches celebrate it as well as families throughout the country, and hardly a schoolhouse, even in the wilds of the distant West, but now has its annual Christmas tree."

Women's magazines of the mid to late 1800s played a major role in spreading the custom of the decorated tree, both in Europe and America. In the 1850s, these magazines ran articles on and descriptions of the novel German tree. By the 1870s-1880s, they were discussing how to set up and decorate a tree of your own. Finally, by the 1880s-1890s, the articles talked about the tree as though it were an age-old and universal custom. Most of the holiday issues were filled with decorating ideas for the home and church as well as do-it-yourself patterns for ornaments and gifts. Periodicals like *Godey's Lady's Book*, *Peterson's Ladies National Magazine* and *Ladies Home Journal*, all published in Philadelphia, were leaders in the Americanization of the decorated Christmas tree. Many other authors and newspapers so praised the tree throughout this period that they encouraged its rapid acceptance by all social classes.

1867 - The counterweighted candle holder was developed by Charles Kirchhof of Newark, New Jersey.

A gas works was built in Lauscha, Germany, which would allow paper-thin glass ornaments to be blown over the steady flame it provided.

1869 - *Harper's Bazaar* gives us a glimpse of early glass ornaments with this description: " . . . the snow-clad veteran, Santa Claus, his bag emptied of its treasures with which he has adorned the tree; globes, fruits, and flowers of colored glass, bright tin reflectors, and innumerable grotesque figures suspended by a rubber string. There were clowns with cap and bells, funny little men concealing their faces behind funnier masks, as they spring up and down; Bismarck leaping up Napoleon's shoulders, exaggerated seraphim with flapping wings, and strange-looking old women with heads larger than their bodies."

1870s - During this decade, trees were still uncommon enough that many newspapers felt it was newsworthy to mention who in town had one. Accounts from this time period steadily increased in local papers.

During this time period, the ornament business in Lauscha and Sonneburg begins its rapid growth into the largest in the world.

1870 - Louis Greiner-Schlotfeger is generally given credit for developing the molded Christmas ornament.

1870-71 - Even in Germany, the decorated tree was not universal at this time. However, the Franco-Prussian War of 1870-71 helped to spread it throughout the countryside. The war brought German soldiers of many regions and social classes together. The decorated tree received a great boost to its widespread popularity when the soldiers returned to their homes and brought with them the beauty of the candle-lit tree. This custom was further enhanced by the idea that the Kaiser had celebrated Christmas with a candle-lit tree. World War I could again bring together soldiers from all areas of Germany and complete the spread of the custom throughout that country.

1871 - William DeMuth of New York advertised some of the first American-made glass ornaments. He produced glass balls and chains of beads for the American market.

Germany was united into one country in 1871 and this political and economic security, coupled with rapid industrial, political and economic growth, gave a boost to the ornament business. Nothing exists in a vacuum: the birth and growth of the ornament business was related to the birth and growth of the German nation.

1874 - The following is a description of a decorated tree from the *Muncy Luminary* (Muncy, Pennsylvania) for the year 1874: "The size of the Christmas tree depends on the number of presents it is to be laden with. For a Sunday-School one or sometimes two trees of quite large size are procured. They may be of pine, hemlock, cedar, arbor vitae, or spruce; any evergreen of suitable shape will answer the purpose. The tree is usually set in a box and firmly fastened in place, the box is covered with white paper or muslin, prettily decorated with greenery, and serves as a resting place for presents too heavy to be hung on the tree. Popcorn strung may be gracefully twined in festoons on the tree; ornamental balls of various colors of shiny surface come on purpose for decoration; also small wax candles with tin candlesticks which are fastened to the tree with wire; also miniature flags, cornucopias of brilliant tints and filled with candies are pleasing to the children. Eggs from which the contents have been carefully removed may be covered with bits of gilt paper cut from the band of envelopes, with flowers or fancy shapes cut out of calico or silk or any highly colored material and pasted on - these suspended from the limbs add beauty to the tree. Red and scarlet apples look well. The presents are labeled with the name of the persons for whom they are intended and hung upon the tree. The distribution takes place after the feast which it crowns and closes; the lighting of the candles in the tree giving the final effect to its beauty, before the gifts are removed."

1876 - On October 10, two Philadelphians, Hermann Albrecht and Abram Mott, patented the first metal Christmas tree stand.

1878 - Icicles, those thin strips of silver that are either thrown or carefully placed onto the tree, were invented in Nuremberg, Germany. At first they were made of silver foil. By the 1920s they were made from lead; but this being harmful to small children if eaten, were changed to plastic mylar in the 1960s.

Eva Stille quotes *The Golden Christmas Book of 1878* as giving these instructions for decorating a tree of the period: "The decorating begins with the heaviest objects, which are best placed near the trunk and in the middle of the limbs. Then one puts on the nuts. Alternating gold and silver ones, they should be placed 3 to 4 on the larger branches, 2 to 3 on the shorter branches and one each on the upper short branches. The gilded and silvered pine cones can then be put closer to the front in the 2nd third of the limb, out from the trunk. Marzipan and sweets are the best between two nuts. Sparkling glass balls, fruits and such are better on the upper branches, in order to enjoy more the radiance of them. Metal spirals and Christmas tree curls are put on the ends of the subsidiary branches, because these are thinner and are easier to bring into motion than the stronger branches. The baskets and nets out of paper are also put on the subsidiary branches. The individual stars are divided equally everywhere, while the chains, nut chains, straw, paper and such, are alternately put on the branches. Paper sacks (cones) are always put on the tips of the branches, best of all beneath the lights. On the top of the tree is usually a large star out of cardboard covered with gold paper, and in the middle is either a self-painted or a store-bought Christmas angel glued on. Also elegant is a white satin ribbon with gold fringe, which carries the Christmas inscription in old gothic script "Glory be to God in the Highest."

"After the lights are put on the tree, the surfaces of the limbs are covered with pulled-apart cotton and these are fastened with silver threads."

1880-1900 - During this time period, the "gaudy tree" was in vogue. The way the tree is decorated will reflect the times and attitudes of the people. During this high Victorian period, empty space was considered a waste. Most furnishings, including those for the tree, were large, highly decorated, and overcrowded. The ornament makers worked hard to fulfill the demands for the current trends. Generally when the trend was gone so were the ornaments of that style. Occasionally ornaments can be dated using these trends.

During this same time period, American toy wholesalers such as Erlich Brothers and Amos Lyon, both of New York, were devoting several pages in their catalogues to Christmas ornaments and decorations.

Scraps, or chromolithograph decorations, were at the height of their popularity during this same period.

1880s - Flat, embossed Kugel caps made of brass are used during these years instead of a cork inserted into the pike.

1880 - Angel hair, another German decoration, hit the market for this year's Christmas season. Made of long fibers of spun glass, it was designed to place an angelic haze over the tree.

Of further interest in this year, Eva Stille quotes the following about a German immigrant family putting up their first tree in Texas: ". . . and I called myself smart that with all of the innumeral and often superfluous packages large and small that I brought along from the homeland to the settlement in Texas, I brought the most necessary things for the decorating of a Christmas tree. There were gold and silver tinsel and wax candles in sufficient quantity. But above all, well-kept, was the most beautiful decoration of the Christmas tree, an angel with golden wings and a long trumpet . . . and in addition with the loyal help of grandmother, even late into the night, the festive preparations for Christmas Eve were begun. An abundance of marvelous things were kept from the curious eyes of the children, blown-out eggs, whose fragile shells were glues with small colorful decorative cut-out lobes decorated with gold tinsel and equipped with threads for hanging, excellent hickory nuts were in abundance, and so that delicious candy did not completely lack for the children, mother had prepared a sweet cake out of honey and flour from a recipe of a neighbor who came from northern Germany, and the creativity of father formed the dough into all kinds of animal figures, stars and hearts.''

During this same year it was estimated that the Christmas tree market in New York's Washington Market alone was 200,000 trees. Such trees were carted and boated in from all over the northeast.

1882 - The first electrically lighted tree was set up in the New York home of Edward R. Johnson, a colleague of Thomas A. Edison. The lights had been hand blown and individually wired. The event was recorded by the Detroit *Post and Tribune*: "Last evening I walked over beyond Fifth Avenue and called at the residence of Edward R. Johnson, vice-president of Edison's electric company. There, at the rear of the beautiful parlors, was a large Christmas tree presenting a most picturesque and uncanny aspect. It was brilliantly lighted with many colored globes about as large as an English walnut and was turning some six times a minute on a little pine box. There were 80 lights in all encased in these dainty glass eggs, and about equally divided between white, red and blue. As the tree turned, the colors alternated, all the lamps going out and being relit at every revolution. The rest was a continuous twinkling of dancing colors, red, white, blue, white, red, blue -- all evening.

I need not tell you that the scintillating evergreen was a pretty sight -- one can hardly imagine anything prettier. The ceiling was crossed obliquely with two wires on which hung 28 more of the tiny lights; and all the lights and the fantastic tree itself with its starry fruit were kept going by the slight electric current brought from the main office on a filmy wire. The tree was kept revolving by a little hidden crank below the floor which was turned by electricity. It was a superb exhibition.''

1887 - John Barth of Louisville, Kentucky, patented a miniature oil lamp for lighting Christmas trees. Although unique and probably safer, it never replaced the candle.

1890s - During this time frame, Christmas became a legal holiday throughout the United States, and the "feather tree", an early artificial tree made of dyed turkey or goose feathers, was developed.

Czechoslovakian beaded ornaments began to be sold in the United States. Fancy bead work was a Victorian fashion that was in this manner transferred to decorations for the tree. Tinsel ornaments were popular during this period. The ornament caps from this period have a domed top with a hole through it. String or wire loops were then passed through the hole. This type of cap was usually glued onto the ornament.

1890 - General Electric buys out Edison's light bulb factory in 1890 and by 1901 are offering Christmas lights for sale. It was not until 1903 that the Ever-Ready Company began marketing strings or "festoons" of lights.

The McKinley Tariff Act passed, requiring a product's country of origin be marked on it. For ornaments, marking the box was sufficient. Shortly after the turn of the century, this act, with its high import taxes, helped put an end to the importation and sale of fancy German paper ornaments.

1892 - Ornament hooks are developed. These replaced the tedious task of hand tying each decoration on a branch.

1893 - Eva Stille quotes the *Arbor* magazine of this year complaining about the disappearance of the old decorations: "Who of we older ones would have believed in his youth, that one could decorate his tree differently than with gilded apples and nuts, that one had coated himself, or with colorful chains and nets, that one with more or less artistic hand had cut himself, or with marzipan and pfefferkachen, which the mother had baked herself. Today that is all different. The tree must sparkle, glitter, blind, until ones eyes fill with tears. There are gold and green candleholders, sparkling icicles, silver shimmering blossoms in whose calyx the lights break their radiance thousand fold, blue blinking stars with silver comets, gold and colored angel hair, ice garlands out of lammetta, in between color-glowing butterflies and flittering humming birds, white doves, black swallows and decorative velvet pieces, colorful glass balls, little bells and innumerable colorful, delightful vanities that make the Christmas tree a fairy present that has a dizzying effect. And this is all available ready-made. It is all in the stores right in front of our astonished eyes.''

1895 - The White House Christmas tree is electrified for the first time during the Cleveland administration.

1900-1915 - The "white tree" became the fashion during these years. This was a reaction against the overcrowded Victorian tree. It was a period of ultra simple and natural. "Fashionable" people placed cotton snow on branches, that held only glass icicles and silver pine cones. Many middle class families imitated the idea of an all white tree by washing the colored paints off their ornaments. Tinsel and lameta-type decorations were also popular as they fit into this basic concept.

1900-1920 - These years marked a period of rapid growth for the decorated tree in the United States. Philip Snyder remarks that one in five families had a tree in 1900. But by 1930 it had become almost universally accepted.

During this 20 year period, a fierce conservation battle against the Christmas tree was waged in the United States. This was spearheaded by the President, himself, during the Theodore Roosevelt administration. Through better conservation measures and policies and the establishment of Christmas tree farms, the custom of the decorated tree not only survived the attack but continued to grow at a phenomenal rate.

1901 - The first Christmas tree farm was established by W. V. McGalliard of New Jersey. Such ventures not only turned out to be profitable but also helped with American conservation measures.

1907 - The series-wired Christmas light strings are marketed by Ever-Ready Co. Such strings usually had eight sockets on them.

1908 - The Paper Novelty Products Company of New York, produced the first honey-combed paper bells.

1909 - The Kremenetzky Electric Co. of Vienna, Austria, begins to market figural light bulbs. Shortly after this General Electric also marketed figural lights. They were, however, never as popular.

F.W. Woolworth filed a successful lawsuit against the American "McKinley Tariff Act" of 1890. He was able to have ornaments classified as glass products instead of toys and thus they avoided the high import taxes that had spelled the demise of fancy paper products.

The United States Forest Service estimated that 5 million trees had been cut for Christmas. By 1920, 5 milliion were cut and exported from Vermont alone. Thus one can graphically see the growth in popularity of the decorated tree in the American home.

1913 - The now familiar metal cap with a spring loop holding inside the ornament was invented about this time.

1914-1918 - World War I. During this period, German ornament exports were cut off and several countries formed ornament businesses of their own. The beauty of the decorated tree began to spread as soldiers from both sides celebrated Christmas around candle-lit trees. In this manner, soldiers from more rural areas carried the tradition home with them. Fortunately, the anti-German feeling of the time had little effect on the acceptance of either the tree or German decorations.

1915-1919 - This time frame could be called the "artistic period" of tree decorations. Most of the free blown, colored glass and Art Deco looking pieces come from this time period. These are characterized by a lot of free blown, annealed, and one-of-a-kind type pieces. Many still have gummed stickers stating they were made in Germany. These types of ornaments were influenced by such designers and artists as Else Wenzvietor, Marianne Allesch, Franz Lampl and J. Berger. This phase was not as popular in America as it became in Europe and there are few good examples found here. Also during this time period, scraps and paper items faded in popularity and disappeared.

1917 - The Socony Co. (Standard Oil Company of New York) marketed the first dripless candles for Christmas trees.

At this same time, European figural lights are cut off by war embargos. Louis Szel goes to Japan to help establish the figural Christmas light industry.

1918 - In reaction to ornament shortages brought on by the war, the United States starts its first significant production of Christmas ornaments since the Kugels.

1920 - The ball and socket, adjustable, clip-on candle holder came into use. It was much safer than regular clip-on holders, but candles were rapidly being replaced by electric lights during this period.

1923 - The first national Christmas tree was set up during the Calvin Coolidge administration.

The Japanese were machine-blowing lights out of milk glass in a wide variety of sizes and shapes.

Lester Haft invented the tri-plug adapter for light strings, allowing them to be connected in one long string.

1925 - At about this time, the now familiar cone or flame shaped light bulb replaces the early pear-shape and round Christmas lights.

1926 - Fifteen small companies joined to form the National Outfit Manufacturers Association or Noma lights. The company, which brought about many innovative changes in Christmas lighting, developed into the largest light outfitters in the United States.

In 1927, the General Electric corporation developed the parallel wiring system for Christmas lights. In this wiring system, one light could burn out and the others remain lighted. However, it would not be until the 1950s that this system came into almost universal use.

1930-1940s - During this time, the German tree went through a simplistic or back-to-basics period. This was strongly encouraged by the Nazi Party as part of their Germanic folk ideology. The simplistic tree which had started in Germany centuries before was created; but, in the place of stars and angels, swastikas were found. Eva Stille shows glass ornaments from this period with such swastikas on them. Other symbols popular with the Nazi party were also used. It is possible that glass ornaments depicting Adolf Hitler were also made during this period. Such political pieces would be extremely rare. Since none were exported to other countries. The quantities would be limited, and many of them were probably "accidently" broken after the war.

1934-1935 - Poland begins exporting beautiful indented ornaments during these years.

1935-1940 - The Premier Glass Works of New Jersey is in operation during these years.

1937-1939 - Max Eckardt founded "The Shiny Brite" Company and begins the largest glass ornament business in United States' history. Eventually this company will surpass even the traditional German industry. His business was greatly enhanced by the ribbon glass blowing machine of the Corning Company which mass produced his clear glass blanks.

1937 - A custom tariff decision, No. 54387, reversed decisions about marking ornaments established by both the McKinley Tariff Act of 1890 and the Smoot-Havley Tariff Act of 1930. Now the ornament had to be marked with its country of origin either by stamping it into the cap or a tag or sticker. Thus caps marked "Germany" indicate a late piece.

1938 - The famous Snow White and the Seven Dwarfs ornaments are produced by Double-Glo, a subsidiary of Paper Novelty Products. When compared to the German pieces, the work was crude, but it remains the most famous of the American figurals.

1939-1945 - World War II. This effectively drew a time line between the "old" and "new" ornaments. A divided Germany found Lauscha in the Communist zone, and ornament making as a viable industry and way of life disappeared.

1943-1945 - War ornaments were produced in the United States. Because of war time shortages, they were unsilvered and often had paper caps and hangers.

1945 - The "bubble-light" developed by Carl Otis in 1936 was marketed by Noma. However, it would not be until the 1950s that it really caught on.

1947-1951 - Japanese products made during this time period will bear the label "Made in Occupied Japan".

1950-1955 - Strings of midget lights are introduced during these years. The first ones came from Italy, Germany, Holland and Japan. These early sets were in series wiring

1960s - The silver aluminum tree with a rotating color wheel makes its appearance. During this time period, it was popular to have all the ornaments the same shape and color. Both in Germany and America, many old ornaments were thrown away at this time. During the late 1960s, Corning Glass begins to market glass ornaments under their own name.

Late 1970s-1980s - During these years the pseudo-country look is popular in decorated trees. Gingham bows, dried flowers and fabric dolls stuffed with foam are some of the decorations that have little resemblance to the true trees of the period.

CHAPTER II

COLLECTOR'S NOTES

This chapter is more or less a collection of ideas and helpful hints for the collectors of Christmas ornaments and decorations. The articles contain those types of ideas that do not really fit into any other section of the book. They are designed to deal primarily with the collecting of ornaments as opposed to the ornaments themselves which will be catalogued and described throughout the rest of the chapters.

Information in the various articles comes from the knowledge and experience of several different collectors; and whether you are new to Christmas collecting or an "old hand" at it, I believe you will find some valuable information that will help make collecting more enjoyable.

IN SEARCH OF THE PERFECT TREE

The first step in search of the "perfect tree' is to decide on the type of tree you want to use. Down through the years almost every member of the pine family (and this contains a considerable variety) has been used for Christmas trees. Besides 35 varieties of true pines, there are 100 other varieties among the spruces, firs, hemlocks and cedars, all of which have probably been used at one time or another. The type used both traditionally and today will vary with the region or area of the country in which they grow.

Cedars and hemlocks, although used in the early history of decorated trees, are very seldom used today. The cedar has practically no needles, as we know them, and dries out quickly. The hemlocks start losing needles right after cutting and the ends of the branches are too weak to hold heavy ornaments or candles.

Of the 25 types of firs, the most commonly used are the balsam fir and the Douglas fir. The balsam has needles that are deep blue-green, flat, blunt and about ¾"-1" long. It is particularly noted for its wonderful aroma. It grows tall and slender with a nice tapering pyramid shape. The tree is full looking, dense with symmetrical branches coming out in an upward angle. Balsam firs make up about 30% of the Christmas trees cut, and they are very popular in the northeastern part of the country.

The Douglas fir, also known as the Douglas spruce and Montana fir, is not a true fir. Although it resembles the fir, it is related to the spruce. They have flat, short, 1" needles. The tree has the nice overall pyramid shape, so necessary to our idea of a Christmas tree. The branches are angled slightly upward and they give the tree a "full" look. The Douglas fir is the largest of the pine family and is found mainly in the Northwest. Out of the group of short needled trees, the Douglas fir maintains its needles and freshness the best. For many years it was the most popular tree for decorating; currently, it is in second place, behind the Scotch pine.

Both the balsam and Douglas firs have a pleasant aroma, they look good, and maintain their needles reasonably long if kept watered.

Spruces are another popular tree used at Christmas time. They are most identifiable by their beautiful pendulous or drooping branches. Their needles are four sided, usually olive or blue/green in color, and are from ½"-1" long. Arranged in compact spirals around the twigs, the needles are more thickly clustered than on the firs. They too, have a nice pyramidal shape, with a symmetric branch system. The "pine cones" of the spruce tree have served as a model for most of the blown glass ornaments. Spruces are found across a large section of the United States, and were popular trees to decorate in Europe, especially the Norway spruce. The color and shape of the spruce is its big draw; however, they do not maintain their freshness and needles as well as the firs and true pines. Spruces are also usually more expensive than either the fir or pine.

Down through the years, true pines have never been as popular for decorating as the spruces and firs. First of all, their needles are on the average of about 4"-5" long, thus making the tree difficult to decorate. Second, the **shape** of the pines never give them the same graceful lines and beauty of the firs or spruces. Pines seldom naturally grow in the ideal pyramidal shape. Branches are not as regular, leaving large holes, gaps and a scraggly appearance. The trunks are sometimes double or crooked, and they do not always come to a single point at the top. But they do have one major advantage: they will maintain their needles many months after being cut and do not dry out as quickly as the firs and spruces.

By far the most popular pine is the Scotch pine. It began to grow in popularity during the 1920s and 1930s until it is currently the most frequently used Christmas tree in the United States. Its needles are 2"-3" long and grayish blue/green in color. Its branches, although not as symmetric as the spruce, are sturdy enough for the heaviest of ornaments, and its natural gaps are ideal for hanging larger decorations. The Scotch pine, which is also misnamed the Scotch fir, is common throughout northern Europe, eastern and midwestern United States.

The type of tree you choose may be modified by several considerations, most important of which is how long you plan to keep your tree up. Traditionally trees went up on Christmas Eve and came down on Twelfth Night, a total of about two weeks in cool, naturally refrigerated Victorian parlors. Today trees that are cut months before they are sold, are put up almost anytime after Thanksgiving and kept in warm houses. As trees could be up for a month or more, it would be important for a person to pick a tree such as a true pine that maintained its freshness and didn't lose needles. Yet another will prefer the traditional look of spruces or firs to display their antique ornaments. Whichever you choose, beauty and safety should go hand in hand, as some of the saddest accidents are those that occur during the holidays. The most unfortunate of these are those involving the symbol if its hope and beauty -- the Christmas tree.

After deciding on the type of tree to look for, the next step is to go buy your tree. The most usual method involves going to the local mall or nursery where, amidst much lifting of trees, shaking apart of branches, twisting, turning and complaining about prices, you search for the perfect tree. Of course, a million other families have been there before you and you have to settle for one that is not quite the right height, width or shape and was cut around the middle of October.

Then there is the adventurer, who, for $20.00, gets to hike up and down row after row of pines over the 30 acres of a tree farm looking for the "perfect tree" (and occasionally for his wandering three year old). This is accompanied by hummed Christmas carols, a nostalgic feeling of the good old days, much measuring and viewing of trees from different angles. There is the crunch of snow beneath your feet, a numbing coldness and a six year old's enthusiasm -- "That's a nice tree, Daddy. Let's go home now." There is the wonderful smell of fresh cut pine as your chosen tree tumbles down and you realize you can't possibly carry it that mile back to the car. Then to top off the afternoon, you can stand around the big iron kettle over a blazing wood fire with friends, family and other "adventurers" and eat a bowl of burnt bean soup. Upon arriving back home you find you have an aching back, sore feet, probably a cold, and a good measure of self satisfaction.

Then there are the folks that already have a perfect tree. It's in boxes out in the garage and for the cost of a few hours of assembly time, interspersed with occasional swearing . . . Presto! they have a perfect plastic tree.

This brings us to the myth of the "perfect tree": the one, straight tree that is just the right height, (usually floor to ceiling), the right width, has close full branches that taper nicely to a single point and is symmetrical all the way around. This is a 20th century American ideal and certainly not the way trees have always looked. Pictures of early trees show them to be about 4' tall and placed on a small table or stand. Branches of various lengths go every which way, there are large gapping holes and many times they are lop-sided. They are, in essence, an ugly "Charlie Brown" tree.

Perfect trees and antique Christmas ornaments do not always work well together. For instance, that beautiful 12" lithographed Santa with tinsel trim needs a corresponding 12" hole or gap to hang in. The perfect tree won't have this hole. If you plan to use candles, you need branches that stick out a good deal further than the ones above them, again not to be found on the perfect tree. Full branches that taper closely together may look good when the tree is bare but it leaves little room for hanging ornaments except at the ends of the branches. Half the fun of looking at a tree covered with ornaments is searching through its nooks and crannies to find the treasures and surprises that are hidden there.

If you have repeatedly turned and repositioned your tree, unsuccessfully trying to find its best side, and if you can't rationalize to yourself or your friends that old fashioned trees are supposed to be lop-sided and uneven; then here's a possible solution to your troubles. Cut a branch from the bottom, back side or another tree. Then tape and wire it into the offending hole or gap. Use thin dark wire and it won't show. Be sure to wire it firmly. If you insert the end into a plastic bag of water next to the tree trunk, the wired branch will stay as fresh as the rest of the tree.

So now your bare tree is up, and has its best face forward. Now it's time to put on your new collection of ornaments. I say your "new collection", because the beautiful ones you had last year were swept up in small glittering pieces after the cat climbed the tree and it came tumbling down -- the cat, of course, was unharmed. The same disasterous scene could be repeated when your toddling two year old pulls on an ornament that doesn't want to come loose and the whole tree comes with it. There is a third more mysterious reason for the tipping over of a Christmas tree -- the no-apparent-reason. Underlying causes for this might be a tree that has been decorated in an unbalanced manner, i.e., all the ornaments on the front side. This is all too easy to do if you place the tree in a corner. Any jar or bump will cause a precariously balanced tree to fall. Collectors might also need to consider the vibrations caused by aircraft, trains and earthquakes.

Several things can be done to help keep your tree from falling. First of all, you will want to get a tree stand that is big enough for your tree. Just because the tree's trunk will fit into the base, doesn't mean it's big enough. You need one that is heavy enough and whose legs spread out far enough to give the tree a good stable base. Most antique tree stands were made for three or four foot trees. They will not securely support a nine or ten footer. After putting the tree and treestand into the desired position, you can fasten the stand down with nails. A nail driven in part way and bent over the "leg" of the tree stand should hold it securely. If you have carpeting underneath, a thin nail shouldn't damage it and the holes will be hidden. If you have wooden floors . . . well, just try to use the same holes every year. This technique will help prevent any tipping of your tree. If you are averse to putting nails in your floor, you might weight the legs down with heavy bricks. Simple laws of physics will tell you that if the top of your tree is knocked far enough off balance, it will pull the rest of the tree down. A cat in the top-most branches has a tendency to create this "off balanced" state. Therefore, I tie the tree to a hook in the wall about 3' down from the top. This can be done with dark wire or sturdy green cord and it will not show. Whether or not you have one of those frisky felines, both of these techniques greatly increase the stability of your tree.

The problems caused by a combination of small children (whether they are yours or just visiting), pets, and Christmas trees decorated with antique ornaments, can be quite disturbing.

Children love the glitter, beauty and mystery of the decorated tree. It's new, different and happens but once a year. Besides, lest we forget, the whole concept of the tree is **designed** to fascinate and delight children. It was invented for them. Therefore, its only natural that they would want to touch and play with these beautiful trinkets. It's also only natural that you cringe when thinking of anyone under 18 years of age handling a $200.00 ornament passed down from your great-grandmother. "Look, but don't touch" is a nice philosophy to try to teach, but it doesn't always work. As insurance, I see how high those inquisitive little hands can go and then begin hanging glass ornaments out of their reach. Non-breakable items such as plastic, celluloid, paper, cardboard, spun cotton, metal, etc., can be placed on the lower branches. These were usually designed to be handled and played with and are quite sturdy. This should also take care of any problems with playful cats batting at your ornaments. I keep mentioning cats because dogs don't seem to cause much trouble except for an occasional wagging tail. However, non-breakable ornaments hung down low will take care of this problem also.

Another possible solution is to keep children and pets away from the tree altogether. This can be accomplished by using the old fashioned Christmas tree fence. This was a little 6″-1′ high wooden fence that surrounded the tree and inside of which were placed the presents or small Christmas village scenes known as a "putz". It's traditional, it's antique . . . it's effective. Keeping cats out of the tree can be a more troublesome problem. I have two possible solutions -- spray the lower trunk with dog or cat repellant, the kind used to keep them away from outdoor plants and trees. If this doesn't work, try the book, *101 Uses for a Dead Cat.*.

As every situation is different, you may want to experiment and find your own solution to the problem of tipping trees. Whatever it might be, remember this old adage -- "Better safe than sorry", and this not so old Murphy's Law -- "If anything can go wrong, it will."

Now to answer the questions you're probably wondering about. Yes, I have a two year old; yes, I have a cat; and no, my tree has never fallen over.

SAFEGUARDING ORNAMENTS ON THE TREE

Once your tree is up and decorated, you will want to help keep your collection safe while it is on display. The most likely time to drop and break an ornament is when it is being put on or taken off the tree.

An ornament's chances for surviving a fall can be increased if some type of padding is placed beneath the tree. I use foam sheets that come out past the edge of the tree. They are then covered with a colorful tree skirt of velvet or some other material. This is helpful not only during the decorating and undecorating process, but it also gives added protection while the ornaments are on display.

The small spring caps from which the ornaments hang should be checked carefully before they are placed on the tree. If they are broken, or if the pike of the ornament is broken, they may no longer fit tightly. This might allow the ornament to slide off the hanger and fall.

If the pike is broken and the cap no longer fits securely, place a larger cap on it. For German ornaments, using the larger caps from American pieces will solve the problem. Some collectors might feel they detract and are not original, but they do safeguard your ornament by hanging it more securely. The other alternative to this is to repair and rebuild the pike. For information on this, see the section on ornament repair.

The hooks that you use to hang your ornaments can be another problem area unless they are attached securely to the branch. Older hooks are made of a heavier wire and thus will be more sturdy. However, the new thinner hooks have an advantage, too. After placing the hook on the branch they can be bent tightly around it, thereby preventing the hook and ornament from slipping or falling off. This is particularly useful if you hang items from the thin wire of your light strings. This same method of wrapping wire around the tree branch to secure the ornament was popular until about the 1920s. Old ornaments can still be found with these strips of crinkle wire attached. It may take longer to put on and take off your ornaments, but you can feel confident that they are securely attached.

For older and heavier decorations, especially kugels, you will want to use sturdy hooks. Ones made out of coat hanger wire might be more appropriate than the thin ones produced today. Making sure that your hook is firmly attached to the limb and not just the needles will help pre-

vent the ornament from slipping as the needles dry out and begin to droop. A few simple precautions such as these will help safeguard your ornaments while they hang on the tree.

STORAGE OF ORNAMENTS

Unless you are one of those fortunate people with a way of displaying your treasured ornaments year round, you will face the dilemma of how to store them. Here are several methods used by various collectors; maybe one will be helpful to you. No matter which method you use, ornaments of all types should be stored in a **cool, dry** area. This can be a problem in itself because basements tend to flood or at best be damp, and attics can get downright hot. The destructive enemies of ornaments in storage are water, dampness, mildew, heat, cold, drastic temperature changes, and the much-feared dropped box or heavy falling object. The terrors of small children and cats will be discussed later.

Water can completely damage almost any old ornament. The exceptions are plastic and glass; but even for the glass ornaments, water will wash away the paint or color leaving a colorless object. If wet, paper objects can be carefully dried and pressed flat again, but water stains and a continual flaking of the colored ink will ruin their beauty and value.

Heat and dampness can do similar types of damage to an ornament. They have a tendency to melt the paint or lacquer coloring, causing it to run, flake, or stick to whatever item in which it is stored. Dampness can also cause warpage in paper, cardboard or wood. Furthermore, it can cause separation of any layers of paper or separation of any glued parts. Moisture also causes damage to paints, inks and lacquers and, of course, it produces rust on metal ornaments or metal parts.

One of the worst things dampness can cause is mildew. Mildew will attack any organic substance or anything that has organic substances in them. This includes the lacquered or painted surface of your glass ornaments, paper items and even spun glass. Mildew, besides ruining the appearance of the ornament by giving it a "fuzzy" look, will eventually cause peeling, flaking, warping or staining. Shortly, we will discuss some methods that will help prevent mildew. However, if you already have some on your ornaments, there is a way to help. Give the ornament a **light** misting with Lysol spray. This must be **light** or the alcohol base will cause the paint, inks and lacquers to dissolve and run. Several coats may be necessary (allowing drying time in between) to kill all the mildew. Since it is a hard mold to kill, you will want to check the ornament in succeeding years and repeat the process as needed.

Extremes in temperature or drastic changes in temperature can cause glass ornaments to crack and even shatter. This is not particularly a problem while they are stored in the home throughout the year; however, it is a factor to consider when newly bought or transported ornaments might be left in a cold car and then brought into a warm house. Decorations hung next to a cold window or a heater could suffer the same fate, and they have been known to discolor in a period of just a few weeks.

Droppage and items falling onto your stored ornaments are hard to prevent. Decorations should be stored on sturdy shelves or in a place where they can't fall. There should be nothing heavy such as paint cans, bricks, anvils, etc., stored above them. Serious collectors might want to look into the various types of household insurance that are available today. This could help financially offset any such disasters, but it certainly couldn't replace a rare collection.

METHODS OF STORAGE

In this first method of storage, the ornaments can be packed in tissue or newspaper inside a small cardboard ornament box, with about a dozen to a box.

The advantage of this system is that it is time proven. Most of your antique ornaments have spent half or three quarters of their existance stored in this manner -- it works. Each ornament when packed in its own cubicle will not rub or bang against others and the box provides additional strength and protection. Thus in case of accidents, one box might be damaged and the other remain intact.

This method also has several disadvantages. If you are like me, you buy lots of individual ornaments and very seldom have enough serviceable ornament boxes to store them all. For large collections, you would also have the extra bulk of the individual boxes. The large commercial ornament boxes being made today can be helpful with this problem. They are sturdy and can hold quite a few ornaments. Finally, this method gives very little protection against wetness, temperature changes, dampness or mildew.

In the second method, the ornaments may be heavily wrapped in newspaper or tissue paper, to form a small padded bundle. They are then layered into boxes.

One advantage of this system is that each ornament has its own protection against hitting other ornaments. If the bottom of the box is padded, all ornaments will stand a good chance of surviving, even if dropped from a great height. This method gives some protection against temperature, dampness, and mildew. Materials are cheap and readily available.

This method too, has several disadvantages. If the paper wrappings should get damp or wet, they will retain the moisture and hold it in against the ornament. This can be complicated by the fact that printers ink from newspapers may rub off and discolor your decorations. It is also time consumming to carefully wrap each ornament. And finally, did you ever try to find that one special ornament, in the middle of the summer, to show a friend? All those little packages look the same and you'll probably end up unwrapping nearly all of them to find the one you want. (One final advantage to this method . . . it provides lots of paper for a blazing holiday fireplace while you put up your tree!)

In this third method, the ornaments are stored inside large boxes between layers of shredded paper.

Again, the ornament's receive a good cushioned "nest" and insulation against temperature changes. This is a good method to use if you are shipping ornaments. But the shredded paper has a tendency to hold dampness and mildew and it also holds in basement odors. Again, finding a particular ornament once it has been packed is like looking through the "grass" of an Easter basket for an elusive jelly bean.

In the fourth method of storing your ornaments, the one I personally prefer, they are packed inside individual cubicles in Zip-lock plastic bags.

I have modified the commercial ornament storage boxes (27″ L. x 17″ W. x 17″ D.) to contain three trays stacked on top of each other and removable by cloth handles. This leaves a top layer 4″ deep which is used for storing bead chains, lights, cardboard ornaments, cotton batting, etc. This could also be used to hold a fourth tray. Each tray

has approximately 28 - 4″ x 4″ cubicals for ornaments. These cubicals can readily be cut and extended for containing longer, larger or odd-shaped ornaments. Each hole is padded with tissue paper and the ornament, inside the plastic bag, is put into its own little section. If some air is put into the bag before it is sealed, the ornament will also have an air bubble (like the air bubble packing material) to protect it. Furthermore, paper, cotton and metal ornaments do not always wrap well in paper, nor do they often fit into the cubicals in ornament boxes. Plastic bags work exceptionally well for these type of pieces, keeping them both clean and dry. This effectively gives your ornaments protection against temperatures, dampness, mildew, droppage and even water. You can also look through your collection and readily find any particular ornament.

Of course, this system too has its disadvantages. There is the initial cost of the ornament box and Zip-lock bags. They are, however, reusable for many years. The plastic bag does not allow the ornament to "breathe", and if moisture is in the bag before it is sealed, it will condense on the ornament. This can be overcome by not blowing air into the bag by mouth. If an air bubble cushion is desired, put dry air in it by means of a blow dryer. If the lacquer or paint becomes tacky due to heat, dampness or sometimes chemical changes in the finish itself due to age and environment, the ornament may stick to the bag. This of course is no worse than sticking to a paper wrapping. With the plastic bag, however, this problem may be eliminated by adding a **light** dusting of talcum or baby powder to the inside of the bag.

I hope one of these methods will be suitable for your storage needs and you can rest assured that your little treasures of yesterday will be safe those other eleven months of the year.

THE ORNAMENT DOCTOR - REPAIRS

When you unpack great-grandmother's most beloved ornament and find it damaged; or when you find that rare, unusual, beautiful . . . but broken ornament in an antique shop, you will face the decision of whether or not to repair. There are several pros and cons to each side.

First, you must face the fact that the ornament is broken. Even if a good repair job is done on it, it will not be as desirable or worth nearly as much as an intact piece. If a poor job is done on the repair, it may cause the piece to be worth even less than if it had been left broken.

Some collectors are not in the least interested in a broken or repaired ornament. Others prefer the piece left untampered with in the "as found" condition. Still others will accept a well-done repair. A "well-done repair" being one that helps to prevent further damage and does not call attention to itself but rather blends in with the overall effect of the ornament. Indeed, some can be so excellently done that they are hard to detect even under close examination. However, very few people are interested in poorly repaired items. Therefore, if you decide to repair, it would be wise to practice first on ornaments that can be thrown away.

Some repairs are not merely cosmetic, but are necessary to help preserve the ornament itself. A good repair will prevent further damage and help the item last longer. Many one of a kind decorations are well worth the time and effort needed to fix them.

If you have decided that a repair will help prevent further structural damage and it will not detract from the ornament's appearance, then here are some helpful repair tips gathered from various collectors.

Cleaning Ornaments

The good news is you have just found a boxful of grandma's old ornaments. The bad news is, they have been in the attic in a box without a lid. How should the dust and soot of 20 years be cleaned? The best advice I can give in this matter is -- don't clean them. Any type of glass cleaner, including water, will completely wash away the finish. The dust or lose dirt can be carefully blown or lightly wiped away, but that's about the only safe help that can be given for dirty finishes on glass ornaments.

In the 1950s and 1960s, a great terror of ornament collectors hit the market -- spray cans of artificial snow. Many old ornaments have globs of this white stuff on them from when it was sprayed on the tree. It can be removed, very slowly and carefully, with photographer's film cleaner. This evaporates so quickly that when used in small quantities, it does not wash away the lacquered finish underneath.

Mildew or mold on the surface of your ornament can hurt its appearance and if left unchecked, it can ruin the finish. Lysol spray will help to kill the mold. It must be sprayed on **very lightly** and allowed to dry thoroughly between treatments or the alcohol base will cause the lacquer to run or the finish to peel. **Do not wipe** the ornament during the process. Wiping will only bring the finish off with it. Simply spray it on and let it dry. It may take several applications over the years to kill this stubborn mold.

In cleaning paper or cardboard, you have a few more options. Surface dust and dirt can be wiped away with a slightly damp cloth. Wiping only small areas at a time and allowing it to dry will bring success. Too much water will cause the paper to warp or curl. The shiny lacquer coat on most scraps will help give them the added protection needed for this type of cleaning. For imbedded dirt, try an eraser bag used by artists and architects to clean dirt off their work.

Dirty or rusty metal items can be wiped with a light coat of oil, taking care not to wipe away any finishes. In cleaning any type of finish, check the color fastness of it on an obscure area before working on the whole ornament.

Other than blowing off surface dirt, don't try to clean cotton items at all. It is possible to clean some fabric ornaments with spot remover or Woolite. However, this is more likely to ruin them than to clean them and is thus not advisable.

Breaks in Glass Ornaments

If you are lucky, the broken ornament may be in several large pieces instead of a thousand small ones. In this case, you won't have to fabricate missing pieces, you will only need to put them back together again. The difficulty lies in the fact that these thin pieces of glass will not support themselves while the glue is drying. This can be overcome if the inside of the ornament is stuffed with cotton or tissue paper. This is then pulled into the contour or shape of the area to be repaired. Then the broken parts can be placed on top of it, matched up with the other pieces, and supported while it dries in place. But even with an exact match up of the parts, noticeable crack lines will be inevitable.

If your broken part shatters into a thousand little pieces, as is most often the case, you will have to use something to fill in the hole. I have found tissue paper to be the best

solution for a variety of reasons. It is cheap and readily available, it comes in a variety of colors, it can take on the same weight and feel of the missing glass, and when wetted with glue it is easily molded. Work with tissue **wrapping** paper -- not toilet paper. The wrapping tissue has a tighter weave, it is stronger and it has no embossed patterns that might show up in the repair.

First, cut the tissue paper in the rough shape of the hole with about ¼"-½" added all the way around. Wet it down with white glue and coat the **inside** edges of the break with glue. Put the paper **into** the ornament through the hole. Next, begin to spread and smooth out the tissue over the inside of the hole. Do this by removing the ornament cap and working from the inside with a long metal wire, bent hair pin, or other similar "tool". Once the wet tissue paper is seated over the opening of the break and smoothed out, it can be given the contour of the broken area by gently blowing into the neck of the ornament. This will also help the glue dry more quickly in that position. For tightly curved parts, you may have to cut lines into one edge of the paper (just like in sewing and dressmaking) to help prevent bunching and wrinkling. Several coats of glue should be built up allowing time for drying in between.

The thin depression left where the glass ornament and paper repair meet can be smoothed out by using nail polish filler. This will even out the edges of your repair with the glass and help prevent it from showing. When you have this matched to your satisfaction, you can begin to match the paint or the finish. By using colored tissue paper, you could be one step ahead in this department. If, however, you have any difficulty in matching hues, your safest route is to stay with the white tissue paper.

When applying the finish over your paper repair, you will find a problem not encountered when the finish is replaced over glass. Your paper repair will not provide the same reflective background as the rest of the ornament and will make the repair more noticeable.

There are several ways that you can simulate the ornament's mirror-like finish. Certain nail polishes and model paints, especially the metallic ones, have their own shiny undercoat. It is for this same reason that they are not recommended for use in repainting on the regular glass parts. They cover the mirror finish and do not allow it to subtly shine through the colors. On the paper repair, however, this opaque shine is exactly what is needed.

In another method of duplicating the shine, strips of thin silver acetate can be cut and glued over the tissue paper. The desired finish can then be applied over this shiny background.

If the break is in the pike area of your ornament, the best thing to do is leave it alone. Slight damage in this area does not detract significantly from the appearance or value of your ornament. Because of the tight curves involved in mending the pike, it is also difficult to get a good unnoticeable repair. If the break has affected the security of the hanging cap, switch to a larger size cap.

If the pike absolutely needs to be repaired, being absent altogether, for instance, the following technique might help. Wrap a piece of tissue paper, wetted with glue, around the end of an appropriate size dowel rod or thin pencil. Allow the glue to set but not dry completely or it will stick to the wooden rod. This will form the open tube of the pike. Flare out the paper at the end of the new paper "pike" into a rough circle and put cuts in it. Again, this will help prevent bunching and wrinkling. This rounded part is then glued inside the ornament. The paper pike can then be trimmed down to an appropriate size, the smaller the better, and painted to match the rest of the ornament.

Here's an alternative method for repairing broken pikes that is also useful for repairing broken masts on ships or balloons, and the long pikes on horns or other musical instruments. A small section of a clear plastic straw can be used to replace or strengthen a damaged pike. When inserted into the broken glass tube of ship masts or balloons, it can be used as a brace for holding the two pieces together. When painted, the straw can also be used to replace any of these missing parts.

Keeping in mind that an ounce of prevention is worth a pound of cure, removing the cap of an ornament correctly will help prevent damage to the pike. Never just pull the cap and spring loop out. As it comes out, the spring will put a great deal of stress against the brittle glass of the pike. The cap and spring loop can be removed safely by squeezing the spring together while pulling it out.

Cracks

Cracks can be caused by bumping, jarring, extreme temperature changes or merely by age. If left unmended, several adverse conditions may begin to develope in the cracked ornament. First, the crack may continue to expand making the ornament look worse and endangering it. Second, the silver finish around the crack will darken, caused by the oxidation of the silver finish, and flake away. This darkened area will slowly spread over the years. Finally, the crack creates a weak point in the glass at which it is likely to break if it is put under even the slightest strain. Fortunately, ornaments that are cracked, but not entirely broken, can be fixed without too much difficulty. To seal and strengthen the crack, apply a coat of white glue to the **inside** of the ornament. Cover the crack and surrounding area. When repaired from the inside, the mend will remain invisible, strengthen the crack, and help prevent further flaking of the silvered interior.

Finish Repairs

This can be a delicate area in which to decide the question of whether or not to repair. You are not preventing further structural damage to the ornament, but rather trying to retain the ornament's beauty. You, as the owner, will have to decide if damage to the finish is distracting enough to warrant tampering with the ornament's authenticity.

Flaking and peeling finishes, especially on pieces covered in crushed glass or "Venetian dew", are a problem. Unless corrected, some of the finish will fall away every time the ornament is handled or stored until there is nothing left. This problem can be solved by spraying the ornament with an artist's fixative used for charcoal or pastel drawings. An example of this is "Tuffilm" by Grumbacher, available in most art supply stores. This holds the finish on nicely and remains totally clear. Large areas of peeling can be carefully pressed down and reattached with white glue or clear fingernail polish.

Missing patches in the "frosted" or crushed glass finishes are not too difficult to replace. First a base coat of flat or antique white paint is applied to the glass. A water base paint is the most authentic. While the paint is still wet, sprinkle glass dust or fine white sand, whichever best matches the finish, over it. Let it dry and shake off the excess. Remember, it is better to have too little than too much. It is difficult to find real glass dust or crushed glass these days. The kind sold in hobby shops is usually made of plastic, and it is not too hard to spot on a repaired ornament. However, you can make your own by grinding up small pieces of glass. Bits and pieces of broken ornaments stripped of their lacquer and silvering are ideal. Besides, this is exactly what the ornament makers originally used -- bits and pieces of their broken ornaments.

As far as missing paints and lacquers, again it is debatable as to whether or not they should be repaired or replaced at all. If the need is there, begin your search for matching finishes in the local hobby shop. There are a multitude of paints and lacquers available today. You can probably find some that are close and then blend colors until you get a match. However, most ornament makers "doctored" their finishes with certain homemaker or secret family formulas to give them a distinctive look. Therefore it is unlikely that you will be able to get an exact match.

For the matte finish pieces, work with water based colors. For the lacquers themselves, try the lacquer based coloring that is used in making stained glass pieces. Certain nail polishes can also match the hues, but not the texture, of the antique finishes. For working with the delicate pastel finishes, some collectors have found a great deal of success with children's markers. They are usually water based and come in a wide variety of shades many of which will match up almost perfectly with the old ornament finishes if the underlying silvering has not been damaged. Experimentation will pay off in this area, but it is best not to experiment on a good ornament. Try your early repairs on pieces you can throw away if necessary.

Paper and Metal Repairs

Never use cellophane or masking tape to make repairs on paper items. They will eventually discolor and are likely to cause further damage when removed. A note to dealers in this same vein, use string tags to price your ornaments. Stick-on labels have a tendency to pull off finishes of both glass and paper. If you have a need to reglue or reattach paper pieces, a light film of white glue such as Elmer's will do a nice job and remain invisible. For larger jobs, use rubber cement as this will not cause the paper to wrinkle like the wet white glue.

Broken metal pieces can often be repaired with Super Glue or solder. Those that are bent can be gently pulled back into position. Remember that these molded pieces are generally made of soft lead and they should be stored in such a manner that they cannot be bent or pushed out of shape.

Wax

Repairs on wax items will usually fall into one of two categories. The first problem area involves the hard sealing wax that was used to fasten clip-ons to birds and other ornaments or to hold various items together. These often break or come loose with the passing of years. If all the wax is still there, it can be heated and reattached. It can also be glued back into place. If the old wax is gone, it can be replaced by using sealing wax purchased at a local stationery store.

The second problem area occurs with the arms and legs of early wax angels. They are often found broken or badly melted. If you have the broken part, it can be reattached with contact cement. This can further be strengthened by inserting a needle into both pieces to act as a brace. For those parts that are missing or badly melted, it is possible to form a new one out of wax. I have also seen some fine reconstruction work done with materials from doll repair kits.

Due to heat and storage, old wax ornaments may be found bent out of their original shape. Warm them by a heater, a blow dryer or even in your hands. When the wax softens, you can gently put it back into shape. Never try this without first warming the piece or the brittle wax will crack and shatter.

Since dust and dirt has a tendency to stick on wax, they are often found in need of cleaning. They can be gently wiped with warm water and a soft cloth, taking care not to wash away any color finish.

Wire

The wire wrapping on balloons, sailboats and Victorian ornaments can be quite beautiful. It can also be quite distracting when it is pulled out of its original shape and lies on the ornament in a tangled heap. Rewrapping a wire ornament is not a task to be lightly undertaken, but it can be done with satisfying results.

Wires that are simply out of place can usually be coaxed back into position by gentle pulling. If, however, you decide that your ornament needs rewiring, the first step is to carefully examine the wire. If it has greenish colored places on it, the wire is corroded and will not survive any attempt at rewiring. It will simply crumble in your hands as you work with it. Also check to see if large sections of wire are missing or falling off. This would indicate that the wire has lost its suppleness and is too brittle to stand the strain of the twisting and pulling required for rewrapping. You might bend back a small end piece of the wire. If it breaks off as it is bent, the wire is too brittle. If it retains the bend, it is probably supple enough for the task of rewiring. If you find you have either of these problems, it is probably best to leave the wire as it is instead of running the risk of losing it completely.

The next step in rewrapping is to take the wire completely off. You will usually find the two ends twisted together somewhere near the top. After you have untangled the wire and straightened it out, you can begin carefully wrapping it back into its original position. You can determine what this original position was by studying pieces in which the wire is still intact. Doing a job like this will lead you to a greater appreciation of the time and talent needed to produce these wire wrapping ornaments. This is especially true of the sailboats where just the right amount of wire tension on all sides is needed to hold the mast in an upright position. While working, don't forget the hanging loop and try to twist the two ends of wire back together to finish off your project.

Resilvering

The silvered interior of an ornament is an integral part of its charm and beauty. The original intent of putting a mirror-like finish on the ornament was to help it reflect the light of the candles which were fastened on the end of the tree branches. This effect is all but lost today as we traditionally place lights on the inside of the tree and the ornaments on the outside. Some of the ornament's beauty fades if this silvering is missing and there are several things that can cause the micro-thin layer of silver nitrate to peel away and disintegrate: dampness, drastic temperature

changes and poor workmanship in the original silvering process. Unfortunately, I know of no way that the individual collector can resilver an ornament themselves. However, if you feel it absolutely needs to be done, you can take it to a glass company that specializes in resilvering old mirrors. The process will not be a cheap one so the question of whether or not the piece is worth the extra cost, effort and chance of getting broken will have to be carefully weighed.

Replacing Eyes in Doll Heads

Ornament eyes were made out of a tear-drop shaped piece of milk glass which then had a round black pupil added to it. These were glued into the eye socket of the doll head. However, the eyes were applied after the face and eye sockets had been painted a flesh color and the problem of missing eyes is caused by the fact that the eyes were glued onto this painted surface instead of directly onto the glass. If dampness caused the paint to weaken or flake, the eyes fell off with it. If you are lucky, the eyes might be found in the bottom of the ornament box. If not, you will face the problem of replacing the ornament or leaving it eyeless. Missing eyes not only affect the price of the ornament, but also hurt its desirability and beauty. Eyes should always be salvaged and saved from any irreparable heads. They may come in handy later and they can always be sold to collectors seeking to replace missing eyes.

Replacement eyes can be made by using elongated, pearl-white beads from a hobby shop. They are football shaped and about ¼" long. When the black pupil is added, they make acceptable substitutes. In fact, one of the doll heads pictured in this book has been repaired with this technique. Can you tell which one? I suggest that you glue your replacement eyes with a water soluble glue such as Elmer's. That way, they could be replaced if some antique originals should become available.

Conclusion

As you can see, a little practice, a little ingenuity and a lot of patience can bring satisfying results in repairing your ornaments. Furthermore, I think you will find it is a good idea to save the parts of irreparable ornaments. Always look through the bottoms of old ornament boxes for missing or broken parts. Often times they were saved and you can use them in your repairs. You never know when you might need to replace caps, clip-ons, eyes, etc., so always save them. Even the broken pieces of glass might come in handy.

This is certainly not a complete list of ideas or possible repair methods; and possibly they are not always the best method. By talking and sharing with others your successes and failures, new and possibly better ways can be found for repairing these fragile treasures of Christmases past.

TELLING OLD ORNAMENTS FROM NEW

As I said, the past few years have brought an increased interest in antique collectibles, things Grandma used to have, Victorian items in general, and of course, Christmas ornaments. This interest has also brought copies and reproductions of these items onto the market and Christmas decorations are no exception. It is important that both collector and dealer have an idea of how to tell the old from the new.

"Old" ornaments are those made before World War II, started in Europe in 1939. "New" ornaments are considered to be those made after the war, from the late 1940s to the present. One could argue that those made in the 1940s and 1950s are not new. This is quite true and pieces from this period are becoming increasingly collectible as the "old" pieces become scarcer. However, there is still a distinctive difference in the style and weight of the glass from this later period; and there is certainly a difference in the prices they command.

Most of these new "old style" ornaments have been blown into the original molds and are exact reproductions. However, there are two reasons why it is important to be able to recognize the difference between old and new pieces. First, like other people who are interested in antiques, ornament collectors are usually looking for the old originals and not their modern reproductions. Second, the prices listed in this book are for the "old" ornaments. New ornaments, on the average, will sell for $2.00 to $10.00. It is true that many of these latter pieces have had only limited production and are as scarce or scarcer than the older versions. For these, prices will be higher but will not equal those from the older productions.

After seeing and handling hundreds of ornaments over the years, a collector develops a kind of "sixth sense" that helps determine whether an ornament is old or new. There are, however, some indicators that will assist in answering the questions of old versus new. However, I would caution that these are only clues and certainly not infallible. The more indicators that are present, the more confident you can be about your decision, but ultimately it is up to the collector's personal judgment.

Weight of the Glass

Probably the single most noticeable difference between old and new ornaments is the weight of the glass from which the ornament is made. Older pieces were blown from a thinwalled glass tube; thus they are lightweight and often feel paper thin. After the War, the glass was a thicker, stronger variety. This leads to a heavier, sometimes plastic, feel in the newer pieces.

Caps and Method of Hanging

The metal cap or the manner in which the ornament is hung can be another source of information. The cap and ring device that held early Kugels is very distinctive of an early period and they are fully discussed in the Kugel section. Another cap and ring device was used before the turn of the century. In this system, the cap was often brass and gold colored, and was fastened onto the glass pike. It had a domed top through which the hanging ring was inserted. Other early methods of hanging the ornament include an annealed glass hook and wire loops, which were popular on tinsel and wire-wrapped pieces. Hangers made of string or thread were common on early paper decorations.

Around the turn of the century, the familiar metal cap with a spring-like metal loop appeared. Early caps are soft, often corroded, and appear to be made of lead. Some of these may have thread or crinkle wire attached to them, which were used before hooks to fasten the ornament to the tree. Caps from the 1920s and 1930s were made of tin or steel. Another old method of using paper and string hangers was revived during World War II when the metal for the metal parts was used for the war effort. Many new caps are made of a gold foil with a stamped filigree design. The caps on newer pieces are usually shiny while those on older ornaments are dull or even rusty.

Labels

Some caps, especially from the 1930s, may be stamped with the word "Germany". American import laws from about 1890 state that all foreign manufactured goods needed to have the name of the country of origin on them. Most glass ornaments satisfied this requirement by having the name stamped on the box in which they were shipped. Others, notably the Art Deco-type pieces from the 1920s, that were made of free blown and annealed glass, had a gummed label stating "Made in Germany". Some rarer glass pieces actually had the word "Germany" molded into them, as did many metal ornaments. Paper pieces may have the country or origin embossed into them or stamped on with ink. After the war, the word "Germany" was no longer used. "The U.S. Zone" and, eventually, the term "West Germany" were used to signify the divided status of the country.

Today almost all ornament caps are marked with the country of their origin. Those scarce pieces of East German origin are marked "Made in GDR". When trying to determine age or country of origin by the type of cap, remember that they are easy to replace and move from one ornament to another.

The Pike

The glass pike in the area of the metal cap can give additional information. In most old ornaments, this area will be dark, discolored and perhaps chipped. This can be caused by a reaction of the metal cap and the silvered interior; or by a slow rubbing-away of the silver every time the cap is twisted or moved. Chipping is caused by the stress that is put on the glass by the cap. It can also be caused when the top is turned, twisted or pulled out.

Taste Test

A more unusual method of helping to determine age is the "taste test". Many, but not all, old ornaments will have a salty taste when touched to the tip of the tongue. The exact reason for this is unknown, but it has been suggested that it might be caused by the chemical makeup of the ornament's finish. It has also been suggested that the taste is made by body salts left on the ornament from many years of handling. Whatever the cause, newer ornaments do not have this distinctive salty taste.

Condition

Since time will also bring wear on the finish, the condition of an ornament can give a clue to its age. This can be a difficult area to judge because some old ornaments that have had good care can be in excellent condition. Similarly, new ones that have been abused can look rather worn and old. There are certain distinctive problems found in the condition of old ornaments. The loss of silvering inside the ornament will result in darkened or unreflective areas. Paint wear caused by years of handling and storage is also likely. Once brilliant colors may be faded or muted. This is caused by wear, dust accumulation and age. Newer ornaments will more than likely have a shine to their finish that has not been worn off by hears of handling.

Wax drips although unsightly can possibly date your ornament to when candles were used instead of electric lights.

Paint and Finish

Besides condition, the actual paint and finish can be helpful in determining the age of an ornament. Many new ornaments have large unpainted areas which shows its shiny mirrored surface. The lacquer paints used in more recent years also have a shiny appearance. On the other hand, many old ornaments were dipped into a base coat of light gold or silver tint. This mellows the harsh mirror finish and leaves a warm, more subtle, glow. Additional colors, which also picked up the subtle hue, were then layered on top of this as highlights. These finishes of "doctored" lacquer are more likely to flake off than wear off. They are also much more susceptible to dampness and water damage than many other finishes. These base coats are seldom used today.

Certain colors and paints will indicate a newer ornament. The flesh colors on faces and hands are a good example. Early pieces were painted in a flat or matte, water based color. Later pieces were painted with an enamel which left them with a shiny appearance. Deep forest green is a color that was not popularly used until the 1950s; and a shining brown-bronze was not common until the 1960s-1980s.

Finally, in the search for clues to determine an ornament's age, we find that certain pieces and types have never been reproduced and thus any that are found could be considered old. Dresdens, lithographed scraps, cotton batting and paper candy containers fall into this category. As an aid to collectors, I have tried to list with the individual ornament descriptions whether or not the piece has been reproduced. But like the other methods listed here, this too is not infallible. It is difficult to determine all the pieces that were reblown in the 1950s and as new ones are reblown every year, it is impossible to project what will be available in the next few years.

As this book contains more than just glass ornaments, here are some ideas for determining age in ornaments other than glass:

Metal - They may have a dull or even rusty appearance unless they were given good care. Older pieces are likely to be stamped "Germany", and very few metal pieces have been reissued.

Lights - Older lights were made of clear glass and then painted. Ones from the 1920s, 1930s and 1950s were made of milk glass. Lights with a small base were designed to fit the old strings popular before World War II. The country of origin stamped on the metal base can also help determine age of a light, with the European pieces being generally older. The attempt to revive the figural light business in the 1950s was not very successful and they are no longer being produced. Thus figural lights are not grouped in the same pre-war, post-war categories of glass ornaments.

Further information on the question of old or new can be found in the respective ornament sections.

Throughout this article, it may sound as though I am against the new ornaments. Far from it! I am only against collectors buying new ornaments believing them to be old. I feel that the newer pieces are collectible in themselves and they will certainly be the antiques of the future. This is especially true if the originals become so expensive that they become unobtainable by the average collector. Sometimes I wonder why we pay $100.00 for an ornament when an exact piece, blown in the same mold, can be bought at a Christmas shop for $3.00. For a reasonably small investment, a collector can obtain quite a large variety of these old style ornaments. Several authors have also discussed the idea that even the newer figural ornaments are getting fewer each year, as the desire for other types of ornaments increase and the makers of the mouth-blown ornaments find more lucrative trades. If this is true, the current production of figural ornaments may provide one last, relatively-inexpensive way to recapture the beauty of yesterday's tree; and allow another generation to rejoice in the virtual fairyland of ornaments that grace its branches. Besides, for children of all ages, to whom the Christmas ornament is really dedicated, it matters not whether these glittering trinkets are old or new.

A WORD ABOUT COLLECTIBILITY AND PRICE

Pricing and price lists are perhaps a major draw for a book of this nature; it is also a major drawback. The author is invariably set up as some final authority on the worth, value, or collectibility of an object. This is not the way I hope this book is used, for determining the value and desirability of something for other people is always a tricky business. Use the book as it is meant, a price **guide**.

How much something is worth is based on several factors: condition, desirability, rarity, age and current market prices.

The condition of an ornament is very important to its price. The value of a damaged ornament will vary with its rarity and the amount of damage anywhere from about half price to worthless. The prices listed in the guide are for ornaments in good condition.

What Constitutes "Good Condition"?

Breaks: In glass ornaments, there should be no breaks, chips or cracks in the glass. Some small chips out of the neck or pike (where the cap is inserted) are generally acceptable. However, if these are long enough to show badly, if they extend into the ornament itself, or affect the secureness of the cap and the hanging ability, then the price will be affected.

Silvering and Paint: The silvering inside an ornament and the paint or finish on the outside must be intact for the ornament to be considered in good condition. With age, the reflective silver surface inside the ornament will tarnish or darken. This process gives it the patina of age. This, along with the muting and fading of the once bright laquered colors, gives the glass a warm golden glow that only age can bring. This, of course, is not an undesirable process. However, if the silvering starts to flake away, leaving dark or unreflective parts, the ornament cannot be considered in good condition. Likewise, paint or lacquer **wear** is expected. But if there are areas of missing paint or chipping and flaking, this will distract from its appearance and thus its value. Paint that is missing from an unsilvered ornament is more distracting than the same problem on a silvered one. This is because it leaves a darkened, unreflective spot in the glass.

Repairs: A good repair can save an ornament from total destruction and improve its appearance once it has been broken. However, once damaged or repaired, the value (if it still has any at all) will be considerably less than for an intact ornament. (See section on repairing ornaments in "Collector Tips".)

For items made from paper, good condition would indicate that they were intact and free from creases, stains or tears. If they were colored in any way or lithographed, the colors should be reasonably brilliant and not faded. There should be no chipping or flaking of the colored surface. If there is any tinsel or wire, this includes glass ornaments, it may be tarnished with age; however, it should not be broken or corroded or pulled loose from its original position.

On metal items, tarnish is to be expected; but, they should be intact and rust-free. Many metal items are easily bent; but, unless there is serious damage, they can easily be bent back into their original position.

Spun glass and fabric items should be intact, free of stains and tears. Both should retain their original full shape with any applied parts also being in good condition.

Lights should meet the same general conditions as glass ornaments. They should be free of breaks and cracks and have good paint. To some collectors, it is important that the light work; to others, it is not a consideration.

Most areas of discussion that follow apply not only to the blown glass ornaments, but to all these other forms as well.

The final decision in the area of condition is more or less a personal one. Does the damage - missing silver or missing paint - affect the overall appearance and desirability of the ornament? If your answer is "yes", then the ornament should not be considered in good condition.

What Consitututes "Desirability"?

A second factor contributing to the price of an ornament is its desirability. This "desirability" is an elusive thing, and yet it is so extremely important when it comes to the price that if an item had no desirability it would have no value. Typical ideas that reflect this are: "I want this because no one else has it." . . . "It's so cute." . . . "It's so beautiful." . . . or "I don't have one like it."

Desirability can be influence by several things:

Rarity: This will be discussed later in greater detail, but it is mentioned here because many collectors hunt for/desire the rare item that no one else has in their collection.

Uniqueness: Items that are unusual are generally more sought after. Whimsical ornaments fall into this category. They are desirable because of their comic nature, childlike charm or unusual combination of ideas. It is for this reason that a kitten in a bag is more desirable than a pine cone.

Beauty: The aesthetic appeal that an item has, especially to a broad audience, will increase its value. If an ornament is considered bizarre or ugly, it has already lost some of its collectibility.

Finishes: The way in which an ornament is finished or decorated can affect its beauty and thus its value. It seems that the most desirable finish is the painted or lacquered one. Although the "sandy" finish, the "frosted" (crushed glass), and the "Venetian Dew" (tiny glass beads) finishes are rarer than the lacquered finish, they demand a lesser price. This can possibly be accounted for by the fact that such finishes tend to distort or cover the delicate molding, thereby making the ornament appear to be more crudely made.

Molding: Ornaments that have been blown into molds are generally more desirable and valuable than those which have been free-blown. However, the fineness or sharpness of this molded detail is very important. The European glass blowers in general and the Lauchan ones in particular were considered the masters at making the fine, delicately molded ornaments. Those ornaments blown in Japan and the United States were generally of a heavier, thicker glass, and the molding was of a cruder nature, i.e., of less detail. This accounts for the substantially lower prices on the ornaments from these two countries. Even though many figurals from the United States are much rarer than their German/European counterparts, desirability has overridden rarity and the price remains low. Here it should be mentioned that the country of origin has little affect on the price of an ornament. It is often very difficult to tell the difference between quality German, Austrian or Czech blown ornaments and although the German-made are traditionally preferred, most collectors do not care what country the ornament is from. Rather, they judge the item and its price on its beauty, detail, molding, uniqueness and the other areas I am outlining.

A second problem area in molding is that of the poorly blown ornament. No matter how fine the detailing on a **mold** is, if the hot glass ball is not properly blown and pressed tightly against each part of the mold, the detail will be lost on the finished product. This is especially true of the fine detailing found on faces, hands, etc. Day after day, working upwards of 12 or more hours over a glowing burner, the cottage worker would blow his glowing orange glass into those small two piece molds. It is obvious that sometimes the hot glass would blow well and fill the mold perfectly, picking up the sharp detail; and that other times, for whatever reason, the hot glass would not expand well into the mold and the detailing would be blurred or lost. It is for this reason that I see a fallacy in the idea that molding can be used to determine age.

Some authorities have suggested that down through the years of use, the fine detailing of the molds was worn away. Thus the "newer" ornaments blown into the old molds would be more blurred on these fine details. I have several "new" ornaments, blown in the old molds, in which the detail is much sharper and clearer than in its antique counterpart. I would suggest that some of the poorly molded "newer" ornaments are caused by this problem of improper expansion coupled with a lack of the care and concern that was shown by the self-employed cottage worker of yesterday. If their ornaments were not carefully made, they would not be bought by the wholesaler. The cottage worker's whole livelihood depended on the quality of his own work. This is not always the case with the ornaments being produced in the factories of today. Furthermore, the glass being used today is heavier than the paper thin type used before the war. This heavier/thicker glass would be harder to blow into the fine lines of a mold, thus causing details to be blurred or lost altogether. I feel these are more likely the cause of poor molding on ornaments than the wearing away of various parts of those sturdy little molds. Regardless of the causes of this problem, a poorly molded piece cannot compete with the desirability or price of a fine, delicately detailed ornament.

A Question of Rarity

A third factor that will affect the price of an ornament is its rarity. This area is a difficult one to establish. Since there is to way to determine the exact number of ornaments blown into a given mold, rarity in the area of Christmas ornaments has to be determined on how often an item is seen. Whenever two collectors get together, they are bound to see something new. This is part of the intrigue of this hobby -- not knowing what will turn up next. It is also what makes it so difficult to establish a firm rating system. There are several interesting ideas that need to be taken into account when considering the rarity of an ornament.

Establishment: An ornament that no one has ever seen before and is truly rare, may not bring as high a price as one which has been seen many times. The difference is, **one has been established** as being rare by collectors and the other has not. Therefore, rarity is often not an established fact, but rather a commonly believed idea. Many items which five years ago were believed to be rare, have turned out to be quite common.

Popularity: This brings us back to the idea of desirability. Those popular ornaments that sold well year after year, would have been produced in great quantities. Because of their popularity and consequent large numbers, they could hardly be considered rare. Those ornaments that did not sell well, would be discontinued early, their numbers would be limited and they could be rare. However, since human tastes have not drastically changed in the last hundred years, those items that were not desirable or popular then, probably are not that desirable now, either. Since we have already shown the important relationship of desirability to price, the outcome of the following situation is fairly obvious. You proudly point to a strange and grotesque little ornament and say, "There were only three dozen of these ever produced." If the answer is something like "I can see why," or "Who cares?", you can forget about your "rare" ornament being worth a fortune. In the same thought, it has already been shown that finishes such as the "sandy" and "frosted" finish, although rarer, do not increase the value because they are less desirable. The same idea of rarer doesn't mean more valuable can be applied to the free blown ornament. Each of these is a one of a kind piece of art, but the mass-produced molded ornament is still more desirable. You will readily find that the prices on rare, unique, free blowns are not as high as its rare molded counterpart. Popularity among collectors is an important factor, important enough to override rarity. Therefore, the best ornament will be both popular and rare.

Variations: A popular selling theme would often be copied and used, with slight variations, by other glass blowers. Every family had its own versions of Santa Claus, flowers, birds, clowns, etc. And perhaps some families would concentrate heavily on variations of one of these themes. However, unless these variations are very obvious and set the ornament apart, even a rare variation on a common theme will not bring an increase in price. An example of this might be the common song birds. There are probably over a hundred molded variations, some probably much rarer than others, but the price for the general group of song birds, rare and otherwise, remains at about $10.00 to $20.00. To be placed in a separate pricing or rarity category, the variation must be major and one that is easily identified. Even though each glass producing family had its own variation on the popular themes, they would also strive to have a special item like no one else's. It would be one of these beautiful special items produced by only one family for perhaps only one season that would be the truly rare and valuable ornament.

A Question of Age

A fourth main factor in the collectibility and pricing of Christmas ornaments is the item's age. The major dividing line is 1939. The one family cottage industry which grew and developed during the 70 "Golden Years" (1870-1939), died with the advent of World War II. Germany, the world, and the ornament business have not been the same since. Those ornaments produced during the Golden Years are more desirable and are referred to as the antique or old ornaments. Those ornaments made after the war lost much of their fragile beauty when mass-produced in factories. Those ornaments from the 1940s-1970s are referred to as "new" ornaments. Although many "newer" ornaments have rising values, they are not as expensive as the "older" versions. (See "Collector Tips" - telling old ornaments from new.)

Current Market Value

The final factor in this consideration of prices is that of the current market value. The fair market value is what an item sells for on a continuing basis. That is to say, you throw out the bargain prices as well as the ridiculously high ones. The real value of something is what you can get out of it when you need the money. In making up the price list for this book, I have tried to arrive at this current market value. Many lists merely report the price for which an item was seen **offered** for sale. They do not tell you at what price they are **selling**, or that those items which were overpriced took ten years to sell (by that time inflation had caught up to it), or that eventually the seller "wised up" and sold the item at a lower price.

One of the lamest excuses I've heard for overpricing is, "That's what the book says it's worth." If it doesn't sell at a given price, it obviously is not worth that price. Besides, one could counter, "What book?" and "Is this the exact same item as described?" Many times descriptions are so vague that they could cover a hundred different items. For example, "silvered glass bird - $40.00." Granted some rarer bird forms are worth $40.00; however, it is not wise to price all your birds (whose current market value is $10.00 to $20.00) at $40.00 unless you really want to keep them.

The fair market value of an item will also vary with the regions of the country. For example, the prices on both the East and West coasts have a tendency to be higher than those in the Midwest. In compiling this guide, I have taken prices from all these areas. I have also had the prices listed here checked by collectors in all three regions. If in the end, people on the coasts say that the prices are too low and the collectors in the Midwest say they are too high, then perhaps I've succeeded in establishing somewhat of a fair price country wide. The important thing to always bear in mind about this or any other price guide is that they are just that -- a price **guide**, not a pricing appraisal list. Currently, ornament prices are in a state of flux. Prices have dropped on common pieces and dropped or stayed the same on average ornaments. Only on the rare and beautiful ornaments have prices steadily risen.

One final thing that price guides unfortunately tend to do is slowly raise the price of its listed items. If an item's listed price is $20.00-30.00, everybody wants to price theirs at the $30.00 level. Originally meant to represent top dollar for fine pieces in excellent condition, it soon becomes the standard price because "that is what the book says." Collectors will eventually have to pay the new inflated price with the finer items going to $40.00, which in turn eventually becomes the standard price because "that's what everyone is asking," etc., etc., etc. So the prices slowly rise in a type of self-fulfilling prophesy until . . . the bottom drops out of the market.

Now that this economics lesson on pricing is over, let me say this. I sometimes wonder if some of these child-like pieces of colored glass are really worth $100.00 or $200.00, especially since they are so easily broken into a thousand worthless pieces. It makes one stop and think when about to buy one of these now tarnished baubles. But, in its soft golden reflection, I see them as a form of folk art that has vanished with its storybook life style into the pages of history. I imagine nostalgically all those many Christmases of yesterday; and the stories those pieces of glass, scraps of paper and bits of tinsel could tell of children's faces full of awe and wonder, of Christmas hopes and dreams come true. That special magic that only Christmas can possess wells up within me and suddenly they are more than colored glass and paper, they are treasured links with a more romantic past . . . I buy the ornament. I think it must be pretty much the same with most collectors.

A LIST OF TERMS
AND ABBREVIATIONS
USED IN THIS BOOK

In the catalogue of ornaments, the reader will find these terms and abbreviations commonly used to help describe the pieces:

(M) - Molded - blown into a detailed mold.

(FB) - Free Blown - made by twisting, turning and blowing into the desired shape rather than with a mold.

(M&FB) - made using a combination of a mold and freeblown techniques.

(BEAD) - Pieces made of small beads strung on thin wire.

SG - Spun Glass - has added parts made from thin glass fiber, i.e., bird tails and angel wings.

Approx. 3″ - Approximately 3″ - size of the ornament measuring only the glass, not clip-ons or hangers. All sizes given are approximate because the pike or stem left on the ornament could vary up to ½″ in length. H, W and L stand for height, width and length. European ornaments were made and marketed in the metric measurements of millimeters and centimeters. Most sizes are ¼″ variances.

2″, 3″ and 4″ - indicates the ornament had separate moldings in these sizes.

Germany, Czech., Japan, U.S., etc. - country in which the ornament was made. No listing indicates the author is not positive of the country or origin.

p28a - Picture 28a - indicates the ornament described is in picture 28 of this volume. The "A", "B", "C", etc., is used when more than one ornament is in the picture with "A" indicating the first ornament on the left, "B" the second ornament from the left, etc.

Snyder p24, Rogers p68, Stille p23, Schiffer p88 - indicates that the described ornament is pictured in *The Christmas Book*, by P. Snyder or *The Glass Christmas Ornament* by Rogers & Hawkins, *Alter Christbaumschmuck* by E. Stille, or *Christmas Ornaments* by M. Schiffer, on the page or picture number indicated.

Standard Form - form or molding most commonly found.

Scrap - small chromolithographed pictured added to an ornament; also called glanzbilder.

Dresden - piece made of embossed and detailed cardboard usually colored gold or silver. Such pieces were often made in Dresden, Germany, hence their sobriquet.

Annealed - two separate pieces of glass melted or fused together rather than molded in one piece.

TYPE I, II, III, etc. - a means of separating ornaments made in different molds but which have the same name or idea. The type number or order in which they are listed has nothing to do with rarity, desirability or price.

Embossed - indicates that the design described is molded into the shape or raised in bas relief.

OP - Old Production - the ornament was produced before 1940; any mold usage since then is unknown.

NP - New Production - ornament mold was made and used since 1940, no known ''old'' ones exists.

OP-NP - the ornament and mold are old but it has also been reused since 1940, i.e., new ornaments of it can be found.

Rarity rating system: - 1. Very Rare; 2. Rare; 3. Scarce; 4. Uncommon; 5. Common

This will give the collector some idea as to how often they might expect to see a given ornament. The system is based on collectors, their collections and how often the given item has been seen for sale.

This seemingly haphazard way of determining rarity is the only option the collector has, because we have no records as to how many ornaments were blown in a given mold or how many of these have survived. Rarity does not always affect the value of a given ornament, nor does it reflect its beauty or desirability.

Reprint from an old catalog.

31

CHAPTER III

GLASS CHRISTMAS ORNAMENTS

HISTORY

Glass Christmas ornaments as we know them have only been produced for a little more than a hundred years, and it has not been until the last 60 years that they were the major type of decoration on the tree. For most Americans, however, the glass decoration whether made in a mold or free blown, has come to symbolize THE Christmas ornament.

Until 1940, the glass ornament capital of the world was the small German town of Lauscha. In its day, this village and its surrounding area produced 95% of the ornaments decorating American Christmas trees.

The early history of the glass ornament is lost in a cerain amount of obscurity and confusion. They began almost as a whim or playful pastime for the German glassmakers. Even after some were sold commercially, they were considered only a secondary occupation to the glassblower's main business of making and selling scientific and pharmaceutical equiment, such as beakers, tubes, retorts, etc.; and glass toys which included marbles and glass eyes for dolls. By the 1880s, this picture would change drastically.

Lauscha's glassblowing business began in 1590 when a group of Protestant glassmakers left their homes in the German region of Swabia because of religious persecution. Lead by the Greiner and Muller families, they settled in the Thuringian Mountains, some 60 miles north of Nuremburg. Lauscha was able to provide the natural resources of wood, volcanic limestone and sand that were necessary to the glass-making business. By 1597, they had founded a glass "house" or factory there with the help of the Duke of Coburg. It must be remembered that during this late medieval period, the backing of a powerful noble was extremely important to such undertakings. Germany was essentially run by such dukes and princes until its unification in the 1880s.

Over the next few decades, Lauscha became an important glass center, producing drinking glasses, bulls' eye window glass (round concentric circles embossed into panes of glass) and the toys and instruments previously listed.

This increased business brought increasing numbers of glassmakers to the area. This in turn put a strain on the wood resources that were necessary to fire the large kilns. By the eighteenth century, many glassmakers were working out of a home workshop. Instead of using the large furnaces of the factory, they began using a small flame produced by burning vegetable oils, such as turnip or grape seed oil, or parafin. Air was forced into the flame by mouth or by a goat skin bellows. This provided a clumsy but effective way of getting different temperatures into the small flame.

In 1867, a gas works was build in Lauscha which provided not only a reliable source of fuel, but also a steady and adjustable flame. Until the development of the gas flame, the glass which was produced at the kiln was of a heavy, utilitarian nature. It was now possible to blow thinner, more delicate, glass items. This was the beginning of the home cottage industry which was destined to become the backbone of the ornament business and the source of a unique style of folk art.

As I previously mentioned, Lauscha was producing a wide variety of glass items, including toys; however, none of them were directly related to the idea of the glass Christmas ornament. The product that eventually lead to the development of Christmas ornaments was the small "silvered" beads and glass tubes that were used in the clothing and fashion industry of the day. In the eighteenth century, Lauschan workers began making tubes of connected beads and "silvering" them with zinc or lead. By the early 1800s, it was their primary business, and the small village of only several thousand inhabitants was supplying the entire European millinery trade.

Glassmakers in Bohemia (now Czechoslovakia) began to errode Lauscha's business in 1845 with a superior bead product known as "pearls of Paris". By 1857, they had also developed a silvering process, based on silver nitrate, which gave the beads a mirror-like shine. The Germans promptly lost most of their market and were not able to recapture it until Louis Greiner-Schlotfeger duplicated the Czechoslovakian process.

By the early years of the nineteenth century, the individual cottage industry was already well established, and the art of silvered decorations, albeit small beads, had been mastered. Now the stage was set for the development of the silvered glass ornament. By the early 1800s, the decorated tree was an established and fast-growing custom; however, the decorations did not include glass items. Most early decorations were cookies, cakes, candies, fruit, nuts, paper and Christmas gifts themselves. Very few, if any, were designed to be reused year after year. At this same time, Lauschan glassmakers were making large glass balls or "Kugels" which they silvered on the inside with zinc or lead. Contrary to the popular title "mercury glass", no known pieces were made with mercury silvering. These early Kugels were made for amusement but were also sold as window decorations, "witches balls", or garden "panorama" balls. These last pieces were fastened on pikes in the garden and served the same function as large silvered lawn decorations do today. These garden balls look almost exactly like the early Kugel ornaments which still had a short pike attached to them and are highly collected in Germany today, bringing prices in the hundreds of dollars.

During the next 20 years, someone decided that these reflective balls also looked great on a candle-lit tree. Who it was and how it happened we will probably never know, but by 1848 we find the first **recorded** order of silvered kugels for use as Christmas ornaments -- "six dozen of Christmas tree ornaments in three sizes." Even the nonchalant way of describing them as Christmas tree ornaments would certainly indicate that the kugels were commonly being sold as ornaments even before that date. (For a more complete history of the kugel ornaments themselves, see the section "Kugels" in this chapter.)

These early pieces were made of thick-walled glass and do not resemble the ornaments known today. The wood-fired kilns had made thick glass a necessity. However, with the establishment of the gas works, the glass tubes could be blown and expanded into a much thinner decoration.

There seems to be some confusion over the first use of molds in Christmas ornaments. Some suggest that Louis Greiner-Schlotfeger developed them in 1870 by blowing glass into a pine cone-shaped pastry mold. However, this does not take into account the molded kugel, such as grapes and "ribbed" pieces, which were certainly created much earlier. Nor does it explain an 1869 account in *Harper's Bazaar* that describes the tree decorated with glass "globes, fruit, and flowers of colored glass". A full description of this tree is given in the section "A History of the Decorated Christmas Tree". Other glass objects, such as the thick "fairy lamps", had been mold-made for many years. It is hard to believe that it would take almost thirty years (1848-1870) for this same technology to be applied to Christmas ornaments.

What Louis Greiner-Schlotfeger probably did do in 1870 was to make the first **thin-walled**, silver-nitrate finished ornament that was mold-blown.

Regardless of the exact dates, the general sequence of events for ornament development was certainly overlapping. First came the heavy glass kugels -- some "silvered" with lead or zinc and coated with wax while others were unsilvered. Some were made of colored glass and some painted with glitter decorations. Then came thick-walled kugels, such as grapes, that were made in molds. Next came the thin-walled ornaments with silver nitrate silvering; and finally the paper-thin, **mold-blown** ornament. It is only natural that there would be several years of overlap in each area of transition or development. The kugels, for example, which were made in a factory's kiln, would not cease to be made just because the cottage workers were making thin-walled ornaments. Like any new product, the new thinner pieces had to stand the test of time and public acceptance. In the meantime, the older kugels were still being sold. As you can see, it is very difficult to assign any definite time frame to the major changes in development.

Even after the development of the molds for making fancy forms, the vast majority of ornaments continued to be free-blown, i.e., made without the use of a mold. This is a fact that is often forgotten by collectors who are more interested in those rarer molded pieces.

By the 1880s, the ornament business had superseded all other glass products of Lauscha and its neighboring villages of Steinheid and Ernstthal. At the same time, the popularity of the glass Christmas ornament developed very quickly, both in Europe and more importantly, in America. Ornaments were offered for sale by large importers and toy dealers such as Erlich Brothers and Amos M. Lyon, both of New York. The single most influential figure in the marketing of the glass ornament, however, was F. W. Woolworth of the "Five and Dime" fame.

America was the glassblower's largest market, and Woolworth was America's largest importer, bringing in hundreds of thousands of ornaments a year. His first encounter with the glass decorations, however, was quite different. Snyder quotes the following autobiographical sketch:

"In the fall of 1880 I went to an importing firm on Strawberry Street, Philadelphia, Meyer & Schoenaman, to buy some toys and about the first thing they did was drag out a lot of colored glass ornaments the like of which I had never seen. 'What are those things?' I asked. They explained that these goods were, oh, such fine sellers, but I laughed. 'You can't sell me any foolish thing like that,' I said. 'I don't believe they would sell and most of them would be smashed anyway before there was a chance to sell them.' They explained the profit was big enough to offset the breakage, but I was incredulous. It was hard to understand what the people would want of those colored glass things. We argued back and forth a long time and finally the house made me the proposition that it would guarantee the sale at retail, of twenty-five dollars worth of Christmas tree ornaments. 'All right,' I agreed. 'You can send them to me wholly at your own risk.'

The goods arrived a few days before Christmas and, with a good deal of indifference, I put them on my counters. In two days they were gone, and I woke up. But it was too late to order any more, and I had to turn away a big demand. The next Christmas season I was on hand early with what I considered a large order, but it was not large enough. They proved to be the best sellers in my store for the holidays."

Woolworth made a substantial fortune (estimated at $25 million) in glass Christmas ornaments, most of which were sold one at a time.

Until the 1890s, Lauscha and the surrounding villages of Steinheid and Ernstthal, had little or no competition in the world's ornament trade. William DeMuth of New York blew and marketed some kugel-like balls and beads in 1870, but this posed no serious threat to the German business. However, in the last decade of the nineteenth century, Lauscha's arch rivel, Goblanz, Czechoslovakia, began to turn their famous bead business into a Christmas business. Stringing their silvered beads on thin wire, they formed them into a wide variety of geometric shapes as well as recognizable objects.

In 1914, a glass factory which made molded ornaments was established in Vienna, Austria, by Josef Eggeling, himself a transplanted German. The Wiener Christbaumschmuck - Fabrik (Viennese Christmas Ornament Factory) supported a cottage industry of German immigrants who blew ornaments very similar to Lauscha's. In the 1920s, Czechoslovakia (now called by that name) moved into the area of molded and blown ornaments. During this same decade, Japan also joined in the competition for the American market. By the mid 1930s, Poland was exporting its product, mostly balls and indents, to the United States.

American glassmakers had dabbled in the ornament market as early as 1871 and again during World War I. Neither of these attempts had been very successful, the 1918 attempt being a crude and poorly colored ornament. During the 1930s, American glassmakers began to establish themselves; and one, Max Echardt, would eventually dominate the business.

Echardt, himself a German immigrant, had been an importer of German toys and Christmas ornaments for many years. By 1937 he was convinced of an upcoming war in Europe which would, as in the past, disrupt the German ornament trade. During the next two years, he laid the groundwork for a new American ornament business. In 1939 he was able to make use of the Corning Glass Company's "ribbon" glassblowing machine. This equipment

run down the pike. The boards were then placed in the rafters or over the oven so the ornaments would dry. The next day, they were lacquered and painted by the family. Other pieces were dipped into clear gelatine to act as an adhesive and rolled in starch to create "snow" or a frosted appearance. Still others were rolled in tiny glass balls to give them a "Venetian Dew" finish.

After more drying, the spears or spikes were scored and snapped off by one of the younger children using a grit-covered knife. Grandmothers added wire wrappings to create beautiful flower baskets, balloons, sailboats, stars and other fancy shapes. Fabric flowers or leaves, spun glass, tucksheer, tinsel, chenille, thread and scraps are examples of other items added during this finishing process.

Finally, the youngest children added the metal caps and put the ornaments into boxes of a dozen each. Working as long as 15 hours a day during "the season", from June to November, a family could produce three to five hundred ornaments a day and earn about three dollars a week.

Fridays were the traditional day for the wife to take the finished ornaments to the collector or wholesaler. They were packed into a tall wicker basket which was then strapped to her back. Another long basketful, often five feet long, was placed lengthwise on top of the first. She might also hand-carry additional bundles. Then came several train trips to Sonneberg where the ornament warehouses were located. In later years, the wholesaler's trucks would pick up the ornaments and deliver the necessary supplies. At this time most ornament makers were working for specific wholesalers and were pretty much told what kinds and quantities of ornaments to produce.

These wholesalers played an important role in the development of the glass ornament. In the earliest system of distribution, peddlers or "wheel barrow sellers" went from town to town and sold the ornaments on street corners. Next the ornaments were handled by the "publisher" system.

Book publishers in Sonneberg, who already had a distribution system, and toy dealers, who already had an export system, became the middleman between the ornament maker and the importer. They also served as mail order houses for distribution in Germany. This system gave the glassblowers a central point of contact with the American buyers, and year around warehouses helped to eliminate the bust-boom cycle of earlier years. The wholesalers, of course, made their share of the profit, often at the expense of the ornament maker. During slow years, volume kept the profit low. During boom years, fierce competition for buyers kept prices (and thus profits) down. The wholesaler's first loyalty was to the buyer and not the individual glassblower.

At Sonneberg's warehouses, showrooms, and exhibitions, the major importers selected their wares. From Sonneberg and Nuremburg, the ornaments were sent by rail to Bremen and Bremerhaven where they were used as a light "topping off" cargo in America-bound ships.

In the final stage, the glass ornaments were sold individually in stores like Woolworths or in sets from mail order companies like Sears and Roebuck. In the 1920s, prices ranged from two cents for 1½" diameter balls to ten cents for large figural or wire wrapped ornaments. It is easy to see why there is such a profusion of round balls.

A wide variety of Christmas ornaments have been made over the last 200 years. Metal, wax, fabric, paper and cardboard have all come and gone. Ironically, the most enduring form of ornament was also the most fragile. The glass ornament has survived the test of time and today is the most popular of all Christmas decorations.

ANIMALS

Animals are among the most popular and collectible of the glass Christmas ornaments. They come in a wide variety of forms ranging from pets and barnyard animals to the more exotic creatures of the jungle.

Animals have found popularity as tree decorations for several reasons. Many, like cats and dogs, represented beloved household pets that were often given as Christmas gifts. Others were considered "cuddly" or were popular because people already collected them in other forms. Owls, bears, elephants, etc., fall into this category. Still other animals such as fish, doves and spiders, represented aspects of the Christian faith or Christmas legends.

It seems that the more common an animal was in real life, the more often it was copied, thus making the ornament more common also. A prime example of this idea is the bird ornaments. Ornaments of the more exotic animals are, like their real life counterparts, harder to find.

Mythological creatures are rare in animal ornaments. However, animals were a popular media for pieces that have commonly been called "fantasy and whimsical". During the past few years, there has been considerable confusion of these terms. Furthermore, it has had the unfortunate result of inflating prices on those pieces that sellers claim are "fantasy or whimsical". These should not be some kind of magic title that instantly bring bigger bucks. In fact, fantasy pieces are in no way uncommon. A fantasy piece is simply one in which the ornament maker used his imagination to create unusual ideas or forms. Animals dressed or acting as people and most characters from fairy tales are fantasy pieces. Technically, fantasy items are any that do not reflect real life things. In that case, it is easy to see that many ornaments are indeed fantasy pieces.

Doubtless, there were many times when a glassblower got tired of blowing the same form thousands of times. Perhaps by design or as a whim (hence the title "whimsical" pieces) to combat boredom, some standard pieces were modified with free-blown additions. Thus molded Santas, dogs, snowmen, etc., were attached to or put into free-blown shapes such as ovals or balls. Similarly, molded heads may have stylized bodies added as a change of pace and a way of expanding a glassmaker's inventory. Many early free-blown pieces also fall into this category having been created on a whim or sudden inspiration.

The end result, however, is that fantasy and whimsical pieces are only titles of explanation and certainly not a basis for increasing prices. Collectors should buy a piece for its own merits and because they like it; not because some often misused title has been applied to it.

ALLIGATOR - (FB), Approx. 8" - The alligator is shown in the prone position with a clip-on in the stomach area. It has four "bumps" on the body and two on either side of the head. No legs show. Although previously thought to be a German piece, an original tag shows this to be a Czech piece. (Czech., p1, OP, R2) $300.00-350.00

VARIATION: STANDING ALLIGATOR - (FB) - This is a 1950s production but still scarce. $70.00-80.00

ANTELOPE (EMBOSSED) - (M), Approx. 2" - This antelope with large curved horns stands embossed onto a square. There is a flower on the reverse. This was perhaps designed to look like an early decorated cookie. (p60c, OP, R2) $45.00-55.00

Bears

Bears were a popular animal theme with the early glassblowers. Popularized by Teddy Roosevelt, the cuddly teddy bear idea became popular after the turn of the century. The bear is also the symbol of the German city of Berlin. Bears are almost always found standing or sitting on their haunches, with a hanging cap in the head area. Since this was also a popular position for dogs, they are sometimes hard to tell apart.

BEAR CARRYING A STICK - (M), Approx. 2″, 2½″ & 4″ - The bear sits on its haunches and holds a slender stick against its chest with its right paw. It has molded fur and a ruffle around its neck that has led to speculation that the piece is a monkey. Since the tail is short and stubby, it is probably a bear. The larger piece is better detailed and appears to be wearing a flat cap. (Germany, p2c and p3a, OP, R3)   Smaller $50.00-75.00
Large (scarcer) $175.00-200.00

BEAR HOLDING A HEART - (M), Approx. 3″ & 3¾″ - This squatting bear is shown with a heart embossed onto its chest. Both paws hold the heart. It has a ribbon around its neck which ties in a bow at the back. (Germany, p5a, OP-NP Small size only, R2)   Smaller $100.00-125.00
Large $150.00-175.00

BEAR IN A CLOWN SUIT - (M), Approx. 2½″, 4″ & 4½″ - This bear is dressed in a two-buttoned clown suit with a ruffled collar. It wears a small hat that covers its right ear, and its paws are in its pockets. (Germany, p5c, p7c, OP, R3)   Small $50.00-75.00
Medium $100.00-125.00
Large $125.00-150.00

BEAR IN A CAP - (M), Approx. 4″ - The bear wears a cone-shaped hat. His right paw is at the ear, and his left is on the stomach. There is no molded fur. This piece has also been described as a dog. (p8a, OP-NP, [1950s], R2-3)
$80.00-90.00
1950s form $25.00-35.00

BEAR IN LEATHER SHORTS AND SUSPENDERS - (M), Approx. 3½″ - This bear is dressed in a traditional Bavarian outfit. It also has a bow at his neck and a conical hat. He has molded fur but is most often found covered in crushed glass. (Germany, p2b, NP 1950s only, R3)
$30.00-40.00

BEAR IN A VEST AND BOW TIE - (M), Approx. 2½″ & 3″ - This standing bear wears a buttoned vest with a bow tie and collar at his neck. He has good molded fur; its right paw is at the hip, and its left is near the stomach. The molds are now in East Germany. (Germany, p4d, p4e, OP-NP limited, R2) $75.00-90.00

BEAR ON A MOTORCYCLE - (M) - Rogers lists this as a post-war piece. (West Germany, NP, R2) $30.00-40.00

BEAR WITH ANNEALED LEGS - (M&FB), Approx. 4″ - This standing bear has molded fur and its arms at the side. Two free-blown, tubular legs are annealed to the round-ed bottom. (p7b, OP, R1) $300.00-350.00

VARIATION: BEAR WITH ARMS AT THE SIDES - (M), Approx. 2¾″ - This is the same bear described above without the annealed legs. $150.00-175.00

BEAR WITH A BOW - (M), Approx. 3¼″ & 3½″ - This standing bear has a ribbon around its neck which is tied in a bow on its left side. Both arms reach down to the thighs. (Germany, p7a, OP-NP [3″ size only], R2)
Small $50.00-60.00
Large $70.00-80.00

BEAR WITH CHENILLE ARMS AND LEGS - (M), Approx. 3½″ - The bear shows molded fur and has a ribbon with a bow tied around its neck. The body has holes through which the chenille arms and legs pass. (Germany, p6a, OP, R1) $275.00-300.00

BEAR WITH A CLUB - (M), Approx. 2½″ - The bear sits on its haunches and holds a club to its chest with both front paws. It has molded fur and a long snout. When viewed from the front, this appears to be a thin piece. (Germany, p2a, OP, R2) $60.00-75.00

BEAR WITH A MUFF - (M), Approx. 3½″ - Shown standing with both paws inside a muff. Molded fur shows on the bear, and the muff is often covered with crushed glass. (p6b, OP, R3) $80.00-100.00

DANCING BEAR ON A BALL - (M) - Rogers lists this as a rare ornament but gives no further description of it. (Germany, OP, R1) $175.00-200.00

STANDING BEAR - (M), Approx. 4″ - The bear is shown standing on bent legs with its paws on its knees. It has molded fur. (p4c, OP, R2-3)
$125.00-150.00

SITTING "TEDDY" BEAR - (M), Approx. 2″ - This bear is in a usual sitting position with its legs out and its arms at the sides. It has molded fur. The molds are now in East Germany. (Germany, p4b, OP-NP, R2) $50.00-60.00

Birds

Birds are probably the most common form of the blown glass ornaments and come in possibly a hundred different forms. With their clip-on "feet" and spun glass tails, it is hard to imagine any tree of yesteryear without at least one of these beautiful ornaments gracing its branches. The bird form was so popular that they are found as ornaments not only from glass, but also from cotton, metal, lithograph, "Dresdens", etc. A bird could be found as one of the forms of almost any medium in which an ornament was made. The relatively low prices for many birds, (especially song birds) do not reflect the delicacy of their molding, beauty of the paint work or their overall aesthetic appeal. Rather they reflect the relative abundance of this type of ornament.

NOTES:
1. SG stands for spun glass, out of which most bird tails were made, although other items were also used. Real feathers and dried plants, which gave the bird a broom-like tail, were used on early ornaments. Crinkle wire and soft tinsel sprays were also used. Additionally the SG tails might be tinted or painted for more color.

2. SG tails are not measured as part of the overall length of an ornament.

3. It was common for the same bird form to be made in several different sizes.

4. Some birds, especially parrots, cockatoos, canaries, etc., might be found in wire hoops or swings that were often found in bird cages.

5. Side wings might be made of wire, glass or tinsel. These make the piece more desirable, and the price is affected accordingly.

BIRD BATH - (M&FB), Approx. 4″W x 3″H - This was made in several pieces. The bowl of the bird bath is a free-blown ball with a clip-on on the bottom and indented on the top. The indentation was done with a form so as to make a geometric reflecting surface. In the center of the bowl is an indented "fountain" that "shoots" up a tinsel spray. A 2½″ molded bird is attached to the side of the bath by a spring. Because of the spring, the bird has a tendency to bang against the side of the bath. Thus, it is likely many were broken. (p9c, OP, R1) $125.00-150.00

BIRD BATH WITH WATER - (M), Approx. 2″H x 2″W - The bowl of this bird bath has ten ribbed edges around it. The "fountain" in the center looks like a small crown with a long top pike. It is filled with water. This reflects off the inside of the bath making it appear as if the entire piece was filled with water. A scrap bird attached to the side is "bathing". It has a clip-on at the bottom. (p9b, OP, R1) $100.00-125.00

BIRDCAGE, PEDESTAL - (FB), Approx. 7½″ but sizes can vary - This earlier cage is cylinder shaped and comes to a point. The pike forms the pedestal that has wire feet. The entire piece is wrapped in wire and has a Dresden bird. (Germany, p10, OP, R2) $125.00-135.00

BIRDCAGE, ROUND - (M), Approx. 3″ - It has molded bars and a bird molded on the side. (OP, R3)$20.00-30.00

BIRDCAGE, SQUARE - (M), Approx. 2″H x 1″W - It is square shaped with molded bars and a molded bird on two sides. (Germany, p12b, OP, R3-4) $10.00-15.00

BIRDCAGE OF ANNEALED GLASS - (FB), Approx. 3″ but sizes vary - The cage is made of bars which are small annealed rods of glass. The cage could be round or square and have colored glass rods incorporated in them. The birds were usually made of colored glass. These were probably made during the Art Deco period from about 1915 to 1930. (Schiffer p.108, OP, R2) $75.00-85.00

BIRDHOUSE - (M), Approx. 1½″, 2″ & 3½″ - The bird appears to be resting on a pole coming out of a round door. The birdhouse is cylinder shaped with the bird embossed on the side. The back slopes at a sharp angle. A 2″ 1950s version is covered with raised bumps. It is rarer than the older version. (Germany, p11b, OP-NP, R4)
1950s & Small $20.00-30.00
Larger $35.00-45.00

BIRDHOUSE WITH DOVES - (M), Approx. 3″ - The roofed birdhouse is square with two doves or pigeons on its sides. One bird is sitting, and one is flying away. A branch with leaves spreads across all four sides. (p12d, OP, R4) $20.00-30.00

BIRD AND GNOME ON A TREE TRUNK - (M), Approx. 3″ x 1″ - A nicely raised gnome or dwarf figure stands in front of a tree trunk. The bird is approx. 1¾″ with a SG tail. It was blown separately and attached to the trunk by a spring. The trunk has an indented socket on both sides so that the bird could be on either or both sides. (Germany, p9a, OP, R2) $80.00-90.00

Bird Nests

Tradition says if you find a bird nest in the Christmas tree you cut, it will bring good luck to the house for the whole year.

BIRD ON A NEST - (M&FB), Approx. 4½″H x 3″W - Nest is a free-blown ball that is indented. The indent is filled with straw, cotton or SG on which rests a molded bird; both are covered with crinkle wire. Later pieces are usually clip-ons. (Czech., Germany, Austria, p13b, OP-NP, R4)$30.00-40.00

VARIATION: (1) Unsilvered - Approx. 3″ - The nest is an indented ball, a molded bird rests on wood shavings and red berries with the whole piece wrapped in wire. Circa 1910, it is hung by a tinsel wire loop. (p14, R3) $75.00-100.00

VARIATION: (2) An earlier form of the above two, this bird is made of paper and chenille. A tinsel hoop forms the hanger. (p13a, R3) $40.00-50.00

VARIATION: (3) New moldings have lace trim and SG in the nest; are usually clip-on. (p13c) $5.00-10.00

BABY BIRDS IN A NEST - (M), Approx. 3¼″ - This molded clip-on is the nest and three baby birds inside. (Germany, Snyder p89, OP, R2-3) $85.00-95.00

VARIATION: (1) Mother and babies in a nest - (M) - Same molded nest with the mother bird, a regular molded song bird, attached to the side. It has a clip at the bottom of the nest. (Germany, p16a, OP, R2-3) $125.00-150.00

VARIATION: (2) Same nest but with molded mother and father birds attached on opposite sides. (Germany, p16a, OP, R2) $150.00-175.00

VARIATION: (3) This comes in the same forms listed above except the molded nest is slightly different. The center baby has its head and beak raised, and the sides of the nest show molded leaves. The same varying prices apply. (p15b, OP, R2)

BIRD ON A DISC (EMBOSSED) - (M), Approx. 3¼″ dia. - The crude bird is shown flying to the left. There is a geometric flower design on the back. (p20b, OP, R2) $15.00-25.00

BIRD ON A PINE CONE (EMBOSSED) - (M), Approx. 3″L - The embossed bird stands on a pine bough, facing right. (Germany, OP, R3-4) $30.00-40.00

BIRD ON THREE PINE CONES (EMBOSSED) - (M), Approx. 2¼″ - This bird with raised wings faces left on a grouping of three pine cones. (p30a, OP, R2-3)$20.00-25.00.

CANARY - (M), Approx. 3½″ L - It is painted a bright yellow with a SG tail. Clip-on. (Germany, OP, R3-4) $20.00-30.00

Chickens

CHICK - (M), Approx. 2″ - This nicely detailed piece shows the tiny wings and a beak on a slightly upturned head. It is usually found as a clip-on. (Germany, p17b, OP, R2) $125.00-150.00.

CHICK ON AN EGG - (M), Approx. 3½″L - The ornament is egg-shaped. On one side it is "cracked" and shows an embossed baby chick coming out. (Germany, p19c, OP-NP [limited], R1) $125.00-150.00

HEN ON A BASKET - (M), Approx. 3″L - She is shown sitting with wings folded on a wicker basket or nest. The hanger is in the tail. (p18b, OP, R2) $175.00-200.00

ROOSTER - (M), Approx. 3″ - This is similar to song bird type ornaments, with the wings folded at the sides and a SG tail. However, this rooster has a large red comb annealed on its head. (OP, R2) $60.00-75.00

ROOSTER EMBOSSED ON AN OVAL - (M), Approx. 2″ - The rooster stands on a limb and faces to the left. There is a geometric design on the reverse. (Germany, p28d, OP, R3-4) $20.00-25.00

ROOSTER ON A CHICKEN COOP - (M), Approx. 2¾″H AND 3¾″ - The rooster is embossed onto the side of a cylinder shaped coop. He is shown climbing a ladder. Flowers and leaves are also embossed about the ornament. There is also a small crude version which is possibly Japanese. (Germany, p11a, OP-NP, R3-4)
Small $20.00-30.00
Larger $40.00-50.00

"COCK ROBIN" - (M), Approx. 3″L - He is dressed in a coat from which the wings show at the sides; he wears a tie and carries a cane in the left wing. Conical hat holds the hanger. It has also been called a weather vane bird. It may also be found as a clip-on. (Germany, p17a, OP-NP [limited], R1-2) $200.00-225.00

COCKATEEL - (M), Approx. 3″ & 4″ - It is very similar to the cockatoo described below; however, the cockateel has a large protruding top feather which is represented in the ornament by a short pike. (Germany, p21a & c, OP, R3-4)
All sizes $15.00-25.00

COCKATOO - (M), Approx. 3″, 4″ & 5″ - It is in the usual bird position with folded wings. Identifiable by the high comb-like head feathers; it has a SG tail. They clip-on or have an annealed hook in back. They are usually beautifully painted. (Germany, OP, R3-4)   All sizes $15.00-25.00

CRANE - (FB), Approx. 3″ - The crane is in a flying position. It has annealed blue wings, feet and beak; a hanger in the back and a tubular type body. Circa 1920s. (Germany, Rogers p141, R3) $20.00-25.00

DOVE WITH A LETTER - (M), Approx. 1¾″ dia. - A flying dove with a letter in its beak is embossed on a round disc. The reverse shows a cross geometric design. (p12a, OP, R2-3) $10.00-15.00

SOARING DOVE - (M), Approx. 4½″ - This piece has nicely detailed feathers. Its molded wings are raised away from the body making the bird appear to be soaring. The position of the wings made this a difficult piece to mold. (Germany, p23d, OP, R1-2) $40.00-50.00

Ducks

DUCK - (FB), Approx. 2½″ - It has annealed orange feet and bill; is in a swimming position. Circa 1920s. (German, OP, R2) $25.00-35.00

DUCK - (M), Approx. 3″ x 1½″ - It is in a standing position, wings at its side, head tucked and its bill resting on the chest. The new version has a "bumpy" pattern on the body and molded feathers. (Germany, P28b, OP-NP [1950s], R3) $25.00-30.00

DUCK, MALLARD - (M&FB), Approx. 3½″ - The body is molded to show the folded wings. It has a curved neck and an annealed beak. It is realistically painted and usually found as a clip-on. (p24b, OP, R1-2) $60.00-70.00

DUCK IN AN EGG - (M), Approx. 3¼″ - The small duckling with its bill tucked to its chest is coming out of the end of an egg. Near the bottom of the egg, the webbed feet have pushed through. (Germany, p18a, OP, R1)$175.00-200.00

DUCK IN A BONNET - "Baby Huey" - (M), Approx. 4½″H - His face is framed by the bonnet, and around the neck is a ribbon that ties in a bow at the front. He has embossed feathers, and his wings are at the side. It could have a clip-on or a hanger in the head. (Germany, p25, OP, R1) $250.00-275.00

DUCK IN TOP HAT - (FB), Approx. 5″ - It is shown in a flying position with annealed wings, wearing a top hat and tails. Clip-on. Circa 1920s. (OP, R2) $30.00-40.00

DUCK IN A VEST - (M), Approx. 3¾″ - The duck has its long bill tucked to its chest. It wears a waist length vest, and the folded wings show on the sides. Seen from the side and back, it appears to be standing in front of a stump. The piece has been described as looking like an early Donald Duck. (p17c, OP, R1-2) $125.00-150.00.

EAGLE WITH LIBERTY SHIELD ON ITS CHEST - (M), Approx. 4″L x 1½″W - The bird is nicely molded on top and bottom with feathers and folded wings. A liberty shield (American flag) is embossed and painted on the chest. Its head is slightly turned, and it has a metal clip-on. (Germany, p26 & p27, OP, R1) $300.00-350.00

EAGLE AND LIBERTY SHIELD - (M), Approx. 3½″ - The eagle with the liberty shield on its chest is embossed on both sides of an egg shape. A laurel wreath runs up both sides of the egg. (p20a, OP, R1-2) $90.00-100.00

EAGLE ON TOP OF A BALL - (M), Approx. 5½″ - It has its wings folded and its head turned to the left. The feathers are nicely molded, but the ball it stands atop is smooth.

(Germany, p28a, OP-NP, R1) $100.00-125.00

EAGLE EMBOSSED ON A BALL - It's attached to the top of a bell - See BELLS.

FLAMINGO - (M&FB) - Sizes will vary because it is free-blown, but the common size is approx. 3″. Identifiable from storks, swans and peacocks by a curved "topknot" on their head. Their long neck is usually bent in an "S" shape, and they have a longer beak. Most often the body is molded to show wings and feathers. The neck and head are free-blown with the topknot and beak annealed on. The most common form is a clip-on. (Germany, Czech., Austria, p47c, OP-NP, R4)   Standard form $15.00-20.00

VARIATION: FLAMINGO WITH ANNEALED LEGS - (FB) - Various sizes. They are free-blown with an annealed "topknot", beak, and long fragile legs. The hanger is usually found in a looped topknot. The annealed parts are often in colored glass. Circa 1920s. (Germany, p29a & p29c, OP, R3)   Small $35.00-40.00
Larger $60.00-75.00

HUMMINGBIRD - (M), Approx. 3½″L - This molded bird has indentations on the sides and SG wings. This perhaps portrays the blurred motion of the bird's wings. (p42, OP, R3) $25.00-35.00

OSTRICH - (M&FB), Approx. 3¼″ - The body is molded; the head and neck are free-blown. It has large fluffs of plumes at the tail and at the legs. It has an SG tail and is a clip-on. (p22c, OP, R2) $75.00-100.00

Owls

Owls are a symbol of wisdom and are commonly associated with forests and trees, so it is only natural that they became a part of the Christmas tree tradition. In the most common form, owls are depicted as if standing on a branch, wings folded at their side, stomach showing and looking straight ahead. The hanger and cap are in the top of their heads. They may be silvered or mat painted. The most common sizes are approximately 3¼″ and 3¾″. This form is fairly common. Those in the common bird position, leaning forward with wings and tail swept back behind them, with clip-on and SG tail are less common. (Germany, Austria, Czech., p33, OP-NP, R4)   Standard form $25.00-35.00

VARIATION: (1) - (M), Approx. 2¼″H x 1″W - This piece is smaller than usual, with smaller eyes, and feet on a rounded bottom. (p34c, OP, R3) $20.00-30.00

VARIATION: (2) - (M), Approx. 2½″ x 1″W - Less molded feathers than usual and smaller eyes. It has the hanger in the top. (p34a, OP, R3) $20.00-30.00

OWL (TYPE I) - (M), Approx. 2½″ & 3″L - Its elongated body ends with a SG tail. It is a clip-on or has an annealed hanger in the back. This is rarer than the standard form. (p23a & p34B, OP, R3) $30.00-40.00

OWL (TYPE II) - (M), Approx. 3″L - It has a SG tail, clips on to the tree, and the head is cocked to the left looking out. (Rogers p77, OP-NP, R3-4)
$30.00-40.00

OWL - (FB), Approx. 3″H - Its beak, short wings, feet and hook are all annealed to a tubular body. Circa 1920s. (Germany, OP, R2) $25.00-30.00

OWL HEAD (TYPE I) - (M), Approx. 3½″ - It shows a detailed feathered head with large deep set eyes and a small beak. The eyes have a small feathered "look" above them. (Germany, p35B, OP, R2) $150.00-175.00

OWL HEAD (TYPE II) - (M), Approx. 3″ dia. - This is similar to the above, except it has little detailing on the feathers and the larger eyes slope at an angle to the sides of the head. (p36a, OP, R2) $150.00-175.00

MILK GLASS OWL HEAD - (M), Approx. 3″ - This ornament is made out of milk glass. The large areas around the eyes extend at an angle along the side of the ornament. The beak is large and well defined. (Schiffer p102, OP, R1)
$130.00-150.00

OWL HEAD ON THREE FACED ORNAMENT - (M), Approx. 2¼″ & 2½″ - Other faces are a cat and a bulldog. (German, p54, OP-NP [limited], R2) $130.00-150.00

OWL ON A BALL - (M), Approx. 3¼″H - a finely molded owl with its wings at the side, sits atop a globe or ball. (p31c, OP, R2) $60.00-70.00

VARIATION: OWL ON AN INDENT - (M), Approx. 3¼″ - This is the same piece as above only the ball is indented. All other information and prices apply. (p32a)

OWN ON LEAF - (M), Approx. 3″ x 2¼″ - The owl, in a flying position, is embossed onto the leaf. (Germany, p30b, OP-NP, R2) $75.00-85.00

OWL WITH TOP HAT AND BEER STEIN - (M), Approx. 4½″ x 2″ - Its facial features are not prominent. Embossed into the chest area, he holds a stein in his left foot. (Germany, p31a, OP-NP [limited], R1) $150.00-175.00

OWL WITH A TOP HAT AND VEST - (M), Approx. 3¼″H - He has large indented eyes. He wears a top hat, bow tie, vest and cummerbund. His wings are folded at the side, and his feet show at the bottom. (Germany, p31b, OP-NP [1950s], R2-3) $60.00-75.00

PASSENGER PIGEON - (M), Approx. 3½″L - It has a small smooth head with the beak tucked back so it does not extend out like most birds. It has a distinctive ruffle of feathers on the throat and chest. It is a clip-on and has a SG tail. The mold was supposedly broken in the 1920s. (Germany, Snyder p135, OP, R2) $60.00-75.00

PARROTS - (M), Approx. size variations are 3″, 3½″, 4″, 4½″ & 5½″ - The larger sizes are more common. It is in the usual bird position with wings folded leaning forward on clip-on "legs". It has an identifiable topknot or head feather that has been pulled to a point. (This was also the exhaust end of the tube while it was molded.) Its back is short and thick. They are usually beautifully painted and have a clip-on, but they may also have an annealed hanger in back or the topknot on the head. While these are rarer forms, placement of the hanger has little affect on prices. (Germany, p37a-d & p47a, OP-NP, R3) $25.00-30.00
Larger $35.00-50.00

VARIATION: (2) - PARROT IN A WIRE OR TINSEL RING - The bird is standard form. (Rogers p10, OP, R2-3) $40.00-50.00

VARIATION: (3) - Same basic form but the head is turned to the left instead of forward/down. (OP, R3) $25.00-30.00

VARIATION: (4) - The head is round and smooth without any identifying "topknot". It has a large parrot-like beak. Same sizes and beautiful colors as above. (Rogers p55,OP, R3) $25.00-30.00

PARROT HEAD - (M), Approx. 3″ - It has well defined feathers covering the head and a large beak tucked against the neck. (Germany, p36b, OP, R1-2) $225.00-250.00

PEACOCKS - (M&FB) - Sizes vary from about 1½″ to 10″, but the most common size is approx. 3″ - The peacock is a common bird form which usually has a molded oval body formed of wings and feathers, with a free-blown neck and head that rise from it in a "J" shape. The head and neck are usually painted a realistic blue. Peacocks can usually be identified from other bird forms by the two or three pronged "crown" on their head. They usually have SG tails and are attached by clip-ons, although some older ones have annealed hooks in their back. (Germany, Czech., Austria, p38a & p38d, OP-NP, R5) Small $5.00-15.00
Medium size $10.00-25.00
Large 5″ and bigger $30.00-40.00

VARIATION: (1) - The same molded piece but the tail is fanned out and raised behind the peacock. (p38b, OP, R3) $35.00-45.00

VARIATION: (2) - The SG tail is shaped and beautifully painted to show the tail in closed or trailing position. It has various colors, and the feather's "eyes" are painted in. (p38c, OP, R2-3) $35.00-45.00

VARIATION: (3) - TWO PEACOCKS ON A CLIP - (M&FB), Approx. 2″ - These are the smaller birds. (p38e, OP, R2) $40.00-50.00

PEACOCK - (M), Approx. sizes are 2¼″ and 2¾″, 3¼″ & 3¾″ - They are molded in the standing position but have no legs showing. Their fanned-out tail feathers make up most of the ornament. The head, with typical peacock crown, and neck are in relief on the tail feathers. It may have a clip-on at the base or a hanger in the top of feathers. This is a fairly common form and sometimes mistakenly called a turkey. (Germany, p41a, OP-NP, R4-5)$15.00-25.00
Larger size $35.00-45.00

PEACOCK ON A BALL - (M&FB), Approx. 3½″ - It is the same molded peacock as above, connected by a short neck to a free-blown ball. Sizes may vary. (Germany, Schiffer p102, OP, R2) $30.00-40.00

PEACOCK BABY RATTLE - (M), Approx. 8″L - The tail feathers are spread to form the background with the head and neck embossed on them. The back side is a sunflower. The handle is formed by the pike which has been left on. Beautiful colors. (Germany, p39 & p40, OP, R1) $300.00-325.00

PELICAN - (M), Approx. 3″ - It is shown in the standing position with its large bill tucked against its chest and wings at the side. It has a fat, squat body that appears out of proportion and feet that show. (Germany, p15a, OP, R2-3) $80.00-100.00

VARIATION: (1) - This ornament is described by Rogers as made in Japan during the 1920s and 1930s. $20.00-25.00

PENGUIN (TYPE I) - (M), Approx. 4½″H - Molded feathers on its back and its flippers at its side. Its beak is tucked to its chest, and it is covered by a "bumpy" pattern that may represent feathers. (Germany, p19b, OP, R1-2) $90.00-100.00

PENGUIN (TYPE II) - (M), Approx. 3½″ - Molded wings at its side, a feather bib around its neck and chest, beak tucked to the chest. Little detail and no molded feathers. (p43a, OP, R2) $60.00-75.00

FREE-BLOWN PENGUIN - (FB), Approx. 1¾″ & 4½″ but sizes can vary - It has a colored glass head and wings with a tubular type body. The flippers, beak and hanging hook are annealed onto the body. It can also be found in silvered glass as opposed to the colored glass. Circa 1920s. (Germany, p43b, OP, R3-4) Small $10.00-20.00
Large $20.00-30.00

Song Birds

There is a wide variety of birds in this category and unless one is a bird expert, they are difficult to tell apart. If there is nothing special or distinctive about them, they have been placed together into the general category known as "song birds". The pricing remains pretty much the same within this general group of birds. They usually have SG tails and metal clip-ons; however, some earlier versions may have annealed hooks in their backs. They are molded, and sizes vary from 1½″ to 7″L. (Germany, Austria, Czech., p44a, p45 & p46, OP-NP, R5+)
Usual form $10.00-15.00
Larger birds $15.00-25.00

VARIATION: (1) - TWO BIRDS ON A CLIP-ON - (M), Approx. 2″ - 3″ - They are usually smaller types of birds. They have one spring attached to each stomach area and joining at the metal clip. Because of banging together, many have been broken. (p3b, OP-NP, R3)
Small $25.00-35.00
Medium $45.00-55.00

VARIATION: (2) - BIRD WITH A BERRY - (M), Approx. 4″ - The molded bird has an annealed loop in the beak. A small plaster "berry" hangs from the beak. (p28e, OP, R3) $35.00-45.00

VARIATION: (3) - BIRD WITH SG WINGS - (M), Approx. 3½″L - The bird hangs from an annealed hook or has a clip-on. It comes in various sizes and bird types. They are often called Hummingbirds. (Germany, Czech., p42, OP, R3) $25.00-35.00

VARIATION: (4) - BIRD WITH A CREST - (M), Approx. 3″ - The bird has a SG comb or "crest" on its head. Clip-on. (OP, R3) $15.00-20.00

VARIATION: (5) - BIRD INDENT - (M&FB) - Sizes vary with the free-blown form. Bird in the flying position. It may be indented into free-blown balls or egg shapes. (p12c, OP, R3) $10.00-15.00

VARIATION: (6) - BEADED BIRD - (Beads) - Approx. 2" - 3" - The bird is in an outlined shape made of small beads. (Czech., OP, R3) $5.00-10.00

VARIATION: (7) - JAPANESE BIRD - Plain and simple balls form this free-blown bird. (Japan, Rogers p72, NP [1950s], R3) $2.00-6.00

VARIATION: (8) - BIRD ON A BRANCH (EMBOSSED) - (M), Approx. 1" & 2" dia. - Bird on a branch, molded onto a disc shape. The reverse side has a geometric design. (OP, R3-4) $10.00-20.00

VARIATION: (9) - BIRD WITH A TOPKNOT - (M), Approx. 5" - This large bird has well defined feathers. Its head is turned almost to the rear, and it has an annealed topknot of red glass. (p23c, OP, R1-2)$30.00-40.00

STORK - (M&FB) - Sizes vary because it is free-blown, but approx. 3" is the common size. The body is molded to show wings and feathers. Neck, head and bill are free-blown and thus can be found in a variety of poses. Storks are similar to the swans, peacocks and flamingos. They can be distinguished by the fact that they have a smooth head with no topknot or crown and they have a long bill which is generally painted orange. The body is often painted white and black. In the standard form, the bird has a SG tail and clip-on holder. In Germany, it is good luck to have a stork nesting on your house or barn. (Germany, Czech., Austria, p21d, OP-NP, R4)   Standard size $30.00-40.00
          Larger $50.00-60.00

VARIATION: (1) - Stork - (FB) - Various sizes - The stork is entirely free-blown with a tubular body, long annealed legs and bill. It may have an annealed hook in the head. Colored glass may be used with no silvering inside. Circa 1920. (p29a, OP, R3)Small $40.00-50.00
          Larger $50.00-75.00

VARIATION: (2) - Milk Glass Stork - (FB) - Sizes vary because it is free-blown - The stork is blown from milk glass and painted. It has a clip-on at the base. (p21b, OP, R2-3) $50.00-60.00

VARIATION: (3) - Mother and Baby Storks - (M&FB), Approx. 3" - Two molded storks on the same clip-on, one larger than the other. (Germany, Rogers p77, OP, R2) $70.00-80.00

VARIATION: (4) - TWO STORKS ON A CLIP - (M) - These are two small size storks on the same clip-on. (p22a, OP, R2) $65.00-75.00

VARIATION: (5) - STORK WITH A BABY - (M&FB), Approx. 3½" - Has a molded body with a free-blown neck and head. In its annealed beak is a tiny molded baby. (p22b, OP, R1) $150.00-175.00

SWAN - (FB), Sizes can vary anywhere from 1½" to 7" - Most common size is approx. 3"L - This is one of the most common and simplistic of the bird forms. It is depicted on trees as early as 1866. It is sometimes referred to as a turkey, which of course it is not. The body is a simple oblong with the neck bent upwards and expanded at the end to form a head. It usually has a SG tail. These are almost always hung from annealed hooks in the back. (Germany, Czech., Austrian, p48a & p49b, OP-NP, R5+)
          Standard form $5.00-15.00

VARIATION: (1) - SWAN MOUNTED IN TINSEL - (FB) - Varying sizes - This is a standard swan mounted in a tinsel hoop or spray. (p48c, OP, R3-4)$20.00-25.00

VARIATION: (2) - SWAN WITH INDENTS - (FB)- Varying sizes - They have different types and sizes of indents in their sides. (p48e & p49a, OP-NP, R5)
          $10.00-15.00

VARIATION: (3) - SWAN WITH TWISTED BODY - (FB) - Varying sizes - The body had twists put in it while the glass was hot. (OP-NP, R4) $10.00-15.00

VARIATION: (4) - SWAN WITH TINSEL WINGS - (FB) - Varying sizes - The side wings and tail are made of tinsel sprays or crinkle wire. Many were blown with holes in the side to accommodate the tinsel wings. (Probably Czech., p48d, OP, R4) $15.00-20.00

VARIATION: (5) - FLYING SWAN - (FB) - Varying sizes - Its neck is stretched out as if flying, and it has small annealed wings. Possible 1920s. (p44b, OP, R3)
          $15.00-20.00

VARIATION: (6) - SWAN BOAT - (FB) - Varying sizes - They have an indent in their back which is filled with cotton or "straw". A pike rises from the back with a scrap rider of an angel, Santa, etc., or a billowing paper sail. This "mast" and the bird are encased in wire, and it may have tinsel wings. This was constructed in the same manner as sailboats. (p51a, p52, OP-NP [smaller version only], R2-3)   Smaller $40.00-50.00
          Larger $85.00-95.00
          With sails $100.00-125.00

VARIATION: (7) - SWAN WITH RIDER - (FB) - Varying sizes, but 4" is most common - It is similar to the swan boat but without the mast. The rider is a scrap person. (p50a & p50b, OP, R3-4)   Small $40.00-50.00
          Larger $65.00-75.00

VARIATION: (8) - SWAN CART - (FB), Approx. 3½" - The free-blown swan forms the body of the cart. It has applied 1¾" wheels in the back. It holds a scrap rider in its indented back, and it is hung by a tinsel loop. (Germany, OP, R1) $175.00-200.00

VARIATION: (9) - SWAN WITH A MOLDED BODY - (M&FB), Usual size 3"L - The body was blown into a mold thus showing nicely detailed feathers and wings. The neck and head remain free-blown. (p47b & p48b, OP, R4) $10.00-15.00
          Larger $25.00-35.00

VARIATION: (10) - SWAN SLEIGH WITH COTTON RIDER - (FB), Approx. 6½" but sizes vary - The bird is a free-blown swan with the sleigh "runners" made of wire. There is an indentation in the bird's back in which sits a cotton batting figure. The whole bird is wire wrapped. (p53, OP, R1) $225.00-250.00

VARIATION: (11) - SWAN WITH SPUN COTTON RIDER - (FB), Approx. 4″ but sizes vary - This wire encased, free-blown swan has a spun cotton rider on its back. The one pictured shows a girl holding a Christmas tree, but the form will undoubtably vary. (p32b, OP, R1) $225.00-250.00

"GERMANY" SWAN - (M&FB) - Approx. 3″L - This is similar to the standard piece, except that it has "Germany" embossed into the glass where the chest and neck meet. This mold was possibly made at the turn of the century when foreign countries were required to mark their products. Ornaments were marked on the box due to their fragile quality, but this ornament maker obviously took it to heart. See also "Germany" woodpecker. (Germany, p28c, OP, R2) $30.00-35.00

SWAN WITH SG WINGS - (M&FB) - Approx. 3½″L - The body is molded, but the head and neck are free-blown. It has a SG tail and SG wings which are inserted into indentations in the sides. (p41b, OP, R2-3) $40.00-50.00

"GERMANY" SWAN WITH SG WINGS - (M&FB) - Approx. 3″L x 2½″H - Its molded body shows feathers and has indentations for its SG wings and tail. Its free-blown neck and head are in an "S" shape. the word "Germany" is molded into the body under the SG wing. (Germany, OP, R2) $50.00-60.00

MILK GLASS SWAN - (M&FB) - Approx. 2¾″ - The head and neck are free-blown but the body has molded wings and feathers. It is indented on the bottom so that it could also sit flat on a table or shelf. Circa 1920. (Germany, p62d, OP, R2-3) $15.00-20.00

SWAN AND "THOR FACE" - (M&FB) - It is similar to the above two pieces with a molded body and free-blown neck and head. On the stomach area is molded a face, and the SG tail makes its beard. The bird's neck and head make a cap for the face. (Germany, Rogers p103, OP, R1-2) $250.00-275.00

SWAN - (FB) - Approx. 2½″ & 3½″ - "S" shaped neck with small annealed wings and hanger. The annealed parts may be of colored glass. The swan is in a swimming position. (Germany, 1920s, OP, R3) $20.00-30.00

SWIMMING SWAN - (M) - Approx. 2½″ - It is shown in a swimming position with its head tucked. The cap is in the back. (Germany, Rogers p61, OP, R2-3) $90.00-100.00

TROPICAL BIRD WITH A LONG BILL - (M&FB) - Approx. 6″ - This bird has a square and angular appearance rather than round. It has no detailed feathers. Its free-blown beak is as long as the body. (p24a, OP, R2) $60.00-75.00

TURKEY (TYPE I) - (M) - Approx. 3¼″H x 2¼″W - The bird is in a standing position with its head tucked to the chest. Its wings are back with the tail feathers up, forming back and upper part; the cap is in the top. This is an unusual form as they are most often found embossed on other shapes. Some other types of ornaments are referred to as turkeys when in reality they are not. Most notable among these are the molded peacocks because of their upright tail feathers and the free-blown swans. Neither of these in reality look like turkeys, but this ornament does. (Germany, p19a, OP-NP, R2) $50.00-75.00

TURKEY (TYPE II) - (M) - Approx. 2″L - This is a plump looking bird with spread tail feathers and a beak tucked to its chest. It resembles, and is often mistaken for the "Swimming Swan". (Germany, p30c, OP, R2) $60.00-70.00

TURKEY EMBOSSED ON AN OVAL - (M) - Approx. 2″ - This fat turkey is embossed on a bumpy oval. (Schiffer p102, OP, R2-3) $15.00-25.00

TURKEY ON A HOUSE - See HOUSES

"GERMANY" WOODPECKER - (M) - Approx. 3½″L - He has a long beak and a hooded crest. He has indents in the sides in which are SG wings; he also has a SG tail. In the side, under his left wing is embossed "Germany". It hangs from an annealed hook in the back. (Germany, OP, R2) $40.00-50.00

WOODPECKER ON A TREE TRUNK - (M) - Approx. 4″ - The tree trunk has a nicely molded bark effect and a "hole" the woodpecker has been making. The bird is a separately molded piece attached to the side of the trunk by a small spring. The hanger is in the top of the trunk. (Germany, p16b, OP, R1-2) $150.00-175.00

VARIATION: TWO WOODPECKERS ON A TREE TRUNK - (M), Approx. 4″ - This is the same piece described above, but another bird has been added to the opposite side of the trunk. $175.00-200.00

Cats

CAT AND DOG HEADED HORN - (M) - Approx. 2½″ - The tiny round head shows a cat face on one side and a bulldog face on the other. The small horn, with a noise maker in the end, extends out from the chin area. (p90a, OP, R1) $75.00-100.00

CAT FACE - (M) - Approx. 2¼″ & 2½″ - This is part of a three faced ornament. The other faces are an owl and a bulldog. (Germany, p55, OP-NP [very limited], R2) $130.00-150.00

CAT HEAD - (M) - Approx. 1¾″ dia. - This is a round looking piece with the ears, eyes, nose and mouth embossed on it. The head is covered with molded fur into which the cat's whiskers easily blend. (p35a, OP-NP, R2-3) $150.00-175.00

VARIATION: CAT HEAD RATTLE - (M) - Approx. 5½″ overall, head 1¾″ dia. - This is the same piece described above. The long blowing pike has been left on to form the handle of the rattle and small pebbles may be inserted for sound. (p337b, OP, R1-2) $175.00-200.00

CAT IN A BAG - (M) - Approx. 3½″ - The bag is square at the bottom and has a gathered ruffle at the top. It has a stylized "M" and heart embossed into it that may indicate it was made by the Muller family. The cat's head and front paws show out of the top of the bag. (Germany, p57c, OP-NP [very limited], R3) $90.00-100.00

CAT IN A NIGHT CAP - (M) - Approx. 3″ dia. - This well detailed head shows molded fur and a ribbon around the neck. The cat's ears show in front of the cap which has a small tassel on the right side. (Germany, p61a, OP, R2)
$175.00-200.00

CAT IN A SHOE - (M), Approx. 3½″ - Cat lying on its stomach facing the toe of the shoe with shoe's strap over its back. The shoe has "stitches" embossed into it and the hanger is in the heel. (Germany, p59a & p201a, OP-NP, R3)
$125.00-150.00

SLEEPING CAT IN A SHOE (TYPE I) - (M) - Approx. 3½″ - This cat lies on its right side inside the shoe. It faces out the open end of the shoe, and one paw shows. Shoe has a wing-tip, a bow, and decoration around the opening. This is the older version of the two types. (Germany, p59b, OP, R3) $60.00-75.00

SLEEPING CAT IN A SHOE (TYPE II) - (M) - Approx. 3½″ - At first glance the piece appears to be the same as the one above, but on closer inspection we find several differences which show this to be a separate molding. There is no wing-tip decoration on the toe of the shoe; the bow has been moved from the top to near the toe; the above has straight line decorations around the shoe opening and this has scallops; the cat's right paw shows and there are deep creases in the side of the shoe. (Germany, p202a, OP-NP, R3) $35.00-45.00

CAT IN A STOCKING - (M) - Approx. 4½″ - The long stocking has lines of dimples that give it a knotted look. Only the cat's head and paws show out of the top. (p58b, OP, R2) $200.00-225.00

CAT IN A "WINDOW" - (M) - Approx. 2″ dia. - Two cat faces look from a round "window" on either side of this ball-shaped ornament. The window has four embossed petals coming out of the sides, and the ball has a bumpy texture. (p59c, OP, R3) $90.00-100.00

CAT PLAYING WITH A BALL - (M) - Approx. 3½″ - The cat appears to be lying on its back with both the front and rear paws holding the ball to its stomach. It has a wide ruffle of fur around its neck but no ribbon. This could also be a bear. (Germany, OP, R1) $275.00-300.00

CROUCHED CAT WITH A BALL - (M) - Approx. 3¾″ - The cat is shown full length in a crouched position. It holds a small ball between its front paws. The exhaust tip is in the face thus it may be poorly molded. The hanger is in the tail. (Germany, p57b, OP-NP [very limited], R1-2)
$200.00-225.00

CAT WITH A CARDBOARD HAT - (M) - Approx. 3½″ - Cat sitting on its haunches with its front legs straight, a thin ribbon and bow around its neck. The top hat is made from heavy printed cardboard held on the head by a protruding glass pike. Found only as a clip-on. It has a dog in a hat companion piece, but the cat is somewhat rarer. (Germany, p63a, OP, R1) $225.00-250.00

MILK GLASS CAT - (FB) - Approx. 3″ - This cat has a

tubular body and tail with annealed legs, ears and whiskers. It also has an annealed hanger in its back. Circa 1920s. (Germany, p62a, OP, R2-3) $20.00-30.00

MINIATURE CAT HEAD - (M) - Approx. 1″ - This resembles the standard size heads. It was part of a set of miniatures made for small trees. The molds are now in East Germany. (Germany, p442, OP-NP 1940s only, R1)
$10.00-15.00

ROLY-POLY CAT - (M) - Approx. 3¼″ - The cat's head, with large eyes, is well-molded with fur. The lower body is embossed onto a rounded ball which shows no fur. It shows the cat sitting on its haunches with the front legs straight and standing on its long tail. The cat has a ribbon and large bow at its neck. (p58a, OP, R1-2)$125.00-150.00

SITTING CAT - (M) - Approx. 4″ - The cat sits on its haunches with the front legs straight. Fur is shown by small indentations. The long tail wraps around the right front leg. No bow or collar show. (Germany, OP, R1-2)
$150.00-175.00

STUDENT CAT - (M) - Approx. 3½″ - This sitting cat holds a mandolin in its left paw and plays it with its right. It wears a "student" cap and has molded fur. (Germany, p57a, OP, R2) $90.00-100.00

TWO KITTENS IN A BASKET - (M) - Approx. 2″ & 2¾″ - The two kitten's heads and paws show over the top of the woven basket. The hood or lid of the basket shows on the rear. There is a similar "Three Mice in a Basket" ornament. (Czech., p58c, OP-NP, R2-3)   Small $45.00-60.00
Large $75.00-85.00

CLAM SHELL - (M) - Approx. 2″ - The shell shows stylized ribbing on the top and bottom to portray a closed shell. There are several slightly different moldings. (p78c, OP-NP, R3) $15.00-25.00

VARIATION: CLAM SHELL WITH EMBOSSED BUMPS - (M), Approx. 2″ - The ribbing shows rows of bumps. (Rogers p186, OP, R2-3) $25.00-35.00

OYSTER SHELL WITH A PEARL - (M) - Approx. 2½″ & 3″ - This nicely detailed shell has a hollow spot in the front in which rests the pearl. It is usually found as a clip-on. (Italy, p443b, NP [1950s], R2-3) $40.00-50.00

CRAB - (M) - Rogers describes it as being made in two movable pieces held together by a pin. (Germany, OP, R1)
$350.00-400.00

Deer

LEAPING DEER - (FB) - Sizes may vary but 3½″L is common - This free-blown deer has a tubular body with annealed legs, ears and antlers. His legs are bent as if running or leaping. Circa 1920. (Germany, p72a, p73b & p73c, OP, R3) $25.00-35.00

VARIATION: LEAPING DEER IN COLORED GLASS - (FB), Varying sizes - This is the same basic piece mentioned above, except blown in colored glass. Brown, milk glass, blue and amber are the common colors. The colored glass ornaments are usually not silvered. (Germany, OP, R3) $30.00-40.00

STANDING DEER - (FB) - Sizes vary but 3″-4″ are most common - These free-blown pieces have tubular bodies with annealed legs, ears, tail and antler. They usually have annealed stands at the feet so they could be used as table decorations. For hanging on the tree, a cap was inserted in the open mouth. Circa 1920. (Germany, p73a, OP, R4) $40.00-50.00

VARIATION: (1) DEER IN COLORED GLASS - This is the same deer described above except it is blown from colored glass. Light brown and milk glass were common colors but blue and amber are also known. (Germany, p71b & p72b, OP, R3 $45.00-55.00

VARIATION: (2) DOE - This is the same basic deer but missing the annealed antlers. Care should be taken to make sure they were never there and not just broken off. (Germany, p72c, OP, R3) $30.00-40.00

Dogs

Man's best friend has been molded and free-blown in a variety of breeds. Although they can be shown standing, the sitting or begging position is the most common. Dogs were a favorite media for whimsical ornaments, and they are often difficult to tell from bear ornaments. All caps are in head area unless otherwise noted. Dog heads are rarer than full body pieces, but most dog ornaments should be considered scarce.

VARIATION: BEGGING DOG (TYPE I) - (M) - Approx. 3″ - It has embossed fur on the head and shoulders, but none from about the waist down. Tail curls up over left leg. This is the piece from which the dog on the ball ornament is blown and is rarer than when blown on a ball. (p65a, OP-NP [limited], R2) $80.00-90.00

BEGGING DOG ON A BALL - (M&FB) - Approx. 4″ - The above listed dog rises out of a free-blown ball. It is shown down to the paws. The size of the ornament may vary with the size of the free-blown ball. (p65b, OP, R3-4)$60.00-70.00

BEGGING DOG (TYPE II) - (M) - Approx. 3½″ - Its head is slightly cocked to the right. It has a smiling face with short upright ears and a ribbon tied on the right side. (p70b, OP, R2) $50.00-60.00

BEGGING DOG WITH A BASKET - (M) - Approx. 5″ - The large dog has a basket of wine and fruits tied around its neck. Nicely molded fur and long ears. (Germany, p64b, OP-NP, R2) $90.00-100.00

SMALL BEGGING DOG WITH A BASKET - (M) - Approx. 4″ - The dog sits on its haunches with its front paws in a begging position. It shows molded fur and holds a small wicker basket in its mouth. The dog has medium length ears. Although the theme is similar to the above, it is an entirely different molding. (Germany, OP, R1-2) $150.00-175.00

BEGGING SPANIEL - (M) - Approx. 3½″ - The dog which is probably a cocker spaniel has long wavy fur, long ears and a bow tie that ties in front. (Germany, p64a, OP-NP [limited], R2-3) $40.00-50.00

BEGGING TERRIER - (M) - Approx. 2¼″ - This dog, possibly a terrier, has short upright ears but no collar or ribbon. (Austria, p4a, OP-NP, R2-3)　New $2.00-10.00
Old $30.00-40.00

BULLDOG HEAD - (M) - Approx. 2½″ - It has heavy facial features and no molded fur. (p67, OP, R2-3)$100.00-125.00

BULLDOG FACE ON THREE-FACE ORNAMENT - (M) - Approx. 2¼″ & 2½″ - The other two faces are an owl and a cat. (Germany, p56, OP-NP [very limited], R2) $130.00-150.00

BULLDOG HEAD (LARGE) - (M) - Approx. 3″ - This has nicely detailed features and fur shows on the back of the head. (Germany, p69b, OP-NP [limited], R2)$125.00-150.00

CIGAR SMOKING DOG - (M) - Approx. 4¾″ - It appears to be squatting on its hind legs with its front paws on its hips. It has a large head, long ears, and a ribbon with a bow at its neck. Its mouth has an indent that holds a wire "cigar". It has been seen as a perfume bottle. (p68, OP, R1-2) $125.00-150.00

DOG BLOWING A HORN - (M) - Approx. 3½″ - This dog, in a sitting position, holds a trumpet in its front paws. It has molded fur and medium length ears. (Germany, p66a, OP, R2) $125.00-150.00

DOG IN A BAG - (M) - Approx. 2½″ & 3½″ - The dog, probably a cocker spaniel, is in a bag labeled "MY DARLING". Only its head and front paws stick out. (Germany, OP-NP [limited], R3-4)　3½″ $40.00-50.00
Scarcer 2½″ $40.00-50.00

DOG IN A COLLAR AND NECKTIE - (M) - Approx. 4″ - This dog is in a sitting position. It has a good facial expression but no molded fur. (p3b, OP, R2-3) $100.00-125.00

DOG IN A DOG HOUSE - (M) - Approx. 3″ - The dog's face fills the square doorway of its cylinder-shaped dog house. The roof is shaped like an acorn cap. (Germany, p61c, OP, R2-3) $60.00-70.00

DOG WITH A CARDBOARD HAT - (M) - Approx. 3½″ - This dog sits up on its hind legs with its front legs held as if begging. It wears a top hat that is made from heavy printed cardboard and is held on by a protruding glass pike. This piece will be found as a clip-on. It has a Cat in a Hat companion piece which is slightly rarer. (Germany, p63a, OP, R2) $225.00-250.00

DOUBLE FACED DOG - (M) - Approx. 2″ - The same face is on both sides in this well-molded piece. (Germany, Rogers p169, OP, R2) $45.00-55.00

GREYHOUND - (FB) - Approx. 3½″ - Blown in milk glass with annealed tail, legs, ears and a glass base. Circa 1920. (Germany, p71a, OP, R2) $20.00-30.00

SCOTTY - (M) - Approx. 3″ & 3½″ - It is in a standing or begging position, with a bow tied around its neck on the left side. Seen from the front, the piece seems narrow. (Germany, p69a & p74b, OP, R3)　Small $60.00-70.00
Large $80.00-90.00

STANDING DOG - (M) - Approx. 4" - This fat dog has both paws clasped over its stomach. There is a ribbon around its neck with a bow that ties in front. It has long hanging ears but no molded fur. (Germany, p69c, OP-NP, R2-3)

New $2.00-10.00

Older $50.00-60.00

SITTING DOG - (M) - Approx. 3½" - Both front legs are straight in the front. No molded fur and little other detail. (Rogers p28, OP, R2) $80.00-90.00

SITTING SPANIEL - (M) - Approx. 2½", 3" & 4¼" - This chubby dog has long hanging ears but no molded fur. It has a ribbon around the neck that ties on its right side. On the larger piece, a heart is formed on the stomach by the position of the two front legs. (p66b, p66c & p61b, OP, R3)

Small $40.00-50.00

Medium $50.00-60.00

Large $125.00-150.00

VARIATION: SITTING SPANIEL WITH BUMPS - (M), Approx. 3" - Similar to the above piece except the ears and the base have a bumpy texture. This is a 1950s version. (NP [limited to the 1950s], R3) $35.00-45.00

SMILING DOG - (M) - Approx. 3" - This slender looking dog is in a sitting position. He wears a ribbon and bow that ties on the left side. It has large inset eyes and a wide smile that gives it an almost comical look. (Germany, p64c, OP-NP [very limited], R2) $40.00-50.00

"STAFFORDSHIRE" DOG - (M) - Approx. 3½" - It is sitting facing to the right, but the head is turned to look straight out. There is a ribbon that ties in front. This piece was probably modeled after the Staffordshire porcelain dogs. It has the word "Cesar" embossed between the haunch and the front foot. (Germany, p101a, OP, R1-2)

$125.00-150.00

WHIPPET - (FB) - Approx. 3" L - This figure looks a little like a greyhound. The piece is free-blown with annealed legs and tail. Circa 1920. (Germany, p62b & p62c, OP, R2-3)

$25.00-35.00

Elephants

Elephants were a popular circus animal during the Victorian era, and elephant ornaments are shown as if on parade.

ELEPHANT SITTING ON A BALL - (M) - Approx. 4¼" - The elephant sits on a small ball with its front legs raised and its trunk hanging down. There are many detailed wrinkles. No early copies are known. (West Germany, NP)

$2.00-10.00

ELEPHANT STANDING ON A BALL - (M) - Approx. 2¾" - This elephant has all four feet on a small ball. Its trunk is curled to the left leg. It wears a decorative piece on its head and back. (Austria, p75c, OP-NP, R2)

$75.00-90.00

WALKING ELEPHANT - (M) - Approx. 2½" & 3" - This elephant is shown with large ears and tusks. Its trunk is curled to its left leg. Molded grass shows between its legs, and on its back it has a decorative blanket with small

tassels hanging down. The ornament has a square look to it, and the hanger is in the back. (Germany, p75a & p75b, OP, R2-3)

Small $75.00-90.00

Large $100.00-125.00

VARIATION: ELEPHANT WITH FRINGED BLANKET - (M), Approx. 2½" - This is the same elephant as described above except the blanket on its back has molded fringe around the edges. (Germany, p74a, OP-NP, R2-3) $75.00-90.00

Fish

The fish is an ancient Christian symbol, and thus has an appropriate place on the Christmas tree. They came in a variety of shapes, and unless one is an expert, they are hard to tell apart. The cardboard or Dresden fish has all the intricate detail needed to identify the fish. This detail was not always possible in blown glass, and they are, therefore, more generic in nature. Some pieces have enough identifiable characteristics that they can be listed separately. Many, however, are listed in one general category.

FISH - (M), Approx. from 2" to 6" - The fish show embossed scales and fins, but they do not always show a tail. The hangers are usually found in the tail area; however, some versions have annealed hooks in the back and SG tails. Some older variations can be found wrapped in wire or in tinsel wreathes. (Germany, Czech., Austria, Japan, p78a-b, p79a, p80a-b, p81a-b-d-e, p82a-c, p84-a-b-c-d, p85a, OP-NP, R3-4)

Small 2"-3" $15.00-25.00

Medium 3"-4" $20.00-35.00

Large 5"-6" $35.00-50.00

ANGEL FISH - (M), Approx. 1¾"H x 3½"W - This unusual fish is fatter than it is long. The mouth is slightly open and has a small fin below it. The scales are well-detailed, and the tail is embossed into the end of the fish. The hanger is in its back. The smaller version is slightly rarer. (p86a, OP, R2-3) Small $60.00-80.00

Large $150.00-175.00

FISH WITH A CURVED BODY - (M) - Approx. 3½" & 4" - This fish is very similar to most, except the body is curved to the right which gives the piece a realistic sense of movement. The hanger is in the tail. (p81c, OP-NP [small only], R3) $40.00-50.00

FISH WITH EMBOSSED WAVES - (M) - Approx. 4½" - This fish has three embossed "waves" curling around the stomach area, plus three on the back and one behind the gills. (p83, OP, R3) $30.00-40.00

FISH WITH A DRESDEN TAIL - (M) - Approx. 3½" - This slender fish has its hanging hook in the mouth and a gold cardboard tail fastened in the rear. It also has paper fins on the top and bottom which are not shown in the picture. (Germany, p82b, OP, R2) $90.00-100.00

FISH WITH A LONG DORSAL FIN - (M) - Approx. 3" - This piece has the basic appearance of many other fish; however, it has a long dorsal fin that runs from the head to the tail area. (p79b, OP, R3-4) $20.00-30.00

"THUMB PRINT" FISH - (M) - Approx. 3½" - This fish has embossed scales, a fin behind the gills and two on the bottom. The most identifiable element is an indented area with a raised edge found near the tail. It has the appearance of a thumb-print pushed into the hot glass. (Schiffer p110, OP, R2-3) $40.00-50.00

MERMAIDS - see "PEOPLE" SECTION "WOMEN AND GIRLS"

PORPOISE - (M&FB) - Approx. 5" - The molded head area shows the porpoise with an open mouth with a place for the hanger. The rest of the "body" is a tapering free-blown tube much the same as a Dublin pipe or hunting horn. The piece shown is unsilvered and wire wrapped. (p76b, OP, R1-2) $200.00-225.00

SHARK - (M) - Approx. 4½" - This piece is made of heavy glass and has no embossed scales. A fin shows behind the gills and underneath. It has an annealed hanger in the back and a SG tail. This piece is commonly believed to be Japanese. (p85b, OP, R2-3) $50.00-60.00

FOX - See LEOPARD

Frogs

FROG - (M) - Approx. 3" & 4" - This frog has its back feet under its body and its front "hands" crossed on the chest. The cap is on the rear. (Germany, p88a & p88c, OP-NP, R3) $55.00-75.00

FROG CLIMBING A LADDER (EMBOSSED) - (M) - Approx. 2½" - This piece is very similar to the ornament which shows a rooster climbing a ladder into a chicken coop. On this cylinder-shaped ornament, a large embossed frog climbs the ladder. (Germany, OP-NP, R1-2) $90.00-100.00

FROG ON A LEAF - (M) - Approx. 2½" - A small frog is embossed onto a leaf which has stylized ribbing. This piece has sometimes been called a Frog on a Tulip. (p88b, OP, R2-3) $55.00-65.00

FROG PLAYING A BANJO - (M) - Approx. 3" - Frog is in a sitting position playing a banjo. (Austria, OP-NP, R2) $50.00-60.00

FROG PLAYING A CONCERTINA - (M) - Approx. 2¾" - The frog is shown sitting on its hind legs and holding the concertina at the stomach area. The eyes are on the sides of the head, and the mouth is wide open as if singing. (p89b, OP, R-2) $50.00-60.00

FROG PLAYING A VIOLIN - (M) - Approx. 2¾" - This is a mate to the one above. It is in the same position but holds a violin at its chest and stomach area. (p89a, OP, R2) $50.00-60.00

FROG UNDER A MUSHROOM - (M&FB) - Approx. 4" - The mushroom is free-blown and has a large rounded "bowl" underneath. A 1½" molded frog is fastened to the bowl under the mushroom, and the whole piece is wrapped in wire. (p90b, OP, R1) $90.00-100.00

HOPPING FROG - (M) - Approx. 3" & 3½" - The frog is shown as if ready to hop. The hind legs are bent, and the front legs are out-stretched. Beneath the frog is embossed ground and grass. (p87a & p87b, OP-NP [large size only], R2-3) $70.00-80.00

SINGING FROG - (M) - Approx. 2¾" & 3½" - Frog is shown sitting with its back feet meeting under its stomach and its front legs on its stomach. It wears a bow tie and a high collar which shows on the back. Its mouth is wide, round and deeply indented, making it look as if it were singing. (p86b, OP, R2) Small $100.00-125.00
Large $150.00-175.00

GIRAFFE - (FB) - Approx. 2½" but sizes can vary - It has a free-blown tubular body with annealed legs, ears and tail. Circa 1920. (Germany, OP, R3) $20.00-30.00

HEDGEHOG - (M) - Approx. 4" - This animal has a long pointed snout and stands on all fours. Ground and grass are embossed between the legs. The hanger is in the tail area. (p101b, OP, R1-2) $250.00-300.00

HORSE - (FB) - Approx. 2½"-3"L but sizes can vary - The horse has a free-blown tubular body with annealed ears and legs. They are difficult to tell from deer without the antlers. Circa 1920. (Germany, OP, R3) $20.00-30.00

VARIATION: (1) - HORSE OF COLORED GLASS - (FB), Sizes vary - This is the same horse form blown in colored glass such as blue or brown. (Germany, OP, R3) $25.00-35.00

VARIATION: (2) - ZEBRA - (FB), Approx. 2½"-3" but size can vary - This is the same free-blown horse form blown from colored glass with elongated stripes incorporated into the glass. (Germany, OP, R2-3) $25.00-35.00

HORSE HEAD IN A HORSESHOE - (M) - Approx. 2½" - The shape of the ornament is formed by an inverted horseshoe. The horse head, with bridle, looks through the horseshoe to the left. (p384c, OP, R1-2) $60.00-75.00

RUNNING HORSE - (M) - Approx. 3" - The horse's legs are bent as if running or jumping. It wears a bridle and saddle. The hanger is in the head. No early copies are known. (West Germany, NP) $2.00-10.00

Insects

BEE ON A FLOWER - (M) - Approx. 2" dia. - This bee or beetle is embossed onto a round flower shape. The petals on the front are ill-defined and thus have been called spider's web. The reverse side, however, clearly shows a daisy. Spiders have eight legs and this insect is shown with six. This piece has mistakenly been called a spider on a web. (p91b, OP, R3) $50.00-65.00

BEETLE (TYPE I) - (M) - Approx. 2¼" - The ornament has an overall oval shape to it. Most of the insect's back is taken up by large wings that meet in the center. Two eyes show on the very short head and six well-defined legs show on the reverse. (p91c, OP, R3) $35.00-45.00

BEETLE (TYPE II) - (M) - Approx. 2¾" - This beetle has a much larger head. Its wings are shorter and do not meet in the back. It has six embossed legs that show on the reverse. (p91a, OP, R2) $30.00-40.00

BEETLE ON A PEAR - (M) - Approx. 3" - The pear has a bumpy surface, and two molded leaves show at the top. The large beetle is embossed across the front of the pea

and is shown with large "pinchers". (p95a, OP, R2)
$100.00-125.00

BEETLE WITH PAPER LEGS - (M) - Approx. 3" - It has two well-defined wings and two concentric circles for eyes. The underneath is smooth, and a set of eight paper legs are glued onto it. (p90c, OP, R2) $90.00-100.00

BUTTERFLY (EMBOSSED) - (M) - Approx. 2"-3" - The butterfly with spread wings is often found embossed onto geometric shapes such as rectangles and ovals and on balls and a fan. (OP-NP, R3-4) $15.00-25.00

DRAGONFLY - (FB) - Approx. 6½" length and wingspan - The body is a free-blown tubular shape with annealed antenna. Painted SG wings are attached to the sides, and it has a SG tail. (p94, OP, R1) $100.00-125.00

MOTH - (M) - Approx. 2"-2½" for the body, but the wing span can vary greatly. The chubby body is molded and shows a head, antenna and ribbing on the lower body. It has indents in the sides for SG wings which are usually elaborately painted. The price will be affected by the size of the wings and the quality of their painting. Larger pieces have a suspension system that hold them in the flying position and some have SG tails. They are often given the more delicate sounding name of "butterfly", but their bodies show them to be the moths which doubtless flitted about the glassblower's flame on late summer nights. (p93a, p93b & p93c, OP, R2-3)   Smaller $80.00-100.00
Larger $125.00-150.00

MOTH (EMBOSSED) - (M) - Approx. 2¼" & 2¾" dia. - A moth is embossed into both sides of this disc-shaped ornament. It shows the segmented body and wings which also show the embossed antenna. (p8b, OP-NP [1950s only], R3) $10.00-20.00

SPIDER IN A WEB (TYPE I) - (FB) - Approx. 4½" - The web is made of three silvered glass rods bound together at the center. They and the rest of the web are covered with wire and tinsel. The spider is made up of two small beads and wire legs. (p92b, OP, R1-2) $80.00-100.00

SPIDER IN A WEB (TYPE II) - (FB) - Approx. 5½" - The web is made of small silvered glass tubes that form eight spokes. Tinsel and wire form the connecting threads. The spider's body is composed of two large beads and its eight legs of five tiny beads each. (p92a, OP, R1-2)$100.00-125.00

SPIDER IN A WEB - (M) - See BEE ON A FLOWER

SPIDER IN A WEB - (BEADED) - Approx. 3½" - The six spokes of the web and the spider are made of small beads. Spokes are connected by thin milk glass tubes. (Czech., p420a, OP, R2) $40.00-50.00

Lions

LION HEAD - (M) - Approx. 2¾" - This is a well-detailed piece with the mame showing around the face and in the back. (p96c, OP, R1) $275.00-300.00

ROARING LION HEAD - (M) - Approx. 3" - This piece is not as delicately molded as the above piece. Ears do not

show, and its mouth is open wide as if roaring. (p96a, OP, R2) $225.00-250.00

SITTING LION - (M) - Approx. 3¼" - This lion sits on its haunches with its front legs straight. A large mane frames the face, and the tail is shown at the back. (Germany, p97a & p97b, OP, R1-2) $250.00-275.00

TEDDY LION - (M) - Approx. 2½" - This fierce lion face is embossed on front and back. It shows a nicely detailed mane. The seam of the ornament shows stylized ribs and bumps. The words "Teddy Lion" are written in script on the lower edge of both sides. (OP, R1) $275.00-300.00

LEOPARD HEAD - (M) - Approx. 3" - This piece has large cat-like eyes, and its mouth is open as if roaring. Ears show on the sides of the head, but no fur shows except for some molding on the forehead. The back of the piece is smooth. This piece has been mistakenly called a fox. The eyes show that it belongs to the cat family. Furthermore, a similar leopard head was found in King Tut's tomb in 1922. The pieces are so identical that the ornament was doubtless molded after it. (Germany, p96b, OP, R1-2)
$300.00-350.00

LOBSTER - (M) - Approx. 3¼" - The segmented tail has a slight downward curve. The claws are molded along side the head area. The reverse shows the segmented underside of the lobster. (Germany, p78d, OP-NP [limited], R1)
$200.00-225.00

Monkeys

MONKEY IN A CLOWN SUIT - (M) - Approx. 3" - This monkey is shown in a standing position with its legs slightly bent. It wears a clown suit with a ruffled collar. Its right hand is on the stomach, and its left is at the side. (p100, OP, R1-2) $150.00-175.00

MONKEY WITH A FUR RUFFLE - (M) - Approx. 3" - This large monkey, which is perhaps a baboon, is shown sitting on its hind legs. Its hands are clasped at the stomach area. It has a wide fur ruffle that frames the face. (Germany, p99b, OP-NP [very limited], R1) $125.00-150.00

MONKEY WITH A VINE - (M) - Approx. 3¼" - The ornament has an overall oval shape with the monkey sitting on its hind legs. Its long arms are wrapped around a thin vine or branch. (Germany, p98b, OP, R2) $100.00-125.00

"RADIO" MONKEY - (M) - Approx. 3½" & 4½" - The monkey is shown sitting in a high back wicker chair. Its long fingered hands hold earphones at its head. It wears a rounded cap which has the word "RADIO" embossed into it on the larger piece. (Germany, p98a & p99a, OP, R2)
Small$100.00-125.00
Large $175.00-200.00

SQUATTING MONKEY - (M) - Approx. 2½" - It is sitting or squatting with its knees pulled up to the stomach area. Its hands are at its sides. (Germany, p99c, OP-NP [limited], R1-2) $70.00-80.00

"CHURCH" MOUSE (EMBOSSED) - (M) - Approx. 3½" - The mouse stands dressed in a short choir robe. A large church window shows on the back and the whole ornament has a dimpled effect. The mouse looks like Mickey Mouse. (p60b, OP, R2) $100.00-125.00

Pigs

BEGGING PIG - (M), Approx. 3¼" - It is sitting on its haunches with its front feet in a begging position. Its ears hang down, and its skin is smooth. Often has a design painted on the stomach. (p102a, OP, R2-3) $90.00-100.00

BUILDER PIG - (M), Approx. 3¼" - This is the pig who built his house of bricks, shown standing in coveralls, a bricklayer's hat and a handkerchief tied in a bow around its neck. The other two pigs of this Three Pig set supposedly exist. (p102c, OP, R1-2) $100.00-125.00

PIG IN A STUDENT CAP - (M) - Approx. 3" - This upright pig has a rounded bottom with no feet showing. Its front hooves rest on the stomach. It has a bow at the neck and wears a student cap with its ears showing in front. This may represent one of the Three Pigs set, a companion to Builder Pig. (Rogers p4, OP, R1-2) $100.00-125.00

PIG IN A TUXEDO - (M) - Approx. 2¾" - This fat pig has no real arms or legs showing. It wears a vest, a cummerbund and bow tie. (p290b, OP, R2) $50.00-60.00

PIG IN CLOVER - (M) - Approx. 3¾" - This upright pig is shown to the waist area with the front legs showing. Below the waist, the ornament widens and is embossed with a four leaf clover. The reverse shows the same clover. (p101c, OP, R1) $175.00-200.00

Rabbits

RABBIT EATING A CARROT - (M) - Approx. 3½" - This full length rabbit sits on its back legs and holds a large carrot in its front paws. The rabbit's ears are lying down, and it has molded fur. Poor molding often distorts the delicate facial features which are best seen from the front instead of the side. (Germany, p104a & p104b, OP-NP [very limited], R3-4) $80.00-100.00

RABBIT EMERGING FROM AN EGG - (M&FB) - Approx. 4¼" but sizes vary with the egg - The molded rabbit is the "Rabbit Eating a Carrot" piece. Below the arms, the free-blown eggs starts, making the piece look like a rabbit rising out of the top of an egg. (Germany, Rogers p20, OP, R1-2) $300.00-350.00

RABBIT IN AN EGG - (M) - Approx. 3½" - Shown breaking through the side of an egg. His head, ears and front paws show in this early piece. It may come as a clip-on. (p5b, OP, R1) $150.00-175.00

RABBIT WITH ANNEALED EARS - (M) - Approx. 2"L - It has a small molded body with annealed ears and front legs. The example shown was not silvered or painted. (p105, OP, R1-2) $35.00-50.00

RABBIT WITH AN UMBRELLA (EMBOSSED) - (M) - Approx. 3" - The rabbit stands on its hind legs and holds an open umbrella in its front paw. It is embossed onto the front of a six-sided house. Bricks and windows show on the house. (p60a, OP, R2) $90.00-100.00

RABBIT WITHOUT A CARROT - (M) - Approx. 3¾" - This is similar to the Rabbit Eating a Carrot piece but does not have a carrot. It sits on its haunches with the front paws at the chest and stomach area. It has molded fur, and the ears are lying down. (Germany, p104c, OP-NP, R2) $60.00-80.00

REINDEER - See DEER

SEA HORSE - (M&FB) - Approx. 5" - The upper half of the sea horse is molded, showing ribbing, and its snout is tucked to the chest. The lower half is a free-blown tube that curls into the tail. (p77, OP, R2) $90.00-100.00

SNAKES - (M&FB) - Approx. 6"-7" but sizes vary since they are free-blown - The head may have molded eyes and markings or may be a simple free-blown egg shape. The body is the long glass pike which has been twisted and spiraled into various lengths. Snakes with molded heads are more desirable. The presence of a snake on the tree probably relates to the medieval passion plays and the Tree of Paradise. (p106, OP, R-3) $30.00-40.00
                    Molded head $35.00-45.00

AUSTRIAN SQUIRREL - (M) - Approx. 3" - In this nicely detailed piece, the busy tail rises past the top of the head and two well-defined ears show. It sits on its hind legs and holds a large nut in the front paws. (Austria, p103a, OP-NP, R2-3) $40.00-50.00

SQUIRREL EATING A NUT (TYPE I) - (M) - Approx. 2½" & 3¼" - The squirrel sits up on its hind legs and holds a nut in its front paws. It has a long thin tail that comes up to the back of its head. This thin looking piece shows molded fur and may be found as a clip-on. (p102b & p103b, OP, R3-4 small, R2 larger)   Small $45.00-55.00
                    Large $60.00-80.00

VARIATION: SQUIRREL WITH A NUT (TYPE II) - (M), Approx. 2¾" - This is very similar to the above but is a different molding. The tail is bushier and stops short of the neck. It is a wider piece and the arms are in a different position. (p103c, OP-NP, R3) $45.00-55.00

ZEBRA - See HORSES

FLOWERS

Flower ornaments on the decorated tree served several purposes. They emulated some of the very earliest tree decorations and were connected with the idea that all the trees and flowers bloomed at Christ's birth. In a more pagan sense, they represented the beauty and promise of spring during the darkest days of winter.

It was a popular theme to put children's heads and faces into flowers. These are listed under "People and Faces in Flowers, Fruits, etc." Flowers were also a popular decoration on other pieces. Those pieces listed here have the flower as the main element of the ornament.

CALLA LILY - (FB) - Approx. 4" but sizes can vary - This free-blown piece is similar to the trumpet flower, but it has a wide, rounded form instead of a slender tapering one. The wide edge is fluted, and the whole flower is hollow. It may have wire or paper stamens, and it is unsilvered. Early versions may be wire wrapped. (Rogers 77, OP, R1-2) $100.00-125.00

Daisies

This title is usually given to any type of flower with long radiating petals and a center "button". Daisies were commonly embossed onto other shapes.

DAISY - (M) - Approx. 1¾" dia. - Six petals radiate from a raised center button. The front and reverse are identical. (p116a, OP, R3-4) $5.00-15.00

DAISY AND PEACOCK BABY RATTLE - See BIRDS - PEACOCK BABY RATTLE

DAISIES (EMBOSSED) - (M) - Approx. 1"-3" - Daisies and stylized daisies are embossed onto a wide variety of geometric forms. The most common is a disc shape but others include balls and eggs. (Germany, Czech., Austria, p107b-d-f, p108a-c-d-e, OP-NP, R4-5) $2.00-15.00

FOXGLOVE - (M) - Approx. 2¾" - This long slender flower has four leaves at the base and has a four-lobed blossom at the end. (Schiffer p111, OP, R2) $50.00-60.00

LOTUS - (M) - Approx. 2" & 2½" - These flowers usually have six evenly spaced leaves at the base and have an overall bell shape to them. There are no detailed petals. (p113c, OP-NP, R3) $15.00-25.00

  VARIATION: LOTUS WITH STAMENS - (M), Approx. 2½" - This is the same form as above. The end is deeply indented and wire or paper stamens are inserted. (p113b, OP, R2-3) $30.00-40.00

"PILLOW" FLOWER - (M) - Approx. 2" - This well-detailed piece has an overall square shape to it. It has four large and detailed petals. It has three well-defined embossed stamens. The back of the ornament is smooth. (p114c, OP, R1-2) $60.00-70.00

Roses

These were the single most popular flower theme in ornaments. Not only have they long been considered a symbol of love and beauty, but they were also sacred to the Virgin Mary.

ROSES (EMBOSSED) - (M&FB) - Approx. 1¼"-3" - Roses were a common form to be embossed onto geometric shapes such as discs, balls and eggs. They are almost always shown in rosette form and often have stems and leaves. (Germany, Czech., Austria, p115c, OP-NP, R5) $5.00-15.00

HOLLOW ROSE - (M) - Approx. 2" - The rose shows many molded petals and leaves at the base. The top has a wide fluted edge. The flower is hollow or open and unsilvered. It is usually found as a clip-on. (p109b & 109c, OP, R2-3) $75.00-85.00

ROSE BUDS - (M) - Approx. 1¼"-3" - There are several varying molds of the rose bud. They have a general egg-shape showing the individual petals in a closed position. They were made by most European glassmakers. (p107c, p110a, p111b & p111c, OP-NP, R3-4) $10.00-20.00

ROSE BUD - (FB) - Approx. 2½" - A free-blown egg shape is the center of the bud. It has three large petals annealed

onto it. The piece is made of milk glass and tinted red, pink or yellow. It has fabric leaves and a fabric wrapped wire stem. The piece could be hung from the bud, or the stem could be wrapped around the branch. This Circa 1920 piece was also sold as perfume holder. (Germany, OP, R2) $30.00-40.00

OPEN ROSES - (M) - Approx. 1¼"-2" dia. - They have a generalized ball shape and come in a wide variety of separate moldings. Most are excellently molded, showing many individual petals. They were made by most of the European glassmakers. (p110, OP-NP, R5)
                      Small $5.00-10.00
                      Larger $10.00-15.00

  VARIATION: OPEN ROSE WITH STAMENS - (M), Approx. 2"-3" - These are usually larger than the standard open rose. The center is deeply indented and wire or paper stamens are inserted. Of course, real roses do not have such stamens, but they look nice. The pieces are often covered in crushed glass and found as a clip-on. (p115b, OP, R3-4) $45.00-55.00

ROSE AND DAISY DOUBLE FLOWER - (M) - Approx. 2" dia. - The front shows an unfolded rosette (round, front view) with many embossed petals. The reverse shows a daisy with a large center button. (p107a, p107e, OP, R2) $20.00-30.00

ROSE GOBLET - (M&FB) - Approx. 7" but sizes can vary-The bowl of the goblet is a molded rose with a fluted rim. It has a long stem and a flat circular base. The whole piece is hollow and unsilvered. (p109a, OP, R1) $175.00-200.00

ROSE ON A LEAF - (M) - Approx. 2¾"H - A rose in rosette form is embossed on a large leaf form. The leaf is veined and has serrated edges. (Germany, p116b, OP, R2-3) $70.00-80.00

ROSETTE - (M) - Approx. 3" dia. - The rosette is in a disc shape viewing the center of the rose. In the "open rose" ornament, the center of the flower is underneath the ornament. The rosette is made of concentric swirls of petals. The front and back are the same. The older piece shown is unsilvered. (p110f, OP, R2-3) $40.00-50.00

ROSE WITH A HIP OF LEAVES - (M) - Approx. 2"-3½" (larger sizes more common) - This piece shows a standard form open rose, beneath which is attached a large group of molded leaves. This gives the ornament a general hour glass or figure 8 shape. They can be found with a hanger or clip-on. (p115a, OP-NP, R3-4) $15.00-25.00

  VARIATION: (1) WITH STAMENS - This is the same piece described above. The top is deeply indented, and a group of paper or wire stamens are inserted. This form is usually found as a clip-on. (OP, R2-3) $30.00-40.00

  VARIATION: (2) AMERICAN ROSE WITH A HIP OF LEAVES - (M), Approx. 2½" - It is similar in style and shape to the European version. However, the glass is heavier and the pike opening is wider. (U.S., p450c, OP, R3) $2.00-6.00

STYLIZED FLOWERS OR "PADULAS" - (M) - Approx. 1½"-2½" - These flowers come in a variety of shapes. They often have a bumpy, dimpled or quilted pattern instead of petals. Often the only way to identify them as flowers is by the fact they have leaves at the top. (Germany, Czech., Austria, p107g, OP-NP, R4) $5.00-10.00

TRUMPET FLOWER - (M) - Approx. 2¾" - The base shows leaves and four large petals. The upper part shows many upright petals. The center is indented. (p114a, OP, R2-3) $30.00-40.00

TRUMPET FLOWER - (FB) - Approx. 4"-5" but sizes can vary - In this free-blown piece, the flower is hollow. It has a wide top that tapers to the metal clip-on. The sides may have hand-added embossing or twists for decoration. Other than being glass flowers, it has been suggested that such pieces might have also served as candle shades or vases for small bouquets of real or artificial flowers. These pieces are also called Morning Gloves. (p113a & p113d, OP, R2-3) $60.00-75.00

HOLLOW TRUMPET FLOWER - (M) - Approx. 3"H - This piece shows flower molded leaves at the base and embossed creases on the side. The wide rim is fluted. The flower is hollow and unsilvered. Usually found as a clip-on. (p112a, OP, R2-3) $100.00-125.00

TULIP - (M) - Approx. 2", 3" & 3¼" - These flowers have an overall cupcake shape to them. They have three or four large petals around the outside. The area inside the petals is undetailed and may be flat or indented. (p111a & p112b, OP-NP, R3) $15.00-25.00

VARIATION: TULIP WITH STAMENS - (M) - The same form as above but has the indentation filled with wire or paper stamens. (p111d, OP, R2-3)$25.00-35.00

FRUIT AND FLOWER BASKETS

Flowers and fruit baskets were a common ornament theme. Doubtless, they represent one of the common Christmas gifts among friends.

AMERICAN FRUIT BASKET - (M) - Approx. 2" - In this piece, the glass is thick, and it has a large pike opening. The basket has a quilted or diamond pattern. The apples and grapes are hard to make out. It is not as delicate as its German counterpart but it is rarer. (U.S., p450d, OP, R2) $10.00-15.00

ANGEL IN A BASKET OF FLOWERS - see ANGELS

BASKET OF APPLES AND GRAPES - (M) - Approx. 2½" - The basket has a quilted or diamond pattern on it. One apple shows on either side, and bunches of grapes hang down the sides. The piece is not very thick. (Germany, p118f, OP-NP, R3) $15.00-25.00

BASKET OF FLOWERS ON A DISC - (M) - Approx. 1¾" dia. - A flower basket is embossed onto a disc-shaped ornament. It has a bumpy pattern around the edges and a geometric shape on the back. (OP, R4) $5.00-10.00

BASKET OF GRAPES - (M) - Approx. 3½" - The oval basket is woven and holds large bunches of grapes. Grape leaves also show. (p117b, OP, R3-4) $20.00-30.00

BASKET OF GRAPES AND PEARS - (M) - Approx. 2½" - The woven basket is smaller than its contents which are heaped high upon it. Two pears show, and larger bunches of grapes hang down the side. (p117a, OP, R3)$30.00-40.00

BASKET WITH FABRIC FLOWERS - (M) - Approx. 2"W x 1½"H - The basket is embossed with vertical, rope-like lines. There are no fruits or flowers embossed into it. It is often wire wrapped and has a wire or chenille hanging loop. A fabric flower is inserted into the open pike. (p119c, p122a, p123c, OP-NP, R3-4) $20.00-30.00

VARIATION: The basket may contain a "bouquet" of fabric or dried flowers. The flower may also be made out of foil.

BOUQUET OF FLOWERS - (M&FB) - Approx. 3½"-4" but sizes can vary - The molded top shows a round group or basket of flowers. A free-blown cone or "handle" extends from the bottom. This has the appearance of the "stems" wrapped into a cone. (OP, R3) $25.00-35.00

CORNUCOPIA OF FLOWERS - (M&FB) - Approx. 4"-5" but sizes can vary - This has the same shape as the hunting horns found in the music section. The large end is a molded group of large flowers. The free-blown "S" shaped pike tapers in size to the end. (OP, R2-3) $30.00-40.00

DAISY BASKET - (M) - Approx. 2" - The basket is made of six "woven" panels and has six large daisies in the basket. (Germany, p118e, OP-NP, R3) $20.00-30.00

VARIATION: The above described basket is wire wrapped and has a chenille hanging loop. It has fabric flowers inserted into the pike. (Germany, p121a, OP-NP, R3) $35.00-40.00

FLOWER BASKETS - (FB) - Approx. 2"-5" but sizes vary - These pieces come in a variety of shapes and sizes. The earliest ones are unsilvered and all are usually wire wrapped with a wire loop for hanging. The flowers may be dried, fabric or foil. They may also have scraps of flowers, angels or children. Small Dresden pieces may also be added as decoration. Tucksheer is often added for greenery. Some shapes include: cone, ball with long pikes, ball with the pike area indented, cylinder, disc, goblet, egg, mushroom and "pacifier" shape. Rogers pictures a pacifier which is in reality a flower basket with the wire and flower missing. (See the one pictured.) Indeed many old flower baskets can be found missing their wire and flowers; this, however, will detract from their price. Prices will be affected by condition, coloring and uniqueness of the shape. (Germany, Czech., Austria, p123, p124, p126, p174b, OP, R4-5)
Small $20.00-30.00
Medium $25.00-35.00
Large $40.00-50.00
With Scraps or Dresdens $50.00-65.00

FLOWER POT - (M) - Approx. 3½" - This piece does not show a basket at all but rather a "pot" with five embossed rings. It is wire wrapped and holds a fabric flower. (p122b, OP, R2-3) $25.00-35.00

FRUIT BASKET - (M) - Approx. 3" - Various fruits are piled high on this wicker basket. The fruits are about twice as high as the basket. (p119b, OP, R2) $15.00-20.00

HEART SHAPED FLOWER BASKET - see HEARTS

HOODED BASKET OF FLOWERS - (M) - Approx. 2" - The woven basket has three roses under a raised back or hood. (Rogers p6, OP, R2) $20.00-30.00

LARGE "EGG" SHAPED BASKET - (FB) - Approx. 6½" - Of an overall egg shape with the pike area indented, wire wrapped and with four wire "legs". In the indented area at the top are dried flowers, a small free-blown deer and a small cotton batting bird. (Germany, p125, OP, R1-2) $125.00-150.00

MINIATURE BASKETS - (M) - Approx. 1¼" - The baskets are embossed to show they are woven and may contain molded fruits or flowers. (Germany, Japan, p120a, p120b, OP, R4) $2.00-5.00

PAPER AND GLASS FRUIT BASKET - (M&FB) - Approx. 3¼" - The basket has an oval shape and is made of cardboard covered with foil. It is filled with free-blown and molded fruit about ½" long. The basket is also filled with angel hair. (p121b, OP, R2-3) $30.00-40.00

ROSE BASKET (TYPE I) - (M) - Approx. 1½", 2" & 2¼"W - Basket is made of vertical lines embossed to look like roping, with four large roses around the top with embossed leaves between them. (Germany, p118a, p118b, p118c, OP-NP, R5) $5.00-12.00

ROSE BASKET (TYPE II) - (M) - Approx. 2¼" - The basket is not woven but rather made up of vertical lines. It has four embossed roses with large leaves on the side. (p120c, OP, R2-3) $10.00-15.00

ROSE BASKET (TYPE III) - (M) - Approx. 2" - The woven basket contains three embossed roses on each side and large leaves hanging down the side. (p119a, OP-NP, R3) $5.00-10.00

ROUND BASKET OF FRUIT (TYPE I) - (M) - Approx. 2½" dia. - The basket is embossed to show it is woven, and it has an embossed rose on the side. Apples and pears show with grapes hanging down the sides. (p117c, OP, R3) $20.00-30.00

ROUND BASKET OF FRUIT (TYPE II) - (M) - Approx. 2½" - The weaving on this basket is much larger, and it has nothing embossed into it. Apples, berries and grapes show inside the basket. (p118d, OP, R3) $25.00-35.00

WOOD AND GLASS FRUIT BASKET - (M&FB) - Approx. 2"-4" but sizes can vary - This small basket with a handle is woven out of wood and is filled with small free-blown and molded glass fruit. (Schiffer p101, OP, R3)
Small $35.00-45.00
Large $75.00-90.00

FRUITS AND VEGETABLES

Real fruits were among the first ornaments to grace the branches of the Christmas tree. Some were gilted with real gold leaf to make them dazzling decorations. Fruit, especially the tropical kinds such as oranges and bananas, were considered a real treat at this time of year. This is a tradition which we carry on today with our gifts. Many fruits were blown in glass, the most common being the grapes and berries. Vegetables as a whole were a little unusual for the tree and hence today are scarcer than the fruits. Baskets of fruit will be found in the section "Fruit and Flower Baskets". Fruits and vegetables with faces embossed into them will be found in the section "People and Faces in Flowers, Fruits, Etc."

Apples

The concept of the apple as an ornament is very old and dates back to the medieval Paradise Play. Real apples -- red, green, yellow and artificially gilted -- hung on the tree centuries before their glass representatives. It is likely that all ball forms were originally designed as an interpretation of the apple; however, molded versions are scarce.

ARTISTIC PERIOD APPLE - (M) - Approx. 2¾" - This molded apple shows a dimpled area on the bottom and creases. It has a free-blown pike and leaves made of amethyst and colored glass and annealed onto the apple. Unlike most apples, this piece is silvered. Circa 1915-1925. (Germany, p132d, OP, R1-2) $60.00-75.00

APPLES - (FB) - Approx. 1"-2" dia. - Usually in the form of a free-blown ball that may have slight indentations in the top and bottom. They are often unsilvered, painted yellow with a characteristic red or pink blush. To add some luster to this otherwise plain piece, they were often covered in crushed glass or Venetian Dew. (p143b, OP-NP, R4) $15.00-25.00

APPLES - (M) - Approx. 1½", 2½" & 2¾" - These molded pieces are not quite round and the most significant "apple" molding occurs at the top and bottom. Bumps, indentations and creases are added to give it a realistic look. These pieces are usually unsilvered. (p643b, OP-NP [small only], R2-3)   Small $15.00-25.00
Large $30.00-45.00

ARTISTIC PERIOD CRAB APPLE - (M&FB) - Approx. 1½" dia. - This piece has a small molded crab apple with a free-blown pike and leaves out of amethyst glass. Few of these pieces were exported to the U.S. Circa 1915-1925. (Germany, p133b, OP, R1-2) $35.00-45.00

Bananas

ARTISTIC PERIOD BANANA - (M) - Approx. 6" - This long, slightly curving piece shows five sides. It has a pike and two leaves of amethyst glass annealed onto the top. This ornament is silvered and dates circa 1915-1925. Such pieces are rare in the U.S. (Germany, p132c, OP, R1-2) $90.00-100.00

BANANA (TYPE I) - (M) - Approx. 3" & 4" x 1"W - This piece has a long, narrow and curved look to it. It has five ill-defined sides, but is very realistic looking. The piece is unsilvered. (Germany, p136a, OP, R3) Small $45.00-55.00
Large $60.00-75.00

BANANA (TYPE II) - (M) - Approx. 3" & 4¼" x 1½"W - This thick looking piece is composed of four flat sections or sides which are easy to distinguish. This piece has only a slight curve to it. It is unsilvered. (p130a, OP, R2)   Small $50.00-60.00
Large $70.00-80.00

GENERIC BERRIES - (M) - Approx. 1"-2" - There is a wide variety of moldings of the common berry. They are generally shown in a cluster or group and have a bumpy or dimpled appearance. More lusterous pieces may be covered with Venetian Dew. Early versions may be unsilvered and have fabric leaves. (Germany, Czech., Austria, Japan, p127a, p127b, p127d, OP-NP, R5) $2.00-10.00

CARROT (TYPE I) - (M) - Approx. 3½" & 3¾" - The piece appears to be long and slender. The top is slightly larger than the rest of the tapering root. It is embossed with creases and indentations for a realistic look. Carrots are usually silvered and painted orange. (Germany, p130c, OP-NP, R3) $65.00-75.00

CARROT (TYPE II) - (M) - Approx. 2¾" & 3" - This piece has a general oval shape which tapers to a point at the bottom. The round sides are embossed to show the creases and indentations of this root. It is usually painted orange. (Germany, p131c, OP, R2) $60.00-70.00

CARROT - (FB) - Approx. 3½" but sizes can vary - It has a rounded top with a long tapering pike below it. This shape is seldom found in orange. Early pieces may be wire wrapped. (Schiffer p112, OP, R3-4) $35.00-45.00

Corn

CORN INSIDE LEAVES - (M) - Approx. 3¼" - The corn cob shows between two long and large leaves. The leaves have embossed veins. (p129e, OP-NP, R2) $30.00-40.00

CORN WITH LARGE LEAVES - (M) - Approx. 3" - In this crudely molded piece, the flattened corn cob shows between two large leaves. No early pieces are known. (p129b, NP) $2.00-5.00

CORN WITH LEAVES - (M) - Approx. 1½", 2¾", 3¼", 4", 4¾" & 5" - This piece shows the corn cob with individual molded kernals. It has molded leaves at the sides. The molds are now in East Germany. Once thought to be rare, this piece is fairly common. (Germany, p128, p129a, p129c, p129d, OP, R3)   Small $20.00-30.00
Medium $50.00-60.00
Large $75.00-90.00

CORN WITHOUT LEAVES - (M) - Approx. 3" & 4" - This is very similar to the corn with leaves piece. It shows small individual kernals but has no embossed leaves. (Schiffer p112, OP, R2) $45.00-55.00

Grapes

AMERICAN GRAPE BUNCH (TYPE I) - (M) - Approx. 1½" - This bunch has an egg shape with embossed grapes. It has a line of stylized leaves around the top. Made by Corning . (U.S., p451f, OP-NP, R5) $.50-2.00

AMERICAN GRAPE BUNCH (TYPE II) - (M) - Approx. 3" - This piece is long and slender. It has an irregular appearance with molded grapes sticking out in various areas. It has no embossed leaves. The glass is thick, and it has a wide pike opening. (U.S., p451e, OP, R3) $3.00-8.00

AMERICAN GRAPES ON A HEART - (M) - Approx. 3" - This shows a bunch of grapes embossed onto a heart shape. No leaves show. The sides of the heart are very ornate. (U.S., p451b, OP, R2) $20.00-30.00

BUNCH OF GRAPES - (M) - Approx. 2¾" & 3¼" - The grapes are shown in a realistic bunch with the top larger than the bottom. The grapes are embossed balls. A large leaf comes about halfway down the ornament. (Germany, p127h, OP-NP, R4)   Small $15.00-20.00
Large $25.00-30.00

BUNCH OF GRAPES - (FB) - Approx. 4"-5" but sizes can vary - The grapes are composed of small free-blown balls held together in a cluster by wire and are wire wrapped. They usually have fabric or foil leaves. (Schiffer p114, OP, R3) $10.00-20.00
Large with fabric leaves $20.00-35.00

GENERIC BUNCH OF GRAPES - (M) - Approx. 1"-4" - Made in a wide variety of different molds. Generally oval, composed of small embossed balls that represent the grapes. (U.S., Germany, Czech., Austria, Japan, p127g, OP-NP, R5)   Small $2.00-6.00
Large $5.00-10.00

GRAPE KUGELS - see KUGELS

GRAPES EMBOSSED ONTO A HEART - (M) - Approx. 2¾" - A bunch of grapes with two large leaves is embossed onto the side of a heart shape. The heart has a quilted pattern and a thick band along the edge. (p141a, OP, R3) $20.00-30.00

HEAVY GRAPES - (M) - Approx. 3½" - This piece shows a long bunch of embossed grapes without leaves. The piece looks like some early Kugels, and the silvered glass is thick. It is possibly an early American or Japanese ornament. (p146a, OP, R3) $10.00-15.00

ROUND BUNCH OF GRAPES - (M) - Approx. 2", 2½", 2¾" & 3" - This is an oval or egg shaped bunch of grapes. There are several different moldings of this form, some showing leaves at the top and others without them. The grapes are shown as embossed balls. (p127f, OP-NP, R5)   Small $2.00-10.00
Large $15.00-20.00

KUMQUAT - (FB) - Approx. 1¼" & 1½" but sizes can vary - This is basically a small free-blown ball that has been painted to resemble the fruit. They are usually unsilvered and are painted yellow with a pink or gold blush. (OP, R4) $2.00-4.00

LEMON - (M) - Approx. 2", 2¼", 2¾" & 3½" - Has general oval shape and a realistic nipple at the bottom, embossed to show a dimpled skin. They are usually unsilvered. (Germany, p136d, p140c, p143c, OP, R3) Small $10.00-20.00
Larger $30.00-45.00

MINIATURE FRUIT - (M&FB) - Approx. ½"-1" - These small berries, balls (apples or kumquats) and nuts are usually found in baskets. However, some were also sold as decorations for miniature trees. (OP, R2-3) $.50-1.00

ORANGE - (M) - Approx. 1¾" & 3" dia. - This piece is blown into a ball shape. It has embossed dimples to represent the skin of the orange. These pieces were generally unsilvered. (p136c, p142a, OP, R3)   Small $20.00-30.00
Large $40.00-50.00

Peaches

ARTISTIC PERIOD PEACH - (M) - Approx. 2¾" - It has the typical look and crease of other peaches. It has a stem and leaves of amethyst colored glass annealed to the top. Circa 1915-1925. This silvered piece may have a sticker stating "Made in Germany". (Germany, p132b, OP, R1-2) $60.00-75.00

FUZZY PEACH - (M) - Approx. 2" - This round piece has the traditional crease and has an added fabric flower. It is unusual in the fact that it is covered with flocking for a colorful but soft velvet finish that resembles real peach skin. (p453a, OP, R1-2) $20.00-30.00

PEACH - (M) - Approx. 2½" & 3" - This ornament has a general egg shape with a sharp vertical crease in one side. No leaves show, although early unsilvered pieces may have fabric leaves. (p134a, OP, R3-4) $15.00-25.00

PEACH WITH LARGE LEAVES - (M) - Approx. 1¾" - This piece has the typical shape and crease; however, its four long leaves run the full length of the ornament. (p134b, OP, R2) $20.00-30.00

PEACH WITH LEAVES - (M) - Approx. 2½" - It can be identified by its squat look and sharp crease running down one side. It has four embossed leaves at the top. (Germany, OP, R3-4) $20.00-30.00

Pears

Pears, a late fall fruit, were very popular as early decorations second only to the apple. Their natural golden color added a wonderful glow to the tree without the trouble of gilding the fruit. Pears were also a popular theme with the ornament makers, with each family having their own slightly different version. Most pears were unsilvered; they were simply painted yellow and given a red or pink blush. Some were covered in crushed glass while others were covered with tiny glass balls or Venetian Dew. Other pieces may have fabric leaves attached. Pears were a popular medium for embossing faces.

PEARS - (FB) - Approx. 2"-4" are common but sizes vary - The pear was an easy ornament to be free-blown with its rounded bottom and tapering top. They can be identified because they have no seam along the sides. They are not as detailed or as popular as the molded variety. Because they had less detail, they were often covered with crushed glass or Venetian Dew. They were made by most ornament-producing countries. (p139b, p140b, OP-NP, R4-5) $10.00-20.00
With Venetian Dew $15.00-30.00

VARIATION: COLORED GLASS PEAR - (FB) - Approx. 4" but sizes vary - Blown from gold or amber glass with annealed leaves. Produced in the 1920s and again in the early 1970s. Unsilvered. (Germany, OP-NP, R3) $25.00-35.00

PEARS - (M) - Approx. 1½"-5" - These have a nice pear shape with embossed creases, a dimple in the bottom and seam marks along the sides. They are usually unsilvered. They were made by most ornament producing countries. (p139d, p139e, p397b, OP-NP, R4-5) Small $10.00-15.00
Medium $20.00-30.00
Large $35.00-45.00

ARTISTIC PERIOD PEAR - (M) - Approx. 4½" - This silvered pear has an annealed stem and leaves of colored glass. Made during the period from 1915 to the early 1920s. They were not as popular in America and thus are scarce. (Germany, p132e, OP, R1-2) $70.00-85.00

HALF A PEAR - (M) - Approx. 3½" - The pear is shown split lengthwise. The back is rounded; the flat front shows a dimpled surface and embossed seeds. Unsilvered. (p139c, OP, R1-2) $65.00-75.00

PEAR WITH A BEETLE - see INSECTS

PEAR WITH A FACE - see PEOPLE AND FACES IN FLOWERS, FRUIT, ETC.

PEAR KUGEL - see KUGELS

PEAR WITH LEAVES - (M) - Approx. 3" - This pear has a split branch with two leaves embossed on the top of it. It is silvered. (Stille p25, OP, R3) $30.00-45.00

"RIBBED" PEAR - (M) - Approx. 2½" - This pear has four embossed leaves at the top and six beaded seams with "ribs" running between them. (p139a, OP, R2-3) $20.00-30.00

PEAS IN A POD - (M) - Approx. 3" - The thick pod is "split" open to show the peas inside. The pike forms the stem of the pod. Early pieces may have fabric leaves and be wire wrapped. (Germany, OP, R1) $400.00-425.00

GHERKIN PICKLE - (M) - Approx. 3½", 4" & 4½" - This piece has an easily identifiable curve to it. It is covered by embossed bumps to give it a realistic look. Of course, the ornament could also be considered a cucumber. These are not as rare as once thought. (p135, OP, R3)
Small $40.00-50.00
Medium $50.00-60.00
Large $70.00-85.00

"HEINZ" PICKLE - (M) - Approx. 3¾" - This is more or less a straight looking pickle. It has molded sections and is covered with realistic bumps. It resembles the pickle that the Heinz Co. used as their trademark. The ornament pictured is unsilvered but silvered versions are also known. (p136b, OP, R2) $75.00-90.00

PINEAPPLE - (M) - Approx. 3" - At first glance, this piece appears to be a bunch of small flowers; however, these represent the texture of the pineapple. It also shows eight long slender leaves. This piece is unsilvered. (p137a, OP, R2) $60.00-75.00

Plums

PLUM - (FB) - Approx. 2"-3" but sizes can vary - Along with apples, real and sugared plums were popular decorations on early trees. Most of the long oval shaped pieces that come to a point could be plums. However, they are seldom appropriately colored and lack the characteristic crease down one side. They are often considered just geometric shapes and were a popular form for indents. Such forms were made by all glassmakers. (p449, OP-NP, R5) $.50-2.00

ARTISTIC PERIOD PLUM - (M) - Approx. 2¼" - This piece has a long oval shape with a crease in the front side. It has a stem and leaves of amethyst colored glass annealed to the top. Circa 1915-1925. (Germany, p132a, OP, R1-2) $35.00-45.00

PLUM - (M) - Approx. 2" - This piece is similar to and often mistaken for a peach. It has a long oval appearance with a deep vertical crease in one side. It usually doesn't have leaves. (OP, R3) $10.00-15.00

POTATO - (M) - Approx. 3" - This rather plain looking piece has a flat square look to it. It has realistic "eyes" and creases embossed into it. (p137b, OP, R2) $80.00-100.00

PUMPKIN - (M) - Approx. 1", 2" & 3" - The squat round piece has thick ribs embossed into the sides. It may have embossed leaves at the top. (Germany, OP, R3)
Small $5.00-15.00
Large $10.00-20.00

JACK-O'-LANTERN - (M) - Approx. 2" - This round piece shows embossed ribs, large round eyes, a triangle nose and a wide grinning mouth. (p395c, OP, R1-2)$150.00-175.00

RADISH - (FB) - Approx. 2½" but sizes can vary - This is a free-blown ball with a long narrow spike on the bottom to represent the main root. It is often painted red and may have a tinsel spray or fabric leaves at the top. (p131a, OP, R2-3) $20.00-30.00

SQUASH - (M) - Approx. 3¼" - This oblong piece has thin "ribs" embossed into the sides. A group of leaves show at the top. (p131b, OP, R2) $25.00-35.00

ARTISTIC PERIOD STRAWBERRY - (M&FB) - Approx. 2½" - The strawberry is molded showing the embossed seeds covering it. It has a free-blown pike and annealed leaves of amethyst colored glass. Circa 1915-1925. (Germany, p133c, OP, R1-2) $40.00-55.00

STRAWBERRIES - (M) - Approx. 1¾", 2", 2¼" & 2¾" - The strawberry was a popular piece and was made in several different moldings. The pieces have the typical berry shape with embossed seeds. It usually has several embossed leaves showing at the top. Early versions may be unsilvered. (p127c, p127e, p143d, p138, p140a, p143d, OP-NP, R4) Small and Medium $10.00-20.00
Large $25.00-35.00

ARTISTIC PERIOD TOMATO - (M&FB) - Approx. 2½" - The tomato is molded and has a stem which is a short free-blown pike. It has two free-blown, annealed leaves attached to the stem. This piece was made during the artistic period from about 1915 to the early 1920s. (Germany, p133a, OP, R1-2) $75.00-85.00

TOMATO - (M) - Approx. 2" dia., 2½" & 2¾" - The piece has the characteristic tomato shape to include creases and folds. The piece is painted red and is usually unsilvered.

(Germany, p130b, OP, R3)
Small $25.00-35.00
Medium $50.00-60.00
Large $70.00-80.00

WATERMELON SLICE - (M) - Approx. 3½" & 4½" - This piece has a curved banana shape to it. The back is rounded and the front is wedge shaped. Down the center of the wedge is a line of embossed seeds. (Germany, p141b, p142b, OP, R2-3) Small $80.00-100.00
Large $100.00-125.00

HEARTS

Hearts used as a symbol of love were a very popular motif used by most of the glassmakers. It was a favorite form onto which other shapes were embossed. Those listed here have the heart shape as the major element.

BERRIES ON A HEART - (M) - Approx. 1¾" - Small berry-like shapes are embossed onto the heart. (p144b, OP, R3-4) $2.00-5.00

BUMPY HEART - (M) - Approx. 2½" - The heart is embossed with a beaded or bumpy pattern. (p145c, OP-NP, R4) $8.00-12.00

BUST OF A LADY ON A HEART - see "WOMEN AND GIRLS" - BUST OF A VICTORIAN LADY IN A HEART

DAISY ON A HEART - (M) - Approx. 2¼" - A large flower with radiating petals is embossed onto both sides. (p144d, OP, R3-4) $8.00-12.00

HEART ON A HEART - (M) - Approx. 2" - A small heart is embossed onto the center of a larger heart shape. The same shape is on both sides and the rest of the piece is covered with a bumpy pattern. (Germany, p144a, OP, R3-4) $10.00-18.00

HEART WITH ANGEL - see ANGELS

HEART WITH EMBOSSED STARS - (M) - Approx. 2" - Both sides of the piece show three embossed stars and a center band of embossed triangles. (Germany, p144c, OP, R3) $8.00-12.00

VARIATION: HEART FLOWER BASKET - (M), Approx. 2" - The above described heart is wire wrapped and has fabric flowers inserted into the open pike. (Germany, p144c, OP, R2-3) $20.00-30.00

HEART WITH GRAPES - see "FRUITS AND VEGETABLES" - GRAPES

HEAVY GLASS HEART - (M) - Approx. 3½" - This large heart has a quilted pattern and five pointed star embossed into both sides. The glass on this piece is heavy. It is not European but possibly an early Japanese or American piece. (p146b, OP, R3) $15.00-20.00

INDENTED HEART - (M) - Approx. 1¾" - A heart indent is embossed onto a molded heart. (p145b, OP, R3)$2.00-5.00

IRIS ON A HEART - (M) - Approx. 2½" - The flower, showing a stem and leaves, is embossed onto the front of the heart. The rest of the piece is covered by a bumpy pattern. (p144e, OP, R3) $10.00-20.00

MERRY CHRISTMAS HEART - (M) - Approx. 3½" - The front of this heart has a wide band with the words "Merry Christmas" embossed into it. The back has a dimpled effect. (Germany, OP-NP, R2-3) $35.00-45.00

QUILTED HEART - (M) - Approx. 1¾" & 2½" - The heart has a quilted or diamond pattern embossed into it. (p145a, p145b, OP-NP, R4) $2.00-10.00
                                    Large $15.00-25.00

SANTA HEAD ON A HEART - see SANTAS

HEAVENLY BODIES

Heavenly bodies such as the sun, moon and stars have always played an important role in man's life. Many legends and stories, including Christmas-related ones, have sprung up about them. Stars and comets, doubtless, represent the Star of Bethlehem and were a popular item to emboss onto other shapes and objects. Those listed here have the star as the main element.

Crescent Shaped Man In The Moon

MAN IN THE MOON (TYPE I) - (M) - Approx. 2¾" & 4" - The ornament is crescent shaped with a face embossed into it. The face is well detailed and shows the eyes, nose and mouth as prominent features. The back side of the crescent shows flat vertical ribs. The ornament's seam runs vertically through the face and nose. (Germany, p147a, OP-NP, R2-3)   Small $50.00-60.00
                                    Large $75.00-90.00

VARIATION: - (M), Approx. 3" - This piece is similar to the above except the seam runs between the face and the back of the crescent instead of through the face. (p148a, OP, R2-3) $60.00-75.00

MAN IN THE MOON (TYPE II) - (M) - Approx. 2" & 2¾" - The ornament has a crescent shape with a face embossed into it. The detailed face has prominent eyes, nose, mouth and cheeks. The back side of the crescent has a bumpy pattern on it. The ornament's seam runs vertically through the face and nose. (Germany, p147c, OP-NP, R2-3)
                                    Small $25.00-35.00
                                    Medium $45.00-55.00

MAN IN THE MOON (TYPE III) - (M) - Approx. 3"H x 2"W - This crescent shaped piece has a deeply embossed face in one side. The back of the crescent is very wide, wedge shaped and has thin horizontal lines embossed into it. The ornament's seam is on the side, between the face and the back of the crescent. Thus placed, the seam does not distort the face. (p147b, p149c, OP-NP [limited], R3)
                                    $45.00-55.00

BOY CLOWN IN THE MOON - see CLOWNS

FROWNING MAN IN THE MOON - (M) - Approx. 2¾" - This piece has the traditional crescent shape and embossed face. The face has a stern or frowning expression, no cheeks and a large prominent nose. The back of the crescent has thick horizontal ribs. The seam is on the side between the face and the back of the crescent. (p149a, OP, R1-2)
                                    $75.00-85.00

ROUND MAN IN THE MOON - (M) - Approx. 2¼" - This double faced piece is rounded and shows the smiling face wearing a close fitting nightcap. This piece was also made as a squeeze toy. (Germany, p329a, OP, R1)$125.00-135.00

ROUND MAN IN THE MOON WITH ARMS - see FICTIONAL CHARACTERS - HUMPTY DUMPTY

Stars

COMET - (M&FB) - Approx. 3¼" - The stylized eight pointed star has a small indented center and a free-blown "tail" that is cone shaped. Comets not only represented the Star of Bethlehem but would have also been popular in 1910 when Haley's Comet made an appearance. (p150a, OP, R2) $30.00-40.00

STAR - (M) - Approx. 1½" & 2½" - This piece shows a six pointed star with a similar star embossed in the center. (p150b, p151d, OP-NP, R2-3 large, R4 small)
                                    Small $5.00-8.00
                                    Large $10.00-20.00

BEADED STAR - (BEADS) - Approx. 3" - These come in both a flat and three dimensional form. Some have five and other have six points. They are composed of small glass tubes and beads. (Czech., Japan, p456c, OP-NP, R4)
                                    $2.00-10.00

GERMAN BEAD STARS AND COMETS - (M&FB BEADS) - Approx. 3" but sizes can vary - These pieces, which also resemble snowflakes, are composed of beads and tubes that may be molded or free-blown. They often have six or eight "arms" with tinsel in the center. When long strips of tinsel wire are added, the star becomes a comet. (Germany, Stille p192, OP, R1-2)   Star $10.00-15.00
                                    Comet $20.00-30.00

LARGE STAR EMBOSSED ON A DISC - (M) - Approx. 2"-3" - There are several varying forms of this type. They are almost always embossed into either side of a disc shape. They include five, six and eight pointed stars. (U.S., Germany, Czech., Austria, p151c, OP-NP, R4-5) $5.00-15.00

SPIKED STARS - (FB) - Approx. 2" to 4½" dia. - This is a free-blown ball with six or eight tubular points or spikes annealed onto it. The center ball may be indented. Larger versions were made for tree top stars. (p151a, OP, R3)
                                    Small $2.00-5.00
                                    Medium $8.00-12.00
                                    Large $15.00-25.00

VARIATION: SPIKED STAR AND HOUSE - A spiked star about 2" in dia. is attached by a short pike to a molded house. The house is usually the 2" size of the House With Pine Roping. (See Houses) (OP, R3)
                                    $40.00-50.00

WIRE AND GLASS STAR - (FB) - Approx. 2"-3½" dia. but sizes can vary - The glass is a free-blown ball of varying sizes which is usually indented. Wire and wire wrapping form a six, eight or ten pointed star with the ball at

its center. Small beads may provide added decoration. (Germany, Czech., p152, OP-NP, R3-4)   Small $15.00-20.00
Large $20.00-30.00

SUN AND MOON ON A BALL - (M) - Approx. 2″ - Faces of a sun and crescent moon are embossed onto either side of the ball, surrounded by six embossed stars and lines that radiate to the edge of the ball. (Germany, p150c, OP-NP, R3) $60.00-70.00

SUN AND MOON ON A DISC - (M) - Approx. 2¼″ - Both the sun and moon have faces and they are embossed into either side of the disc. Web-like lines radiate out to the edge of the ornament. (Germany, p151b, OP-NP, R2-3) $60.00-70.00

SUN FACE ON A BALL - (M) - Approx. 2″ - The front shows a detailed sun face with radiating lines. The back is bumpy and shows a geometric pattern that resembles a flower. (Germany, OP, R2) $50.00-60.00

SUN FACE ON A DISC - (M) - Approx. 2″ - A round sun with a smiling face is embossed into one side of a round disc. No early examples are known. (Germany, NP) $2.00-10.00

THE NORTHWIND - (M) - Approx. 3″ - The ornament has an overall egg shape. The right side has an embossed face that resembles a man in the moon. The chin and forehead show embossed hair. The egg shows a frosty finish coming from his mouth portraying the cold north wind. The reverse has the same face. (p148c, OP, R1-2) $125.00-150.00

HOUSES AND BUILDINGS

The style of houses range from simple cottages to mansions and castles. They include, of course, churches which were an important part of the community. Some houses may represent the homes of the glassblowers, themselves. Others are certainly modeled after houses in their villages.

STANDARD COTTAGE - (M) - Approx. 2¼″, 2½″ & 2¾″ - This small house has a pine tree to the left of the door and two pine trees on the back. One side shows two windows and an embossed fence. The other has two windows and a door. (Germany, p154a, p154b, p156a, OP-NP, R5) $10.00-20.00

VARIATION: COTTAGE WITH A MILL WHEEL - (M), Approx. 2½″ - The front appears exactly like the standard cottage; however, a large waterwheel is embossed on the back. (Germany, OP-NP, R2)$25.00-35.00

CHALET - (M) - Approx. 2¾″ - It has a long steep sloping roof. Three windows show on the front and back but no doors appear. (p166b, OP-NP, R3) $15.00-25.00

GINGERBREAD HOUSE - (M) - Approx. 3″ - This is similar in style to the standard cottage. However, it has a heart at the gable and is covered with designs that make it look as if it were made of gingerbread. (p155a, OP, R2) $30.00-40.00

LARGE STUCCO HOUSE - (M) - Approx. 3″H x 1¾″W - The surface of the house has a rough texture like stucco.

The roof has a diamond pattern embossed into it. The front shows two windows and a door with six panels. The side shows three large windows. Opposite sides are identical. (Probably Czech., p166c, OP, R2-3) $30.00-40.00

LIGHTHOUSE - (M) - Approx. 3″ - The building has six sides with windows in them. Near the top of the ornament, it expands out to form the walkway around the light. The top is also six sided with small windows in each panel. (p160a, p 172a, OP-NP, R3-4) $30.00-40.00

HOUSE UNDER A TREE - see TREES

HOUSE WITH PINE ROPING - (M) - Approx. 1″, 2″, 2½″ & 3″ - The square-looking piece has four sides. Each side shows a window with a swag of pine rope underneath. No doors show. (Germany, p164a, p164b, p165a, OP-NP, R4)
Small $5.00-15.00
Large $15.00-20.00

VARIATION: Above house with a free blown star above it. $40.00-50.00

HOUSE WITH A TURKEY - (M) - Approx. 2″, 2½″ & 2¾″ - The cottage with a thatched roof has a large turkey embossed in the front. A picket fence goes all the way around. There is a large tree on the right side and a smaller on the left. This is found in both German and Austrian versions. The two are practically identical except for the detail between the gables. The Austrian shows brickwork, and the German several smooth panels. (Germany, Austria, p156c, p157a, p157c, p163b, OP-NP, R3-4)   Small $25.00-35.00
Large $30.00-40.00

CZECH. HOUSE WITH A TURKEY - (M) - Approx. 2½″ - This is very similar to the above pieces. They are round where this has a flatter shape. A large tree on the right side comes halfway up the roof. (Czech., OP-NP, R3)$20.00-30.00

SQUARE HOUSE - (M) - Approx. 2½″ - The front shows two windows and a doorway flanked by two pine trees. The back shows a bay window. (p165c, OP-NP, R4)$10.00-15.00

TALL HOUSE - (M) - Approx. 3″ - This piece has a tall narrow appearance. It has a dimpled roof with a circle design in the gable. Opposite sides are the same with the front and back showing a door and large four-paned window. Only the corners are embossed to show brickwork. (p165b, OP, R3) $15.00-20.00

"TREE HOUSE" (TYPE I) - (M) - Approx. 2½″ - A highly detailed square-looking piece. On opposite corners, it has an embossed tree that covers the corner and stops at the roof line. The front shows a roofed porch, two windows and a ladder leading to a gabled window. The back shows an arched door, two windows and a window in the gable. All sides show embossed stonework. (p154c, OP, R2)
$25.00-35.00

"TREE HOUSE" (TYPE II) - (M) - Approx. 2½″ - On this piece, the thick embossed tree on the right corner comes up past the roof line. House has a sloped roof with no added gables. The doorways are not elaborate, and embossed stonework shows only at the base. (p156b, OP, R2)
$25.00-35.00

VICTORIAN HOUSE - (M) - Approx. 3¼″ - It has a tall tower in the front with an arched doorway in it. The tower rises above the regular roof. The back shows two windows and a door. The piece is embossed to show brickwork. This has also been called a church. (p162d, OP, R2-3)$25.00-35.00

ROUND, SNOW-COVERED HOUSE - (M) - Approx. 2½″ & 3½″ - It is embossed to show brick-work and four arched windows with six panes. The roof is embossed to show snow, with large piles hanging down between the windows. (Germany, p161a, OP, R2-3) $20.00-30.00

CHURCH - (M) - Approx. 1¾″W x 3″H - It has three large arched windows on either side and double doors in the front. The short steeple is offset to the front and the roof has a diamond pattern. (Germany, p162a, OP, R3) $15.00-25.00

CZECH. CHURCH - (M) - Approx. 1¾″W x 3″H - This is very similar to the above German church. However, the steeple is centered on the roof and there is a small half-circle window in the back. (Czech., p162b, OP-NP R3)$15.00-25.00

CHURCH ON A BELL - (M) - Approx. 2¼″ - The church, with the steeple in front, has a pattern of stars embossed around it and on the back. The bell has a glass clapper. (Germany, p227a, OP, R3) $25.00-35.00

CHURCH ON AN EGG - (M) - Approx. 3½″ - The church, surrounded by trees and a fence, is embossed on an egg-shaped ornament. It has a bumpy pattern along the seams. (p161c, OP, R2-3) $55.00-65.00

CHURCH ON A DISC - (M) - Approx. 2½″ dia. - The small church is shown with a tall steeple at the side. Trees are shown on either side of the church. (p163a, OP, R2-3)
          $20.00-30.00

LARGE CHURCH - (M) - Approx. 1¾″W x 4″H - The steeple is centered on the roof, and it has three large, arched windows on either side. The front shows a large detailed door flanked by two windows. The back shows one large and two small arched windows. (Germany, p162c, OP-NP, R3) $30.00-40.00

CASTLE TOWER - (M) - Approx. 4″ - It is round with a funnel-shaped roof. It is molded to show square stonework and pairs of windows. (p155b, OP, R2) $60.00-80.00

TOWN HALL BUILDING - (M) - Approx. 1½″ & 2″ - This square looking piece has a large two story front section with a gabled roof. The door has two small windows above it and a half-circle window in the gable. (Probably Czech., p155c, p166a, OP, R3)   Small $10.00-20.00
          Large $20.00-30.00

WINDMILL (TYPE I) - (FB) - Approx. 4¼″ but sizes can vary - It has a domed roof with a large sloping lower portion. The arms are made of tinsel. The whole piece is wrapped in wire and is unsilvered. (p153, OP, R1-2)$90.00-100.00

WINDMILL (TYPE II) - (FB) - Approx. 5½″ but sizes can vary - The top and bottom are ball shaped with a connecting pike between them. The arms are made of wire, and the whole piece is wrapped in wire. A scrap figure may be attached to the pike. (p159b, OP, R2-3) $50.00-60.00

WINDMILL - (M) - Approx. 4¾″ - It shows embossed stonework, an arched door and a rounded window. There is a wide indented band going around the center. Dresden windmill arms are added. (Germany, p158b, p159a, OP, R2)
          $50.00-75.00

WINDMILL (TYPE II) - (M) - Approx. 3¾″ - It has four sides with embossed stonework. It has windows in three sides, but no door shows. The ribbed bottom comes to a point. It has Dresden cardboard arms. (p157b, OP-NP, R3)
          $50.00-60.00.

WINDMILL ON A DISC - (M) - Approx. 2¼″ - The windmill is embossed onto a disc. It shows a bumpy pattern underneath along the seams. (p161b, OP, R2-3)$25.00-35.00

WINDMILL WITH EMBOSSED ARMS - (M) - Approx. 2¼″ - The molding shows stonework, several windows and a door. The roof is domed and the arms of the mill are embossed into the front. (p160b, OP-NP [1950s], R3)
          $20.00-25.00

HOUSEHOLD ITEMS

This section represents items that were commonly found in homes both in Europe and America, the same type of items that were also commonly sold by the large mailorder houses of the day. Many ornaments were copied directly from the popular-selling household wares of the time.

As tastes changed over the seventy Golden Years of ornament making, so did the styles of household utensils. Such changes and developments were also reflected by the ornament makers. Hence, in early years we find the Gramophone ornament, and in later years we find it has been replaced by a box radio ornament.

This section also includes many personal items such as shoes, purses, baby items, etc. Many decorations in this area represented some of the common toys of childhood and may have been designed to replace those toys which once hung on the tree.

Baby and Children Items

This section represents items belonging to children. The babies and children themselves will be listed in separate sections.

BABY BUGGY - see BABIES - BABY IN A BUGGY

BABY SHOE - see SHOES, BOOTS AND STOCKINGS

BEAD PACIFIER - (BEADS) - Approx. 2¼″ - This three dimensional piece is made of small glass beads and rods. (Czech., Rogers 150a, OP, R2) $15.00-25.00

PACIFIER - (FB) - Approx. 2¼″ - Rogers pictures and describes this piece as a pacifier. In reality, it has a general pacifier shape, but was commonly used as a flower basket or hanging vase. In such a case, it has fabric flowers and wire wrapping. It is possible that the shape was marketed as a pacifier as well as a vase; however, it is more likely that such pieces are ones in which the original flowers and wire are missing. In either case, the piece must be priced considerably **lower** than the more highly decorated vase. Also see FLOWER BASKETS. (p124b, OP, R4)
          $15.00-25.00

CORNUCOPIA OF TOYS - (M) - Approx. 3¼" & 3¾" - This piece has an overall cone shape. The cone or cornucopia has a "waffle" pattern to it, and various toys are embossed into the top. Most distinguishable among the toys is a large doll. (p173, OP-NP, R2-3) $75.00-100.00

BOY HEAD BABY RATTLE - see MEN AND BOYS

CAT HEAD BABY RATTLE - see ANIMALS - CATS

DOUBLE HEADED BABY IN A RATTLE - see BABIES

RATTLES - (FB) - Approx. 5"-6" but sizes can vary - This is a free-blown ball with the long slender pike left on. The ball is often painted and contains pebbles that make it rattle. (OP, R2-3) $25.00-35.00

"MERRY XMAS" RATTLE - (M&FB) - Approx. 5" but sizes can vary - The rattle end is pear-shaped with an embossed, checked pattern. It has a wide band going around the middle with the words "Merry Xmas" embossed into it. The handle is a long free-blown pike. Small bits of glass, clay or gravel may be added to make it rattle. (p167, OP, R2) $50.00-60.00

PEACOCK BABY RATTLE - see BIRDS - PEACOCKS

PEAR-SHAPED RATTLE - (M&FB) - Approx. 3½"-4½" but sizes can vary with the free-blown pike - The molded rattle has an overall pear-shape and has an embossed design of raised squares. The free-blown pike forms the handle of the rattle. (OP-NP, R3) $30.00-40.00

TEDDY BEARS - see ANIMALS - BEARS

TOPS - (FB) - Approx. 3"-4" but sizes can vary - There are a wide variety of these as they are free-blown. The bottom has a cone or funnel shape, followed by a thin "neck" and a larger top. (p445c, OP-NP, R4) $5.00-10.00

Barrels and Casks

Barrels and casks were used for storage of many items and the aging of beer and wine. They were a part of everyday life throughout the golden age of ornament making.

BARREL - (M) - Approx. 2¼" - The barrel is molded to show individual staves and end hoops. One side may have an embossed bunghole. (OP-NP, R3) $20.00-30.00

BARREL BABY RATTLE - (M&FB) - Approx. 6½" but sizes can vary - The molded barrel shows embossed staves and hoops on the end. A long free-blown pike extends from the side, giving it a handle. Glass, clay or pebbles may be inserted to make it rattle. This piece has also been described as a gavel. Early versions may be unsilvered and wire wrapped. (p168, OP, R2) $70.00-80.00

BARREL WITH A ROSE - (M) - Approx. 1½"L - The barrel has embossed staves and two hoops. A large flower with leaves is embossed between the two hoops. The hanger is in the barrel's side. (Germany, OP-NP, R3) $10.00-20.00

BARREL - (FB) - Approx. 3¼"L - It is free-blown into a fat cylinder shape. They are often unsilvered and wire wrapped. (p158a, OP, R2-3) $50.00-60.00

BASEBALL - (M) - Approx. 3" dia. - The appropriate stitching shows at the top and the bottom. It has an embossed anchor on the top near the pike. (OP, R1-2)$175.00-200.00

BEER STEIN - Rogers lists such an ornament but gives no description. (Germany, OP, R1) $150.00-175.00

Bottles, Flasks, Jugs, Etc.

Most bottles and flasks are free-blown and have a flattened bottom like their real-life counterparts. The most popular are the bottles with paper labels.

BOTTLES - (FB) - Approx. 4"-5" but sizes vary - Most often they have a round body with the long pike forming the neck of the bottle. They may have a flat bottom and a wire handle, with early versions being unsilvered and wire wrapped. They may have artificial flowers or scraps added for decoration. Other than round, they can be found in an oval or tear-drop shape that is hard to distinguish from mandolins. (p170a, p170c, OP, R3-4) $50.00-60.00

BOTTLES WITH PAPER LABELS - (M&FB) - Approx. 2"-3" but sizes may vary - These small bottles, some of which are free-blown and other molded, have applied paper labels. They represent wine and champagne bottles, and some have foil or metallic paint around the top near the hanger. The labels are often written in German or French and may represent actual brands. Labels include: "Malaga" and "Erdener Treppchen". The value of a bottle is drastically reduced if the label is missing. (p169, p177c, OP, R2) $40.00-50.00

Carrousels

CARROUSEL - (M) - Approx. 2½" & 3" (2¼" dia.) - This piece has a six paneled roof and six panels on the carrousel. Animals include a running horse and a lion pulling a chariot (one in each panel). Each panel shows riders and a swagged cord with tassels at the top. (Germany, p171b, OP-NP [limited], R3) $35.00-45.00

CARROUSEL WITH A ROUND TOP - (M) - Approx. 3½" & 4" [2½" dia.] - This piece has six panels showing chair and swans. The top is rounded instead of flattened into panels. (p172b, OP, R2-3)   Small $40.00-50.00
Large $65.00-75.00

REVERSE CARROUSEL - (M) - Approx. 2¾" (2" dia.) - This piece has six panels with horses and chairs alternating. In other carrousels the animals move to the right. In this piece they move to the left. (p171a, OP, R2-3)$35.00-45.00

SMALL CARROUSEL - (M) - Approx. 2½" (1½" dia.) - This carrousel has only four panels. It has two running horses and two walking lions, and each has riders. (p171c, OP-NP, R2) $15.00-25.00

CAULDRON - (FB) - Approx. 2"-3" but sizes can vary - The piece is round with a wide rim. They are hollow inside and not silvered. Other than representing a cauldron or cooking pot, the same piece has been used as a "nest" for a bird's nest ornament, and they held fabric flowers thus becoming a flower basket. Finally these hollow cauldrons were used as lighting. Hanging from a metal loop, they held water and a floating wick. (p191d, OP, R2-3)

Small $15.00-25.00
Larger $30.00-40.00

Clocks

CLOCK AND SUNDIAL - (M) - Approx. 2½″ dia. - The embossed clock face, which has no numerals, shows 12:15. There is a ribbon-like design under the face on the rim. The back shows a sundial. (p179a, OP, R2) $70.00-80.00

CUCKOO CLOCK - (M) - Approx. 2¾″ & 3½″ - It has a slanted "roof" at the top and embossed leaves around the clock face. The cuckoo bird sits atop the clock face. The back shows the clock weights - pine cones and leaves. The sides also show pine cones. The smaller piece had an embossed clock face and the larger one out of paper. Only the smaller version has been remade. (Germany, p175c, p176b, OP-NP, R3)   Small $25.00-35.00
Larger $45.00-55.00

"EGG INDENT" CLOCK - (FB) - Approx. 3″ but sizes can vary - A large indentation was placed in a free-blown egg shape. Spun glass was fastened inside the glass, and a paper clock face placed on the outside. (p178, OP, R2)$15.00-25.00

FLOWER CLOCK - (M) - Approx. 2″ dia. - Wall clock with eight lobes or petals around an indented center and a paper face attached. (p177a, OP, R2) $30.00-40.00

POCKET WATCH - (M) - Approx. 1¾″ dia. - This watch has an embossed clock face with Roman numerals; the hands show 10 o'clock. (p176a, OP, R2) $35.00-45.00

POCKET WATCH WITH A PAPER DIAL - (M) - Approx. 1¾″ - The watch is a flat disc shape with a rough ridge along the seam. A paper clock face is applied to the center of one side. The reverse shows a rose with leaves. The value is drastically reduced if the paper face is missing. (p175b, OP, R2) $30.00-40.00

RECTANGULAR CLOCK - (M) - Approx. 3″ - It shows a rectangular clock case with raised areas at the top and bottom. It has three embossed panels on each side. The embossed clock face shows four o'clock, and it shows a short pendulum underneath. (Germany, p179b, OP-NP, R2) $35.00-45.00

WALL CLOCK - (M) - Approx. 3¾″ - This molded piece shows a carved wooden case. There are carved triangular pieces at the top and bottom. The clock face is paper, and below it is a long swinging pendulum. (Germany, p175a, OP, R2) $55.00-65.00

DICE - (M) - Approx. 2″ - They are square looking with their six sides embossed circles around the embossed dots. The hanger is in the corner. (Germany, p182b, OP-NP, R2) $20.00-30.00

FOOTBALL - (M) - Approx. 3¼″L - This ornament is oval in shape with the hanger in the top. It shows embossed seams and stitching near the pike. (p180a, OP, R2) $60.00-75.00

Goblets and Wine Glasses

These represent the richer side of life and were often free-blown. They may have artificial flowers or scraps added as decoration.

CHAMPAGNE GLASS - (FB) - Approx. 5″ but sizes may vary - It has a wide shallow bowl with a long stem and flattened base. It is unsilvered and wire wrapped. (p183b, OP, R2) $50.00-60.00

ROSE GOBLET - (M&FB) - Approx. 7″ but sizes may vary - The bowl of the goblet is a molded rose with a fluted rim. It has a long stem and a flat circular base. The whole piece is hollow and unsilvered. (p109a, OP, R1)$175.00-200.00

WINE GLASS - (FB) - Approx. 5¾″ but sizes may vary - This has a tall oval bowl with a stem and flattened base. It is unsilvered and wire wrapped. (p183a, OP, R2) $50.00-60.00

GRAMOPHONE - (FB) - Approx. 4¾″ - The base can be barrel or box shaped, and it has a large "morning glory" type horn coming out of it. The horn and base are blown separately. The piece is unsilvered and wire wrapped. (p174a, OP, R2) $125.00-150.00

Guns and Weapons

Guns have not been very popular in the past or with collectors today. They seem to clash with the peaceful child-like nature of the tree.

CANNON - (M&FB) - Approx. 5½″ - The cannon shows the carriage and two wheels. It shows embossed designs and raised "rivets". The barrel of the cannon is free-blown, and the hanger is in the rear. (p181c, OP, R1)$125.00-150.00

REVOLVER - (M&FB) - Approx. 5″ - The grip and cylinder are molded; the elongated barrel is a free-blown tube. The hanger is in the grip, but no trigger shows. (p181a, OP, R2) $125.00-150.00

RIFLE - (FB) - Approx. 12″ - This early, unsilvered piece has a fat stock, and a slightly bent hollow tube forms the length of the rifle. The trigger and guard are made of wire, and the whole rifle is wire wrapped. (p181b, OP, R1-2) $200.00-225.00

SEA MINE - (M) - Approx. 2″ - It is round with a raised area near the top. It has two embossed lines between which is written in German "Seemine" (Sea mine). This was produced during World War I and not exported. (Germany, Stille p51, OP, R1) $125.00-150.00

Lamps, Lanterns and Lighting

BANQUET LAMPS - (M&FB) - Approx. 5″-6″ but sizes may vary - The base and tall pedestal rise to the oil holder. The base may be free-blown or molded and the column twisted or indented for added decoration. The oil reservoir sets this off from the more common table lamp. The globe or shade may be free-blown or molded and is added as a separate piece over a thin pike above the oil reservoir. (p184, p187b, p188b, OP, R3) $30.00-40.00

CANDLE - (M) - Approx. 4" - The candle has a well molded flame and shows wax dripping down the sides of the candle. It is a clip-on piece. (Germany, p190b, OP-NP [limited], R2) $80.00-90.00

CANDLE (TYPE I) - (FB) - Approx. 3½"L - This is basically a tubular piece of glass with the "flame" coming to a pencil-like point. The piece is silvered, and a large hanging cap fits over the bottom. (U.S., p450j, OP, R4) $2.00-5.00

CANDLE (TYPE II) - (FB) - Approx. 3½" - This piece is more delicate and not as thick as the one above. It also has a small "bowl" at the base representing the bowl that would catch wax. (Schiffer p117 OP-NP, R2-3) $10.00-20.00

CANDLE CHANDELIER - (FB) - Approx. 4" - The body of the lamp is shaped like a cupcake and has four annealed candles attached to it. The hanger is at the top of the long pike. (p188a, OP, R2-3) $20.00-30.00

GAS LAMP CHANDELIER (TYPE I) - (FB) - Approx. 7¾" but sizes may vary - The long pike ends in a ball to which two shades are attached by short arms. This early piece is wire wrapped and unsilvered. (p185, OP, R1-2) $100.00-125.00

GAS LAMP CHANDELIER (TYPE II) - (FB) - Approx. 4"-5" but sizes may vary - This is similar to the above in construction. Two small balls represent the lamp's globes, and they are placed over two annealed hooks. This piece is silvered and much later. (Schiffer p116, OP, R1-2) $40.00-50.00

HANGING OIL LAMP - (M) - Approx. 4½" - This piece is molded to show the ribbed oil reservoir and a tall chimney. It is held inside a hanging wire bracket. (p188c, OP, R1-2) $30.00-40.00

JAPANESE "GIFU" LANTERN - (M) - Approx. 2¼" & 3" - They have a generalized egg shape with molded ribbing going around it. This is the typical "Japanese lantern" shape. The glass is thick, and the pike is wide. This piece was also made as a light bulb. (U.S., p450e, p450f, OP, R2-3) $2.00-8.00

JAPANESE "ODAWARA" LANTERN - (M) - Approx. 2" & 3" - The ornament has an overall cylinder shape to it. It has deeply indented "ribs" which represent the foldings in the lantern. This piece was also made as a light. (U.S., p452i, p452k, OP-NP, R4) $.50-2.00

AMERICAN LANTERN - (M) - Approx. 2¾" - It has four panels with a star embossed into each one. (U.S., p450d, OP, R3) $4.00-6.00

PANELED LANTERNS - (M) - Approx. 2¼" - Has six panels in both upper and lower halves, each has an embossed design. A folding candle-lantern with celluloid panels was made in this style from 1900- 1920. (Germany, p189a, OP-NP, R4) $2.00-8.00

RAILROAD LANTERN - (M) - Approx. 3" - The lantern's "globe" has six molded "wires" on it. It has a decorated base at the end of a short pike. (Schiffer p117, OP-NP, R1-2) $60.00-75.00

STREET LIGHT - (M&FB) - Approx. 4½" - The lamp has a six paneled shade with a domed top. The "post" is free-blown with a "ridge" in the center. (p177b, OP-NP [1950s], R2) $20.00-30.00

TABLE LAMPS - (FB) - Approx. 3"-4" are most common but sizes may vary - The shades are usually domed, although some have indented "panels". The pedestal is attached to a flattened base. The shades may have fabric or Dresden trim attached. (p187a, p189b, p189c, p189d, OP-NP, R4-5) Small $10.00-20.00
Larger $15.00-25.00

Pipes

"DUBLIN" PIPE - (M&FB) - Approx. 3"-5" but sizes may vary - The round decorative cap is molded. The thick stem is free-blown and has a curve to it. The hanger is in the decorative cap. Molded cap designs include a rose pattern, four panels with crosses in them, arches with three leaves in them, and a series of small arches. (p193b, p194, OP, R4) Small $15.00-25.00
Larger $25.00-35.00

GERMAN PIPE - (FB) - Approx. 4½"-8" but sizes may vary - The bowl may be egg or funnel shaped. The stem attaches under the bowl, makes a curve and goes straight up to a bent mouthpiece. Older versions are unsilvered and wire wrapped. (p195a, OP, R2) Small $20.00-30.00
Larger $100.00-125.00

VARIATION: GERMAN PIPE WITH SMOKE - (FB), Approx. 4½" - This is similar to those described above, however, from the bowl rises a curl of spun glass "smoke". (p195b, OP, R2) $30.00-40.00

MAN'S HEAD PIPE (TYPE I) - (M&FB) - Approx. 3¾" overall, 1½" head only- The man wears a round fur cap that has been indented to form the bowl. He has short hair that shows in the front and rear; and he has a moustache. The straight free-blown stem attaches in the neck area. (Germany, p192a, OP, R1-2) $150.00-185.00

VARIATION: MAN'S HEAD GERMAN PIPE - (M&FB), Approx. 7" - The same head as above is on a long stem. The stem makes a "U" curve under the head, runs straight for about 4" and bends into the mouthpiece. (Germany, OP, R1) $250.00-275.00

MAN'S HEAD PIPE (TYPE II) - (M&FB) - Approx. 3¾" overall & 1½" head only - This is similar to Type I except the smiling head is rather comical and has thick flowing hair in the back of the head. (p199a, OP, R1-2) $150.00-185.00

SAILOR'S HEAD DUBLIN PIPE- (M&FB) - Approx. 3½" - The man wears a short brimmed seaman's cap. Thick wavy hair shows at the sides and rear. The smiling man wears a moustache. A thick free-blown tube, bent in the standard way, forms the stem of the pipe. The hanger is in the man's cap. (Schiffer p117, OP, R1) $225.00-250.00

SANTA HEAD PIPE - see SANTA CLAUS

STRAIGHT STEM PIPE - (FB) - Approx. 3"-5" are common but sizes may vary - These have an egg shaped bowl which has been deeply indented. Inside the bowl is usually a noisemaker similar to those found in horns. The stem comes out of the sides of the bowl and often has a "ridge" or raised ring at the halfway point. (p193a, p196, OP-NP, R4) $15.00-20.00

VARIATION: TWISTED STEM PIPE - (FB), 3″-5″ - This is similar to the one above, except the thick stem has been twisted for a decorative effect. (p196e, OP-NP, R3-4) $15.00-20.00

QUILTED PILLOW (TYPE I) - (M) - Approx. 3½″ - This piece has an overall oval shape to it. It has a raised center area that is quilted and indented with a star and four circles. The reverse is the same. This is a very detailed design. (Germany, p182a, OP, R3) $15.00-25.00

QUILTED PILLOW (TYPE II) - (M) - Approx. 3¼″ - This is very similar to Type I and has an overall oval shape. The raised center is quilted and has an indented flower and two small stars. The sides show four embossed roses each. The reverse side is the same. (Germany, p182c, OP-NP, R3) $15.00-25.00

Purses and Money Bags

"50,000" BAG - (M) - Approx. 2½″ - Tied at the top with a bow and has "50,000" embossed on the front of the bag. (Stille p163, OP, R1-2) $50.00-60.00

"POMPADOUR" BAG - (M) - Approx. 2½″ - This bag is tied at the top with a ribbon. It has an embossed rose and the name "Pompadour" on it. (p192b, OP, R1-2) $50.00-60.00

PURSE WITH EMBOSSED LEAVES - (M) - Approx. 1¾″W - The purse has a dimpled or waffle pattern embossed into it. This perhaps represents small chain links. Such purses were popular in the late Victorian period. The purse shows a "metal" frame at the top and has a three-bladed "leaf" embossed on the front. (p191a, OP-NP, R1-2) $30.00-40.00

PURSE WITH EMBOSSED FLOWER - (M) - Approx. 2″ - This is the same purse described above, except it has an embossed flower instead of a leaf. (p190c, OP, R3) $30.00-40.00

PURSE WITH EMBOSSED ROSES - (M) - Approx. 2¼″W - It shows a "metal" frame at the top. The purse itself has a large diamond pattern and a branch of roses embossed onto it. (Germany, p191c, OP-NP [limited], R2) $40.00-50.00

WRINKLED PURSE - (M) - Approx. 2½″ - This purse shows a "metal" frame on the top and deeply embossed wrinkles in the bag itself. It has a branch of flowers embossed onto it. This was an early piece and may have a wire "handle" as well as a cap. (p190a, OP, R2-3) $40.00-50.00

RADIO - (M) - Approx. 2″L - This square-looking piece shows a large embossed "fabric" square over the speaker and three round knobs underneath. This is a late piece. (p180b, OP, R2-3) $25.00-35.00

SCISSORS - Rogers lists such an ornament but gives no description. They were supposedly made between 1910 and 1914. (Germany, OP, R1) $175.00-200.00

Shoes, Boots and Stockings

BABY IN A SHOE - see BABIES

BEADED STOCKING - (BEADS) - Approx. 3½″ - This is a flat outline shape of a stocking made by small beads. (Probably Czech. or Japan, Rogers p112, OP, R3) $2.00-6.00

BOOT WITH UNCLE SAM - see PEOPLE - UNCLE SAM

CAT IN A STOCKING - see CATS

CAT IN A SHOE - several variations - see CAT

CHRISTMAS STOCKING - (M) - Approx. 4¼″ - It has a dimpled pattern to show it is knitted. Embossed on the front is a bear, doll, trumpet, horse and sword. There is a small decorated panel at the top. (p198, OP, R2) $125.00-150.00

CINDERELLA SHOE - Rogers states that this high heeled shoe was blown in colored glass only. (Germany, OP, R1) $75.00-100.00

CLOWN IN STOCKING - see CLOWNS

DOUBLE STRAPPED SHOE - (M) - Approx. 3¾″ - This woman's shoe shows a wing-tip, a bow, and two straps near the opening. The hanger is in the heel. (p200b, OP, R2) $45.00-55.00

HOLLOW STOCKING - (M) - Approx. 6¼″ - It is completely hollow with a wide opening at the top. It has embossed dimples and marks to represent a knitted sock. It is un-silvered and may be wire wrapped. (p197, OP, R2) $300.00-350.00

PAIR OF SKIS - (FB) - Approx. 5″ overall, 2″ boots - The free-blown boots have applied fabric "laces" and are fastened onto a pair of metal skis. (p203, OP, R1-2) $60.00-75.00

SANTA IN A STOCKING - see PEOPLE - SANTA CLAUS

SADDLE SHOE - (M) - This has a decorated toe, embossed laces and decorations along the sole. (Germany, Rogers p113, NP) $2.00-10.00

SHOE WITH A RIBBED TOE - (M) - Approx. 3″ - A low heeled shoe with no bows. The toe and instep area show embossed ribbing. There are two dimpled panels around the opening. This is perhaps a Dutch wooden shoe. (p201b, OP, R2) $20.00-30.00

STOCKING WITH A BALL - (M) - Approx. 4¼″ - The stocking is embossed to show it was knitted. It has a thick band at the top and a round ball showing at the top. (p187c, OP, R2) $125.00-150.00

STOCKING WITH TOYS - (M) - Approx. 5″ - The fabric of the large stocking is shown with vertical lines and smooth horizontal bands. The top of the stocking shows a bow, doll's head and a candy cane. No early examples are known. (West Germany, NP) $2.00-10.00

STANDARD SHOE - (M) - Approx. 1¾″, 2″ & 3″ - This commonly found shoe has a wing-tip toe and a small bow halfway up the instep. The opening has a dimpled decoration around it. (Germany, p200a, p202b, p202d, OP-NP, R4)
Small $10.00-15.00
Medium $10.00-20.00
Large $20.00-30.00

SKEIN OF YARN - (M) - Approx. 1¾″ & 2¼″ - In this small ornament, the embossed yarn is in an oval shape and wrapped, or tied, around the middle. (Germany, p191b, OP, R2)
Small $20.00-30.00
Large $30.00-40.00

Tea Pots, Coffee Pots, Urns, Etc.

These represent some of the common objects of everyday life as well as some of the fancier versions. Molded pieces are more popular than the free-blown items.

TEA AND COFFEE POTS - (FB) - Approx. 2″-4″ but sizes may vary - The tea pots are squat and rounded, while the coffee pots are taller with a cylinder-like top. They have annealed handles and spouts; they are also flattened on the bottom. (p204b, p204c, OP-NP, R4-5) $8.00-15.00

SUGARS AND URNS - (FB) - Approx. 2″-4″ but sizes may vary - They are usually similar to the pots listed above except they have two annealed handles. (p204a, OP-NP, R4-5)
$8.00-15.00

COFFEE POT WITH A ROSE - (M) - Approx. 3¼″ - The rounded coffee pot has a rose embossed into either side. The handle and spout are annealed. (p170b, OP, R2-3)
$20.00-30.00

TEA POT WITH FLAT SIDES - (M) - Approx. 2″ - It has six flattened sides and a flower embossed on it. The handle and spout are annealed on. (OP, R2-3) $20.00-30.00

TELEPHONE - (M) - Approx. 1¾″ - It has a square base that raises in a pyramidal shape to the receiver's cradle. The receiver is blown separately out of milk glass, and it has a paper dial. (p176c, NP [1950s only], R2)
$35.00-45.00

Umbrellas and Parasols

These were popular during the Victorian period when the parasol was a part of every well-dressed woman's wardrobe.

CLOSED UMBRELLA - (FB) - Approx. 4″-7″ but sizes may vary - These were simply enlargements in the glass pike and easily made. The handle was left straight, and they had long indentations to represent folds in the material. The early ones were often unsilvered and wire wrapped. Some had added scrap pictures. (p205, OP-NP, R4)
$15.00-25.00
With Scraps $35.00-45.00

VARIATION: CLOSED UMBRELLA WITH A HOOK HANDLE - (FB), Approx. 5½″ but sizes may vary - It is similar to those above, except the handle was bent into a hook shape. They were usually silvered. (OP-NP, R4) $10.00-15.00

OPEN UMBRELLA - (FB) - Approx. 4″-6″ but sizes may vary - The open top is formed by a ball shape that has been deeply indented to give it a dome shape. The long pike is left on as the handle and part of it protrudes above the open top. Early pieces are unsilvered and often wire wrapped. They may have additions of fabric or Dresden trim. The more elaborate the piece, the higher its value. (p206, OP-NP, R3)
Plain $15.00-25.00
More Elaborate $45.00-55.00

WATER CAN - (FB) - Approx. 3½″ - This is basically a cylinder shape with a domed top and flat bottom. The handle, hoop and spout are put on in wire. The piece is unsilvered and wire wrapped. (p199b, OP, R1-2) $60.00-70.00

KUGELS

Kugel is a German word that literally means a "ball" However, through the years, collectors have used it to describe any early thick-glass ornament regardless of its shape.

Kugels can be identified in several ways. The most obvious is their weight and thickness of glass. Also, they typically have a round flattened cap that may or may not be embossed. They have been described as looking like the ends of Victorian curtain rods. The caps, which are usually made of brass, are fastened to a hole in the top of the ornament by a stout wire that is bent sideways once it is inside the ornament.

Except for the earliest versions, kugels do not have the short pike that was left from the blowing process. In the later paper-thin ornaments, these short pikes were again left on, and it is here that the hanger and cap were inserted. But in the kugels, the pike or "spear" as it was referred to in German, was cut off flush with the ornament. Those early kugels which retained the pike used a cork and string or wire as the method of hanging. The string or wire was pushed through the center of the cork and tied off at the bottom, while the top was formed into a loop. The cork was then glued inside the pike.

German glassblowers began making kugels as early as 1820. Although similar forms such as rounded bottles, fish floats and witch balls had been made much earlier, these were only distantly related to the kugel Christmas ornament. These early ornaments were used by glassblowers, themselves, as house and tree decorations. Many also hung from wooden crowns mounted on the ceiling. However, it was not until 1848 that we find the first **recorded** sale of the kugel ornaments. Early ornaments were "silvered" with lead or zinc instead of the solution of silver nitrate which would be used in later years.

Although they were a German invention, not all kugels were German made. Some were made in France, some in the United States, some later pieces in Austria, and it is also likely that some were made in the Austria-Hungary area which was divided into Czechoslovakia after World War I. Although there is no direct proof of Czech kugels, certainly the glass works and guilds were there, and they were in direct competition with the German ornament makers. It seems logical that once the kugel ornament began to catch on and sell, that the Bohemian glassmakers would not allow the Germans to go unchallenged.

American versions were produced by both an unnamed New Jersey firm and William Demuth of New York. Very little is known of either of these producers. It has been suggested that they blew replacement ornaments for the early German immigrants. As there is no shortage of kugel ornaments in the United States in spite of their age, these manufacturers seem to have had a prolific production. I find it hard to believe that all the kugel ornaments found in our country were brought here by German immigrants.

I have seen two kugel-like ornaments marked "Made in France". The glass was not quite as thick as on other ornaments, and the flat cap was not embossed. The fact that it was marked "Made in France" shows it to be a later piece, possibly about the turn of the century.

Although kugel means "ball", kugel ornaments were made in several different shapes. The most common of these is, of course, the round ball; but other shapes include grapes, a pear, an egg, a ribbed ball, a turnip and a bell. The different varieties of grapes and the ribbed ornaments were made from molds while the rest were free-blown. The pear and egg are examples of the free-blown ornaments and are very similar in shape. One is usually distinguished from the other by the end in which the hanger is placed.

Sizes of the kugel, especially the free-blown ones, vary drastically. Balls can be found from 1½" to 18" in diameter. However, those in the 2½" to 4" diameter range are the most common and the most popular with collectors today. Most collections are displayed on a tree. Since ornaments over about 4" in diameter are considered too heavy and bulky, larger sizes do not bring proportionally larger prices. These larger sizes were probably used on outdoor trees and as household or store decorations. Big kugels seem to have been blown until a relatively late period expressly for the purpose of hanging on outdoor trees where the paper-thin ornaments, developed in the 1870s, would be too easily broken.

Color is another collectible aspect of kugels. They can be found in silver, light green, green, gold, light blue, cobalt blue, red and amethyst. These colors are listed in order of their rarity and popularity with amethyst being the rarest.

Two other early types of kugels that should be discussed are the German schecken and plumbum. Literally they mean "speckled" and "lead" ornaments. Most kugels have the same mirror-like inner surface found in the later ornaments. However, the earlier schecken and plumbum used different methods for decorating the blown glass balls.

I have seen two methods in which the scheckens were given their speckled appearance. In the first, different colors of paint were dabbed inside the ball. Then the inside was coated with a thin layer of melted wax to give it a solid background. In the second version, small clippings of colored thread were used. Again they were held in place against the inside of the glass ball by a thin coating of melted wax.

Plumbums also used wax as a background color and as a method of holding the other interior decorations in place. In this ornament, hot lead was dropped into the ball. Then with a flick of the wrist, it was swirled in a broad stripe around the inside.

Even though they are among the earliest commercially produced ornaments, kugels are not difficult to find. But their addition to a collection represents one of the important steps in the development of the Christmas ornament.

NOTES:

● Prices given may be slightly affected by the color of the ornament.

● Kugels should be hung on sturdy branches inside your tree.

BALLS - (FB) - Approx. 1½"- 18" but sizes may vary - Most have the typical embossed cap. (U.S., Germany, France, p211, OP, R3-4)

Small $25.00-35.00
Medium $40.00-60.00
Large $70.00-100.00

BALL WITH DOUBLE HANGER - (FB) - Sizes vary - This is the same basic ball form except it has a brass cap and hanger on both ends. Presumably one could hook several together. (Rogers p111, OP, R1) $75.00-100.00

RIBBED BALLS - (M) - Approx. 3" is most common but sizes may vary - Because of the fine evenness of the ribs, this was probably blown in a mold. Later versions of this were blown in thin glass. (p215, OP, R2-3)$100.00-125.00

EARLY KUGEL WITH A PIKE - (FB) - Approx. 2"-4" dia. is common but sizes may vary - It has a cork in the pike with a string or wire loop for hanging. (Predominately Germany, p212b, OP, R1) $75.00-100.00

"SCHECKEN" KUGEL - (FB) - Sizes vary - They have a spotted appearance and are usually coated with wax on the inside. Sometimes colored wax was used for the background. (Germany, p212a, OP, R1) $150.00-175.00

"PLUMBUM" KUGEL - (FB) - Sizes vary - They are "silvered" on the inside with a lead stripe and then coated with wax. (Germany, Snyder p93, OP, R1)$175.00-200.00

EGGS AND PEARS - (FB) - Sizes vary from 2"-10" - If the hanger is in the broad end it looks like an egg. If it is hung from the small end, it resembles a pear. (U.S., Germany, p210, OP, R2)

Small $100.00-125.00
Large $140.00-150.00

RIBBED EGGS - (M) - Approx. 2"-3" are common but sizes may vary - Because of the fine equal ribbing shown on these, it is likely they were blown in a mold. (Schiffer p119, OP, R1) $100.00-125.00

TURNIP SHAPE - (FB) - Sizes vary from 2"-11" - They could also be described as looking like a toy top. Some larger ones were French made. (Schiffer p119, OP, R1)
$100.00-125.00

GRAPES IN A CLUSTER - (M) - Approx. 3", 4", 6" & 6½" - These were undoubtedly blown into a mold. I would suggest that with the abundance of this type of grape kugel in the U.S., that it was made by William Demuth of New York. (Probably U.S., p208, p209, OP, R3)

Small $100.00-125.00
Large $125.00-150.00
Colored Glass $125.00-150.00

GRAPES IN AN OVAL CLUSTER - (M) - Approx. 3" & 4½" - Again these were probably mold made. They are scarcer and thus might be German made. (Possibly Germany, p207, OP, R1-2)   Large and Small $150.00-175.00

GRAPES IN A BALL CLUSTER - (M) - Approx. 3½" dia. - This looks like small knobs or grapes embossed on a ball shape. Later thin-glass ornaments were blown on this same idea. (Schiffer p120, OP, R1-2) $100.00-125.00

GRAPES WITH EMBOSSED LEAVES - (M) - Approx. 3" - Several embossed leaves show at the top around the brass hanger. (Schiffer p120, OP, R1) $125.00-150.00

PACIFIER SHAPED KUGEL - (FB) - Approx. 2½" - This unusual shape resembles an early baby's pacifier. (Schiffer p120, OP, R1) $100.00-125.00

MUSHROOMS

In Germany mushrooms are considered to be a symbol of good luck.

MUSHROOM - (FB) - Approx. 1"-4" but sizes can vary - The rounded "cap" is deeply indented and the tubular "stalk" comes out of it. The hangers are almost always in the cap, although some are clip-ons. Most mushrooms are unsilvered. (p213a-d, OP-NP, R4) 1"-2" $10.00-15.00
Standard 2"-3" $10.00-15.00
3"-4" $20.00-25.00

MUSHROOMS WITH FACES - see GNOMES, DWARVES AND MUSHROOM PEOPLE

MUSHROOM PEOPLE - see GNOMES, DWARVES AND MUSHROOM PEOPLE

THREE MUSHROOM ON A CLIP - (FB) - Approx. 2½" but sizes vary - Three free-blown mushrooms are mounted on the same clip-on holder. One large and two smaller. (Germany, Stille, p163, OP, R2) $30.00-40.00

TWO MUSHROOMS ON A CLIP - (FB), Approx. 2½" but sizes vary - One large and one smaller mushroom are on the same clip-on holder. They are often decorated with tucksheer greenery. (OP-NP, R3) $25.00-35.00

MUSICAL INSTRUMENTS

ACCORDIAN - (M) - Approx. 3" - The piece has the overall appearance of an inverted fan. The bellows show and widen at the bottom while a keyboard shows at the sides. (Germany, Czech., Austria, Rogers p159, OP-NP, R2-3) $25.00-35.00

BANJO - (FB) - Approx. 5"-10" but sizes may vary - This is basically a flattened disc on the end of a long pike. Paper discs or stars and scraps may be added for decoration. Early versions are unsilvered and wire wrapped with wires representing the instrument's strings. (p214, p219a, OP, R2-3) Small $20.00-30.00
Large $40.00-50.00
With Scraps $70.00-90.00

BANJO - (M&FB) - Approx. 4" - The body of the banjo is a molded disc showing decoration and a stretcher bar. A free-blown pike represents the neck of the instrument. It may have wire "strings". (p224d, OP, R2) $30.00-40.00

Bells

Bells were an important part of everyday life up through the late Victorian period. They represented church bells, school bells, hand bells, etc. European bells were usually indented on the bottom and had small glass clappers that "tinkled" when they were shaken. American and Japanese bells were not indented on the bottom and usually had molded clappers. Bells are probably the single most common figural shape.

THE COMMON BELL - (FB) - Approx. 1½"-4" - These were made by all the European glassmakers. Older versions are often wire wrapped. (OP-NP, R5+)
Small and Medium $1.00-5.00
Large $5.00-10.00

VARIATION: COMMON BELL WITH SCRAP DECORATION - (FB), Sizes vary - Scraps of angels, children, flowers, etc., were added to the bell for decoration. In the late 1920s and 30s decals replaced the lithographed scraps. (p228b, OP, R2-3) $35.00-40.00

AMERICAN BELLS - (M) - Approx. 2", 2½" & 2¾" - Almost any American company that made ornaments produced some form of bell. Those from the Corning Glass Company are probably the most common. American bells are made of a heavier glass and have no intricate embossed details. The pike has a wider opening, and the clapper is usually a molded bump on the bottom of the bell. Wartime bells are unsilvered but may have a piece of tinsel inside them. They are very common, and size does not affect the price. (U.S., p450, OP-NP, R5) $1.00-2.00

BELL - (BEADS) - Approx. 3" - The bell shape is shown in a flat outline of small beads. (Czech., Japan, OP, R3-4) $1.00-3.00

BELL WITH A CROWN (TYPE I) - (M&FB) - Approx. 3¾" - A small 1" molded crown is attached to a free-blown bell by a short pike. This makes it a type of hand bell. The bell is the standard shape with an indented bottom and a glass clapper. (Germany, p227f, p228a, OP, R2-3) $40.00-50.00

BELL WITH A CROWN (TYPE II) - (M&FB) - Approx. 3" - A small ¾" molded crown is attached to a bell by a short pike. The bell is a ball shape that has been deeply indented and a glass clapper added. (p227d, OP, R2-3) $30.00-40.00

BELL WITH AN EMBOSSED CHURCH - (M) - Approx. 2½" - A church with a large belfrey is embossed onto a standard bell shape. Embossed stars show on the sides and the back. (p227a, OP, R3) $25.00-35.00

BELL WITH AN EMBOSSED EAGLE - (M&FB) - Approx. 4" - It has a molded 1¼" ball with an embossed eagle and stars on both sides. The ball is attached by a short pike to a free-blown bell in the standard form. This is an early, turn of the century piece. (Germany, p228c, OP, R2) $70.00-90.00

BELLS WITH FLOWERS - (M) - Approx. 1½"-2½" - These bells had different flower themes embossed into them. Daisies were a popular flower form. (Germany, Czech., Austria, p227b, OP-NP, R4) $5.00-10.00

BELL WITH GEOMETRIC DESIGNS - (M) - Approx. 1½"-3½" - There are a wide variety of these types of mold-blown bells. Some have ribbing, dimples, bumps, stars or

other geometric patterns. (Germany, Czech., Austria, p227c, OP-NP, R4-5)   Small $2.00-5.00
Larger $5.00-10.00

HAND BELL (TYPE I) - (FB) - Approx. 4″ - The standard bell shape is attached to a long pike. The tube is shaped into a round handle and often has a ridge around it near the bell. (p227e, OP-NP, R3) $15.00-25.00

HAND BELL (TYPE II) - (FB) - Approx. 4″ - A standard bell shape is attached to a long pike. The pike is left as a long thin tube with no attempt to make it look like a real handle. This is more common on later pieces. (OP-NP, R3-4) $5.00-10.00

"MERRY CHRISTMAS" BELL - (M) - Approx. 3″ - This is a molded bell shape with the words "Merry Christmas" embossed onto ribbon going around the side. This piece should not be confused with bells that merely have the words painted or printed on them. (OP-NP, R2-3) $25.00-35.00

VARIATION: "MERRY XMAS" BELL - This is the same basic form and size as above, except it has the words "Merry Xmas" embossed into it. (OP-NP, R2-3) $25.00-35.00

SANTA BELL - see SANTA CLAUS

GIRL SHAPED BELL - see WOMEN AND GIRLS - GIRL BELL

CAT HEAD HORN - see CATS

CELLOS AND VIOLINS - (M&FB) - Approx. 3″-5″ but sizes may vary with the free-blown pike - It is very difficult to determine the difference between a cello and violin ornament. Both have a well molded case which shows embossed strings and scrollwork. A long free-blown pike represents the neck of the instrument. In some pieces, the pike was cut right above the molded body, giving them an unusual appearance. These are not as popular as those pieces with the pike left on. Cellos may have a small knob or pointed tube in the base which represents its stand; otherwise cellos and violins are the same. There are many slightly different moldings of the popular piece. Older versions are wire wrapped. (p225, OP-NP, R3-4)   Small $15.00-25.00
Larger $20.00-35.00

CLARINET - (FB) - Approx. 3½″-6½″ but sizes may vary - It is a long uncurved horn. A long pike is simply pushed into a funnel shape at the end. Some versions may have flat areas along the pike to represent keys. Early versions are wire wrapped. (p219c, OP, R2)   Small $15.00-25.00
Larger $30.00-40.00

CLOWN IN A MANDOLIN - see CLOWNS

CLOWN IN A DRUM - see CLOWNS

DRUM - (M) - Approx. 2″H (1½″ dia.) & 2½″H (2″ dia.) - These pieces have the typical cylinder shape. They have embossed "ropes" that criss-cross around the side. They show no drumsticks. Toy drums were a popular toy at Christmas time. (Germany, Czech., Austria, p223c, OP-NP, R3-4) $20.00-35.00

FRENCH HORN or TUBA - (FB) - Approx. 2½″-5″ but sizes may vary - These have a funnel shaped bell end and a long pike that loops over itself forming a circle in the center. This shape is generic in that it can represent a French horn, tuba, hunting horn or postal horn, all of which have the same general shape and were popular European instruments. These horns were made by all the European glassmakers. (p223a, p223b, OP-NP, R4-5)   Small $5.00-10.00
Large $10.00-15.00

GUITAR - (M&FB) - Approx. 4″-5″ - These are similar to cello and violin ornaments. However, the guitar has an hour-glass or figure eight shape to the body. They have embossed strings and a circle that represents the hole into the sounding box. The long free-blown pike represents the neck of the instrument. (Germany, Czech., Rogers p156, OP-NP, R2-3) $20.00-30.00

AMERICAN GUITAR - (M) - Approx. 2″ - This has the characteristic figure eight shape, embossed strings and hole. It is made of thick glass with a wide opening, and it has no pike representing the neck of the guitar. (U.S., p450b, OP, R2) $5.00-10.00

HARP WITH AN EMBOSSED ANGEL - (M) - Approx. 3½″ - A cherub-like angel is embossed, in the flying position, onto the strings of a harp. The back shows only the strings. (Germany, p234c, OP-NP, R2) $40.00-50.00

HUNTING HORN - (M&FB) - Approx. 4″-7″ but sizes may vary - The large horn end is blown into a mold and has a checked or diamond pattern that makes it resemble a bud of clover. This large end is deeply indented to give it the appearance of a horn. The rest of the piece is made up of a tapering free-blown tube that has several bends in it. Many ornaments have fabric flowers added to the indentation, making it a type of cornucopia. It could also represent a wall vase which was popular at the time. They were made in the shape of a horn, filled with flowers and hung on the wall. Most of these hunting horns are hung by a length of string that runs from the front to back and are attached to wire wrapping or annealed hooks. A rarer version can be found as a clip-on. (p217a, p217b, p220b, OP, R3)   Small $35.00-45.00
Larger $60.00-80.00
Clip-on $100.00-125.00

VARIATION: HUNTING HORN - (FB), Approx. 4″-7″ but sizes may vary - This is very similar to the above piece, except is has no molded part nor any indentation. One end is large and rounded and tapers back along the pike which also has the characteristic bends in it. The large end often has a small opening with fabric flowers and tucksheer. Again, these pieces are usually hung by a length of string. They are not as desirable as horns with molded parts. (p217c, OP, R3)   Small $25.00-35.00
Large $45.00-60.00

HOLLOW HUNTING HORN - (FB) - Approx. 8″ but sizes may vary - This completely hollow piece is realistic in its portrayal of the hunting horn. It is unsilvered and usually wire wrapped. It may also have flowers and tucksheer added to the horn's opening. (p220a, OP, R2)$125.00-150.00

LYRES - (FB) - Approx. 3"-4½" but sizes may vary - They have a central ball with two curving struts or side frames annealed on the sides. Many have a long center pike onto which scrap children or angels may be attached. Others may have cardboard pieces embossed to represent strings. Some may have indents in the central ball or be wrapped in wire. Because lyres usually have a cap and hanger in the bottom, many have been hung upside down and gone unrecognized as lyres. (p226, OP-NP [1950s-1960s], R3-4)

Small $20.00-30.00
Large $40.00-50.00

LYRE - (M) - Approx. 3" - The lyre is embossed onto both sides of a shape that has the same general form. It has a bumpy pattern around the side and bottom. (Germany, Rogers p159, OP-NP, R2) $20.00-30.00

MANDOLIN - (FB) - Approx. 4"-10" but sizes may vary - This simple form has many small variations; but basically it is an egg shape at the end of a long pike. The front side is usually flattened and may have a paper disc or star added to represent the hole for the sound box. Others may be decorated with scraps of flowers, angels and children. Older versions are usually unsilvered and wire wrapped with wires representing the instrument's strings. Various forms were made by all the European glassmakers. (p219b, p219d, p224c, OP, R4)   Small $25.00-35.00
Larger $40.00-50.00
With Scraps $75.00-90.00

VARIATION: INDENTED MANDOLIN - (FB), Approx. 4"-5½" but sizes may vary - This is basically the same as the above except the "box" is deeply indented. Again, scraps, stars or fabric flowers may be added as decoration. (p216, OP, R3) $45.00-55.00

MANDOLIN - (M&FB) - Approx. 3"-5" but sizes may vary with the length of the free-blown pike - There are many slightly different moldings of this popular piece; however, most have the same general characteristics. The body is a molded egg shape with the front flattened and the back round. The front shows embossed strings and an oval "hole" into the sounding box. The free-blown pike forms the neck of the mandolin. Some pieces were made without the pike, so only the molded body shows. These were not as popular as pieces with the long pike. Earlier versions may have wire "strings" or wire wrapping. Mandolins were a popular European instrument and a common ornament made by all the European glass-blowers. (p224a, p224b, OP-NP, R5) $20.00-30.00

MAN IN A CELLO - see MEN AND BOYS - MAN IN A CELLO

SAXOPHONE - (FB) - Approx. 4" but sizes may vary - This piece has the typical "S" shape to it with an upturned bell. It has several flattened areas along the pike representing keys. Like other horns, the bell of the saxophone has a foil noisemaker inserted into it. (Germany, p222b, OP, R2) $40.00-50.00

TRUMPET - (FB) - Approx. 3"-8½" but sizes may vary, usual sizes 3½"-5½" - These pieces have a funnel-shaped bell and a long free-blown pike that loops over itself in an oval shape. The trumpet usually has a foil noisemaker glued into the bell end, and they were popular as toys as well as ornaments. Like birds, it is hard to imagine a tree that never had a trumpet on it. Toy trumpets were a popular Christmas gift. Trumpets were made by all the European glassmakers. (p221, OP-NP, R5)   Small $5.00-10.00
Medium $10.00-15.00
Large (over 7") $30.00-40.00

VARIATION: TRUMPET WITH A MOLDED BELL - (M&FB), Approx. 4½" but sizes may vary - This is similar to the standard form trumpet in all respects, except the bell has a diamond or "waffle" pattern embossed into it. (p221a, OP, R3) $10.00-15.00

VARIATION: TWISTED TRUMPET - (FB), sizes vary - This is the standard form horn except, while the glass was hot, it was twisted for an extra decorative effect. (OP-NP, R3) $8.00-12.00

VARIATION: TRUMPET WITH INDENTS - (FB), Approx. 5½" but sizes may vary - This is made like the standard form horn except it has a rounded ball behind the horn's bell. This ball has three reflectors indented into it. (p222a, OP, R3) $15.00-25.00

NUTS: ACORNS AND WALNUTS

Acorns

Acorns are considered a symbol of good luck in Germany. This perhaps stems from its connection with the sacred oak tree. It is also an old symbol for the rebirth of life.

STANDARD ACORNS - (M) - Approx. 1", 1½" & 2½" - The acorn often has a ribbed body and a quilted or dimpled cap. (Germany, Austria, Japan, p229b, p229c, p230a, p230b, p230d, OP-NP, R4   Small $2.00-5.00
Large $5.00-10.00

ACORN CHAIN - (M) - Approx. 18" - This chain is made of 1¼" molded acorns strung together. Such strings were looped over the tree branch. (p229a, OP, R1-2) $50.00-60.00

ACORNS ON A LEAF - (M) - Approx. 1¾" & 2¾" - Three acorns are embossed into a stylized oak leaf. The leaf shows veins and serrated edges. The back shows only the leaf. (Germany, p230c, p230e, OP-NP, R3-4)Small $10.00-15.00
Large $15.00-25.00

ACORN WITH EXTENDED ARMS - (M&FB) - Approx. 3½" but sizes may vary - A large size acorn has a free-blown ball annealed to its top. Three tubular arms hang down around the ornament with smaller balls or acorns dangling from each arm. (Rogers p175, OP, R2) $40.00-50.00

AMERICAN ACORN - (M) - Approx. 2" - Although rarer, this piece is not as delicate as its German counterparts. The glass is thicker, and it has a wider pike opening. It was made by Corning Glass circa 1939. (U.S., OP, R2) $5.00-10.00

PANELED ACORN - (M) - Approx. 2½" - The bottom of this stylized acorn is formed by five flat panels. The cap is dimpled. (p230f, OP-NP, R3) $2.00-5.00

Walnuts

Until the turn of the century, real walnuts both silver and gilted were popular tree decorations. They were hung singly or in long chains. Walnut shells have also been used as candy containers and as small oil lamps.

STANDARD WALNUT - (M) - Approx. 1″, 2″ & 2½″ - These are molded and embossed in a very realistic manner. Early pieces may have fabric leaves. (Germany, Czech., Austria, p218c, OP-NP, R4-5)   Small $5.00-10.00
Large $10.00-15.00

ARTISTIC PERIOD WALNUT - (M) - Approx. 2″ - This standard form walnut has a pike and leaves of amethyst colored glass annealed to its top. It was made during Germany's artistic period of ornament making circa 1915-1925. They were not as popular in the U.S. and thus are rare. (Germany, OP, R1-2) $40.00-55.00

EMBOSSED WALNUTS - (M) - Approx. 1½″ - These walnuts are embossed with flower or geometric designs. (OP, R3) $3.00-5.00

LARGE WALNUT - (M) - Approx. 4½″H x 3½″W - This large piece has the typical walnut shape and it has a wide seam where the two shell halves join. It has a bumpy pattern on the shell itself. (p143a, OP, R2) $25.00-35.00

Real Nuts

REAL WALNUT PURSE - Original 1891 directions for making this homemade Victorian piece can be found in Eva Stille's *Christbaumschmuck*. The gilded nut was split open and hung with colorful ribbon. A small bag with tiny presents was fastened to the inside with additional ribbons. The piece pictured still has a spool of silk thread and a tiny porcelain doll in it. (p218e, OP, R1-2) $35.00-45.00

REAL WALNUTS - These can sometimes be found in boxes of old ornaments. They may be gilded or silvered and be decorated with scraps, beads, fabric flowers, etc. The more elaborate this additional decoration, the more desirable the piece. (Homemade, p218a, p218b, OP, R3)
$1.00-10.00

REAL WALNUT WITH A WAX JESUS - Half a walnut shell is used as a manger. A tiny wax Jesus figure lays on top of a halo made with gold crocheted thread. (Germany, p218d, OP, R2) $25.00-35.00

PEOPLE

People are probably the single most collectible form, not only in glass ornaments, but in all other materials as well. These pieces come in a whole host of characters, including angels, babies, storybook people, historical personalities, stars of stage and screen, "just plain folks", and of course, Santa Claus.

People ornaments are among the most beautiful and cleverly made pieces of the German glassblowing art. To have the necessary detail, they were inevitably mold blown.

People ornaments do have one unique problem - names. A few personalities, both historic and fictional, have been immortalized in glass by both European and American ornament makers. In some of these pieces the face, dress or features can unmistakably identify and name the character. In most other cases, however, a certain feature, look or dress have lead collectors to **associate** the piece with some personality. In some cases, the applied name may be correct. But in many other instances, the names are probably totally different from what the ornament maker intended. Many pieces were just general characters and not designed to be anyone in particular. Still others are German folk and fairy tale characters that may go unnamed or misnamed because we, as Americans, are unfamiliar with who they are supposed to represent.

Names, whether correct or not, do provide a convenient point of reference when collectors are describing an ornament. Inasfar as I can determine their accuracy, I have tried to use the names commonly given a certain piece. I have also made comments when discrepancies occur.

By naming an ornament, we gain the advantage of describing it in one or two words. Unfortunately, we also find the unwarranted tendancy for "named" ornaments to escalate in price. This is due partly to the fact that toy and character doll collectors are also interested in these pieces. But, just as important, we find a strong desire in collectors to have an ornament that is generally recognizable. The result is to name pieces, usually incorrectly, and raise the price.

As Shakespeare's Juliet once said, "What's in a name? A rose by any other name would smell as sweet." So should a fine ornament be judged on its own merits and not on some name that is often only arbitrarily attached to it.

People are broken down into major themes which are then listed alphabetically. Those pieces which are general characters will most likely be found under "Men and Boys" or "Women and Girls".

Angels

Surprisingly enough, there are comparatively few religious forms of Christmas ornaments, and angels are probably the most common expression of the religious theme. Almost always, these angels are represented as children with girls being the most favored. Depicting children as happy angels was one small, comforting way the Victorians dealt with a high infant mortality rate. More than one angel was probably molded in memory of a beloved child.

Many times German artists described any child-like ornament as an angel; however, in this section, I have reserved the use of that title for those ornaments that possess angelic wings. These wings may be molded into the ornament or they may be applied paper or spun glass (SG) wings. Putti head forms (heads only, with wings shown under the chin) are scarcer than full-body forms. These head forms were very popular in art and architecture of the period and are often found in wood, clay, plaster and porcelain.

ANGEL BLOWING A TRUMPET - (M) - Approx. 5″ - She blows a trumpet which is embossed onto her chest. Her back is arched, giving the piece an unusual curve. SG or paper wings are attached to indents in her back. (p237a, OP-NP [early 1950s only], R2-3) $70.00-80.00

ANGEL BUST - (M) - Approx. 4″ - This young girl with wavy hair has a nicely detailed face. Her neck and shoulders are covered by molded feathers. She has aplied paper wings. The delicacy and detail would indicate she was blown in an old mold; however, no old examples are known. (Germany, p232a, NP, R3) $2.00-10.00

"PUTTI" ANGEL HEAD - (M) - Approx. 2″, 2½″ & 3″ - This is the head of a small girl in the Putti style. Her molded hair comes down and curls at the jaw. The wings are molded under the chin and are not distinct unless viewed from the bottom. (Germany, p239a, p239b, p240b, OP-NP, R2-3)   Small $35.00-50.00
Large $90.00-100.00

ANGEL HEAD EMBOSSED ON A DISC - (M) - Approx. 2″ dia. - The ornament has slightly scalloped edges with small embossed star and Putti head embossed in center. The reverse shows a stylized eight petaled flower. (p240a, OP-NP [1950s], R3) $20.00-25.00

ANGEL HEAD WITH LARGE WINGS - (M) - Approx. 2½″ - Her face is framed by two large wings that join under the chin. This is probably an Italian piece. (p319a, NP (1950s only), R3) $20.00-30.00

ANGEL IN A BASKET - (M) - Approx. 3″ - The angel is embossed onto a background of stylized flowers. Her outstretched hands hold onto the edges of the wicker basket below. (p114b, OP, R2) $125.00-150.00

ANGEL IN A HOOP SKIRT - (M) - Approx. 4½″ - This girl with her hands clasped in prayer wears a long bell-shaped skirt and apron. Her molded wings can only be seen from the back as they are flat with the ornament. (p241b, NP [1950s only], R3) $50.00-60.00

ANGEL ON A "CLOUD" OF ANGEL HAIR - (M) - Approx. 4″ - This angel with long flowing hair has a dress with a square collar. Both hands rest at the chest area. Below the waist, the glass turns into a tubular spike onto which the angel hair cloud is fastened. The initials DHL are embossed into her back. (Germany, p238a, OP, R1-2) $150.00-175.00

ANGEL ON A HARP - (M) - Approx. 3½″ - The cherub like angel is embossed, in the flying position, onto the strings of the hair. The back shows only the strings of the harp. (Germany, p234c, OP-NP, R2) $30.00-40.00

ANGEL ON A PINE CONE - (M) - Approx. 3½″ - Made during the 1920s and early 1930s. (Germany, OP, R1-2) $50.00-60.00

ANGEL WITH A TREE- (M) - Approx. 4″ - This girl holds an applied paper tree in her right hand and a molded toy horse in her left. Her right arm is unmolded, and the tree covers the whole right side. Her molded wings are folded at the back. (Germany, p242c, NP - no early examples are known) $2.00-10.00

ANGEL WITH A TREE AND HORN - (M) - Approx. 4″ - This chubby little girl carries a tree in the right hand and a horn in the left. Her small wings are folded in the back, and she has a decorative ribbon on the chest. Her sleeves, wing tops and ornament base have a bumpy beaded effect. (Germany, p242b, OP-NP [limited], R3) $30.00-40.00

ANGEL WITH LITHOGRAPHED FACE - (M) - Approx. 3″ & 3½″ - A girl or woman angel, standing in a long robe, holds a flower over the left breast. Molded, spread wings show over the shoulders and along the sides. The face area is flattened, to hold the lithographed face. (p275c, p292a, OP, R2)   Small $90.00-110.00
Large $150.00-175.00

BOY CHERUB - (M) - Approx. 3½″L - Molded only from the waist up, the boy appears to be rising out of a stylized flower. His left hand is on the chin, and the right is across the stomach. Wings are either paper or SG inserted into indents in the back. It can have a clip-on or hanger in the head area. (Germany, p234b, OP-NP, R2) $70.00-80.00

CHERUB BLOWING A TRUMPET - (M) - Approx. 3½″ - This slender bodied child blows a separately molded trumpet that comes out away from the body. He may have an annealed hanger in the back or a clip-on at the base. He may also have SG or paper wings. (Rogers p141, OP, R1-2) $125.00-150.00

CHERUB BLOWING A TRUMPET - (M) - Approx. 3½″ - He is similar to the above except the trumpet is molded onto the chest. (Rogers p137, OP, R1-2) $75.00-100.00

CHUBBY GIRL ANGEL WITH A STAR - (M) - Approx. 3½″ - The six pointed star is embossed on the front of her dress. Small butterfly-like wings show over the shoulders. (Rogers p140, OP, R3) $50.00-60.00

DOUBLE FACED ANGEL HEAD - (M) - Approx. 2¾″ - The ornament has an overall egg-shape with an angel face embossed into both sides. The remainder of the ornament is covered with the feathered wings which surround the faces. (p235d, OP, R2) $50.00-60.00

DOUBLE ORNAMENT ANGEL AND SANTA - (M) - Approx. 3½″L - A chubby girl angel is one side, and a typical Lauchian Santa with a tree is on the other. The angel carries a tree in the right arm and a star in the left. The molded wings are spread over the shoulder and side area. (Germany, p243, OP-NP, R2) $80.00-90.00

FLYING ANGEL ON A DISC - (M) - Approx. 2″ dia. - The small cherub-like angel is shown flying to the left with a wreath in its hand. The back has the same embossed picture. (p235e, OP, R2) $35.00-45.00

GUARDIAN ANGEL WITH TWO CHILDREN - (M) - Approx. 3½″ - This standing woman angel is in a long flowing gown with two molded children standing in front of her. The boy and girl come up to the angel's waist and her hands are on their heads. The "guardian" angel has a scrap face. She has molded indents for SG or paper wings. (Germany, OP-NP [limited], R2) $100.00-125.00

CHERUB ON A BALL - (M&FB) - Approx. 4½″ - The young child has both arms crossed at the chest with the left over the right. The only clothing is a thin sash that runs from the right shoulder. She is molded to the waist, below which is a free-blown ball. Although not shown in the picture, she had applied paper wings. This same torso was used to make a mermaid ornament. (Germany, p231a, OP, R1-2) $75.00-100.00

KNEELING ANGEL (TYPE I) - (M) - Approx. 3¼″ - A young girl in a flowing robe, kneeling on one knee, has her hands pressed together in prayer. The wings are made of paper or SG. (Germany, p233c, OP-NP (limited), R3) $80.00-90.00

VARIATION: KNEELING ANGEL TREE TOP - (M&FB), Approx. 10″ - The above described angel is attached to a free-blown ball or indent. The remaining pike is widened to fit the top of a tree. (Germany, OP-NP, R2) $90.00-110.00

KNEELING ANGEL (TYPE II) - (M) - Approx. 3¾″ - Similar to the above ornament, she too kneels on the left knee. The hair is not as full and curly, and the hands are clasped at the breast, not under the chin. She has SG wings. (p244b, OP, R2-3) $90.00-100.00

KNEELING ANGEL WITH MOLDED WINGS - (M) - Approx. 3½″H x 2″W - The young girl has her hands clasped in prayer with the spread wings showing over the shoulders and along the sides. She kneels on both knees. (Germany, p242a, OP-NP, R2-3) $40.00-50.00

MOTHER AND CHILD ANGEL - (M) - Approx. 3¾″ - Both mother and daughter are dressed in long flowing robes, and they are in a standing position. The child is molded on the front and comes up to chest level. The mother's left hand is on the girl's head, her right hand is at the upper chest. The mother has paper wings. The reverse of the ornament shows the mother to be kneeling. (p233a, OP, R2) $175.00-200.00

"RAPHAEL" ANGEL - (M) - Approx. 3″ & 4″ - The girl angel is shown on a cloud from the waist up. Her left hand is at her chin, her right is across her waist. The ornament was molded after a famous painting by Raphael. There are no indents for SG wings, but some may have had pressed paper ones applied. There are at least three slightly different moldings of this piece. Two have had limited reproduction. They may have a clip-on at the bottom. (Germany, p232b, p233b, p234a, OP-NP, R2-3)$125.00-150.00

"RAPHAEL" ANGEL INDENT - (M&FB) - Approx. 3″ dia. - Facing to the left, this angel on a cloud is indented into a free-blown ball. The indentation is about 1¾″. The ball may be indented on both sides. (OP-NP [1950s only], R3-4) $20.00-30.00

"RAPHAEL" ANGEL ON A DISC - (M) - Approx. 2″ - She is shown facing to the left, chin in hand. Wings show over her left shoulder. The reverse has embossed stars. (p239c, OP, R2-3) $30.00-40.00

"RAPHAEL" ANGEL ON A MEDALLION - The angel on the cloud faces to her right and is embossed on a six pointed star or medallion. (Rogers p142, OP, R2-3) $35.00-45.00

"RAPHAEL" ANGEL ON AN EGG - (M) - Approx. 3¼″ - She faces to her left and wings show over her right shoulder. The egg shape is embossed with a feather-like design that radiates from the angel. An embossed cross is on the back. (p235b, OP, R1-2) $70.00-80.00

SEATED ANGEL EMBOSSED ON A HEART - (M) - Approx. 3″ - The angel with wide spread wings appears to be seated on a small chair or throne. The edges of the heart shape are embossed with flowers. The back is ribbed and has an embossed ribbon and bow. (p235a, OP, R2) $40.00-50.00

SNOW ANGEL WITH A BASKET OF FLOWERS - (M) - Approx. 3″ - This young girl angel is shown from the hips up. She wears a long coat with a scarf wrapped around her head. She holds a basket of flowers and her molded wings are folded behind her. This form is common among snow angel lithographs. (Germany, p241a, OP-NP, R2) $60.00-70.00

STANDING ANGEL (TYPE I) - (M) - Approx. 4″ - This slender girl angel has her hands clasped in prayer. She is dressed in a long robe, and the wings are applied paper or SG applied to an indented area in her back. Clip-on or hanger in head area. (Germany, p241c, OP-NP, R2) $60.00-70.00

STANDING ANGEL (TYPE II) - (M) - Approx. 3½″ - She wears a long flowing robe and her hands are pressed together in prayer under her chin. Her shoulder length hair has a circlet of flowers in it, and a sash ties in a bow on the front of her gown. She has applied paper wings. (Germany, p231c, OP, R2) $75.00-90.00

STANDING ANGEL WITH FOLDED WINGS - (M) - Approx. 3″ & 3½″ - Young girl or woman dresed in a robe. Her molded wings are folded at the back and are not distinct unless viewed from the back. (Germany, p237b, OP-NP, R4) $50.00-60.00

VARIATION: ANGEL WITH FOLDED WINGS TREE TOP - (M&FB), Approx. 10″ - The above described angel was attached to a free-blown ball or indent. The remaining pike was widened at the end to fit on top of the tree. (Germany, Schiffer p149, OP, R2) $100.00-110.00

LARGE STANDING ANGEL - (M) - Approx. 6½″ - Her hands are clasped in prayer, and she wears a long flowing robe. There are no indents for SG wings, but she may have had paper ones. (Germany, OP-NP, R2) $50.00-60.00
New $2.00-10.00

STANDING ANGEL TREE TOP - (M) - Approx. 7″ - This angel with her hands pressed together in prayer wears a long flowing robe. Her shoulder length hair frames a face that is not well-detailed but often painted. She has applied paper wings. The bottom pike is widened out to fit on top of the tree and is covered with an angel hair "cloud". (Germany, p231b, OP [1930s], R2) $125.00-150.00

STANDING ANGEL WITH "SPIKE" WINGS - (M&FB) - Approx. 4¼″ - She stands in a long flowing robe with her hands clasped in prayer. She has shoulder-length wavy hair. In her back are four free-blown pikes that may represent wings or a star-burst. (p270a, OP, R2) $90.00-100.00

Babies

BABY GIRL CARRYING A TREE - (M) - Approx. 2½″ & 3½″ - Dressed in a long snow coat and cap, this chubby baby carries a tree in her right arm. Her left arm rests at the stomach area. (Germany, p310b, OP-NP [very limited], R1)

Small $90.00-110.00

Large $125.00-150.00

BABY IN A BATHTUB - (M) - Approx. 2¾" - The ornament has an oval shape. The smiling baby hangs onto the edge of the tub. Her head, chest and feet rise out of the water in this nicely detailed piece. The underneath of the ornament is shaped like a tub. (Germany, p246b, OP, R1)

$275.00-300.00

BABY IN A BUGGY - (M) - Approx. 2¼" & 3" - The four wheeled buggy has a folded hood. The baby girl lies facing to the right with a rattle in her left hand. (Germany, p245a, OP-NP [limited], R2-3)

Small $50.00-75.00

Large $75.00-100.00

BABY IN BUNTING WITH A PACIFIER - (M) - Approx. 2½" & 3½" - The ornament has an overall egg shape. The bottom half is striped and the open upper half shows a baby head with a pacifier in its mouth. (Germany, p309c, OP-NP [limited], R2-3)

Small $60.00-75.00

Large $75.00-100.00

BABY IN BUNTING WITH A SCRAP FACE - (M) - Approx. 3½" - The ornament's shape and the rough texture of the bunting makes it almost look like a pine cone. The upper end shows a ruffled "opening", the center of which is flattened to hold the scrap face. (p246c, OP, R1)

$150.00-175.00

BABY WITH A BOTTLE - (M) - Approx. 3½" - She is dressed in a long baby gown with puffy sleeves and a yoke collar. She holds an old fashion baby bottle in her right hand. (p244c, OP, R1-2) $150.00-175.00

DOUBLE HEADED BABY IN A RATTLE - (M&FB) - Approx. 6½" overall and 2½" on the molded head - One side of the rattle shows the smiling baby in a night cap. The other sides shows a crying baby. The pike comes out of the chin area of the child. (p337a, OP, R1)

$250.00-275.00

Head only $200.00-225.00

SCRAP FACED BABY IN A BABY SHOE - (M) - Approx. 3" - The shoe appears fat and blunt at the toe like a baby shoe. It has a large bow at the opening which also has "stitch" marks around it. In the opening is a ruffled bonnet flattened in the center for the scrap baby face. (p202c, OP, R1-2) $75.00-90.00

SCRAP FACED BABY IN A LADY'S SHOE - (M) - Approx. 4½" - This large shoe has decorations at the pointed toe and a bow at the opening. In the "open" part of the shoe is an embossed baby shown from the chest up. A ruffled bonnet frames the face which is flat glass with a scrap face added. (Germany, p246a, OP, R1) $225.00-250.00

SNOW BABY - (M) - Approx. 2½" - She is dressed in a hooded snowsuit such that only the face shows. The right hand is at the breast and the left is at the side. (Germany, Rogers p152, OP, R1-2) $50.00-75.00

THREE FACED BABY INDENT - (M&FB) - Approx. 3½" - The three baby faces are indented into a free-blown shape. Both round and plum shapes have been used and

thus the size of the ornament might vary. One face is crying, one is smiling and one seems in between. All heads have a ruffled collar at the neck. (p306a, OP, R2)

$175.00-200.00

TWINS IN BUNTING - (M) - Approx. 3" - The ornament has an overall egg shape to it. The bunting has 3 ribbons and bows tied around it. Two children are shown from the shoulders up, nestled in the bunting. (Germany, p245b, OP, R2) $100.00-125.00

FOR THINGS THAT BELONG TO BABIES, see HOUSEHOLD ITEMS

Clowns

Like many other things, the golden age of the circus coincided with that of the ornaments and many circus items were immortalized in glass. Undoubtedly the most popular circus theme with German glassblowers was the clown. Since they sold well to the American market, different clown themes and variations were constantly being molded. Clowns are almost always dressed in a jumper-like clown suit with a ruffle about the neck. Since many are so similar, with only slight variations, they are hard to tell apart.

ANIMALS IN CLOWN SUITS - see respective type in the animals' section

STANDARD FORM CLOWN - (M) - Approx. 2" to 4¾" - He is dressed in a one-piece clown suit with a ruffle around the neck. Arms are straight at the sides, and his hands are in the pockets. His feet blend into the rounded base. On top of the smiling, rounded head, there is a cone shaped hat. The suit shows molded wrinkles, but has no molded stripes or buttons. (Germany, Czech., Austria, p249b, p252b, p252c, p252d, p269b, p269c, OP-NP, R4-5)

Smaller $30.00-40.00

Larger $40.00-50.00

VARIATION: (1) "MY DARLING CLOWN"- (M) - Approx. 3" & 4¾" - Standard form with "My Darling" molded on the front. This was probably made by the same glassblower that made the "My Darling" dog. (Germany, OP, R3) Small $35.00-45.00

Larger $60.00-70.00

VARIATION: (2) "500,000 CLOWN" - (M) - Approx. 3" & 3¾" - Standard form with "500,000" molded on the front. The significance of the number is uncertain. (Germany, p254b, OP, R3-4) Small $40.00-50.00

Larger $50.00-60.00

VARIATION: (3) - (M) - Approx. 3" - The arms are slightly bent and the hands are OUT of the pockets. The suit has three molded buttons on the front, and the ruffle goes higher to the back of the head. (p249b, OP, R3)

$30.00-35.00

VARIATION: (4) "DIAMOND" CLOWN - (M) - Approx. 3" & 3½" - Similar to the standard form, except less detailed. The legs come to a point and so does the hat, giving it a diamond shape. The ruffles are large rounded lobes, and the suit has two buttons. The head is poorly molded and blends into the cap and ruffles. (p263a, p263b, OP-NP, R4) $20.00-25.00

VARIATION: (5) - (M) - Approx. 3″ - This clown has a high collar instead of ruffles, his suit also has molded stripes and three buttons. (Rogers p510, OP, R3)
$40.00-50.00

VARIATION: (6) - CLOWN PLAYING A CONCERTINA - (M) - Approx. 3½″ - He looks like a standard form clown, but holds an accordian across his chest and stomach area. (Czech., p254a. OP-NP, R3)
$30.00-35.00

AMERICAN CLOWN - (M) - Approx. 3″ - Made of heavy glass, this piece shows little detail. He is shown to the feet in a clown suit with two buttons, his hands in his pockets. Both the ruffled collar and hat are ill-defined. This unusual piece is silvered on the outside. (U.S., p266, OP, R1-2)
$25.00-35.00

BALDING CLOWN HEAD - (M) - Approx. 3½″ - In this nicely detailed piece, the clown only has hair on the sides of his head. He wears a small conical hat in the center of his head and a ruffled collar below his chin. The face looks more like a distinguished old gentleman than a clown. This has led to this piece being called Disraeli or Scrooge. This, of course, would be ignoring his hat and ruffled collar. It is very similar to the John Bull ornament. Perhaps turning it into a clown was a political statement by the German glassblower. This piece was also made as a light bulb. Also see John Bull. (p277a, OP, R1) $175.00-200.00

BOY CLOWN - (M) - Approx. 4″ - The boy is dressed in a conical hat and a clown suit with ruffled collar. He has no clown-like or comical face. The suit has three buttons and the boy's hands are in his pockets. (Germany, p249a, OP, R2-3)
$30.00-40.00

BOY CLOWN HEAD - (M) - Approx. 2½″, 3″ & 4″ - The head is shown only from the chin up. The ruffled collar is under the chin, around the base of the ornament. The hat is tall and rounded with a button or pom-pom on the front. He has long hair that "puffs" out at the sides and covers the ears. The face is not comical or painted like a clown. Several different sizes and moldings exist of this popular ornament; however, the differences are subtle and usually in the facial features. (Germany, p317a, OP-NP, R3-4)
$75.00-85.00

BOY CLOWN HEAD ON AN INDENT - (M&FB) - Approx. 6″ - This is a four-inch molded head atop a free-blown ball that has a large indent in the front. (Germany, p255, OP, R1-2) $125.00-175.00

BOY CLOWN IN THE MOON - (M) - Approx. 3″ dia. - The small boy clown sits in a crescent shaped moon, facing left. The moon has two indented stars. The boy's left hand is at the ruffled collar, the right holds the side of the moon. He wears a cone-shaped hat that has the hanger in it. This ornament is often incorrectly called a man or sailor in the moon. However, close examination shows the boy to be dressed as a **clown**. (Germany, p149b, OP, R3-4)
$70.00-90.00

BOY CLOWN ON A BALL - (M) - Approx. 4″ - The boy wears a cap and a waistcoat with three buttons. He has a small ruffled collar. From the knees down is a 1½″ ball

with painted stars. (p252a, NP [1940s and 1950s only], R3)
$50.00-60.00

CLOWN CLIP-ON - (M) - Approx. 3″ (ornament only) - He wears a baggy clown suit with four buttons. The collar is only lightly ruffled. His hands are in his pockets and he wears a conical hat. This piece is similar to some early European figural lights. (p308b, OP, R2) $70.00-80.00

CLOWN HEAD - DOUBLE FACED - (M) - Approx. 3½″ - He wears a tall detailed conical hat with two pom-poms. He has a smiling, nicely-detailed face. The ruffle at his neck is small. The same face is on the opposite side. (p256, OP, R2-3) $150.00-175.00

CLOWN HEAD INDENT - (M&FB) - Approx. 4″, indented clown is 1½″ - This clown in a conical hat with a pom-pom and a ruffled collar is indented into a free-blown ball which is oblong or other shape. (p261b, OP, R3) $40.00-50.00

CLOWN HEAD WITH GLASS EYES - (M) - Approx. 3¾″ - The ornament has an overall egg shape with a large head. The body is rounded and shown to the waist. The suit has two large buttons, a ruffled collar and a conical hat. The right hand is at the ruffles and the left at the stomach area. (Germany, p267a, OP, R1) $150.00-175.00

CLOWN IN A BOOT - (M) - Approx. 3″ - The clown appears to be rising out of a "dimpled" boot or sock. From the waist up he wears a suit with two buttons, a ruffle and conical hat. (Germany, p254c, OP-NP [limited], R2-3)
$60.00-75.00

CLOWN IN A CELLO - see MAN IN A CELLO

CLOWN IN A DRUM - (M) - Approx. 2½″ dia. - The clown head appears to be bursting through the head of the drum. The back of the drum is smooth and the edge shows typical drum roping. (Germany, p264a, OP-NP [very limited], R2)
$100.00-110.00

CLOWN IN A MANDOLIN - (M) - Approx. 5½″ - This is a mandolin with a grinning, bald clown head and arms coming out of the upper part. One hand is plucking the strings. (p267b, OP, R2-3) $125.00-150.00

CLOWN ON A PINE CONE - (M) - Approx. 3″ - The clown is embossed into a standard pine cone made during the 1920s and early 1930s. (Germany, OP, R1-2)
$50.00-65.00

CLOWN ON A **LOG** PLAYING A BANJO - (M) - Approx. 4″ - He sits cross legged on a small log with the banjo going to the right shoulder. He has a small ruffled collar and a hat, but not a clown face. This is a 1950s piece. Also see: GNOMES ON A LOG PLAYING A CONCERTINA in Gnomes, Dwarves & Mushroom People. (p265a, NP, R3-4)
$20.00-30.00

CLOWN ON A **STUMP** PLAYING A BANJO - (M) - Approx. 3″ & 4¼″ - This clown with a suit, ruffled collar and cone-shaped hat, sits up an upright stump. He is playing a banjo and his left leg is crossed over his right. The small size is rarer. (Germany, p262b, OP-NP, R4)Old $40.00-50.00
1950s version $20.00-30.00
New $2.00-10.00

CLOWN PLAYING A BASS FIDDLE - (M) - Approx. 3½"H x 4½" - The clown is shown from head to foot, and the fiddle goes from his foot to his left ear. He holds it with his left hand and plays it with his right. He wears a ruffled clown suit and conical hat. (p309a, NP [only 1950s pieces are known], R3) $15.00-25.00

CLOWN SITTING ON A BALL - (M) - Approx. 3½" - This clown sits with his legs straddling a large ball. He wears a ragged collar and a clown suit with two buttons. His hands are in his pockets. (Germany, p267c, OP, R2-3)
$125.00-150.00

CLOWN TORSO (TYPE I) - (M) - Approx. 3" - In this unusual piece, the clown is shown to the waist only. He wears a conical hat, and his hands are inside his clown suit which has a ruffled collar. (p249c, OP, R2-3)$50.00-60.00

CLOWN TORSO (TYPE II) - (M) - Approx. 2½" - He is shown in a ruffled collared clown suit with his hands in his pockets. His face is often painted dark. (p268b, OP, R3)
$50.00-60.00

CLOWN WITH A CRESCENT MOON - (M) - Approx. 5" - He wears a clown suit with a large crescent moon embossed on the stomach. His hands are in his pockets. His collar is dagged with bells at the end. His hat is conical with a turned up brim. His hair is shoulder length. (p268c, OP, R2-3) $90.00-100.00

COMIC FIGURE - (M) - Approx. 3" - This strange little man does not wear any hat or clown outfit. He is shown to the waist with his skinny arms and hands resting on his stomach. He has two buttons and a bow tie off-centered to the right. He has large ears and nose. His face is painted in such a way as to show an "X" with the nose as the center. (p263c, OP, R2-3) $85.00-95.00

GIRL JESTER - (M) - Approx. 3¼" & 3¾" - This shows a little girl's head on a cylinder or bell shaped "body". Molded on to this "body" is a dagged collar with bells. She has curly hair and wears "pumpkin shell" type hat. (Germany, p343b, p344b, OP, R3)   Small $75.00-100.00
Large $150.00-175.00

GRINNING CLOWN HEAD - (M) - Approx. 4½" - This early piece has an exceptionally wide grin. It has thick areas both over and under the eyes. It may be matte painted instead of silvered. It has a tiny cone shaped hat that almost looks like a horn. It was, in fact, the exhaust end of the glass tube. The back of the head is ribbed like a pumpkin. (p273, OP, R1-2) $225.00-250.00

"HANS" CLOWN HEAD - (M) - Approx. 2" - This head is missing the typical ruffles and cone-shaped hat. He wears a rounded hat with a thick brim. He has a smiling comical face with rounded cheeks. (Germany, Rogers p66, OP, R2-3)
$65.00-75.00

"HANS" CLOWN HEAD ON A BALL - (M&FB) - Approx. 3¾" - Same head as above, but the "body" is a round ball that may be indented. (Germany, p311c, OP, R2-3)
$65.00-75.00

"HANS" CLOWN HEAD ON A SPIKE - (M&FB) - Approx. 4"H and 5"H - This is the same head as above. From the neck down it is a free-blown spike or icicle. (Germany, p253b, OP, R2-3)   Both Sizes $100.00-125.00

"JOEY" CLOWN - I use this term to describe a popular clown-style with several unique variations. He is portrayed in a tight fitting "skull" cap and a ruffled collar. He has arched eyebrows and a learing smile that makes him look almost sinister. "Joey" is a popular term for clowns and is named after the European father of clowns Joseph Grimaldi.

"JOEY" CLOWN HEAD - (M) - Approx. 2¼" & 3½" - The clown is shown from the shoulders up. Most of this is taken up by the large, fluffy ruffles that come up around the face and back of the head. He wears a close fitting skull cap, not the cone-shaped one of most clowns. (Germany, p247a, p268a, OP, R3) $55.00-75.00

"JOEY" CLOWN HEAD WITH CHENILLE ARMS AND LEGS - (M) - Approx. 4" glass portion only, 5½" with chenille legs - The standard head comes down to a large barrel-shaped body. There are indents into the sides and bottom into which are inserted chenille (pipe cleaner) arms and legs. (Germany, p251a, OP, R1-2) $150.00-175.00

"JOEY" CLOWN HEAD WITH STYLIZED BODY - (M&FB) - Approx. 6" - The standard head is blown onto a large round or oval ball that forms the body. The "body" is usually decorated to simulate a suit. (Germany, p251b, OP, R2) $110.00-125.00

"JOEY" CLOWN HEAD ON A BALL - (M&FB) - Approx. 3½" - This is similar to the above, except the ball or oval is not much bigger than the head. It may have curly angel hair ruffle added at the neck. (Germany, OP-NP, R2-3)
$90.00-100.00

"JOEY" CLOWN HEADED SNAKE - (M&FB) - Approx. 7" overall, 2" head alone - A small clown head with a portion of the ruffled collar is blown onto a free-blown "snake" body. This body has been twisted or spiraled like other snakes. This has also been described as a genie head on a wisp of smoke. Sizes can vary with the length of the free-blown body. (Germany, p347b, OP, R2) $100.00-125.00

"JOEY" CLOWN HEAD WITH A SG COLLAR - (M) - Approx. 6" overall, head only 3" - The standard head is shown to the chin. However, the ruffled collar is not molded. It is replaced by SG which is attached to a hole in the bottom of the ornament. (Germany, p247b, OP, R2)
$125.00-150.00

"JOEY" CLOWN WITH ACCORDIAN - (M) - Approx. 3¼" - This clown has the same type head and face as the others, but it also has a molded body. The accordian is held in both hands and covers from the neck down. (Germany, p248c, OP-NP, R3) $40.00-50.00

"JOEY" CLOWN WITH A DRUM - (M) - Approx. 3½" - This clown is in the same style as above. On his chest is a small drum which he beats with his right hand. His left is behind the back. This is the most common of the musical Joey Clowns. (Germany, p248b, OP-NP, R4)
$40.00-50.00

"JOEY" CLOWN WITH A SAXOPHONE - (M) - Approx. 3¼" - He is the same style clown as above, but he blows a saxophone which is held in both hands. This is the rarest of these three. (Germany, p248a, OP-NP, R2-3)
$40.00-50.00

"JUDY" CLOWN HEAD - (M) - Approx. 3" - Judy was the battered half of the Punch and Judy Clowns. This piece is the head only and shows no ruffled collar. The face shows no emotion and has little clown-like look to it. The hat is beehive shaped with little triangles all along the edge and stripes that go to the peak. (Germany, p262a, OP, R2-3)
$60.00-75.00

DOUBLE FACED "JUDY" CLOWN HEAD - (M) - Approx. 3" - Similar to the above except the face is embossed into both sides. (Germany, OP, R2-3)
$75.00-90.00

DOUBLE FACED "JUDY" ON A BODY - (M&FB) - Approx. 5¼" - The head is similar to the above two ornaments. It is shown from the chin down, on top of a free-blown oval. The oval has two large indents that possibly represent buttons. (Germany, p261a, OP, R2)
$75.00-90.00

"JUDY" BELL, DOUBLE FACED - (M&FB) - Approx. 5"H - The molded head, similar to all of the above, but slightly smaller, is attached to a free-blown bell by a short pike. The double faced head forms the handle. (Germany, p253a, OP, R1-2)
$75.00-90.00

LARGE-HEADED CLOWN (TYPE I) - (M) - Approx. 3" - He is similar to the standard clown. His suit has two pompom buttons and one on his hat. His body appears short and wide, and his head is out of proportion to the body. (Schiffer p109, OP, R2-3)
$40.00-50.00

LARGE-HEADED CLOWN (TYPE II) - (M) - Approx. 3¼" - The head is out of proportion to the body which is shown to the waist. His hands are shown at the stomach and chest. His suit has three buttons and a ruffled collar. He wears a conical hat. (p265c, OP, R2-3)
$40.00-50.00

"PUNCH" CLOWN - (M) - Approx. 3½" - He wears a hood that ends in ruffles around the neck. Three bells are on the hood on either side of the face. His hands are on a bulging stomach, and he has a hunch back. He is shown only from the waist up. (Germany, p260, OP-NP [very limited], R2-3)
$75.00-85.00

"PUNCH" CLOWN WITH LEGS - (M&FB) - Approx. 4" overall, 3½" body - He has the traditional hump back and bulging stomach. His left hand is on his stomach and the right at his ruffled collar. (Germany, p291d, OP, R1)
$300.00-350.00

PUNCH AND JUDY SHOW (TYPE I) - (M) - Approx. 3" - These famous slapstick puppet-clowns are shown embossed on a puppet stage. Punch on the right hits Judy with a club. Only the very top of Judy shows. Punch sits with his left leg straddling the stage. The front of the stage has eight molded stripes and curtains. The reverse shows a clown head with ruffled collar. He has large ears and a small cap. The top of the stage has a rounded arch shape, and the sides are plain. The back is covered with small "bubbles". (Germany, p257, p258, p259a, OP, R2)
$90.00-100.00

PUNCH AND JUDY SHOW (TYPE II) - (M) - Approx. 3" - In this version, both Punch and Judy carry clubs and are shown straddling the stage front. The stage shows no curtains and has a roof-like top that slopes to the front and back. Both the front and sides have eight stripes. The reverse side is similar to the above, except the clown hat is more like a small ball instead of a cone. The bottom is "dimpled". (Germany, p259c, OP-NP [very limited], R2)
$90.00-100.00

PUNCH AND JUDY SHOWS (TYPE III) - (M) - Approx. 3"H x 2"W - At first, the stage has the appearance of a square house. Closer examination shows both Punch and Judy astride the curtained stage with a crescent moon at the bottom. The back and sides give the impression of curtains, but has no real features. (Germany, p259b, OP, R2)
$60.00-80.00

ROLY POLY CLOWN - (M) - Approx. 2½" - He wears a tight fitting cap that frames his face, and his large ears show. His hands are resting on his stomach. He also wears a wide collar and tie. The ornament is rounded at the waist, giving it a roly poly look. (Germany, p250a, OP-NP [limited], R2-3)
$40.00-50.00

SNOWMAN CLOWN - (M) - Approx. 4¼" - This clown appears to be made of three rounded balls like a snowman. His arms are bent at the elbow, and his hands are in his pockets. He has a ruffle at the neck, three buttons on the body and one button on the cone-shaped hat. (Germany, p265b, NP [none known prior to 1940s-1950s production], R3-4)
$15.00-25.00

STRAWBERRY NOSED CLOWN - (M) - Approx. 3½" - This out of proportion looking clown has a large head with a strawberry looking nose. He has a small ruffle around the neck and a tiny hat on the right side of his head. (p270c, OP, R2)
$50.00-75.00

Fictional Characters

ALADDIN - (M) - Approx. 3½" - Wearing a large turban and billowing pants, Aladdin stands full length his hands in his pockets. The skin is painted a bronze color. (Germany, p270b, OP, R1-2)
$125.00-150.00

ALI BABA IN A BARREL - (M) - Approx. 4" - The bearded figure rises from the stomach up out of a wooden barrel. His left arm is across the stomach and his right is at his ear. His right hand may be holding a beer stein, and thus it has also been suggested he is a man in a beer barrel. (Germany, p276a, OP, R1)
$225.00-250.00

ANDY GUMP - Rogers states that such a character was produced during the 1920s and 1930s, but gives no description. He is often confused with Happy Hooligan, but Andy Gump should have a long neck and no lower jaw.

BARNEY GOODLE HEAD - (M) - Approx. 2¼" - His head is round and has a tiny hat high on the forehead. He has a heavy moustache and eyebrows. (p327a, OP, R1)
$200.00-250.00

BUSTER BROWN HEAD - (M) - Approx. 2¾" - The boy has flowing shoulder-length hair. Beneath his chin is a high collar and small tie. He resembles the comic strip character popular at this time period. He has also been described as a Charles Dickens' character. (p283c, OP, R1)

$250.00-275.00

BUSTER BROWN WITH ANNEALED LEGS - (M&FB) - Approx. 4½" - He has long shoulder-length hair that curls under, a large ribbon tied at the neck and low-belted pantaloons. His left hand is at the side and his right at the stomach area. He is shown in the typical dress of that cartoon character. (Germany, Schiffer p126, OP, R1)

$300.00-350.00

BUST OF JOHN BULL - (M) - Approx. 3" - The head and shoulder area are shown on this piece. The head is balding with hair showing only at the sides. There is a large bow tie beneath the chin. The nicely detailed face has rosey cheeks and a smile. This is very similar to the Balding Clown Head. This piece, which has also been called Disraeli and Scrooge, was also made as a light bulb. (Germany, OP, R2)

$140.00-160.00

VARIATION: (1) - JOHN BULL WITH CHENILLE LEGS - (M), Approx. 3" glass, 4¼" with legs - This is the same piece described above with the addition of chenille legs below the shoulders. The chenille "legs" may also have composition boots attached to them. (Germany, p283b, OP, R1-2)   Legs Only $160.00-190.00
Legs with Boots $190.00-225.00

VARIATION: (2) JOHN BULL BUST WITH CHENILLE ARMS AND LEGS - This is the same glass piece described above, but chenille arms with wax hands have been added to the shoulders. The chenille legs have wax boots. (Germany, p278a, OP, R1) $300.00-325.00

CAMPBELL SOUP KIDS INDENT - (M&FB) - Approx. 4½" - Two children's heads with glass eyes are indented into a free-blown plum shape. Their faces are almost square looking with ruffles around the edges of the indent. There is a single tuft of hair in the center of the head like the Campbell Soup Kids. (p324a, OP, R2) $150.00-175.00

"DEVIL" HEAD - (M) - Approx. 2½" - This head is almost perfectly round. He has a wide learing grin with six widely spaced teeth showing. He has thick cheeks below the eyes, and three well-defined wrinkles on the forehead between the eyes. Ears show at the sides. No hair shows, but thick ribs (almost like a pumpkin) show on the back. It is unlikely that this was designed as a "devil" head. In fact, it was used as the head of an Uncle Sam ornament. (Germany, p282b, OP, R2) $200.00-225.00

"DEVIL" HEAD WITH A NECK (TYPE I) - (M) - Approx. 3½" - His neck shows below the chin. He has tufts of hair at the sides and very front part of the forehead. He has deep creases around a mouth with a slanted/leering smile. Ears show at the sides. It is unlikely that this piece was designed to be the devil. (p282c, OP, R2)$200.00-225.00

"DEVIL'S HEAD (TYPE II) - (M) - Approx. 3" - This is very similar to the above, except he does not smile. There are heavy creases around the nose and mouth. (OP-R2)

$200.00-225.00

THE DEVIL (HEAD) - (M&FB) - Approx. 2" - The oval shaped head has a learing grin, wide eyes and two annealed horns on the forehead. There is little detail in this piece which is often unsilvered and painted red. Other ornaments may be called devil heads, but this one leaves little doubt as to who it portrays. (Schiffer p116, OP, R1)

$125.00-150.00

DOLLY DINGLE HEAD - (M) - Approx. 3" - This pudgy girl face has short hair turned under at the end. The face has little expression or detail. (p318b, OP, R1-2)

$150.00-175.00

FOXY GRANDPA - (M&FB) - Approx. 4½" - His coat is open showing a vest and tie. The left hand is at the stomach area, and the right is near the lapel. He has hair on the side of his head and wears painted glasses. He was an early comic strip character. He usually has free-blown annealed legs. (Germany, p285b, p291b, OP, R2-3) $175.00-200.00

GENIE FROM THE BOTTLE - (M) - Approx. 4" - The genie with fat cheeks wears a turban hat, baggy trousers and a jacket. His legs are bowed and his chin rests on the finger tips of his folded hands. (Germany, OP-NP [limited], R2) $150.00-175.00

GOLDILOCKS - (M) - Approx. 3" - She has long flowing hair that comes down past her shoulders. Her dress has short puffy sleeves, a square collar, and ties with a large bow in the back. Her right hand is at the collar, and her left is at the breast. (Germany, p244a, OP-NP [limited], R3-4) $45.00-60.00

GOLDILOCKS HEAD - (M) - Approx. 2½" & 3" - She is shown to the chin area with long curly hair framing her face and even bangs coming down into the forehead. She has two bows on either side of the head and a ribbon that joins them. The larger version is much cruder. There is less detail, and the ornament surface is pitted showing the crudeness of the mold. The larger piece is probably not German. (p315b, p315c, p316b, OP-NP [smaller head only], R3 [smaller], R2 [larger])   Smaller $100.00-150.00
Larger $90.00-100.00

GRETEL - (M) - Approx. 3¾" - She has short hair, a blouse and what looks like baggy pants. Her right forefinger is at her mouth, and her left hand is at her side. Also see the companion piece, Hansel. (p294a, OP, R2-3) $80.00-90.00

HANSEL - (M) - Approx. 3" & 3½" - He wears a cap and pants with suspenders. His right hand holds a square cookie or book; his left is in his pocket. He has also been called a schoolboy. Also see Gretel. (p293a, OP, R2-3)

$60.00-70.00

HAPPY HOOLIGAN (TYPE I) - (M&FB) - Approx. 4½" - His jacket is buttoned at the top and open at the bottom, and he wears a tin can as a hat. His right arm is at the waist, and his left is at the lapel of his jacket. He has thin protruding lips and large ears. Like many of the other early comic strip figures, he often has free-blown annealed legs, but many were made with legs and some of these came as clip-ons. He is the most common of the comic strip characters. (Germany, p285a, OP, R3) $175.00-200.00

HAPPY HOOLIGAN (TYPE II) - (M&FB) - Approx. 5¾″ overall & 4¼″ body alone - This is an earlier and rarer version. In this nicely detailed piece, he wears a jacket and both arms are folded at the chest. The face, with large ears, is nicely detailed as is the tin can hat. He has free-blown legs annealed onto the bottom. (Germany, p280b, OP, R1) $250.00-300.00

HAPPY HOOLIGAN HEAD - (M) - Approx. 2¾″ - The face is similar to the above pieces with the large ears and "bump" on the head representing his tin can hat. His skinny neck fastens to a clip-on. (Germany, OP, R1) $250.00-275.00

HUMPTY DUMPTY - (M) - Approx. 2½″ dia. - The ornament is a ball shape with the eyes, nose and mouth embossed into it. No head or hair shows. At the sides are two embossed arms which are bent at the elbow. This piece was made by the Muller-Hipper glassmakers and was for sale in 1926. (Schiffer p132, OP, R1-2) $150.00-175.00

JACK FROST - (M) - Approx. 2½″ & 3½″ - This gnome-like head wears a stocking cap and has a beard. The face is nicely detailed and looks almost like a small boy. The large size is much rarer. (p385c, OP-NP [limited to l950s], R3) Small $40.00-50.00
Large $50.00-75.00

KATE GREENAWAY GIRL - (M) - Approx. 3″ & 4″ - She wears a long full length coat with two large fasteners in the front and a small hood-like hat. Her left arm is at her chin, and her right is at the breast. She also came as a clip-on. (Germany, p275a, p289a, OP, R2) Smaller $100.00-125.00
Larger $150.00-175.00

KAYO - (M) - Approx. 2½″ - This full-figured boy wears a hat and a neck scarf tied in the front. His shirt has molded stripes, and his hands are in his pockets. He has large eyes and an impish looking face. Kayo was in the Moon Mullins comic strip. This piece has also been referred to as Smitty. (p290c, OP, R2) $50.00-60.00

KEYSTONE COP - (M&FB) - Approx. 3¼″ & 4″ body only, 4½″ & 6″ with annealed legs - He wears a high rounded policeman's hat and a double breasted jacket. His left hand is in the belt of his coat, and his right hand is at the side. The Keystone Cops were popular in early silent movies. The piece may or may not have annealed legs and may be a clip-on. (Germany, p285c, p291c, OP, R2-3) Small $175.00-200.00
Large $225.00-250.00

COMIC KEYSTONE COP - (M) - Approx. 4½″ - This full-figure piece has a smiling comic face with large ears. He wears a rounded policeman's hat and a three button jacket that is belted at the waist. Both hands are at his belt, and the right one holds a nightstick. In another slightly different version, the nightstick hangs from the belt. (Germany, p250b, OP, R2) $100.00-125.00

VARIATION: COMIC KEYSTONE COP WITH CHENILLE LEGS - (M), Approx. 4½″ overall, 3″ glass body - This is the same piece described above to the bottom of the coat. The rest of the ornament has been indented and two chenille legs with wax boots have been added. (Germany, p278c, OP, R1) $325.00-350.00

LITTLE BLACK SAMBO - (M) - Approx. 4¼″ - He is bare chested with long striped pants. His short black hair does not cover the ears in which are molded earrings. The skin is usually a golden brown color. The missing clothes perhaps refer to the story in which Sambo loses his clothes to tigers. (Germany, p284a, OP, R1-2) $200.00-225.00

LITTLE MISS MUFFET - (M) - Approx. 3″ & 3½″ - This chubby girl carries a purse in her right arm while both hands rest at the stomach. She wears a long, round shirt with puffy sleeves and a bonnet. She has occasionally been called Mrs. Santa No. 2, but her most accepted name is Little Miss Muffet. (p286, p345c, OP, R4) $60.00-80.00

MISS LIBERTY - (M) - Approx. 3″ - She wears the peaked cap typical of early Miss Liberty pictures. She holds a rolled scroll at the chest with her right hand. Her left arm is covered by draped cloth. The back shows the drapery of her gown and long flowing hair that comes to the middle of her back. (Germany, p287b, OP, R2-3)
$140.00-160.00

MISS LIBERTY IN A FLAG - (M) - Approx. 3½″ - This piece is very similar to the above except the drapery over the left shoulder is molded to show stars and stripes. Her hair is only shoulder length. (Germany, p287c, OP-NP [very limited], R2) $140.00-160.00

MOON MULLINS - (M&FB) - Approx. 4½″ - An early comic strip character dressed in a coat, vest, tie and wearing a rounded hat with a thick brim. His hands are in his pockets, and he is smoking a cigar. He was an early comic strip character. He usually has free-blown annealed legs. (Germany, Schiffer p125, OP, R1-2) $300.00-350.00

MOON MULLINS (TYPE II) - (M&FB) - Approx. 5½″ - He is dressed in a long buttoned coat with a bow tie. His left hand is at his side, and the right is at the lapel of his coat. He wears a rounded cap with a thick brim. He has free blown annealed legs. He has also been referred to as an early 1905 version of "Foxy Grandpa". (Germany, p284b, OP, R1-2) $300.00-350.00

MRS. SANTA CLAUS - (M) - Approx. 4¼″ - She wears a duster-type hat on her head and her short sleeved dress has a low, square collar. The blouse under this is checked and there is a small bow at her neck. Since both her hands rest on the square collar of her dress, she has erroneously been described has holding a purse. (Germany, p346a, OP, R1-2) $250.00-275.00

SANTA CLAUS - see SANTA section

PINOCCHIO - (M) - Approx. 4″ - This boy puppet appears to be molded after the Disney character and is thus probably a late piece. He wears a large bowtie and has three round buttons on the front. He has a "button" nose, a conical hat, and his hands are in his pockets. (p281b, OP, R1) $80.00-90.00

POPEYE - (M&FB) - Approx. 4½″ - He wears a small hat and has a cigar or pipe sticking out of the left side of his mouth. He has muscular arms and a molded striped shirt. He usually has free-blown annealed legs. Rogers states they were only made during the 1930s. (Germany, Schiffer p126, OP, R1) $300.00-350.00

PUNCH AND JUDY CLOWNS - see CLOWNS

RED RIDING HOOD HEAD - (M) - Approx. 1¾" & 2½" - Her flesh painted face with glass eyes is fully enclosed in a hood that even wraps under the chin. This hood is almost always red, hence the name Red Riding Hood. This is probably the most common of the head ornaments. She may also be found as a clip-on. (p324b, OP, R3-4) $65.00-75.00

RED RIDING HOOD AND WOLF - (M) - Approx. 3" - They are shown standing on an oval shaped ornament. There are pine trees on either side and grass underneath. The reverse side shows Grandma's house between two pine trees. There are large bumps along the seam of the ornament. (Germany, p306b, OP-NP [limited], R2) $45.00-60.00

SCROOGE - see BALDING CLOWN HEAD and JOHN BULL

SMITTY (TYPE I) - (M) - Approx. 4½" - The comic strip character's head is out of proportion and is as big as the rest of his full-length body. His hat, which resembles a golf hat, is turned sideways to his left. He has a scarf around his neck, and his hands are in his pants. This piece has been referred to as Skippy, but Skippy did not wear a hat or have an impish look. (Germany, p288, OP, R1) $200.00-225.00

SMITTY (TYPE II) - (M) - Approx. 3½" - This is similar to Type I except smaller. This comic strip character has a head **slightly** out of proportion to his body. He wears a hat that appears to be turned sideways, and a bow tie. His hands are in his pockets. This piece has also been referred to as Skippy. (Germany, p281c, OP, R2) $100.00-125.00

SMITTY HEAD - (M) - Approx. 2½" - This is basically the same head as on the body above, with the hat turned sideways and an impish look. (Germany, p317c, OP-NP [limited], R1-2) $75.00-100.00

SNOW WHITE and THE SEVEN DWARFS - see GNOMES, DWARVES and MUSHROOM PEOPLE

THE MAN IN THE MOON - see HEAVENLY BODIES

THOR FACE ON A BIRD - see BIRDS

THOR - see MEN AND BOYS - THOR FACE

THUMBELINA - see FACES IN FLOWERS

UNCLE SAM ON A BOOT - (M&FB) - Approx. 5" - (Sizes can vary with the pike) - Uncle Sam is shown from head to waist embossed onto a boot or stocking. He is dressed in the typical red, white and blue outfit with a top hat. The long pike is left on this early unsilvered piece, and the whole ornament is wrapped in wire. (Germany, p296, OP, R1-2) $300.00-325.00

GROTESQUE UNCLE SAM - (M&FB) - Approx. 6¾", with hat 9" - The molded head has been listed and described as a devil head with a wide grotesque smile. The body is free-blown and tubular with chenille arms and legs. A 2½" top hat was added. (They are pictured separately.) This piece has been identified as Uncle Sam from old ads. (Germany, p347A and 348 (hat), OP, R1) $375.00-400.00

WITCH - (M) - Approx. 3½" - She looks like a little old lady wearing a shawl. She has a broom in her right hand, a conical hat and a cat at her feet. (OP, R1-2) $275.00-300.00

Gnomes, Dwarves and Mushroom People

With a traditional peaked cap and long beard, these characters are often hard to distinguish from Santas. You may find that some ornaments described as Santas are in fact Dwarves or Gnomes. These little people were not only popular in German folk tales, they are also found in stories throughout Europe and America. Another related theme is the Mushroom People. They are faces or bodies most often found on the stem of the mushroom with the cap becoming their hat. In Germany, the mushroom was a symbol of good luck. These figures and the Gnomes could be considered as representatives of the ancient tree and forest spirits, and their presence on the Christmas tree was thought to bring good luck.

PALMER COX BROWNIE - (M&FB) - Approx. 5" with legs & 3½" body - He has a face typical of Cox brownies and wears a small hat. His arms are crossed at the chest, and he may have free-blown annealed legs. (Germany, p280a, OP, R1-2) $250.00-275.00

DWARF WITH A LANTERN - (M) - Approx. 2½" - This full length piece wears a hooded cap, a jacket and pants. He has a beard and holds a paneled lantern that covers from his stomach to his feet. No old copies are known. (Germany, p300c, NP) $2.00-10.00

DWARF WITH A MONEY BAG - (M) - Approx. 2¾" - This slender piece is well detailed. He wears the traditional pants, jacket and hood. He has a waist length beard and holds a small money bag in his right hand. Both hands rest at the stomach area. (Germany, p300a, OP-NP, R1-2) $60.00-75.00

DWARF WITH A PICK - (M) - Approx. 2½" - This fellow wears pants, jacket and a conical cap. He has a long flowing beard and holds a large pick in his left hand. (Germany, p300b, OP-NP, R1-2) $50.00-75.00

SINGING DWARF - (M) - Approx. 2½" - He has a fat body and squat legs. His long beard reaches to the belt of his jacket, and his mouth is wide open as if singing. His peaked cap hangs down in the back. (Germany, p300d, OP-NP, R1) $80.00-90.00

SNOW WHITE AND THE SEVEN DWARFS - (M) - Approx. sizes: Snow White 4", the Dwarves 3¼" each - All figures are based on Walt Disney's famous cartoon. Snow White is usually painted white and shown in a long dress with short puffy sleeves. Dopey is probably the best molded piece and is painted gold. Sneezy is slender, has his hands on his hips and is usually painted blue. Happy is fat, has his hands on his hips and is cobalt blue. Grumpy is slender, has his arms crossed and is usually green. Doc has the right hand down and the left up, he is usually painted silver. Bashful is fat and has his hands at the hips; he is painted red. Sleepy is slender, has his hands at the side and is painted red. The ornaments are a solid color with no detailed painting and they are made of a thick glass. (American [Double-glo Co. 1938], p301 & 302, OP, R2)

Boxed set of eight $300.00-400.00
Separate pieces $40.00-50.00

ELF ATOP A MUSHROOM - (M) - Approx. 3½" - This small elf with a long beard and holding a pipe, sits upon a large mushroom. He does not straddle it like other pieces, but rather both legs rest atop the mushroom cap. (p299c, OP, R1) $125.00-150.00

ELF HEAD - (M) - Approx. 3" - He wears a peaked cap with hair showing in the front and back. This face has a boyish look, and the small beard on his chin makes it appear painted. The piece appears to be made from an old mold, although no early copies are known. (Germany, p306c, NP) $2.00-10.00

ELF ON A STUMP (EMBOSSED) - (M) - Approx. 2½" - This elf in a peaked cap is embossed onto the front of the stump. He appears to be sitting in a hollow area. Also embossed on the stump is a tree limb and leaves. (Germany, p70a & 299a, OP-NP, R3) $45.00-55.00

ELF UNDER A MUSHROOM (EMBOSSED) - (M) - Approx. 2½" - The elf is embossed onto the stalk of a short, fat mushroom. He is smoking a pipe and his elbow rests on a smaller mushroom. (Germany, p305b, OP-NP, R2) $40.00-60.00

GNOME IN A LARGE HAT - (M) - Approx. 4" - This gnome with a long beard and mustache that falls to his feet, wears a large dome-shaped hat which was perhaps designed as a mushroom cap. His right hand rests on his beard and in his left he holds a pipe. (p276c, OP, R2) $100.00-120.00

GNOME IN TRIANGLE WINDOW - (M) - Approx. 2¼" & 3½" - Wearing a peaked cap and a long beard, he looks through a "window" that is formed by three criss-crossed branches. A rough area underneath may be flowers. The overall shape of the ornament is triangular and with the back being rounded. On the back, the early version has a triangular design with loops at the corners. The 1950s version is a different mold and lacks this design. (Germany, p316a, OP-NP [1950s], R3) Old $50.00-60.00
1950s $35.00-45.00

GIRL ELF IN LEAVES - (M) - Approx. 2¾" - Her dress is made of hanging leaves. She has a collar around her neck made of leaves or petals and a similar type of cap on her head. No early examples are known. (Austria, NP) $2.00-10.00

GNOME PLAYING A CONCERTINA - (M) - Approx. 3¾" - This fat gnome sits on a log and plays a concertina which he holds across his stomach and chest area. He has a short beard and a tall rounded hat. The difference between old and new ornaments can be seen on the ends of the log. Old versions show tree rings; newer versions have raised bumps. (Germany, p299b, OP-NP, R2-3) Old $100.00-125.00
1950s $20.00-30.00
New $2.00-10.00

GNOME ON A TREE TRUNK WITH A BIRD - see BIRDS - BIRD AND GNOME ON A TREE TRUNK

MINIATURE GNOME - (M) - Approx. 2" - He is shown standing with his hand on his hips. He wears a peaked cap and a long beard. Clip-on. (p350d, OP, R1-2) $35.00-45.00

SMALL GNOME HEAD - see FICTIONAL CHARACTERS - JACK FROST

DWARF IN A PINE CONE - see SANTA IN A PINE CONE

MUSHROOM GIRL - (TYPE I) - (M) - Approx. 3½" - This chubby girl has a mushroom cap as her hat. Some of her hair shows in the back, and she has a ruffled collar around her neck. Both hands are in her pockets. (p305c, OP, R2-3) $35.00-45.00

MUSHROOM GIRL WITH A PIPE - (M) - Approx. 4" - She is very similar to the above piece. The ruffled collar goes all the way around the neck, and there are two embossed buttons on her suit. Her arms and hands show, and she holds a long stemmed pipe in her right hand. (p303c, OP, R1-2) $90.00-100.00

MUSHROOM GIRL (TYPE 2) - (M) - Approx. 3½" - The mushroom cap forms her cap. Her body is in the shape of the mushroom's stalk, and there are four stylized leaves at the bottom. She wears a ruffled collar and both her hands rest on a belt around her middle. (Germany, p305a, OP-NP, R2) $75.00-90.00

MUSHROOM MAN - (M) - Approx. 3½" - His hat is a mushroom cap and he appears to be straddling or sitting on the stalk. He has a nicely detailed face, mustache and beard. He wears a jacket and his hands are at his chest and stomach. (Germany, p304, OP, R3) $70.00-80.00

MUSHROOM MAN WITH A PIPE - (M) - Approx. 3¾" - He is very similar to the mushroom man described above. In his right hand he holds a small pipe and in his left a walking stick. (Germany, p303a, OP, R1-2) $90.00-110.00

MUSHROOM WITH A FACE - (M) - Approx. 2¾" - This squat looking mushroom with a thick stem has a smiling face embossed below the cap. No head shows. The stem is so thick that the piece also resembles an acorn. (p369b, OP, R1-2) $125.00-150.00

MUSHROOM MAN WITH A MONKEY BAG - (M) - Approx. 3¼" - In this chubby piece, a smiling face is embossed into the stalk of the mushroom. Arms are shown with the hands resting on the stomach area. The right hand holds a sack. (p303b, OP, R1-2) $100.00-125.00

Historical Figures

AL JOLSON HEAD - (M) - Approx. 3" - He wears a small rounded cap with a brim. Part of the neck shows below the smiling face. (Germany, Rogers 196b, OP, R1) $150.00-175.00

AL JOLSON IN BLACKFACE - (M) - Approx. 2¾" - The smiling face with short dark hair has been painted a purplish-black. (p329c, OP, R1) $175.00-200.00

AMELIA EARHART - "THE EXPLORER" - (M) - Approx. 3½" & 3¾" - She wears a flying suit or artic suit with hood and wide collar. There is a satchel or map hung over the shoulder and resting on the stomach area. Both hands show at the side. Both sizes of the ornaments are pictured. In one she appears to be a woman. In the smaller size, a man with a mustache is shown. (p284c & 298, OP, R2-3)
$125.00-150.00

BABY JESUS EMBOSSED ON AN EGG - (M) - Approx. 3" - The roughened surface of the ball gives it the appearance of straw. He appears to be wearing a type of angelic skirt that comes to the knees. There are several embossed balls around the figure as well as on the side seams. This is an early piece. (p336, OP, R1-2) $100.00-125.00

BABY JESUS HEAD - (M) - Approx. 2¼" & 3" - He is shown to the chin with thick wavy hair coming down only to the ears. He is also simply called a "boy's head". (Germany, p319c & 320b, OP, R2-3) $75.00-100.00

BABY JESUS ON A LEAF - (M) - Approx. 3" - Jesus lies on his back with a radiating star above his head. Lines radiate out from his body to fill in the shape he is embossed on. The back is veined to show the shape to be a leaf. (p235c, OP, R1-2) $175.00-200.00

BEN FRANKLIN - (M) - Approx. 3" - He has straight shoulder length hair with an inward curl and a high balding forehead. His right arm is at his side, and his left is in his pocket. There is a small scarf-like tie at the neck of a long coat. (Germany, OP, R1-2) $250.00-275.00

"BISMARK" - (M) - Approx. 3" - He wears a coat with a high collar and five buttons down the front. He wears a conical hat and has a large handlebar mustache like the pre-Hitler leader of Germany. His hands are at his side. (Germany, p289c, OP, R1) $175.00-200.00

BUST OF JESUS - (M) - Approx. 3" - He is shown to the shoulder area wearing a gown open at the neck. His hair flows down onto the shoulders. A beard, mustache and crown of thorns show on a nicely detailed face. This is probably an early German piece. (p271, OP, R1)
$400.00-450.00

CHARLES LINDBERGH HEAD - (M) - Approx. 2" - The head wears an aviator's cap with goggles on top and ear cups. The cap fastens under the chin of the boyish looking face. (OP, R2) $100.00-125.00

VARIATION: (LINDBERGH WITH CHENILLE ARMS AND LEGS) - (M&FB) - Approx. 4¼" glass and 6¼" with legs - The head described above is molded onto a free-blown, barrel shaped body. Chenille arms and legs are attached to indents in the body. (p272, OP, R1-2)
$250.00-275.00

CHARLIE CHAPLIN - (M) Rogers describes this piece as a dancing figure with a battered hat and cane made from 1912-20. No further information is available. (Germany, OP, R1) $275.00-300.00

CHARLIE CHAPLIN HEAD - (M) - Approx. 3½" - He is shown in the rounded hat that was typical in all his movies. Puffs of hair show at the sides and front of the hat. His nicely detailed face resembles Chaplin and includes a painted mustache. (Germany, p327c OP, R1-2)
$225.00-275.00

DISRAELI - (M) - Approx. 3" - He wears a large top hat, a jacket and a small scarf-like tie. His long hair touches his shoulders. His left hand is at the stomach area and the right is at his side. This is an early piece. (Germany, Rogers, p202, OP, R1) $250.00-275.00

EDDIE CANTOR WITH CHENILLE ARMS AND LEGS - (M) - Approx. 5½" overall, 4" for the glass body. - The smiling face has large eyes and ears, wears a conical hat and has a bowtie at the neck. His jacket has a waffled or checked effect with five buttons. Indentations at the shoulders and bottom hold the chenille arms and legs. (Germany, p228b, OP, R2) $250.00-275.00

"EINSTEIN" FACE ON KITE - (M) - Approx. 3" - The face appears to be old, with heavy eyebrows and moustache. It bears a remarkable resemblance to the mathematical genius Albert Einstein. Perhaps that is why the face is embossed on a geometric shape. There is nothing on the reverse. (p283a, OP, R2) $125.00-150.00

JOAN OF ARC HEAD - (M) - Approx. 2½" - She has glass eyes. She wears a round pillbox shaped hat (arming cap). The rest of her face is enclosed in a coif; both are dimpled to perhaps represent chain mail. She is similar to the Red Riding Hood head. However, this piece has a definite flattened cap. (Germany, p327b, OP, R2-3) $85.00-100.00

JOSEPH, MARY AND CHILD NATIVITY SET - This German set has been produced on a limited basis during the past few years. It has the appearance and detail of an old mold production. However, no old examples are known; unless the child in the manger is the same piece Rogers mentions as being in a German museum. (Germany, p334a, p334b & p334c, NP)   Set $30.00-40.00

JOSEPH - (M) - Approx. 4½" - He is shown kneeling on his left knee with his hands clasped in prayer. He has shoulder length hair and a long flowing robe. Part of the above set.

VIRGIN MARY - (M) - Approx. 4" - She kneels on both knees with her hands clasped in prayer. She wears a long flowing robe and a scarf about her head. Part of the above set.

CHILD IN THE MANGER - (M) - Approx. 3½" - He lays on his back in the manger wrapped in cloth. The straw at his head radiates outward with a halo-like effect. Part of the above set.

MADONNA AND CHILD - (M) - Approx. 3½" - The ornament has an overall pear shape with back being rounded. Mary is shown to the waist holding the young child Jesus at her left side. (Germany, p333b, OP-NP limited, R2) $70.00-80.00

BUST OF MADONNA AND CHILD - (M) - Approx. 2½″ - This ornament has an overall triangular appearance. Mary, who is shown to the lower chest, holds an unclothed Jesus in her right arm. Mary's flowing robe and head scarf show on the back. (p339b, OP, R1-2) $125.00-150.00

STANDING MADONNA AND CHILD (TYPE I) - (M) - Approx. 3″ - Mary stands in a flowing robe and head scarf. She holds the unclothed baby Jesus in her left arm. His right arm appears to go around her. (Germany, p339a, OP, R1) $225.00-250.00

NEW STANDING MADONNA AND CHILD (TYPE II) - (M) - Approx. 5½″ - Shown in a long flowing gown, Mary holds the child at her left side. Her head is slightly bent towards him. No early pieces of this are known. (p333a, NP [1950s only] R2-3) $25.00-35.00

MARY PICKFORD - (M&FB) - Approx. 4½″ with annealed legs - She is dressed in a flowing toga-like gown that is slightly off the shoulders. She has shoulder length wavy hair; her right hand is across the stomach; and her left hand is straight at the side. Although commonly referred to as Mary Pickford, she bears little resemblance to that silent movie star. She may or may not have annealed legs. (Germany, p236 & 280c, OP-NP Some 1950's [without legs], R1).
Old with legs $275.00-300.00
Old without legs $125.00-150.00
Newer $20.00-40.00

MARY PICKFORD HEAD (EMBOSSED) - (M) - Approx. 2½″ - The head, which faces to the right is embossed onto an egg shape. The silhouette shows long flowing hair and hair ornamentation. (Germany, Rogers, p196a, OP, R1) $75.00-100.00

REVOLUTIONARY WAR SOLDIER - See GIRL SOLDIER

WINSTON CHURCHILL - (M) - Approx. 3½″ - Shown only to the waist, he wears a conical hat and jacket. His boyish face resembles Churchill. His right hand holds the jacket lapel, and the left is at the stomach. This is probably a 1950's piece since Churchill would not have been a popular subject prior to WWII. (p279c, NP [1950s] R1-2) $80.00-90.00

Indians

Most Indian ornaments were probably made for the American market. However, the "Cowboys and Indians" theme is a popular one in Europe, possibly influenced by the Wild West Shows that were popular in the late 1800s. Rogers stated in her book that all old Indian molds are now in East Germany. Any of the Indian ornaments should be considered rare.

INDIAN HEAD IN A HEADDRESS (TYPE I) - (M) - Approx. 3½″ - This ornament shows the neck and head, but no shoulders. He wears a large headdress full of feathers and there is a bow or scarf at his neck. The face is painted in a copper-brown. His hair is knotted in a ponytail at the back of his head. The molds are now in East Germany. (Germany, p330a, OP, R2) $275.00-300.00

INDIAN HEAD IN A HEADDRESS (TYPE II) - (M) - Approx. 3¾″ - This is similar to the above piece except the neck area is slightly larger, and it does not have the scarf. The bottom has a bumpy effect. This is perhaps an example of the West Germans remaking a piece for which the East Germans had the mold. Early versions have paper eyes. None are known prior to 1950s. (West Germany, p332b, NP, R4) $2.00-10.00

INDIAN HEAD - (M) - Approx. 3″ - This head has no headdress or feathers. It has a simple headband around its shoulder length, molded hair. The face is elongated. (German, p332c, NP [No early examples known] R4) $2.00-10.00

INDIAN HEAD ON A PINE CONE - (M) - Approx. 3″ & 4″ - The Indian's face has a grim look. He wears a headdress that sweeps back along the sides of the cone. The cone itself has a diamond or quilted pattern. (Germany, p331a, OP, R2)   Small $150.00-175.00
Large $225.00-250.00

GRIM FACED INDIAN WITH A HEADDRESS (TYPE I) - (M) - Approx. 2¼″ - This small head is usually painted an appropriate copper color. He wears a small feathered headdress that encircles the head like a crown. The well molded face has a stern expression. It is usually a clip-on. (Germany, p330b, OP, R2) $225.00-250.00

VARIATION: INDIAN WITH CHENILLE ARMS AND LEGS - (M&FB) - Approx. 4½″ glass - 6″ overall - This is the small head described above molded onto a free-blown, barrel shaped body. Chenille arms and legs are attached to indentations in the "body". (OP, R1) $350.00-400.00

GRIM FACED INDIAN WITH A HEADDRESS (TYPE II) - (M) - Approx. 3¼″ - This is similar to the above piece, with the small headdress and grim expression. He has embossed war paint designs on the cheeks and well defined wrinkles at the mouth, eyes and forehead. (Germany, p335, OP, R1-2)

$200.00-225.00

INDIAN IN A BUST FORM - (M) - Approx. 3¾″ - He is shown from the chest and shoulders up with a shirt draped at the shoulders and open at the neck. The small headdress encircles the head almost like a crown. It has no molded feathers, but they may be painted on. This popular piece is nicely detailed. Large plaster Indian busts, similar to this, were popular around the turn of the century. The 1950s version has a "bumpy" pattern around the shoulders. (Germany, p330c, OP-NP [1950s version is rarer than the prewar], R2-3) $225.00-250.00
1950s $90.00-100.00

INDIAN IN A CANOE - (M) - Approx. 3¾″ - The Indian with a headdress on, sits inside a canoe with his legs outstretched. His hands are on the outside edge and hold paddles. The canoe and the whole ornament have a banana-like curve to it. (Germany, p331b, OP-NP [limited] R2) $200.00-225.00

INDIAN PRINCESS BUST - (M) - Approx. 2½″ - She has a flat pleated collar around the neck and shoulders. Her long flowing hair is tied with a headband which is knotted in the back and has two hanging ends. She has a rose embossed on her chest. (p318a, OP, R2) $80.00-90.00

INDIAN STANDING, SMOKING A PIPE - (M) - Approx. 3½" - This standing Indian smokes a pipe held in the left hand. The headdress goes around the head in a "halo-like" manner. It has little detailed molding. (German, p332a, NP, 1950s, R4)   1950s $20.00-30.00
                                                New $2.00-10.00

STANDING INDIAN - (M) - Approx. 4½" - This Indian shown to the hips, wears a full headdress and a large medallion on his chest. His hands are at his sides. He may have annealed legs and appears to be by the same glassblower who made Happy Hooligan, Foxy Grandpa, etc. (Germany, Schiffer p125, OP, R1) $450.00-500.00

Men and Boys

BEARDED MAN WITH ANNEALED LEGS - (M&FB) - Approx. 4½" - He wears a long sleeved jacket that is folded over and held together with a sash. He has a beard and mustache and a thick rounded hat. (Germany, Schiffer p126, OP, R1) $300.00-350.00

COMIC BABY BOY HEAD - (M) - Approx. 2" - The head is in the shape of a ball with an almost comical face on it. He wears a nightcap with a tassel on the right side of his head. A small tuft of hair hangs onto the forehead. (p325, OP, R2) $75.00-90.00

BLACK BABY - see LITTLE BLACK SAMBO, also
    SQUATTING BLACK BOY

BOY HEAD (TYPE I) - (M) - Approx. 2½" - He has thick wavy hair that frames his face. It is parted on the right side. (p313b, OP, R2) $80.00-95.00

BOY HEAD (TYPE II) - (M) - Approx. 2¾" - His wavy hair appears to be parted on his left side and one curly lock hangs onto the forehead. (p297c, OP, R2-3) $70.00-85.00

BOY HEAD (TYPE III) - see BABY JESUS HEAD

BOY HEAD IN A TOBOGGAN HAT - (M) - Approx. 3" - The short hat has a pom-pom on the front and has a dimpled "fur" edge. Under the boy's chin is a small ruffled collar. A curl of hair hangs onto the forehead. The reverse shows the boy's hair. This piece is often confused with the boy clown head. The clown head does not have the curl of hair on the forehead. (p317b, OP, R3) $65.00-80.00

BOY HEAD RATTLE (DOUBLEFACED) - (M&FB) - Approx. 6½" overall, 2½" head only - The baby boy is shown in a nightcap with bangs hanging down. One side shows a smiling face, the other a crying face. The pike comes out of the chin area. It is likely that this piece could also be found as a clip-on. (p337a & 338a, OP, R1)
                                Clip-on $200.00-225.00
                                Rattle $250.00-275.00

BOY HEAD WITH A CROWN - "THE PRINCE" - (M) - Approx. 2¼" - The small boy's head wears a crown with four peaks. The center of the crown rises up in a cone shape to the ornament's cap. Hair shows along the sides and in the back. This piece has also been referred to as Jesus, the Prince of Peace. (p311b, OP, R2) $80.00-90.00

VARIATION #1: THE PRINCE WITH CHENILLE ARMS AND LEGS - (M&FB) - Approx. 4¼" glass, 5½" with chenille legs. The molded head is attached to a free-blown body in the shape of an egg. Chenille arms and legs are fastened into indents in this "body". (p312b, OP, R1-2) $225.00-250.00

VARIATION #2: - THE PRINCE ON STYLIZED BODY - (M&FB) - Approx. 5¼" - The molded head is blown onto an oval shape, that may represent his body. Many pieces also have an angel hair "collar" around the prince's neck. (p312a, OP, R1-2) $125.00-150.00

VARIATION #3: PRINCE HEAD ON A BALL - (M&FB) - The same head is annealed onto a free-blown ball. Because the ball may vary, the sizes may change. (p311a, OP, R1-2) $100.00-125.00

BOY IN A BAG - (M) - Approx. 3" & 3½" - A boy's head with short curly hair rises out of a round bottomed bag. The bag is tied with a ribbon and bow and has a ruffled opening at the top. This piece is sometimes confused with its companion piece "A GIRL IN A BAG". However, her hair is longer. (Germany, p343a & 344a, OP, R3)
                                        $60.00-85.00

BOY IN A FLOWER BASKET - (M) - Approx. 2¼" & 3½" - The boy rises from the stomach up out of a wicker basket of flowers. All around his waistline are embossed daisies. He wears a hat, a shirt with a wide collar and holds a small stick in his right hand. This same piece was made as a celluloid pull toy with metal wheels. (Germany, p287d, OP, R2)   Small $35.00-55.00
                                Large $60.00-70.00

BOY IN A NIGHTCAP - (M) - Approx. 2½" & 3" - The boy head shown to the chin wears a nightcap with a tassel end hanging down the left side of his head. A curl of hair shows on his forehead and around the edges of the cap. (Czech. p320a, OP-NP, R3-4) $80.00-90.00

VARIATION: BOY IN A NIGHTCAP RATTLE - (M) - Approx. 5½" overall, 2½" for the head - This is the same head described above, but the pike has been left on to form the handle of the baby rattle. Small pebbles have also been inserted to make it "rattle" when shaken. (Czech., p297b, OP, R2) $150.00-175.00

BOY IN A NIGHTCAP WITH A NECK - (M) - Approx. 3" - This is similar to the above piece, except his neck shows beneath the chin. His cap is taller than the one above, but the tassel is still on his left side. Locks of hair show around the edges of the cap. (p297a, OP, R2) $90.00-110.00

BOY IN A SLED - (M) - Approx. 3½" & 4" - The boy carries the sled on his back with his arms through the runners. He wears a toboggan hat and sweater. His arms, legs and feet show at the side of the ornament. The flat riding boards of the sled show on the back of this nicely detailed piece. The mold is now in East Germany. (German, p351b & 352, OP-NP [limited, both sizes], R1-2) $150.00-175.00

BOY OR CHILD IN A SNOWSUIT - (M) - Approx. 4" - The child, the exact sex is hard to determine, is in a snowsuit with a round, tight-fitting hood that ties under the chin. The entire snowsuit has dimpled effect. The right

has been called Santa and Jack Frost. (Germany, p385a, p385b, OP, R2-3)

Small $60.00-80.00
Large $125.00-150.00

FACE IN A PINE CONE (TYPE I) - (M) - Approx. 3½″ - In this long, slender piece, the pine cone effect covers most of the ornament except for a small part in front where the face appears. The face has a long beard and a handlebar mustache. It has been called a Santa in a pine cone, although there is no hat or anything else to indicate it is a Santa. (Germany, p386b, OP-NP, R2-3) $90.00-100.00

FACE IN A PINE CONE (CRUDE) (TYPE II) - (M) - Approx. 3″ - This appears to be a crude copy of the above piece. Neither the face nor beard are deeply embossed or detailed. Both are usually painted. This is probably not a German piece; in fact, Rogers suggested it is Japanese. Also see - "PINE CONE MAN". (OP, R2-3) $40.00-50.00

GIRL IN A BASKET OF FLOWERS - see ANGEL IN A BASKET

GIRL HEAD IN A LARGE PETALED FLOWER - (M) - Approx. 2½″ - This girl with long flowing hair is embossed into the center of a large petaled flower, which is perhaps a rose. The back is veined to resemble a leaf. The overall shape of this piece is round. (Germany, p392c & 396b, OP, R2-3) $125.00-150.00

GIRL IN A TULIP - (M) - Approx. 3½″ - In this chubby looking piece, the girl's head rises out of the flower. Long hair frames her face and the double layer of flower petals is highly detailed. This piece has also been called "Thumbelina". (Germany, p391c, OP, R2) $125.00-150.00

GIRL WITH A HAT IN A TULIP - (M) - Approx. 3¼″ - This girl's head, in a bonnet with a ruffled edge, rises out of a four petaled tulip. Both the head and petals are nicely detailed, and it may be found as a clip-on. (p393a, OP, R2) $175.00-200.00

GIRL'S BUST IN A FLOWER - (M) - Approx. 2½″ - This girl with long wavy hair is shown to the shoulders and appears to have a ruffled collar. The stylized flower has six petals. This piece has also been called "Thumbelina" and is often found as a clip-on. (Germany, p390, OP, R2-3) $125.00-150.00

GIRL'S HEAD IN A DAISY - (M) - Approx. 2½″ - A girl's face with short wavy hair is embossed into the center of a daisy with the petals radiating out from her face. The reverse side shows the full flower. (p392a, OP, R2) $90.00-100.00

GIRL'S HEAD ON A ROSE - (M) - Approx. 2½″ dia. - The head with short wavy hair rises out of the center of a rose with swirled petals. There is nice detailing on the face and rose. There is an embossed flower on the back. (Germany, OP, R1-2) $150.00-175.00

GIRL FACES IN AN EGG - (M) - Approx. 3¼″ - The girl appears to be emerging from the front of an egg shell which frames her face. The reverse shows the same except the face is slightly different. The ornament has an overall egg shape to it. (p314a, OP, R1-2) $150.00-175.00

JACK-O'-LANTERN - (M) - Approx. 2¼″ - This round piece is ribbed to resemble a pumpkin. It has large rounded eyes, a triangle nose and a wide smiling mouth, which are embossed. (p395c, OP, R2) $150.00-175.00

PARSNIP FACE - (M) - Approx. 4″ - The piece is creased and dimpled to show that it is a root crop. The smiling face is nicely detailed but has no outline of a head. Four leaves show at the top. (Germany, p388, OP, R1) $250.00-275.00

GIRL'S HEAD IN A PEAR - (M) - Approx. 3″ - The whole head of this girl with short hair is embossed onto the pear. Above her head is a branch with two large leaves that come down on either side of the head. The girl has a worried look. (Germany, p95b & p400a, OP-NP, R2) $125.00-150.00

PEAR FACE - (M) - Approx. 2″ & 2¾″ - The eyes, nose and mouth show but there is no head outlined. A branch, with two leaves, shows above the face. (Germany, p396a & p400b, OP, R2)

Small $90.00-100.00
Large $125.00-150.00

VARIATION: PEAR FACE WITH "BUMPS" - (M) - Approx. 2″ - This is the same as the above described pieces, except it is covered with small, raised bumps. There are no known early pieces. (West Germany, NP) $2.00-10.00

"PEAR MAN" - (M) - Approx. 3″ - The large deeply embossed face covers the front of the pear and makes it look as though it is a man's head in the shape of a pear. (Germany, p395a, OP, R1-2) $150.00-175.00

PEAR WITH A CLOWN FACE - (M) - Approx. 2½″ - The face is reminiscent of a jack-o'-lantern with its round eyes, triangle nose and wide grinning mouth. (p397a, OP, R1) $75.00-90.00

PIERRE STRAWBERRY - (M) - Approx. 3½″ - This man's head with a thin mustache and a small beard on the chin, rises out of a strawberry. This mustache and beard give him a French look. Embossed leaves around the top of the berry form a kind of collar for him. His head shows no detailing for hair. (Germany, p393b, OP, R1) $300.00-325.00

PINE CONE MAN - (M) - Approx. 3″ - In this chubby looking pine cone, the eyes, nose and mouth show but it has no beard. It has two arms; the left rests at the stomach and the right at the chest. (Germany, p386a, OP, R1) $125.00-150.00

POPCORN HEAD - (M) - Approx. 2½″ & 3″ dia. - The head is rounded and covered with large raised bumps like a kernel of popcorn or a popcorn ball. The face is jack-o'-lantern-like with round eyes, a triangle nose and a wide smiling mouth. (Germany, p389 & p395b, OP, R2)

Small $200.00-250.00
Large $300.00-350.00

"SOUR GRAPES" - (M) - Approx. 2½″ & 3¾″ - This is a full head embossed into a bunch of grapes. A small hat with a tassel shows under the large grape leaves at the top. The man's mouth is twisted in a sour expression. (Germany, p387, OP, R1-2)

Small $175.00-200.00
Large $250.00-300.00

84

FACES IN MUSHROOMS see GNOMES, DWARVES & MUSHROOM PEOPLE

Santa Claus

To children and grown-ups alike, the figure of Santa Claus embodies the spirit of the Christmas legend. Down through the years, the Santa figure has been extremely popular with both the ornament maker and the buying public. Because of this, he was portrayed in a wide variety of forms, as well as variations on a standard form. In German traditions, Santa Claus is represented in one of four ways:

1. St. Nicholas - This form usually wears a bishops' hat and vestments, carries a staff or shepherds' crook and has a cross on his chest. Although many early figural Christmas lights were made as St. Nicholas, no known ornaments were blown in this form. This could possibly be accounted for by the fact that St. Nicholas' Day comes early in the month of December before the tree is up.

2. Father Christmas - In tradition there is very little difference between Father Christmas and just plain Santa Claus. Both are the legendary figures of Christmas Eve, who bring the toys, goodies and in German tradition, the tree itself. This is why many Santa ornaments are depicted carrying a tree. In the molded ornament, Father Christmas is usually dressed in a knee length coat, with a hood and possibly an elbow length cape. Father Christmas is often portrayed as a slender old man with a stern expression.

3. Santa Claus or Weihnachtsman - According to tradition, the name "Santa Claus" started with the early Dutch and English settlers of New England. The English interpreted the heavily accented Dutch pronounciation of St. Nicholas as "Santa Claus". He was also known to the Dutch as "Sinterklaas" - again a name easily corrupted into the English Santa Claus. In this ornament form, Santa is molded with a waist or hip length coat, and cap-like hat. This is the image of Santa Claus that was to be fully developed in the United States based on the famous drawings of Thomas Nast. Although the Santa and Father Chrismas ornaments could have been molded and blown as contemporary pieces, the Father Christmas is an older **form**.

4. Christkind, Christkindle, Kriskindle, Kris Kringle - Literally, this is the "Christ Child" or the spirit of the Christ Child or the Spirit of Christmas. Down through many years and the blending of many traditions, we find the "Kriskindle" represented not only as another version of Santa, but also as a benevolent dwarf, elf, fairy, etc. This is why the American Santa has elf helpers and why dwarves, gnomes, elves and fairies play an important role in Christmas ornaments. These "Kriskindle" type ornaments will not be listed in this section. The reader will find them catalogued under Dwarves, Gnomes, Elves, etc.

NOTES:

1. On some ornaments it is difficult to tell a Santa from an elf, gnome, dwarf, "mountain man" (He was popular in German folk tales as an old bearded, hermit-like figure. The grandfather figure in **Heidi** is a good representation), or simply a bearded old man unless the traditional Santa suit is present. In the past, any long bearded character has been typically referred to as a Santa. I have tried to make distinctions whenever possible.

2. Lithograph paper "scraps" of Father Christmas and Santa Claus are often added to other objects such as balloons and gondolas. This section deals with the blown glass Santas only. Paper Santas added to other objects will be discussed in their relative sections.

3. Santas colored in gold, green, blue or any color other than the traditional **red** are somewhat rarer.

STANDARD FORM SANTA CLAUS - (M) - Approx. 2" to 5½" - This form has many separate variations, showing they were made in separate molds. However, many variations are very slight and are often based on the shape of the beard, width of the ornament, how far down the cap comes, etc. Major variations will be listed separately. In this "standard form", Santa is shown three-quarters length or about from the hip up. He wears a cap and a hip length coat, with no legs or feet showing. He carries an undecorated Christmas tree at his left shoulder. He may have a cap and hanger in the top of the head or a clip-on at the base. Clip-ons are slightly more desirable. (Usually Germany, p353, p354b, p354e & p359a, OP-NP, R4-5)

Standard 3" $25.00-35.00
Larger Sizes $40.00-60.00
Clip-ons add $ 5.00-10.00

VARIATION #1: Father Christmas form - (M) - 3" to 5½" - Same basic form as above, however, the coat appears to be longer and the cap is a hood that comes all the way down in the back and attaches to the coat (no head or hair show in the back). This is only slightly rarer than the standard form. (Usually Germany, p357a, OP-NP, R4)

Standard $25.00-35.00
Larger $40.00-60.00
Clip-ons add $ 5.00-10.00

VARIATION #2: Stern faced Father Christmas - (M) - 3" to 5½" - This is a separate set of moldings based on the above listed Father Christmas. In this form he has an angry, frowning or stern expression on his face. This is somewhat rarer than the above two forms. (Germany, p364b, OP, R3-4)

Small $35.00-45.00
Large $50.00-65.00

SANTA WITH A BASKET (TYPE I) - (M) - Approx. 4" - This Santa carries no tree. His hands are clasped at the waist, and he carries a small basket on the right forearm. He wears a small cape that covers the shoulders. This is an early piece. (Germany, p354c, OP, R3) $40.00-50.00

SANTA WITH A BASKET (TYPE II) - (M) - Approx. 3½" - His arms are at the waist with the hands in opposite sleeves. The basket is on the right forearm, and his hat is conical shaped. (Snyder p134, OP, R3) $30.00-45.00

FROWNING SANTA WITH A BASKET - (M) - Approx. 3" - This Santa with a frown or stern expression carries the basket over his left arm. His hands are butted together at the waist, and he wears a hooded cap. (p365c, OP, R3)
$35.00-45.00

SANTA WITH HIS HANDS IN HIS SLEEVES - (M) - Approx. 2½", 3" & 3½" - This one carries no tree, basket or bag. Arms are at the waist, and his hands do not show as they are placed on the sleeve of the opposite arm. (Germany, Austria and Czech., p354a, d & 360a, b, c & p364a, OP, R4)
$25.00-35.00

JAPANESE SANTA WITH HANDS IN HIS SLEEVES - (M) - Approx. 2″ - This is in the same style as above only smaller, cruder and of heavier glass. (Japan, p350a, OP, R4) $10.00-15.00

JAPANESE SANTA WITH A TREE - (M) - Approx. 4″ - This piece is remarkably well made and detailed. It resembles the German Father Christmas with a hood instead of a cap and carries a tree at the left shoulder. The glass is thicker than in European pieces. (Japan, p365b, OP, R2-3) $75.00-85.00

SANTA WITH LARGE BAG - (M) - Approx. 3″ - This is similar to a standard form Santa, however, he carries a large sack over his left shoulder and has no tree. (Germany, molds now in East Germany, p359c, OP-NP [limited], R3) $25.00-30.00

SANTA WITH A TREE AND DRUM - (M) - Approx. 3¾″ - This hooded Santa with a long beard, has a tree at his left shoulder and carries a small drum in his right. (p363a, OP, R2) $50.00-60.00

FATHER CHRISTMAS HOLDING A SMALL BAG (TYPE I) - (M) - Approx. 3¼″ & 4¾″ - This piece is popularly called ''The Weihnachtsman''. He has a long coat with an elbow-length cape. He holds a small sack in his right hand. His long beard hangs below his belt. (Germany, p364c, OP, R3) Small $75.00-90.00 Large $100.00-125.00

FATHER CHRISTMAS HOLDING A SMALL BAG (TYPE II) - (M) - Approx. 4½″L x 2¾″W - This is very similar to the above except it is not German and is less detailed. The base ends in rounded ''feet''. (p362a, OP, R2-3) $75.00-85.00

FATHER CHRISTMAS WITH A BAG AND TREE - (M) - Approx. 3½″ - He holds a small bag or purse of ''goodies'' in the right hand and a stylized tree at the left shoulder. He holds a small doll in the left hand. Clip-on. (Germany, p357a, OP, R1-2) $75.00-100.00

ROLY-POLY SANTA - (M) - Approx. 3″ - This Santa is shown to the waist which has been rounded to give him a roly-poly look. He has a long beard, his hands rest on his stomach, and his right one holds a doll. (p369a, OP, R1-2) $80.00-90.00

ROLY-POLY SANTA WITH A HEART - (M) - Approx. 4″ - Shown to a rounded waist, this Santa has a roly-poly look. Both hands rest on the stomach area, and he holds a heart in his right hand. (p363b, OP, R2) $80.00-90.00

''SQUARE'' SANTA WITH TREE AND BAG - (M) - Approx. 4½″ - This broad shouldered Santa has a square appearance. He holds a tree in the right hand and a bag over the left shoulder. (**Not** German, p362b, OP, R3) $60.00-70.00

STOOPED OVER FATHER CHRISTMAS - (M) - Approx. 2¾″ & 3½″ - He is dressed in the traditional suit and has a pack over the right shoulder. He is shown in the standard length but bent in the middle, appearing to be stooped over from the weight of the pack. The smaller size is rarer. (Germany, p365a, OP, R2-3) Small $75.00-85.00 Large $85.00-95.00

SANTA WITH A SCRAP FACE - (M) - Approx. 4½″ - Early German, the Santa figure is frosted. (Germany, OP, R1) $125.00-150.00

SANTA WITH A SCRAP FACE - (M) - Approx. 3¾″ - Santa shown in traditional fur trimmed hat and coat coming down to the hips. One arm hangs at side, the other is across his stomach. The scrap face is of Father Christmas. (Germany, p361a, OP, R1-2) $125.00-150.00

VARIATION: This is similar to the above, except Father Christmas wears a hood that comes down to a small cape on his shoulders. (Germany, p292c & 361b, OP, R1-2) $125.00-150.00

SANTA AND ANGEL DOUBLE SIDED ORNAMENT - (M) - Approx. 3½″ - A standard form Santa with a tree is on one side, and a chubby girl angel is on the other. She has a tree in the right arm and a star in the left. (Germany, p243, OP-NP, R1) $125.00-150.00

SANTA WITH AN ACORN CAP - (M) - Approx. 4″ - This piece is made of heavy glass and has no delicate molding. The base is rounded, and his hands are at his chest. His cap is rounded and ribbed like an acorn cap. This is not a German piece; it may be early Japanese or American. (p380c, OP, R2-3) $60.00-75.00

PARACHUTING SANTA - (M&FB) - Approx. 8½″ - The Santa is a 3″ standard form. The parachute is made from a free-blown ball with the bottom side completely indented to give it the chute effect. The Santa is attached to the ''chute'' by four ribbons. Also see Santa in a Parachute. (Germany, NP - limited) $15.00-20.00

SANTA RIDING A HORSE - (M) - Approx. 3″H x 2½″L - Santa leans forward against the horse's neck and carries a small bag on his back. Grass is molded around the legs of the horse, and it is not free standing. Clip-on. (Germany, p378b, OP-NP [NP very limited], R1-2) $250.00-275.00 NP $5.00-10.00

SANTA UNDER A MUSHROOM CAP - (M&FB) - Approx. 4½″ - This is a standard form 3″ Santa under a large free-blown mushroom cap which is made from a ball shape that has been indented at the bottom. Santa is attached to the ''mushroom'' by a short neck of glass. (Germany, OP, R2) $90.00-100.00

SANTA BELL - (M) - Approx. 2½″ - This is a small standard form Santa in which the bottom has been deeply indented. This gave the Santa a typical bell shape. A glass clapper was then added. (Germany, OP, R1) $75.00-90.00

Santa With Legs

The majority of Santas are of three quarter length and no legs or feet show; however, in a few types - legs and feet are stylisticly or accurately added.

SANTA WITH ANNEALED ARMS AND LEGS - (M&FB) - Approx. 4″ - The head and lower body are molded, then hollow, tubular arms and legs were annealed on. Although it is reminiscent of modern Italian ornaments, it is in fact early German. (Germany, Rogers p181, OP, R1-2) $350.00-400.00

SANTA WITH ANNEALED LEGS - (M&FB) - Approx. 3¾" - This early Santa has his arms in his sleeves and wears a hood. Free-blown legs are annealed onto the bottom. (p368b, OP, R1) $275.00-300.00

SANTA WITH BAG AND TOYS - (M) - Approx. 3¾" - He carries a large sack over the right shoulder and back. There are a drum and doll molded on his stomach area. Below the coat, the "feet" end in a square shape. (p362c, OP, R3-4) $50.00-60.00

SANTA WITH CHENILLE LEGS - (M) - Approx. 4½" & 5"; Overall glass bodies 3¾" and 3" - This is a standard form Santa down to the bottom of the coat. Here the ornament has been slightly indented and chenille legs with composition boots added. This is not as rare as originally believed. (Germany, p357b, p367a & p367b, OP, R3)
Small $100.00-125.00
Large $150.00-175.00

SANTA WITH LEGS - (M) - Approx. 3½" - Santa carries a tree at the left shoulder, and short stubby legs show below the hip length coat. The boots, however, do not show as the legs blend to a rounded base. (Germany, Snyder, p134c, OP, R3-4) $40.00-50.00

AMERICAN SANTA WITH A TREE - (M) - Approx. 4½" - This shows a "younger-jollier" type Santa that is typically American. The beard is shorter, and the coat goes only to the waist area. The glass is heavier than in German ornaments. It has also been suggested that this is a Japanese piece. (U.S., p366a, OP, R2) $50.00-75.00

AMERICAN SANTA - (M) - Approx. 3" - He wears a waist length coat that is belted and shows three buttons. His beard is short. His right hand is at the belt, and his left is at the side. The tassel of his cap hangs in the back. The glass is heavy and has no delicate details. It was possibly made by Corning Glass from 1939-1940. (U.S., p366b & p451a, OP, R2) $35.00-45.00

SANTA IN AN AUTOMOBILE - (M) - Approx. 3¼" - The car has no top, and Santa is seen from the chest up in the front. The back is full of toys. There is also another known version of a Santa in a car. (p376, OP, R1) $225.00-250.00

Santa In Various Items

SANTA IN A BALL (TYPE I) - (M&FB) - Approx. 3½" to 4" - A molded Santa head from about the **chin** up, rises out of a free-blown ball. (p382b, OP, R3-4) $45.00-55.00

SANTA IN A BALL (TYPE II) - (M&FB) - Similar to the above ornament, however, the Santa is slenderer and the ball smaller. Not as wide a piece as Type I. (p382a, OP, R3-4) $60.00-75.00

SANTA IN A BALL (TYPE III) - (M&FB) - Similar to the above two ornaments except Santa is shown from the **chest** up. This is a more detailed piece. (p382c, OP, R3) $70.00-85.00

SANTA IN A BALL (TYPE IV) - (M&FB) - Approx. 4" - This molded Santa rises from the free-blown ball from the **stomach** up. His arms show and the hands are in the sleeves. Nice detail. (Snyder p134, OP, R3) $60.00-70.00

SANTA ON A BALL (TYPE I) - (M&FB) - Approx. 5" - Sizes may vary with free-blown ball - This ornament shows the standard Santa from head to knee area, on a free-blown ball. The Santa is attached to the ball by a short neck or pike. (p381a, OP, R3) $125.00-150.00

SANTA ON A BALL (TYPE II) - (M&FB) - Approx. 4½" - This is similar to the above, except the free-blown ball is indented on the bottom. This flattened area would also allow it to stand as a table or mantle decoration. A small glass clapper may have been inserted inside, thus making this a Santa bell. (Germany, p381b, OP, R3, Bell R2)
$125.00-150.00
Bell $135.00-155.00

SANTA ON A BALL (TYPE III) - (M&FB) - Approx. 5" - Sizes will vary with size of the ball - This piece is similar to a "bird on a nest" ornament. A free-blown ball is indented at the top. Cotton and a molded Santa are held in the indentation with crinkle wire. It has a tinsel hoop for a hanger. (Rogers p180c, OP, R3) $60.00-70.00

SANTA ON A BALL (TYPE IV) - (M&FB) - Approx. 3¾" - This standard form Santa is similar to the above except the free-blown ball is small and in proportion with the body. It is also indented on the bottom. (Germany, p380a, OP, R2) $90.00-100.00

DOUBLE SANTA ON A BALL - (M) - Approx. 4½" - The Santa is double sided with his hands in his sleeves. He rises from the waist up out of a free-blown ball. (Germany, p358, OP, R1-2) $75.00-85.00

SANTA IN A BALLOON - (M&FB) - Approx. 4½" overall, Santa 2" - This molded Santa with his hands in his sleeves forms the center between two free-blown ball shapes. This early piece was also wire wrapped similar to early balloons. (p355, OP, R1) $90.00-100.00

SANTA IN A BASKET (TYPE I) - (M) - Approx. 3" - In this squat looking piece, Santa arises from chin up, out of a woven basket. His arms rest on the front edge of the basket, but not all of his beard shows. The basket has molded on it what at first glance appears to be a poinsettia type flower. However, closer examination shows that this is a boy dressed in a hooded monk's robe with arms and legs spread. This is the symbol for the City of Munich. (Germany, p379c, OP-NP, [NP limited], R3-4) $70.00-80.00

SANTA IN A BASKET (TYPE II) - (M) - Approx. 2", 3" & 3½" - This is similar to the above. However, Santa appears from the lower chest up, thus making the ornament taller and slenderer. There is no "Munich Boy" on the woven basket. (p378c, OP, R3-4) $70.00-80.00

SANTA AT THE CHIMNEY - (M) - Approx. 3" - He is shown kneeling beside the chimney and dropping down toys. Below him, a "cut away" of the chimney shows a doll falling through it. This is a finely detailed piece. (Germany, p378a, OP, R1) $150.00-175.00

SANTA IN A CHIMNEY WITH A LEDGE (TYPE I) - (M) - Approx. 3" - From the chest up, a standard form Santa rises from a round brick chimney. He carries a tree at the left shoulder. The second row of bricks stick out forming a ledge or lip around the chimney. There are six to seven large bricks on each layer of the chimney. (Germany, p383c, OP-NP [early & few], R3-4) $75.00-85.00

SANTA IN A CHIMNEY (TYPE II) - (M) - Approx. 3″ - Similar to the above, except not as large in diameter. The second row is smooth with the rest and does not form a ledge. The Santa has good detailing, and his cap has a fur trim that the above Santa does not. There are several slightly different moldings of this piece. (Germany, p383b, OP, R3-4) $50.00-70.00

SANTA IN A SQUARE CHIMNEY - (M) - Approx. 4¼″ - The chimney is a square or diamond shape. Santa rises from it chest high. He has a bag and presents over his right shoulder. His left hand is on the chimney. (Germany, NP, R4) $2.00-10.00

SANTA IN A COACH - (M) - Approx. 3″H x 2½″W - A Santa head with cap rises from the roof of a coach. The head is poorly molded; the beard and hair spread out over the roof. The coach is oval shaped and has four spoked wheels and a window in the center of each side. This has also been called a "Santa in a Tank". (Germany, p377b, OP-NP [very limited], R2) $150.00-175.00

SANTA IN A PARACHUTE - (M) - Approx. 3″ - Santa hangs from an open parachute. He has a tree in his right arm, and both hands are at his chest. (Germany, p377c, OP-NP [limited], R1) $150.00-175.00

SANTA IN A STOCKING - (M) - Approx. 3½″ - This is similar to the clown in a stocking ornament. Santa rises chest high out of what looks like a knitted sock. He has a tree at the right shoulder. (Czech., p380b, OP-NP, R1-2) $70.00-80.00

SANTA IN A TINSEL WREATH - (M) - Approx. 2½″ & 3″ for the Santa - This Santa has holes in the head and base through which passes a wire that holds it in the center of a tinsel wreath. He usually has his hands in his sleeves. A tree carrying, standard form Santa is a rarer form. (p356 & p359b, OP, R4, Large R3)   Small $30.00-40.00
Large $35.00-45.00

SANTA IN A WINDOW - (M) - Approx. 3½″ - This is a ball shape with a "window" in which is a Santa head. Two pine trees are on either side. The back has a small closed window. The bottom has a smaller blown out ball. The figure could also be an elf, dwarf or mountain man. (Germany, OP, R2) $80.00-90.00

SANTA IN A GLASS TRIANGLE - (M&FB) - Approx. 3″ - A miniature Santa is framed by a glass triangle of annealed glass. (Germany, p350b, OP, R1-2) $35.00-40.00

Santas Embossed Onto Other Things:

With the popularity and salability of Santa Claus, it was only natural that they be applied or molded onto other shapes. These are scarcer than standard form Santas.

FATHER CHRISTMAS ON AN EGG SHAPE - (M) - Approx. 3½″ - He stands full bodied on the front of the egg-shape, holding a tree in the right hand and "goodies" in the left. The reverse has a branch embossed on it. (Germany, p375c, OP, R2-3) $45.00-60.00

SANTA ON AN EGG SHAPE - (M) - Approx. 3¼″ - He holds a tree at his right shoulder. On the back is a pine branch with three pine cones. (p350c, OP, R3)$25.00-35.00

SANTA ON A HEART - (M) - Approx. 3″L x 2½″W - The face, beard and hat are molded onto the heart with lines radiating outward from the face. The reverse side has lines similar to a clamshell . (Germany, p379a, OP-NP, R2-3) $50.00-75.00

SANTA INDENT - (M&FB) - Approx. 4″ - Sizes may vary - A molded Santa is embossed onto a free-blown shape. The bowlegged Santa carries a bag of goodies over his right shoulder. (Germany, p374a, OP, R2-3) $25.00-35.00

SANTA IN A SLED - (M) - Approx. 3½″ - This piece is molded like the boy in a sled piece. Santa carries the sled on his back with his arms through the runners. The riding boards show on the back. Santa has a long beard and wears a fur trimmed hat and coat. If made by the same glassblower who made the "Boy in the Sled", the molds would be in East Germany. (Germany, p351a, OP, R1) $300.00-350.00

SANTA ON A LEAF - (M) - Approx. 3″ - A full bodied, standing Santa is portrayed on a stylized leaf. He holds a crude tree in the right hand and a small bag in the left. The reverse is the same as the front. (p375a & p451c, OP, R2-3) $35.00-45.00

FATHER CHRISTMAS ON AN OAK LEAF - (M) - Approx. 3½″ - He is shown from the hips up and molded on a stylized leaf. The back shows the leaf pattern. (U.S., p374b, OP, R3) $35.00-45.00

FATHER CHRISTMAS ON A PINE CONE - (M) - Approx. 4½″ - He is shown standing embossed on the pine cone. He holds nothing. Little detail. (p375b, OP, R2-3) $40.00-50.00

SANTA **FACE** ON A PINE CONE - see FACE IN A PINE CONE

SANTA **HEAD** ON A PINE CONE - (M) - Approx. 3¼″ - This pine cone has leaves at the top. The head has a cone shaped hat and long beard. This could also be a dwarf or "mountain man". (Germany, Rogers p84, OP, R2-3) $65.00-75.00

VARIATION: SMALL HEAD ON A PINE CONE - (M) - Approx. 3½″ - This is very similar to the above described piece; however, the embossed head is smaller allowing more of the pine cone to show. (Germany, p373c, OP, R2) $65.00-75.00

SANTA **IN** A PINE CONE - (M) - Approx. 3½″ - He rises from the chest up out of a pine cone. He wears a Father Christmas type hood. Arms and hands show at the top of the cone. The cone has four leaves at the base. Santa's back is "bumpy", but the hood is smooth. He could also be a dwarf. (p262c, OP-NP [limited], R1) $75.00-100.00

SANTA ON AN OVAL - (M) - Approx. 2½″ - Oval shape with two large panels on each side. A standing Santa with a bag and tree on one side and a tree with candles on the other. (p373c, OP, R2-3) $25.00-35.00

SANTA HEAD PIPE - (M&FB) - Approx. 6″ - Santa's head and beard form the bowl of this early pipe. Because the stem was free-blown, it could be longer or shorter, straight or bent. (Germany, OP, R1) $230.00-250.00

SANTA FACE ON A PINE TREE - (M) - Approx. 3″ - The face, with no hat, is embossed into the upper part of what appears to be a standard pine tree. His beard flows nearly to the base. The embossing is not deep nor detailed. (p384b, OP-NP, R1-2) $75.00-90.00

SANTA FACE UNDER A PINE TREE - (M) - Approx. 3½″ - An inch high Santa face is molded at the base of the tree with three molded mushrooms around the sides and back. (Germany, p379b & p438c, OP, R3) $90.00-100.00

Santa Heads

Santa heads are considered more desirable than most other Santa forms; they are also rarer. The heads are often in an oval or egg shape. Santa forms usually have the traditional fur cap perched atop their heads and hair showing in the back of the head. Father Christmas forms usually have the hood coming all the way down the back of the head and sometimes even under the chin.

STANDARD FATHER CHRISTMAS HEAD - (M) - Approx. 1½″, 2½″ & 3½″ - It is oval shaped. The hood encases the entire head and may have frosting/crushed glass trim. (Germany, p370b, p370c & p372b, OP-NP [only the medium size was reproduced. It was limited to 1940s and 1950s], Small & large R3, Medium R3-4)
Small $35.00-45.00
Medium $50.00-65.00
Large $75.00-90.00

VARIATION: FATHER CHRISTMAS HEAD - (M) - Approx. 2½″ - It has the same oval shape and hood; but the face is longer, and may be flesh painted. This has the appearance of being larger than the medium of above. (p372c, OP-NP, [limited to 1940s and 1950s], R3-4) $35.00-45.00

FATHER CHRISTMAS HEAD WITH GLASS EYES - (M) - Approx. 3½″ - The head is egg shaped and surrounded by the hood. He has a beard and well defined mustache. It may be found as a clip-on. (Germany, p368a & p370a, OP, R1-2) $175.00-200.00

SANTA HEAD WITH GLASS EYES - (M) - Approx. 3½″ - This piece has an overall pine cone shape. His fur trimmed cap has "flaps" which cover the ears. He has a long pointed beard and blown glass eyes. (Germany, p368c, OP, R1-2) $175.00-200.00

JOLLY SANTA IN A TASSEL CAP (TYPE I) - (M) - Approx. 3½″ - He has a short beard with large round cheeks and nose. The cap has a small rounded fur trim and the tassel is on the right side. (p367c & p370d, OP-NP, R3-4) $45.00-55.00

JOLLY SANTA IN A TASSEL CAP (TYPE II) - (M) - Approx. 3½″ - Similar to the above except the fur on the cap is much wider, and the cap and tassel hang down the left side. He looks like the modern American Santa. Newer

pieces show the mold was broken and repaired on the reverse side. (Germany, p372d, OP-NP, R3) $45.00-55.00

CZECH SANTA HEAD - (M) - Approx. 3″ - This head is flatter and wider than many others and with plain cap has a seashell type look. The cap comes halfway down the back, the rest is "hair". Beard and hair may be frosted. (Czechoslovakia, p372a, OP-NP, R3) $35.00-45.00

DOUBLE FACED SANTA HEAD - (M) - Approx. 2¾″ - The Santa is shown in a round fur cap and has a long flowing beard. The same face is on both sides. (OP-NP, R1) $75.00-90.00

DOUBLE FACED SANTA IN A TINSEL WREATH - (M) - The overall size is approx. 5″, however, the molded Santa head is only about 1½″ - The same cap covers both heads. This can also be found as a small ornament or strung together to form a short strand of "beads".
(OP, R2-3) Tinsel form $30.00-40.00
(OP, R2-3) Ornament $25.00-30.00
(OP, R1) Beads $175.00-200.00

SANTA HEAD WITH A CAP - (M) - Approx. 3″ - This head wears a close-fitting cap with no trim or tassel. His face is excellently molded and detailed with a large mustache and eyebrows being prominent. The ornament has an overall egg shape and molded hair shows on the reverse. (Germany, p373a, OP, R2-3) $75.00-90.00

VARIATION: SANTA HEAD ON A PIKE - (M) - Approx. 4½″ - This is the same head described above. His chin or beard ends in a hollow blown "pike" that comes to a point and makes the beard look extra long. (Snyder p123, OP, R2) $150.00-175.00

SANTA HEAD WITH A LEAF CAP - (M) - Approx. 4″ - This head with a heavy mustache and beard wears a cap made of leaves or pine branches. It has an overall pine cone shape and has also been called "Jack Frost". (Germany, p371a, OP, R2) $250.00-275.00

SANTA IN A FUR CAP - (M) - Approx. 3¾″ - He wears a round pillbox shaped fur hat. His hair and beard are both short. As a slight variation, he may have a short pike extending from under the head. (p371b, OP, R1-2) $150.00-175.00

MINIATURE FATHER CHRISTMAS HEAD - (M) - Approx. 1″ - This shows the head inside a hood. It is part of a miniature set made for small trees. The mold is now in East Germany. (Germany, p442, OP-NP [1940s only], R2) $15.00-20.00

WEIHNACHTSMAN'S HEAD - (M) - Approx. 2″ x 1″, 3″, 3½″ x 1½″ & 4″ x 2″ - Most of the ornament is made up of a long flowing beard. A small, round fur trimmed cap is on the head. The cap has no "tail" or fur ball like American Santas. The reverse shows long flowing hair. Examination of the back of newer versions of the 4″ head show the mold was broken and repaired. (Germany & Czech., p372e & p372f, OP-NP, Small & Large R3-4, Medium R4)
Small & medium $55.00-65.00
Larger $65.00-75.00

Snowmen

A popular winter pastime in both Europe and America is the building of snowmen. Therefore, it is only natural that they would appear on the Christmas tree. Snowmen were also a popular form of figural lights.

STANDARD FORM:

SNOWMAN HOLDING A BROOM - (M) - Approx. 3", 3½" & 4" - These snowmen hold a broom, bristle end up, at the right shoulder. They wear a small cone shaped cap and have an elongated body, with a rounded head. Their arms meet at the chest, but no hands are shown. Many times they have a sandy or frosted finish. These were made in several different moldings with only minor changes. (p398b, p401a, b, c & d, OP-NP, R4) Small $20.00-30.00
Larger $25.00-35.00

AMERICAN SNOWMAN - (M) - Approx. 3½" - This American ornament is molded to look like three consecutively smaller balls stacked on top of each other. It is unsilvered heavy glass that has a matte white finish. It is less delicate, but rarer than the German form. (U.S., p402c, OP, R1-2) $40.00-50.00

DIMPLED SNOWMAN - (M) - Approx. 3" - This snowman is very similar to the standard form; however, it is more detailed. It has small "dimples" covering the body to simulate rough snow and a rounded cap with a small brim. The head is larger than the standard form, and he carries a broom in the right hand. (p398a & p399c, OP, R3-4) $35.00-45.00

SNOWMAN IN A CHIMNEY - (M) - Approx. 3" - This shows the standard form snowman from the waist up. The bottom is a round, bricked chimney with a ledge. It is similar to the Santa in a chimney except rarer. (Germany, p383a, OP, R1-2) $150.00-175.00

SNOWMAN CLOWN - see CLOWNS

SNOWMAN IN A BALL - (M&FB) - Approx. 5" overall, 3" for snowman - This snowman, without a broom, is molded with a large free-blown ball at the base. (p349, OP, R2) $75.00-100.00

SNOWMAN ON A BALL - (M&FB) - Approx. 3¾" - A snowman with a conical hat, two buttons, and a broom in the right hand stands on a free-blown ball. (Germany, p399a, OP, R2) $75.00-100.00

SNOWMAN WITH A BROOM IN A BALL - (M&FB) - Approx. 4" - This shows the standard form snowman from the waist up. The bottom is a large free-blown ball. This is similar to the Santa on a ball ornament except it is rarer. (Germany, p402a, OP, R2) $75.00-100.00

SNOWMAN WITH A CONCERTINA - (M) - Approx. 4" - His mouth is open as though singing. He plays the concertina with both hands. (p269a, NP [1950s only], R3) $25.00-35.00

SNOWMAN WITH A TOP HAT - (M) - Approx. 3¼" - He looks similar to the standard form and carries an upright broom at his right shoulder. He wears a battered top hat

and may represent Frosty the snowman. He may also be found as a clip-on. (OP, R2) $50.00-75.00

SNOWMAN WITH CHILDREN - (M) - Approx. 3¾" - The snowman has a ring of molded children dancing around it. Two well molded arms are bent in at the waist, and the left holds a broom. The rounded head has no molded cap. (Germany, Snyder p130, OP, R1) $400.00-450.00

WALKING SNOWMAN - (M) - Approx. 4½" - This long snowman has molded legs with one slightly in front of the other giving a "walking" appearance. He has a sprig of holly in one hand and a wide brim hat on his head. (Germany, p402b, NP [Blown in 1950s only], R3) $30.00-40.00

Women and Girls

ANGELIC GIRL - (M) - Approx. 3½" - She is dressed in what looks like a robe or nightgown with a square collar. Her left hand is at the collar, and her right is near the stomach area. Long, curly hair rests on her shoulders and comes down the back. (Germany, p341c, OP, R2) $75.00-100.00

BUST OF A LADY WITH FLOWERS - (M) - Approx. 3¼" - She is shown to the lower chest area although no arms show. Her long wavy hair comes down past the shoulders and completely covers the back of the ornament. There is a branch of three roses embossed across her chest. (Germany, p326c, OP-NP [Very limited], R1) $100.00-125.00

BUST OF A VICTORIAN GIRL - (M) - Approx. 2¾" - Although shown to the lower chest, no arms are shown. She has a ruffled collar and long wavy hair that comes onto the shoulder. In the back, her hair is tied in a bun and a ribbon shows. This piece is similar to the "Indian princess". (Germany, p326b, OP-NP [Very limited], R2) $125.00-150.00

BUST OF A VICTORIAN LADY IN A HEART - (M) - Approx. 3" - The ornament has an overall heart shape with extra geometric embossing along the sides. The silhouette lady's head is embossed in the center. The reverse side shows a slightly different head facing the opposite direction. (p392b, OP, R2) $80.00-100.00

DUTCH GIRL HEAD - (M) - Approx. 2", 2½" & 3½" - She wears a dutch hat that frames her face like a triangle. The front edges of the hat are shown folded back. Hair frames her face inside the hat. (Czech., p313a, OP-NP [limited to the 1950s], R2-3) Small $50.00-70.00
Medium $75.00-90.00
Large $125.00-150.00
1950s production $20.00-30.00

FLAPPER GIRL HEAD - (M) - Approx. 2¾" - She wears a close fitting hat that was popular during the 1920s. The edges of the hat appear turned back, and its seams join in the back of the girl's head which is seen best on the reverse. Her hair shows at the sides and forehead. (Germany, p315a, OP, R2-3) $125.00-150.00

"FLUFFY" - (M) - Approx. 3½" - This full length girl stands fluffing her long wavy hair. Her hands, up to the elbow, are in the hair. She wears a short sleeve nightgown, belted at the waist and with three embossed flowers or

stars. (Germany, p310c, OP-NP [Very limited], R1)
$150.00-175.00

BUST OF AN ART NOUVEAU LADY - (M) - Approx. 3″ - Her nicely detailed face is inset into her long hair which flows down across her shoulders. A flower is shown at her chest. She is very reminiscent of Art Nouveau ladies depicted in the statues and jewelry of the period. (Germany, p318c, OP, R2)
$150.00-175.00

BABY GIRL'S HEAD (TYPE I) - (M) - Approx. 2½″ - She has glass eyes and short hair. She has two bows in her hair on either side of the head. (Germany, p321b, OP, R2-3)
$70.00-80.00

BABY GIRL'S HEAD (TYPE II) - (M) - Approx. 2¾″ - She has glass eyes and is similar to the one above. She has a small ruffled collar below the chin. She has more hair and the bows are lower than in Type I. (p323b, OP, R2-3)
$75.00-90.00

GIRL'S HEAD (TYPE I) - (M) - Approx. 2½″ - She has glass eyes (they are missing in the pictured example). Curly hair frames her face and is shown on the reverse. (Germany, p321a, OP, R2-3)
$75.00-90.00

GIRL'S HEAD (TYPE II) - (M) - Approx. 2¾″ - Her wavy hair frames her face which is shown to the chin. Her uneven bangs are brushed to the right. Dimples show on either side of her mouth. (p314c, OP, R2)
$75.00-90.00

GIRL HEAD (TYPE III) - (M) - Approx. 2¼″ - She is shown to the chin with what looks like a ruffled collar under it. Her long straight hair is parted in the middle and has a slight flip on the ends. Her face shows little detail. This is a crudely done piece. (p319b, OP, R2)
$65.00-75.00

GIRL HEAD IN A HOOD WITH GLASS EYES - see LITTLE RED RIDING HOOD

GIRL HEAD WITH RIBBONS IN HER HAIR - see FICTIONAL CHARACTERS - GOLDILOCKS HEAD

GIRL HEAD IN A TOBOGGAN CAP - (M) - Approx. 2½″ - She has glass eyes and her face is framed by wavy hair. A small toboggan cap with a bow in front sits atop her head. Her hair shows on the reverse. (p323a, OP, R2-3)
$75.00-90.00

GIRL HEAD WEARING A DUST CAP - (M) - Approx. 2½″ - She has glass eyes and a duster cap that frames most of her face with ruffles. Because of the cap the reverse is smooth and shows no hair. (Germany, p321c, OP, R2-3)
$75.00-90.00

GIRL'S HEAD ON A HEART - (M) - Approx. 3½″ - The ornament is roughly heart shaped with the girl's head, coming out of three leaf clover, embossed on it. The clover leaves make it look as though she had large ears. The front of the ornament has horizontal lines across it, while on the back is an embossed rose and leaves. (p341b, OP, R2)
$50.00-60.00

GIRL HOLDING A TEDDY BEAR - (M) - Approx. 3½″ - She wears a rounded hat with thick trim on the edge.

Below the waist, she is rounded into almost a ball shape. On her stomach she holds a teddy bear stretched between her hands. She is similar to the Miss Muffet ornament. (p293b, OP, R2)
$100.00-125.00

GIRL BELL - (M&FB) - Approx. 3″ - The head is molded, but the dress is free-blown and deeply indented on the bottom. This forms the bell, and a small glass clapper is added. She has outstretched, annealed arms. (p309b, OP, R1)
$90.00-100.00

GIRL IN A BAG - (M) - Approx. 2¾″ & 3¼″ - Only the girl's head, with long curly hair, shows out of the top of the bag. The bag has a round bottom and a ribbon tied in a bow around the ruffled opening. For its companion piece see "Boy in a Bag." (Germany, p343c & p345b, OP, R3)
$60.00-85.00

GIRL IN A BASKET OF FLOWERS - see ANGEL IN A BASKET

GIRL IN A BEEHIVE - (M) - Approx. 3″ - The beehive has embossed ribs going around it. The top of the hive is lifted and the girl's head and arm stick out. There is also an embossed bee on the front of the hive. (Germany, p391a, OP, R2)
$100.00-125.00

GIRL IN A FUR COAT - (M) - Approx. 3¾″ - She wears a scarf over her head which ties under the chin. From her shoulders to her waist is a heavy coat or cape that appears to be fur. Her hands are crossed at the stomach area. (p289b, OP, R2)
$100.00-125.00

GIRL IN A "LM" SACK - (M) - Approx. 3¾″ - The girl's head and two arms rise out of what looks like a money bag with the initials "L.M." on it. She has long curly hair, and her arms rest on the outside of the bag. The initials may indicate the piece is made by the Muller family of glassblowers. (Germany, p345a, OP, R1-2) $50.00-75.00

GIRL JESTER - see CLOWNS

GIRL SOLDIER - (M) - Approx. 4¾″ - This piece with its long hair tied in the back could also be a boy, but the facial features are more feminine. She wears boots and a military coat with braided fasteners on the chest. She also wears a beehive shaped hat with a star embossed on it. Both arms are at her sides, and there is a sword hanging on her left side. (Germany, p274, OP, R1-2)
$275.00-300.00

GIRL'S TORSO WITH A PRESENT - (M) - Approx. 4½″ - The girl, who wears no clothes, is shown to the waist. She has medium length curly hair and both hands are at the chest, holding a present wrapped with a bow. (p346b, OP, R1)
$225.00-250.00

LARGE HEADED GIRL WITH ANNEALED LEGS - (M&FB) - Approx. 3½″ - Her head is out of proportion to her body. She has thick curly hair that is tied in a bun in the back and large cheeks. Her left arm is at her breast. She has been called "ZaZu", but she is possibly a comic strip or movie character. (Germany, p291a, OP, R1-2)
$300.00-350.00

ANGELIC MERMAID - (M&FB) - Approx. 4″ - The body form is from a cherub angel. Both arms are crossed at the

chest, left over right, and she wears only a small sash. Below the waist, the ornament is pulled into a bent free-blown tapering tube to represent the fish body. This part is very similar to a Dublin pipe. (Germany, p394, OP, R1)
$150.00-175.00

"GOLDILOCKS" MERMAID - (M&FB) - Approx. 4″ - The upper torso is that of the Goldilocks ornament. The piece begins to taper into the free-blown fish tail right below the square collar of her dress. (Germany, p76a, OP, R1)
$150.00-175.00

OLD WOMAN WITH ANNEALED LEGS - (M&FB) - Approx. 4½″ - She appears to have a scarf around her head, both hands are clasped at the stomach area and she carries a purse over her left arm. (Germany, Schiffer p125, OP, R2)
$250.00-300.00

PEASANT LADY - (M) - Approx. 4¼″ - A head scarf ties under her comic looking face with a large smiling mouth. She wears an apron that ties in the back, and both hands rest on the apron. This piece has also been referred to as a folktale witch, although there seems to be no basis for it and another unmistakable witch ornament exists. (Germany, p346c, OP, R1-2)
$150.00-175.00

PEASANT WOMAN WITH A SPOON - (M) - Approx. 3½″ - She wears a scarf that ties under her chin and an apron that ties in the back. She holds a large spoon in her right hand and a carrot in her left. (Czech., p340b, OP-NP [limited], R2)
$60.00-80.00

SNOW GIRL WITH A ROSE - (M) - Approx. 3″ - She is dressed in a coat with a hood and short cape. Her skirt shows beneath the waist length coat. Her hands are at her breasts, and the right one holds a rose. (Germany, p341a, OP, R2)
$75.00-100.00

VICTORIAN LADY ON AN URN - (M) - Approx. 3¼″ - This bust of a Victorian lady, with her hair in a bun, is embossed onto a fancy shape that resembles an urn. A rose is embossed on the back. (Germany, p326a, OP-NP, R2-3)
$35.00-40.00

WOMAN PLAYING A GUITAR - (M) - Approx. 3¾″ - She holds a guitar in both hands, and her mouth is wide open as if singing. She wears a hat and a short sleeved dress with a square collar. The mold for this ornament is now in East Germany. (Germany, p342a, OP-NP [limited], R1)
$125.00-150.00

PINE CONES

Pine cones are the "fruit" of the evergreen and part of its natural decoration. In many ancient religions, they were considered a symbol of fertility. Cones were one of the earliest decorations for the tree, and they were often gilded or painted silver and tied with bright ribbons. Pine cones were supposedly the first molded ornaments to be produced by Louis Greiner-Schlotfeger in 1870.

Regular pine cones are very common, but they were also a popular form onto which other things were embossed. The embossed items will be found in their relative sections.

STANDARD PINE CONES - (M) - Approx. 1″- 5″ - There are a wide variety of sizes and molding on the cones. However, there is little to distinguish them. Almost every glassblower had his own version of this popular piece, and it was sold by all the major ornament producing countries. (p435, OP-NP, R5)   Small & medium $1.00-8.00
Larger $5.00-15.00

AMERICAN PINE CONES - (M) - Approx. 1¾″, 2¾″ & 4″ - The glass is heavier than in their European counterparts and they usually have a wider pike opening. Some of the largest of the cones are American made. One producer was Corning glass in the late 1930s. American cones are somewhat rarer than European ones. (U.S., p435b, p435d, p451g & p451h, OP, R3-4)
Small & medium $2.00-10.00
Large $5.00-15.00

BIRD ON A PINE CONE - see BIRDS

CLOWN ON A PINE CONE - see CLOWNS

FACE ON A PINE CONE - There are several versions - see PEOPLE AND FACES IN FLOWERS, FRUITS, ETC.

"FINGER" CONE - (M) - Approx. 3″ - This is modeled after the cone of the white pine. It has a sharp bend in it about halfway down the length. (Rogers p83, OP, R3-4)
$15.00-25.00

FIR CONE - (M) - Approx. 4″ - This cone is long and slender with a slight curve to it. The molds are now in East Germany. (Germany, Rogers p70, OP-NP [limited], R3)
$15.00-25.00

INDIAN ON A PINE CONE - see INDIANS

SANTA ON A PINE CONE - There are several varieties - see SANTAS

THREE CONES ON A BRANCH - (M) - Approx. 2½″ - A group of three pine cones is embossed onto a three branched pine limb. The branches show the needles on the front and back. (OP, R2-3) $15.00-20.00

SCRAP AND GLASS ORNAMENTS

In these unusual pieces, the scrap is not merely added as a decoration such as the riders on balloons, boats, gondolas, etc. In these decorations, the scrap, itself, is an integral part of the molded or blown glass ornament. These are also considerably rarer and more desirable than other glass pieces with added scraps. During the 1920s, the distinctive lithographed scraps were replaced by printed ones. Therefore, it can be determined that ornaments of this type are rather early pieces. Some are repeated here from their respective sections while others seem to fit only under this heading.

ANGEL WITH A SCRAP FACE - (M) - Approx. 3″ & 3½″ - The girl or woman angel stands in a long gown with a flower held over her left breast. Her molded wings are shown at the shoulders and down the sides. The glass at the face is flattened and a scrap attached. (p275c & p292a, OP, R2)   Small $90.00-110.00
Large $150.00-175.00

SANTA WITH A SCRAP FACE (TYPE I) - (M) - Approx. 3½" - He wears a hood and short shoulder cape. His right arm is across his stomach, and his left arm hangs at his side. He carries nothing. The glass at the face area has been flattened, and a scrap face is applied. (p292c, OP, R1-2)
$125.00-150.00

SANTA WITH A SCRAP FACE (TYPE II) - (M) - Approx. 3½" - He is very similar to the above except he wears a fur cap instead of a hood. All other prices and information apply.

GUARDIAN ANGEL WITH TWO CHILDREN - (M) - Approx. 3½" - The lady angel stands in a long flowing gown. She has her hands on the heads of a boy and girl. Although the angel's flowing hair shows at the sides, the glass is smooth from the breasts up for a scrap head or bust to be applied. (Germany, OP-NP [limited and without the scrap], R1-2)
$100.00-125.00

SCRAP GIRL WITH A BLOWN GLASS SKIRT - (FB) - Approx. 4½" but sizes could vary - On this piece, the scrap torso of a woman or girl is applied to a free-blown skirt. The scrap is attached to the pike which has been left on the skirt. Feet and shoes may be attached to an indentation in the bottom of the skirt. The exact scrap used could vary, but they are often the same ones used to make scrap doll ornaments. (p292b, OP, R1-2)
$150.00-175.00

SCRAP INSIDE A BLOWN GLASS BALL - (FB) - Approx. 2" but sizes will vary with the free-blown ball - These pieces can be found with several variations. In some, a ball is blown with a large open end which is flattened out. A scrap, mounted up-right on a cardboard disc, is then glued into the bottom with the scrap inside. The ball is often painted leaving one section clear. The scrap can be seen through this "window". The scrap, itself, may be decorated with cotton, tinsel or spun glass. Another version, based on the same principle, shows a mirror image scrap and a double "window". In a third version, a clear glass sphere was painted to show a house. A large window was left clear. When looking through the window a scrap of two children at play can be seen. (p436 & p439, OP, R1-2)
$60.00-80.00

SCRAP FIGURE SEALED INSIDE A GLASS ORNAMENT - (FB) - Approx. 3" but sizes can vary - A small glass ball was blown, and a short pike was left on it. The ball was silvered, painted and a scrap was added to the pike. Then another glass oblong was blown over the scrap and annealed onto the small glass ball, thus leaving the scrap totally enclosed. The back was painted, and the front left clear as a window for viewing the scrap figure. (p436, OP, R1-2)
$60.00-80.00

TRANSPORTATION

During the golden age of ornament making many forms of transportation such as sailboats, steam ships, trains and coaches reached the zenith of their popularity. Still other forms such as hot air balloons, airplanes and cars were new inventions which captured the imagination of the ornament maker and buying public alike. Transportation was a popular ornament theme and various forms were immortalized in paper and cardboard, as well as glass.

Airplanes

People in both the United States and Europe had been experimenting with "flying machines" prior to the famous 1903 flight of the Wright brothers. However, most "aeroplane" type ornaments are no earlier than this time period. Airplane ornaments are usually constructed of free-blown oval or cigar shapes with tinsel wings added to them. The tail and propeller were also added by loops of tinsel, and the whole piece was usually wrapped in crinkle wire. Although biplanes were used into the 1930s, most ornaments only show one wing. Because they are free-blown, sizes can vary from approximately 3½" to 6½". No early examples of molded airplanes are known.

SIMPLE AIRPLANE SHAPE - (FB&Wire) - Approx. 3½"-6½" - A free-blown cigar shape forms the fuselage. Wire forms the wings, propeller and tail. It often has a scrap rider attached. (p434b, OP, R2-3)
$70.00-80.00

FREE-BLOWN AIRPLANE WITH WHEELS - (FB) - Approx. 4"-5" - The elongated body is free-blown and has an indented cockpit. The wings, propeller and tail are made of tinsel wire. Small wheels of brass or "Dresden" cardboard are added as an undercarriage. The piece is usually unsilvered and wire wrapped. (Rogers 211, OP, R2)
$185.00-225.00

AIRPLANE WITH A PLASTER SANTA - (FB) - Approx. 5"-6" - A free-blown airplane like the one above has a small plaster and scrap faced Santa added to it. The small 1½" Santa sits as the pilot in an indented cockpit. The piece is usually unsilvered and wire wrapped. (p404, OP, R2-3)
$200.00-250.00

VARIATION: BIPLANE WITH SANTA - (FB), Approx. 5"-6" - This is basically the same piece described above. However, two wings are added to make it a biplane. (OP, R2)
$200.00-250.00

BEADED AIRPLANE - (Beads), 4" & 7" sizes can vary - The three dimensional airplane is made of small beads. It may be a Czech. or Japanese piece. (p405, OP, R2-3)
Small $20.00-30.00
Large $25.00-35.00

SANTA IN AN AIRPLANE - (M) - Approx. 3"L - This piece shows a molded fuselage with Santa and bags sitting inside. The wings and propeller are tinsel wire. The molding shows the engine and wheels. No early examples of this piece are known. (Germany, NP)
$2.00-10.00

"SPIRIT OF ST. LOUIS" AIRPLANE - (FB) - Approx. 3" - The fuselage is a free-blown cigar shape that is usually unsilvered. Spun glass wings are attached at the top and rear of the plane. It has a paper propeller and paper or tinsel wheels. (Germany, p403, OP, R2-3)
$125.00-150.00

ANCHORS - (FB) - Approx. 3½" to 5" but sizes can vary - The anchor shape with a cross bar at the top. It is made of free-blown and annealed glass tubes. They often have a scrap angel and wire wrapping. (Germany, OP, R1-2)
$150.00-175.00

Automobiles

Most ornaments portray cars from the 1920s and 1930s. Molds changed every few years or were redesigned to show the latest models. Exact years and models are hard to determine since they include United States, foreign and fantasy types. Hangers appear in the roof, front and rear bumper. Cars often have more than one hanger.

AUTOMOBILE (TYPE I) - (M) - Approx. 3″ - The roof is gently rounded and two windows, with rounded sides, show. The fenders are rounded and teardrop headlights show on the front ones. (p414a, OP, R2-3) $50.00-65.00

VARIATION: POLICE CAR - (M) - Approx. 3″ - This is the same piece described above. On the roof a small pike, sometimes used for hanging the car, has been sealed. This gives the piece its "cherry" or flashing light. (p414b, OP, R2-3) $50.00-65.00

AUTOMOBILE (TYPE II) - (M) - Approx. 3″ - It has a square body with **two** square windows and a spare tire on the back. (p415a & p417c, OP, R2-3) $65.00-75.00

COMIC CAR - (M) - Approx. 2½″ - This short looking car has a domed roof with only one window showing. Its rounded back shows an embossed rumble seat. It looks like cars depicted in cartoons. (p416c, OP, R1-2) $100.00-125.00

SANTA IN AN AUTOMOBILE - see SANTAS

SANTA IN A COACH - see SANTAS

"SQUARE" CAR - (M) - Approx. 2¼″ & 2¾″ - This piece has a short hood and an overall square look to it. It has **three** square windows. (p418, OP, R2-3) $65.00-75.00

TOURING CAR (TYPE I) - (M) - Approx. 2¾″ - This has a long engine hood. The roof of the body slopes back and shows three windows. There is a spare wheel on the back. There is a sharp crease, perhaps a mold seam, that goes down the first window and door. (p415b, OP, R2)
$100.00-125.00

TOURING CAR (TYPE II) - (M) - Approx. 3″ - This has a long engine hood with embossed air vents. The body is square and shows two doors. There is a spare wheel on the back. (p416a, OP, R2) $100.00-125.00

TRUCK - (M) - Approx. 2½″ - This piece has a short hood and cab. The long truck bed is covered by a rounded "canvas" top. Wheels are embossed into the area under the truck. (p416b, OP, R1-2) $125.00-150.00

VW CAR - (M) - Approx. 2¾″ & 3½″ - It has a short hood and long body with a sloping roof. Three windows and one door show. None are known prior to the 1950s. (West Germany, p417a, NP)   1950s $20.00-30.00
Newer $ 2.00-10.00

Balloons

During the last half of the 1800s, hot air ballooning became popular in both Europe and the United States. At this same time, glassblowers began producing their versions of the balloon. The ornament comes in two distinct forms, single and double balloons, both of which are generally free-blown. Both styles are usually wire wrapped and may carry a scrap rider in the form of Santa, angels, children, etc. Balloons were popular pieces throughout the pre-war years and are still being produced and collected today. The double balloon is usually preferred over the single and both types are more desirable with the scrap riders. In either case, prices are based on desirability as opposed to rarity.

SINGLE BALLOON - (FB) - Approx. 2¾″ to 12″ but sizes can vary since they are free-blown. The piece is usually formed by a free-blown ball with the long blowing pike left attached. A lithographed scrap is usually attached to the pike, and the whole piece is wrapped in wire. Prices given are for wire wrapped pieces with scraps. How elaborate and beautiful a piece is also affects its price. (Germany, Austria, Czech., p406, p408 & p409b, OP-NP, R4)
Small $30.00-50.00
Medium $50.00-75.00
Large $90.00-110.00

VARIATION #1: - MOLDED BALLOONS - (M&FB) - Approx. 2¾″ to 8″ - A long free-blown pike is left attached to a ball or geometric shape which was mold blown. Again, they often have added decorations of tinsel, wire and scraps. (p406d, p406e, p407c & p413, OP-NP, R3)
Small $30.00-50.00
Medium $50.00-75.00
Large $90.00-110.00

VARIATION #2: PATRIOTIC BALLOONS - (M&FB) - Approx. 2¾″-12″ - These can be either of the above two forms. The pieces may be painted red, white and blue; have American flags; or patriotic scraps such as Miss Liberty, George Washington, Uncle Sam, etc. (OP, R2-3)
Small $50.00-60.00
Medium $75.00-90.00
Large $100.00-125.00

VARIATION #3: INDENTED BALLOON - (FB), Sizes vary - This is basically the same form as those listed above, except the free-blown ball has a reflective indentation in it. (p419b, OP-NP, R2-3) $25.00-40.00

DOUBLE BALLOONS - (FB) - Approx. 3″ to 12″, Sizes can vary because they are free-blown. This piece is formed by two balls, a larger one on top and a smaller one, representing the basket, on the bottom. Both are connected by a short pike. They usually have wire or tinsel decorations, as well as a scrap rider. Early versions are often unsilvered. Prices are affected by the condition of the wire, the beauty and how elaborately the piece is constructed. (Germany, Austria, Czech., p407a, p407b, p409a, p411 & p412a, OP-NP, R3-4)
Small $30.00-45.00
Medium $75.00-100.00
Large $140.00-175.00

VARIATION #1: PATRIOTIC BALLOON - (FB) - Approx. 3″-8″ - These pieces are formed in the same manner as those above. They may be painted red, white and blue; have American flags; or patriotic scraps. (OP, R2-3)
Small $30.00-50.00
Medium $90.00-110.00
Large $140.00-175.00

VARIATION #2: INDENTED BALLOON - This double balloon shape has one or two reflective indents in the top balloon. (p419b, OP, R3) $15.00-25.00

Balloons With Baskets

BALLOONS WITH "BASKETS" - (FB) - Sizes vary - The "balloon" is a free-blown ball with a basket of tinsel, cardboard or metal suspended underneath. The basket is held on by string, wire or tinsel. (p412b, OP, R1-2)
$100.00-125.00

BALLOON WITH A BASKET OF FLOWERS - (M&FB) - Approx. 3¼" - A free-blown ball forms the balloon. A molded basket of flowers is attached to it by a short pike. (p419a, OP, R2) $35.00-45.00

BALLOON RIDING SANTA - (M&FB) - Approx. 6½" - A free-blown ball with a long pike has a 2" molded Santa in a basket suspended from it as a rider. (p433c, OP, R1-2)
$80.00-90.00

BICYCLE - (Beads) - Approx. 3½" - This three dimensional piece is constructed of small glass beads and tubes. It is nicely detailed and probably Czech. made. (p420b, OP, R2)
$25.00-35.00

Boats

During the many years of ornament productions, boats went through many transformations. They went from sails to steamboats to modern oceanliners. All of these were portrayed in glass by the ornament makers. By far, the most common were the free-blown sailboats; but several versions of molded boats also exist.

SAILBOATS - (FB) - Approx. 3" to 12" sizes can vary since they are free-blown - The boat, itself, is formed by an oval or egg shape that has a deep indentation in one side. Into the indentation was placed cotton and a separate unblown glass rod which formed the "mast". The whole piece was held together with wrapping of crinkle wire which also represented the rigging. Broken or loose wire will cause the mast to lean or come completely off. Scrap riders of children, angels and Santas were often attached to the mast. Older versions are often unsilvered. (Germany, Czech., p422c, p425 & p426, OP-NP, R3-4)
Small $40.00-55.00
Medium $75.00-100.00
Large $125.00-150.00

VARIATION #1: SAILBOATS WITH SAILS - (FB) - sizes vary - This is basically the same as the above piece, however, instead of a scrap figure, there are paper sails or a miniature Dresden sail boat attached to the mast. (p425a, p425d & p427a, p427b, OP-NP, R2-3)
Small $40.00-60.00
Medium $75.00-90.00
Large $150.00-175.00

VARIATION #2: MUSHROOM SAILBOAT - (FB) - Approx. 4½", Sizes vary - This is a traditional sailboat form, but it has small plaster mushrooms and angel hair added around the mast. $40.00-50.00

VARIATION #3: "CROWN" SAILBOAT - (FB&M) - Approx. 5" but sizes can vary - The boat is formed in the traditional manner, but the mast has a large molded base. This piece resembles a crown and fits into the indentation in the boat. This piece was offered by Sears as early as 1910. (Germany, p423, OP, R2-3)
$75.00-90.00

VARIATION #4: PATRIOTIC BOAT - (FB), Sizes can vary - This is formed like the traditional sailboat; it is painted red, white and blue; may have American flags or patriotic scraps. (p422a, OP, R2) $75.00-90.00

STEAMSHIP - (FB) - Approx. 5½" but sizes can vary - This is very similar in construction to sailboats. It has two added smokestacks in the front and rear which have wire and SG smoke. (p424, OP, R1-2) $100.00-125.00

"BREMEN" STEAMSHIP - (M) - Approx. 3¾" - The hull of the ship shows embossed portholes and the name "Bremen" which is a famous ship and important German port city. It has a raised top deck with lifeboats and smokestacks. It is usually found unsilvered, and the example pictured has tinsel on the inside. (Germany, p429, OP, R1-2) $100.00-125.00

PASSENGER SHIP - (M) - Approx. 3½" - The hull shows four embossed portholes and an anchor. The upper deck has portholes, lifeboat and three smoke-stacks. The center smokestack may be used for a hanger. (Germany, p428a & p430a, OP-NP [1950s], R3)   Old $90.00-100.00
1950s $30.00-45.00

AUSTRIAN PASSENGER SHIP - (M) - Approx. 2¾" - The well defined hull shows six portholes. The upper deck shows two levels and two smokestacks. No early examples are known. (Austria, p428b, NP) $2.00-10.00

U-BOAT - (M) - Approx. 2" - This elongated shape has embossed "plates" and the words "U. Boot 9". "Boot" is German for boat. U-boat stands for underwater boat or submarine. This piece was made during World War I but not exported to the United States. (Germany, Stille p51, OP, R1) $250.00-275.00

CINDERELLA CARRIAGE - (M&tinsel) - Approx. 3" - The body of the carriage is molded showing side doors and curtained windows. Wire tinsel make up the undercarriage and wheels of the ornament. (Germany, p422b, OP, R2)
$50.00-60.00

Dirigibles and Zeppelins

From about the turn of the century until the great "Hindenburg" disaster, dirigibles and the zeppelins were the transportation craze. This was reflected in the ornaments from the same time period. The most popular form for exporting to the United States was the "Los Angeles". The real airship had been made in Germany for the United States as part of Germany's World War I reparations. Dirigibles come in both a free-blown and molded form, with the molded pieces being much more popular.

FREE-BLOWN DIRIGIBLES - (FB&Wire) - Approx. 2½" to 6" but sizes can vary - The "body" of the piece is usually blown in a cigar or cylinder shape. It has a tinsel wire propeller in the front or rear, and a tinsel undercarriage or gondola that usually holds a scrap rider. The whole piece is wire wrapped, and early versions are unsilvered. The body of the ornament is a common glass form, and the only thing that makes it a dirigible is the added wire tinsel. For this reason, they are not as popular as molded pieces. (p433a & p434d, OP, R3) $125.00-150.00

VARIATION #1: FREE-BLOWN "GRAF ZEPPELIN" - (FB) - Approx. 5¼″ - This cigar-shaped piece has a painted American flag and the printed name "Graf Zeppelin" on the side. It usually has an annealed hook in one side and a SG tail in the end. (Germany, p431b, OP, R2-3) $125.00-150.00

VARIATION #2: PATRIOTIC ZEPPELIN - (FB) - Sizes can vary - Usually found in a free-blown cigar shape, these pieces are painted red, white and blue, have American flags or a patriotic scrap such as Miss Liberty riding in them. (p434a, OP, R2) $175.00-200.00

PSUEDO - DIRIGIBLE - (FB) - Approx. 4″-6″ but sizes vary - The most common form for these is oblong or cigar-shaped. Early versions are often unsilvered and wire wrapped. They are often called dirigibles with a substantial price attached to them. However, they lack the propeller, undercarriage and gondola that make them true dirigibles. They are in fact common free-blown shapes. (OP-NP, R5)
$1.00-8.00

ZEPPELIN (TYPE I) - (M) - The super structure is covered by embossed panels. There are two small gondolas underneath and it has "Zeppelin" embossed into the side. It may be wire wrapped and have a wire propeller. (Germany, Stille p176, OP, R1-2) $275.00-300.00

ZEPPELIN (TYPE II) - (M) - Approx. 3¼″ - This piece has eight elongated panels and is embossed with thin vertical lines. It has one large and one small gondola underneath and an annealed hook for hanging. (Germany, p434c, OP-NP, R2) $100.00-125.00

"GRAF ZEPPELIN DL 127" - (M) - Approx. 3½″ - This molded piece shows six smooth side panels and four stabilizers in the rear. A gondola with portholes hangs underneath. "Graf Zeppelin DL 127" is embossed into the side of the airship. (Germany, p430b & p431a, OP, R3)
$225.00-250.00

"LOS ANGELES" - (M) - Approx. 4″ - This long cylinder shape is covered with embossed panels, and it has an embossed propeller in the front. It has two small gondolas underneath. It has molded flags above the gondolas and a paper label printed "Los Angeles". (p431c, OP, R2)
$250.00-275.00

"ZR III" - (M) - Approx. 5¾″L & 2¼″W - This piece has eight elongated panels and is embossed with thin vertical lines. The front has an extended motor or prop with an acorn shape. It has a gondola underneath and the marking "ZR III" embossed into it. (p432, OP, R1)
$175.00-200.00

"Z.R.3" - (M) - It is composed of many elongated panels and has two gondolas underneath. It shows four molded stabilizers in the rear and has "Z.R.3" written on it. (Rogers p207, OP, R1-2) $225.00-250.00

GONDOLAS - (FB) - Approx. 3½″-5″ but sizes can vary - These are generally made of free-blown pieces in the form of an oval or egg shape. They are deeply indented, much the same as sailboats and carry a scrap rider. They are generally wire wrapped and have a tinsel hoop for hanging. These are a simple ornament and not as rare as once believed. Since they are simpler than the similarly constructed sailboats, which could easily be modified into a gondola, their price should be in line with them. (p410 & p433b, OP, R3) $50.00-75.00

LOCOMOTIVE - (M) - Approx. 3″ - This piece shows the wheels, engine, cab and coal car. It is nicely detailed. (Germany, p417b, OP-NP, R1) $100.00-125.00

SLEIGH WITH A COTTON FIGURE - (FB&Wire) - Approx. 6″ - The sleigh is made of a free-blown oval with a deeply embossed "seat". The runners are formed on the outside by tinsel wire. A cotton batting Santa rides in the sleigh. (Germany, p421, OP, R1-2)
Sleigh only $50.00-60.00
Sleigh with figure $225.00-250.00

TRAFFIC LIGHTS - (M) - These pieces are described by Rogers. The molds are now in East Germany. (OP-NP, R1-2)
$40.00-50.00

TOONERVILLE TROLLEY - (M) - Approx. 2½″ - This is molded after the famous tin toy of the same name. Santa rides in the front, and it has a capital "T" and "Depot Line" embossed into the side. It shows three windows and wheels. (Germany, OP, R1) $300.00-350.00

COVERED WAGON - (M) - Approx. 2″L - This is a Conestoga type wagon. The wheels, side boards and hooped cover all show. (Germany, p417d, OP-NP, R2)
$20.00-30.00

TREES

Trees represented as ornaments have always been of the pine or evergreen family. Their link with Christmas is obvious and the source of many stories and legends. Most trees are shown undecorated; however, any of them could have the addition of bright colored dots representing ornaments.

STANDARD TREE - (M) - Approx. 2″, 3″ & 3½″- There are several slightly different versions of the molded tree. These variations lie in the length and shape of the individually molded limbs. The branches are usually layered on top of each other in an alternating pattern. Trees are often found as clip-ons. (Germany, p437b & p438a, OP-NP, R3-4) $25.00-35.00

VARIATION #1: TREE WITH A TRUNK - (M&FB) - Approx. 3½″-4½″, sizes can vary - This is a molded standard form tree with a free-blown pike protruding from the bottom. This represents the tree's trunk. (Germany, Rogers p220, OP, R3) $25.00-35.00

VARIATION #2: TREE ON A BALL - (M&FB) - Approx. 3″-4½″, sizes can vary with the free-blown ball - This is a molded standard form tree attached to a free-blown ball by a short pike. (Germany, Schiffer p143, OP, R2-3) $35.00-50.00

VARIATION #3: DECORATED TREE - (M) - Approx. 3″ - This tree has small indented "holes" in the ends of alternating branches. These indentations are painted to resemble colored ornaments (red and pink are usual). Any of the standard trees could be painted for the same results regardless of whether they had the indentations. (Germany, p437c, OP-NP, R3) $25.00-35.00

VARIATION #4: TREE WITH "ARMS" - (M&FB) - Approx. 3″-4″, sizes can vary - The basis of the ornament is a standard form tree. It has a free-blown ball attached to the top from which extend three tubular "arms". These hang down around the tree and hold small ball or bell ornaments. (Germany, Rogers p219, OP, R2) $50.00-60.00

AMERICAN TREE - (M) - Approx. 3″ - This piece has a long and a narrow appearance, and there is no delicate detail on the brances. The glass is heavier, and it has a wider opening in the pike. It has a characteristic "button" shape at the base. This was made by Corning Glass in 1939-40. (U.S., p437a & p451d, OP, R2) $20.00-30.00

BEADED TREE - (BEADS) - This piece is the flat outline of a tree made with small beads or glass tubes. (Japan, Czech., OP, R2-3) $5.00-12.00

FREE-BLOWN TREE - (FB) - Approx. 5″ - This piece is made of three concentric cones. The trunk is represented by the pike, and it has been flattened into a round base. The piece shown has plaster mushrooms at the base and is wire wrapped. This is probably a Czech. piece. (p440, NP [1950s], R2-3) $10.00-20.00

HOLLOW, FILLED TREE - (M&FB) - Approx. 3″ but sizes can vary - The tree itself is molded, but it has a free-blown "trunk", base and tree top ball. The piece was left hollow at the circular base and filled with what looks like green sawdust. There is no hanger or clip-on included in this piece. (p443a, OP, R2) $20.00-30.00

HOUSE UNDER A TREE - (M) - Approx. 3″ - The tree is a standard form with a cottage embossed into one side. The house shows two sides, a door and windows. It comes halfway up the length of the tree. (p438b, OP-NP, R2) $35.00-45.00

MUSHROOMS UNDER A TREE - (M) - Approx. 2½″ - Four mushrooms are embossed around the base of a standard tree. One is on each of the four sides. (Schiffer p143, OP, R2) $30.00-40.00

NARROW LIMB TREE - (M) - Approx. 2¾″ - This is a common variation of the standard tree form. The limbs are narrow and ill-defined. They are basically made up of a pattern of zig-zag lines as opposed to individually molded branches. (Germany, p116c, OP, R3) $25.00-35.00

SANTA FACE **ON** A PINE TREE - see SANTAS

SANTA FACE **UNDER** A PINE TREE - see SANTAS

TREE WITH FLAT SIDES - (M) - Approx. 3″ - This is a variation of the standard form tree. The four rows of "limbs" are long and flat almost like shingles. Each limb

is embossed with long vertical lines. (Germany, Rogers p220d, OP-NP, R2-3) $25.00-35.00

MISCELLANEOUS GLASS ORNAMENTS

This section is used to include those items that don't fit into sections of their own.

BALL OR SPHERE SHAPES - (FB) - Approx. ¾″ to 8″ dia. - These pieces were the mainstay of the ornament maker's business. The original concept represented the apple on the Tree of Paradise. Glass balls are the oldest form known to have been blown (see Kugels). These shapes were lacquered and painted in a variety of ways, and this is what establishes their desirability and value. Some were wrapped in wire, tinsel, string and fabric. The ball is by far the most common shape and was manufactured by ornament makers worldwide. Value ranges from impossible to give away to ten dollars for large and elaborate pieces.

FANCY MOLDED SHAPES - (M) - Approx. ¾″ to 5″ - the common sizes are 2″-4″ - These come in hundreds of various shapes and geometric figures. They are mold-blown with embossed shapes and designs, but fall into no recognizable category. No doubt some were designed to be some specific, but as yet unrecognized object. Most, however, are simply pretty molded shapes. These shapes were made by glassblowers worldwide and range from rare to very common. Even the rare ones fall into one generic price grouping since they are not considered very collectible. (p448 & p452, OP-NP, R5) $.50-8.00

FANCY FREE-BLOWN SHAPES - (FB) - Approx. 1½″ to 8″ - This grouping includes those pieces which are not balls or molded forms. They come in a vast variety of shapes including: teardrop, egg, oval, cigar, plum, disc, cone, cylinders, etc. Older pieces may be unsilvered and wire wrapped. Such shapes were often used with wire to form other recognizable forms. Many of these are twisted and pulled into interesting shapes, but their price and desirability rest on their age, beauty and size. They were produced by ornament makers worldwide. (p449, OP-NP, R5) $.50-10.00

BEADED ORNAMENTS - Approx. 2″-6″ - These pieces were produced by Czech., Japanese and German ornament makers. They were first produced by the Czech's in the 1890s and have become so much associated with them that most beaded ornaments are referred to as "Czech. ornaments", regardless of the real country of origin. Other than labels, there is no absolute way to tell in which country the ornament was made. However, here are some **general** guidelines: German beads are often faceted; Japanese are usually round beads only; and Czech. pieces often incorporate glass tubes. These pieces are constructed of small silvered beads and colored glass tubes which are strung on thin wires. The wires are then bent and twisted together to form objects and geometric figures, both in two and three dimensions. Recognizable objects are more desirable and are generally listed in their respective sections. (Germany, Czech. & Japan, p455, p456 & p457, OP-NP, R4)   Flat Shapes $1.00- 8.00   3-Dimensional $10.00-20.00

STRING OF BEADS - (FB&M) - Approx. 1'-12' - Chains of nuts, candy, popcorn and cranberries have long been popular adornments for the Christmas tree. In the late 1800s chains or glass beads also began to appear. These beads were a natural offshoot from the millinery trade which already used silvered beads and glass tubes in Victorian hats, purses and clothing. The first chains were made of large beads (¾"-1" balls) or oblong shapes. They were usually unsilvered and strung in small one to two foot chains that were designed to dangle or loop over the ends of branches. Some of these were mold blown and some were even indented. In later years, smaller beads were blown or molded into long tubes. After being silvered as one piece, the individual beads were cut apart. Bead sizes can range from ¼" to 1½" in size. This large bead is on an occupied Japan piece that is ten feet long. The most popular of these strings had faceted beads and embossed oblong shapes; they resemble the beaded glass necklaces often given away at carnivals. Any small (¾"-1½") molded ornament could have been found as a chain. Examples include acorns, crowns and Santa heads; they are listed in their respective sections. Although most strings of beads are glass, some post-war strings are made of faceted plastic. William DeMuth of New York also made some chains of balls in the 1870s. These would be heavy Kugel-like ornaments. (p454)

Old 1'-2' Chains of Large Beads $5.00-10.00
Chain of huge 1½" beads $20.00-30.00
String of Round Beads $2.00-8.00
String of Faceted or Fancy Shapes $5.00-15.00
DeMuth Chain $100.00-125.00

Cross

The cross is an unusual item for the Christmas tree since it is associated with Easter and the crucifiction rather than the birth of Jesus.

CROSS - (M) - Rogers describes these as being mold made and often embossed with designs. (Germany, Czech., OP, R1) $100.00-125.00

BEADED CROSS - (Beads) - Approx. 4" - This three dimensional piece is composed of small glass beads on a wire. It is Czech. or Japanese. (p457b, OP, R2-3) $10.00-15.00

FREE-BLOWN CROSS - (FB) - Sizes can vary - This piece is composed of hollow glass tubes which are annealed together to form a cross. (OP, R1-2) $30.00-45.00

IRON CROSS (EMBOSSED) - (M) - Approx. 1¾" - The Iron Cross was a military honor in both world wars and held in high esteem by the Germans. This equal armed Maltese cross is embossed onto a disc with a bumpy pattern. This type of piece was not exported to the United States and is thus rare. (Germany, Stille p51, OP, R1)
$75.00-100.00

JESUS ON A CROSS (EMBOSSED) - (M) - Approx. 1½" dia. - Christ hanging on the cross is embossed onto this small disc shape. (OP, R1-2) $35.00-45.00

SWASTIKA (EMBOSSED) - (M) - Approx. 2" - The swastika was an ancient cross and solar symbol long before its sinister connection with the Third Reich. However, this piece is probably politically connected. It is embossed onto a disc with its arms bent in a clockwise position. This

piece was not exported to the United States, at least in any significant numbers. Many ornaments of this nature were "accidently" broken after the war. A piece like this, although rare is difficult to price since many collectors would refuse to have it and especially to hang on a Christmas tree. (Germany, Stille p51, OP, R1)
$150.00-175.00

Crowns

Crowns could be used in connection with royalty, the Wise men, or as a symbol of Christ.

CROWNS - (M) - Approx. ¾", 1¼" & 2¼"W - This molded piece is round with a domed top. Small embossed bumps represent gems. The small size is usually found attached to other objects such as balls. (Germany, p444, p445b, OP-NP [1¼" size only], R3)   Small $2.00-10.00
Large $20.00-35.00

CHAIN OF CROWNS - (M) - Approx. 1-1½ feet - The small molded crowns described above are strung together into a loop or chain to hang over the tree's branches. (Germany, OP, R1) $75.00-100.00

CROWN ON A BELL - see MUSICAL INSTRUMENTS - BELLS

CROWN ON A BOY - see MAN AND BOYS - THE PRINCE

CROWN ON AN EGG - (FB&M) - Approx. 3½" but sizes can vary - A 1¼" crown is molded onto a free-blown egg shape. (Germany, p445a, OP, R1-2) $60.00-75.00

DECORATED EGGS - (FB) - Approx. 3½"-4½" - This free-blown egg shape is usually made of milk glass and resembles early glass Easter eggs. They have a heavy brass hanger (circa 1890) and probably did double duty as Christmas and Easter decorations. They were decorated with Dresden trim and often had scrap pictures applied. The type and elaborateness of the decoration will affect the price. (p441, OP, R2) $50.00-75.00

CRUSHED GLASS AND CARDBOARD ORNAMENTS - Approx. 2" - The piece is made out of embossed, three dimensional cardboard that has been covered with crushed glass. Unless the cap is removed, these look exactly like glass ornaments with a frosted finish; this is the reason for including them in the glass section. It is likely that the embossed cardboard is a type of "Dresden" ornament, as they are the right size, time period and theme for that style of German ornament. The embossing on the cardboard must be very deep and detailed for it to show as well as it does through the layer of crushed glass. (Germany, (?), p453b, c & d, OP [circa 1910], R1-2) $55.00-75.00

GLASS BALL WITH MINIATURE ORNAMENTS INSIDE - (M&FB) - Approx. 2½" - To make the ornament, a free-blown ball, with a large opening in the bottom, was formed. Smaller ornaments were fastened onto a paper disc and placed inside the ball. The disc covers and seals the large opening. Ornaments pictured show a molded 1½" bird; a molded 1½" Santa; a free formed 1½" swan. The same idea has been used in later years using plastic figures. Earlier versions used wax or scrap figures. (Germany, p446,

OP, R1-2) $50.00-60.00

ICE CREAM CONES - (FB) - Approx. 4″ but sizes can vary
- A free-blown ball is attached to a cone or funnel shape.
Ice cream cones were introduced at the St. Louis World's
Fair. (p445d, OP, R3-4) $5.00-10.00

Icicles

Icicles were a common wintertime sight both at home
and in the forests. They have their own natural beauty and
sparkle in the light. It is little wonder they were copied in
glass and adapted to use on the Christmas tree. They come
in two different forms, solid glass and hollow blown. They
are thought to be the first glass ornament.

SOLID GLASS ICICLES - Approx. 2½″-8″, sizes can vary
- These are formed out of a solid piece of glass that is
twisted and grooved to resemble the real thing. This type
of ornament is one of the first, if not the first, type of glass
ornaments to be marketed commercially. (OP-NP, R3)
                          Small $5.00-8.00
                          Medium $7.00-10.00
                          Large $10.00-15.00

VARIATION #1: GROUPS OF ICICLES - Two or three
solid glass icicles, usually of varying lengths, are annealed together at the top to form a hanging cluster. (Rogers
p120, OP, R1-2)   Group of 2 $20.00-30.00
                          Group of 3 $25.00-35.00

VARIATION #2: COLORED GLASS ICICLES - These
were twisted out of solid glass in red, green or amber.
(OP, R1-2) $10.00-20.00

HOLLOW BLOWN ICICLES - (FB) - Approx. 2″-18″ - A
long, slender cone of funnel shape is pulled and twisted to
give it the appearance of an icicle. Some versions may be
clear with tinsel trim inside them, but most pieces are
silvered. (OP-NP, R3-4)   Small 2″-4″ $1.00-5.00
                          Medium 4″-8″ $10.00-15.00
                          Large over 10″ $20.00-30.00

ORNAMENTS WITH EXTENDED "ARMS" OR
HANGING PIECES - (FB&M) - Approx. 3″-5″ but sizes
vary - These can come in a wide variety of shapes and styles
both free-blown and molded. Some have a hanging center
piece, often a molded object such as a tree or acorn, with
three or four tubular arms hanging down. Small ornaments
dangle from the ends of these annealed "arms". Other
pieces have annealed hooks with shapes hanging from
them. The price will be affected by the size and overall appearance of the piece. Molded pieces are more popular than
free-blown ones. (p447, OP, R3)   Small $10.00-20.00
                          Large $20.00-30.00
                          With Molded Parts $50.00-60.00

REFLECTIVE OR INDENTED ORNAMENTS - (FB&M)
- Approx. 1″-8″ - The most common are the 2″-4″ sizes. The
basic ornament shape includes balls, ovals, cigar shaped,
discs, plums, cylinders, etc. They have a geometric pattern
composed of small reflective surfaces indented into them.
In early versions, these "reflectors" were pushed in by
sticks or shaped lumps of coal. Later multi-faceted patterns
were achieved with carved wood or plaster forms which
were pushed into the ornament while the glass was still hot.
Still others were mold blown reflectors. These are rarer and
can be identified by the presence of "seam" marks. Flower
and berry patterns are common at the center of the reflector. Larger ornaments may have three or four large indents
in them or many smaller ones. Polish reflectors are considered the most beautiful of this type of ornament. By
their very nature, reflectors are always silvered and may
also be found wire and tinsel wrapped. (p449, OP-NP, R5+)
                          Small $ .50-2.00
                          Medium $1.00-5.00
                          Large $2.00-10.00

VARIATION #1: KNOBBY INDENTS - (FB) Sizes can
vary - A free-blown shape is covered by small balls or
knobs which have been annealed onto it. The body of
the ornament contains several indents or reflectors. Such
work was very time consuming. (p449d, OP, R3)
                          $10.00-20.00

VARIATION #2: REFLECTOR ORNAMENT AND
ICICLES - (FB) - Approx. 5″, sizes can vary - A free-
blown shape with three reflective sides is inside a
pyramid of solid glass icicles. (p449c, OP, R2)
                          $25.00-35.00

SWINGS - (M) - These are described by Rogers as having
a clear glass seat and a boy or girl rider blown out of glass.
It had tinsel ropes that would allow it to swing on the tree.
(Germany, OP, R1) $275.00-300.00

TREETOP SPIKES - (FB) - Approx. 4″-12″ but sizes vary
- These free-blown treetops often have an indented ball with
a long tapering pike. Common variations include: several
reflectors in the ball; two or three balls "stacked"; and a
tinsel spray coming from the top of the spikes. Some versions may be wire wrapped. Although very beautiful,
treetop spikes are not often collected for the simple reason
that there is room for only one treetop on a tree. However,
some collectors place wire hangers in the bottom and hang
them upside down like long icicles. (p442, OP-NP, R5)
                          Small $1.00-5.00
                          Medium $5.00-10.00
                          Large $15.00-25.00

CHAPTER IV

PAPER ORNAMENTS

From the earliest descriptions of Christmas trees until the 1920s, paper played a major role in the decorating of trees. After World War I, for various reasons that will be discussed later, paper and cardboard were surpassed and indeed replaced by the blown glass ornaments.

The earliest record of a decorated tree, which was in Strasbourg in 1605, mentioned paper roses as part of the ornamentation. Doubtless, paper had also played a major role in the Paradise and other Christmas time trees of the Middle Ages. So, for many centuries, paper provided an easily made and colorful addition to the tree. It proved to be a cheap medium in which the creative mind could run free and mistakes could simply be thrown away. Furthermore, paper did not require a special talent to create beautiful decorations.

The use of paper ornaments reached its pinnacle of popularity from the 1870s to 1900. During this time, new printing and forming processes brought commercially made "fancy German paper" flooding onto the international market. These intricate and beautiful manufactured items such as scraps, paper dolls, "Dresdens" and candy containers hung side by side on the tree with their homemade counterparts. Ladies' magazines of this period, both in the United States and Germany, abounded with descriptions and suggestions for making these homemade paper ornaments and candy holders. Some of the finest examples of these come from *Godey's Ladies Book* of 1880.

While the commercially made decorations are more sought after by collectors, the homemade ones are just as rare. They also have their own special homespun appeal, and indeed, finely made ones are often difficult to tell from commercial versions.

There were many popular themes in both the commercial and handmade paper ornaments. Flowers, stars, crescent moons, crosses, hearts, anchors, horses, horseshoes, lyres, harps, dolls, fairies, sleighs, shoes, boats, trolley cars, Jacob's ladder, boats, hot air balloons, vases, urns, coffeepots, baskets, butterflies, carriages, fish, birds, dogs, cats and other animals both of the exotic and barnyard type, all found their place on the holiday tree. And we should not forget one of the earliest and longest lasting ornaments - the paper chain, still made in the elementary school of today.

During periods of high national pride such as the Spanish American War and World War I, patriotic themes became popular. These included items such as flags, scrap dolls of Miss Liberty and Uncle Sam, stars, American eagles and shields. The Centennial Celebration in 1876 was also a time of patriotic outpouring such as was seen during our more recent Bicentennial.

Most "store bought" ornaments were assembled and finished by German cottage laborers who received the parts from the manufacturer and assembled them for forty to eighty cents a gross. Thus, even they, in reality, were homemade. But not all fancy paper ornaments were being made in Germany. Flat paper ornaments resembling homemade versions were being manufactured by "W.C. and Co." and the "Novelty Ornament Co." of Philadelphia as early as 1878. And by the turn of the century, honeycomb bells and decorations were being made by the "Biestle Co." of Shipensburg, PA, and the "Paper Novelty Products Co." of New York.

For further information on the history and construction of the homemade ornaments, I would recommend Nada Grey's book - *Holidays*. She even includes patterns for reproducing the more popular Victorian designs.

By the late 1880s paper ornaments of all kinds had become so popular on the Victorian tree that the stylish *Ladies Home Journal* of 1887 condemned them saying:

"Have no paper articles on the tree, except receptacles made to hold something, such as bonbons, fancy boxes, baskets and cornucopias are allowable, but the time wasted over chains, gondolas and tinsel ornaments in recent years, has been something to contemplate. Real dressed dolls look more sensible than caricature fairies or angels, as they can be used, besides which, they are likely to be more beautiful . . . Cover a bare spot by a Japanese fan which, if paper, is paper put to a use."

However, the paper ornaments survived such attacks and remained popular until after the turn of the century when tariffs, embargoes and anti-German feelings, generated by the war, cut deeply into both the supplies and demand. The glass ornament had made steady progress in its popularity since the 1870s. And now it eclipsed the paper ornament both in its demand and cheapness. Although late advertising campaigns praised them as being more colorful and nearly unbreakable, paper decorations never regained their prominence and gradually faded from the twentieth century tree.

This chapter on paper ornaments has been divided into three major sections: "Scraps", which will also include dolls and spun glass ornaments; "Dresden ornaments"; and "Paper candy containers".

This chapter deals with those paper items that would be generally found **on the tree**. Other items made of paper or cardboard that were designed for house or table decorations can be found in the "Other Christmas Collectibles" section.

SCRAP ORNAMENTS

"Scraps", or as they more accurately should be called - chromolithographs, were a product of the industrial and technological revolution of the nineteenth century. These beautiful full-color pictures were found in almost every aspect of daily Victorian life - from advertising products to scrap books, from calendars to cake decorations; from trading cards to school or church rewards; from pictures in the parlor to pretty paper dolls and from Valentines to . . . of course, Christmas ornaments. They were traded, collected, pasted, decoupaged, given away, played with and used to create other items. They were versatile and virtually everywhere.

These colorful prints have been given several different names. In Germany, they were called "glanzbilder", literally "beautiful picture" which referred to their glossy look; or "oblaten", literally "wafers", referring to their early use as decorations on cakes or cookies. In France, they were known as "Chromos" referring, of course, to chromolithographs. In England and America, they became known simply as "scraps". The original scrapbook was designed to hold and display collections of these wonderful pictures.

Before discussing the use of scraps as Christmas ornaments, let us first look at their general history and method of manufacture.

Scrap ornaments and indeed scrap collecting, in general, reached their height of popularity during the last half of the nineteenth century. Prior to 1800, pictures were printed by carving the desired scene into wooden blocks (woodcuts) or later, by engraving the picture into steel plates ("steel engravings"). Any color on these pictures had to be added by hand. Both of these processes were time consuming and very expensive. Then around 1800, German printers discovered lithography. Using a grease crayon to draw on limestone, they were able to attract or repel ink in the appropriate areas of a print. The result was a beautiful picture, with little or no wear on the printing plates; and more importantly, an economical system of mass-producing the prints or pictures. At about the same time, German chemists discovered new methods for developing colored inks and dyes. Soon Germany, and Berlin in particular, became the center of this new chromolithographic process. At first these new colored pictures were flat and square. Later in the century, however, machines were developed that embossed and cut the pictures in intricate patterns. Power driven machines and the new concept of mass production kept prices low; putting the "scraps" into the reach of even the poorest class.

The "Golden Age" of the richly colored, embossed and die cut "scrap" lasted from about 1870 to 1905. In 1905 high tariffs on "fancy German paper" began to cut back the supplies in both the United States and Europe. These same tariffs also spelled the demise of the already expensive "Dresden" ornament; and they died out just as manufactured ornaments were becoming extremely popular in the United States. By World War I, war embargoes and anti-German feeling had cut off scrap supplies and scrap buying. By the end of the war, the "scrap craze" was over; and in a few years, the four color printing process rendered chromolithography obsolete and expensive, just as it had done to its predecessors the woodcut and steel engraving. However, the new printing processes were never able to capture the same rich, beautiful colors nor the delicate shadings that are found in the scraps of the nineteenth century. Now the angelic children, sad Santas and dress-up dolls with their tarnished tinsel are only a nostalgic part of the Victorian Christmas.

Chromolithographs were manufactured in a multi-step process. After the appropriate drawing had been placed on the limestone negative (later steel plates would be used), it was linked with one of the desired colors. This was then printed onto heavy paper. The paper was removed and the next color added to the plate. Each separate color on the scrap required a separate printing; and each time it was inked, the paper had to be lined up exactly as before or the printing would look blurred. This color was layered upon color, up to twenty-six times to give a richness and depth of hues never achieved before or since.

Next the printed surface was coated with a colloidal glue. After dyeing, the print was covered with a gum-mastic based lacquer. These two steps protected the initial surface, gave the scrap its glossy look, and prepared it for embossing.

The embossing process gave the scrap a slightly three dimensional look with its textured surface of raised and depressed areas. As in the printing process, the chromo would have to be lined up carefully on the embossing machine so that the embossed pattern would match the inked picture.

After the steel embossing dies, came the cutting dies. These cut away the unused paper and usually cut the scrap into a silhouette or outline form. Later the embossing and cutting process would be combined into one step. The individual scraps were often connected together in larger sheets, or "swags", by thin strips of paper which were left by the cutting die. These thin strips, or "ladders", often contained the name of the manufacturer, the country that produced them and the product's number (ladder number) for ordering purposes.

The "Scraps" were now ready to be sold. Some went directly to book and paper sellers and were sold to the eagerly buying public for $.3 to $.15 a sheet. Others went to "middlemen" where they were embellished, or glued onto other items to create such things as Valentines cards and Christmas ornaments.

Taking into account the extreme popularity of the colorful scrap, and the rapid growth of the commercial ornament business during the same time period, it is only natural that the two ideas would combine and scraps would find their way onto the holiday tree in varying forms.

As Christmas ornaments, scraps are most often found as small angels, Santas or children "riders" which were glued onto blown glass airplanes, balloons, dirigibles, sailboats, swan boats, cotton, "Dresden" ornaments, glass or other types of material in order to add the fine colored detail that could not otherwise be captured in the medium of the ornament itself. Hence, blown glass or cotton batting angels might have beautiful lithographed faces or wings. Plain cardboard cornucopias or candy containers would become marvelously decorated treasure boxes, ready to be filled with sugary delights when colorful scraps were added.

Sometimes the scrap was not merely added for color, but rather became an integral part of the ornament itself. Examples, such as a scrap girl with a blown glass skirt, a scrap bird on a glass birdbath, or ornaments with scraps inside them, were a creative combining of the two elements and show the ingenuity of the German ornament makers. These pieces will be found listed in the glass section.

Finally, the scraps themselves often became ornaments. Twists of wire tinsel, colored cellophane, crepé paper, cotton batting or mica "snow" might be added for further decoration. In such cases, the scrap was often backed by a heavier piece of cardboard.

In other instances, a Christmas-like scrap, or any other beautiful chromo, would simply be placed on the branches of the tree or hung by thread to slowly twirl on the air currents.

Many scrap ornaments were commercially made by the cottage industry of Germany. However, there were also "homemade" versions, created from store bought scraps, postcards or the advertising cards which were popular giveaways from local businesses. The value of a scrap ornament is not based on whether it is store bought or homemade, but rather on its overall appearance and subject matter. The commercial variety are usually more elaborate and decorative, but the homemade ones, as always, have a certain rustic warmth and sentimental charm that also attract collectors. In either case, they added color and vogue to the Victorian tree.

Dating The Age Of A Scrap

There has been a recent increase of interest in scraps and many types, including Christmas ornaments, have been reproduced. Since it is true that the older the scrap is, the more desirable/valuable it is, it becomes important to be able to date the age of a scrap.

Older scraps were generally printed on heavy paper which was sometimes the thickness of light cardboard; they were also more heavily embossed. Pieces from the 1920s to the present were generally printed on thin paper, and less deeply embossed. Old scraps were lithographed while newer ones have been printed or screened. A magnifying glass will reveal that lithographs have points of different colors while printed ones are all the same color. The colors on old pieces are also richer and deeper than on new. Even if the colors are strong and vibrant, the white backing on older scraps will probably be yellowed with age.

Older scraps had the name of the maker printed on the ladder and not the scrap itself. Many newer pieces will have the name of the manufacturer in small print, on the front or the back. To a certain extent, any ornament the scrap is attached to can be dated by the age of the scrap itself.

Small scraps that are applied to items such as glass, cotton, "Dresdens", etc., will be catalogued and priced in their appropriate areas. This section will list only those items in which the "scrap" is the major element of the ornament. This includes scraps with and without tinsel trim; dolls; scraps with trim of spun glass, cotton, crepe paper, etc; and new scrap ornaments.

Scrap Ornaments With and Without Tinsel Trim

This type is most commonly referred to as a scrap ornament, because the scrap itself is the main element with the tinsel being only a decorative frame for the picture. It was also the most enduring, being produced until about 1927.

Sometimes the scrap was wired or glued onto a simple tinsel ring. Other times, wire loops were pushed through the paper scrap itself. Most often, however, the tinsel was looped in a clover leaf pattern and stapled, sewed, glued or punched through a cardboard backing that the scrap was then glued onto. Then cellophane, crepe paper, "Dresden" trim, tinsel sprays or smaller chromos might also be added to make the piece more elaborate. Since it may vary greatly, the exact arrangement of tinsel, cellophane, etc., is not mentioned and only the scrap itself is described. However, the tinsel decoration is an integral part of the ornament, and the price will be affected if it is not esthetically pleasing or it is not in good condition. Without the tinsel trim, the scrap alone might sell for 25%-50% less. As always, the more elaborate the ornament, the higher its price will probably be.

There were thousands of differing scraps used as Christmas ornaments, and it would be very difficult to catalogue them all. However, they can be grouped into some major categories with enough specific examples to give the reader price guidance.

NOTES:

1.) Double scraps, that is an ornament with a scrap on either side whether exactly the same or different, will be worth more. They were made so that if seen through the tree, or if they turned on their hanger, the plain cardboard would not show. Mirror image scraps are even rarer than the double. These were made during the 1890s, and were designed to give exactly the same appearance on both sides. Because they are mirror images of each other, they fit back to back perfectly.

2.) Sizes given are for the scrap and not the overall ornament. Scrap sizes can vary from ½" to 2 feet or more. Popular scraps were also printed in various sizes. Therefore, you might find a scrap larger or smaller than the ones listed here. It should be noted that this was before photographed reductions and enlargements. Each scrap size had to be completely redrawn in all its intricate detail. Large scraps, seven inches and larger, demand a higher price than those of medium size, 2"-6", or the small size ½"-2". Most ornaments were made from the medium size, while the smaller sizes were used as "riders".

3.) Prices are also given for only the scrap only because many were used plain with only a string or thread hanger. They may be found as a "Scrap only" even today. "With tinsel" indicates that they have been turned into ornaments in some manner, usually by adding tinsel, cellophane, etc. These are more desirable than scraps alone.

4.) Prices reflect scraps in fine shape. Creases, stains, tears, fading, flaking paint or ink, etc., will bring substantially reduced prices.

Santa Claus

The best "find" in this type of scrap is the old fashioned, German "Father Christmas". He is a slender, bearded old man in a long coat. Most often he is shown carrying an evergreen tree and a bag or basket of toys. Generally, he is portrayed as walking. Santas dressed in colors other than red are only slightly rarer.

SANTA WITH TOYS (TYPE I) - Approx. 4¾" x 2½" - He faces left, and both arms are full of toys and a tree. There is a small bag of toys at his hip and a sword is held across the front. He is dressed in a redish-brown coat with a fur trimmed cap.   Scrap only $15.00-25.00
With tinsel $25.00-35.00

SANTA WITH TOYS (TYPE II) - (M) - Approx. 5½" x 3" - He faces to his right and holds a string of toys in his right hand which include a trumpet, sword and book. He carries a small bag at the left which includes a clown and circus animal. At the left shoulder, he carries a tree and a toy rifle. He wears a long fur trimmed coat and a hood.
Scrap only $25.00-35.00
With tinsel $35.00-40.00

SANTA WITH TOYS (TYPE III) - Approx. 8¼" x 3½" - He stands facing the right with switches in his right hand and a cane in his left. He has a basket full of toys on his back, and he wears a long red coat, a hood and old fashioned glasses.   Scrap only $35.00-45.00
With tinsel $75.00-90.00

SANTA WITH TREE (TYPE I) - Approx. 6¼" x 2½" - He faces to his right and wears a long red or white coat with a wide fur collar; and a small satchel hangs at this right side. He carries a snow covered tree and bag over the left shoulder. He carries switches in his belt, but no toys show. (Made by E. Heller of Vienna, one of the few scrap manufacturers outside Germany). (p459)

Scrap only $10.00-25.00
With tinsel $30.00-40.00

SANTA WITH TREE (TYPE II) - Approx. 4" x 1¼" - He walks to his right in a knee length red coat. He carries a blue satchel in his left hand and a toy sword in his right. An undecorated tree appears over his left shoulder.

Scrap only $10.00-25.00
With tinsel $25.00-35.00

SANTA WITH TREE AND CAKES - 6½"L - He wears a knee length fur trimmed coat and hat. His beard is short, and he looks jollier than the traditional Father Christmas. He carries a small bag of apples and presents in his right hand and a square cake in the arm. A snow covered tree is at his left shoulder. His belt is made of rope, and a heart shaped cake appears in the left pocket. This is a later piece, probably used as decorative scraps on cakes.

Scrap only $10.00-15.00
With tinsel $30.00-40.00

SANTA WITH TREE AND TOYS (TYPE I) - Approx. 6½" x 2¼" - He stands full to the front in a long brown-green coat and hood. He has a wicker basket of toys and presents on his back. His right hand is in a satchel, and his left holds a tree.

Scrap only $20.00-30.00
With tinsel $40.00-55.00

SANTA WITH TREE AND TOYS (TYPE II) - Approx. 4¾" x 2" & 6¾" x 3" - He is walking to the right, wearing a blue coat and fur cap. He carries a snow covered tree on his right shoulder and a pack over his left. Switches and toys hang from his belt. This was a popular/common piece. (p466a & p466b)

Scrap only (small) $10.00-15.00
(large) $25.00-35.00
With tinsel (small) $20.00-30.00
(large) $40.00-55.00

SANTA WITH TREES AND TOYS (TYPE III) - Approx. 9" x 4½" - He stands facing forward in a light red coat, shoulder length cape and hood. An undecorated tree is in his left hand, and he is emptying a bag of toys with the right. (p460)

Scrap only $40.00-50.00
With tinsel $70.00-80.00

SANTA WITH TREE AND TOYS (TYPE IV) - Approx. 6½" x 3½" - He is walking to the left, wearing a long red coat, hip-length cape and hood. There is no fur trim. He carries an undecorated tree in his right hand and a basket full of toys on his left arm. (p458)

Scrap only $25.00-35.00
With tinsel $40.00-55.00

ADVERTISING SANTA WITH TREE AND TOYS - Approx. 9¾" x 5¾" - He stands to the right in a long red coat and hood. He holds a decorated tree in his right hand and a puppet in his left. He has a large sack of toys on his back. Advertising says "Now get your stocking ready with the compliments of Matthew Newkirk." This is an American

piece and is not embossed. (p461) (Made by Aug. Gast and Co., New York) $40.00-55.00

SANTA WITH TOYS AND A DECORATED TREE - He stands facing full forward in the traditional outfit. He carries a basketful of toys that show at the right shoulder. The right hand has toys and cakes. The left hand holds a small tree decorated with candles. His pockets are full of fruit and "Lebkuchen" cakes. This piece was designed for cakes. (Germany, Circa. 1910, pic. Stille p20)

Scrap only $15.00-25.00
With tinsel $25.00-35.00

SANTA - Approx. 4½" x 1¼" - He stands facing his left. He wears a long red coat with a bag at the right shoulder and switches on the left hand. It is a swag mate to Santa listed below. (p504a, Printed in Germany by "FWKB" #1236)

Scrap only $5.00-10.00
With tinsel $20.00-30.00

SANTA - Approx. 4½" x 1¼" - He stands facing his right in a blue coat and red hood. He has a decorated tree at the left shoulder and a basket of goodies on his arm. A bear and doll are in his right arm. He is the swag mate to the above. (p504a, Germany, "FWKB") Scrap only $5.00-10.00
With tinsel $20.00-30.00

SANTA WITH A BOOK - Approx. 4¾" x 2½" - He appears to be walking to his right holding a book in his raised right hand. He carries a pack or basket of toys on his back. He has a rocking horse under his left arm. He wears a long red coat and small hat. Scrap only $15.00-25.00
With tinsel $25.00-35.00

SANTA WITH CHILDREN (TYPE I) - Approx. 10¼"W x 7½"H - Santa in a blue coat and hood walks to the right followed by four children, one of whom is crawling. He has wicker baskets on his hip and back that are full of toys. He carries a tree in his right hand. This is a swag mate to the one below. Scrap only $45.00-55.00
With tinsel $75.00-90.00

SANTA WITH CHILDREN (TYPE II) - Approx. 10¼" x 7¾" - He walks to the left with three children, one of whom is crawling. He wears a long red coat and hood decorated with holly. He carries an undecorated tree in the right hand and a basket full of toys on his left arm. He has a pack of toys on his back. This is a swag mate to the above piece. (p465) Scrap only $45.00-55.00
With tinsel $75.00-90.00

SANTA WITH A CHILD AND TOYS - He wears a long coat and hood-like hat. He wears a large bundle on his back, but toys don't show from it. He has toys hanging from both hips including a drum, dolls, a trumpet, a clown and switches. He holds a small girl in a dress in his right arm. His left hand is pulling a doll from the bag at his hip. There is a cut tree laying in the background. (Germany, Circa. 1890, pic. Stille p40) Scrap only $25.00-40.00
With tinsel $45.00-60.00

SANTA WITH CHILDREN (TYPE III) - 10" - Santa in a white outfit holds a child in his left arm, showing him a toy soldier. To his right stand two other children dressed in coats. To his left is a basket of toys and a dog sitting and watching. (ladder number #2862)

Scrap only $45.00-55.00
With tinsel $75.00-90.00

ST. NICHOLAS - Approx. 4½" x 1¾" & 6½" x 2½" - He faces to his left and has a Bishop's staff, hat and robe. He carries a bag of fruit over his right shoulder and has a Bible in his right arm. This is a later piece. (Made by Littauer and Boysen "L&B" #33,692&93 - 1887-1927. Their speciality was scraps for cookies and gingerbread men.)

Scrap only $7.00-15.00
With tinsel $20.00-35.00

SANTA IN A WICKER BASKET - 5½"H x 7"W - A small Santa appears in the center of the basket full of holly and mistletoe. He holds a card that says "Xmas basket"; this piece is not embossed. (p464)

Scrap only $7.00-15.00
With tinsel $20.00-30.00

SANTA HEAD (TYPE I) - His face is framed by a blue hood with holly sprigs. The piece is not embossed. (p469b)

Scrap only $1.00-3.00
With tinsel $5.00-10.00

SANTA HEADS (TYPE II) (Swag of Six) - Approx. 3" x 1½" each - He wears a small fur-trimmed cap that is red, blue or green. He has rosey cheeks and a long beard that is half the length of the scrap. This was a latter German piece made by Littauer & Boysen ("L&B", 1887-1927, #32004) (p463a)

Single scrap only $1.00-2.00
Swag of Six $6.00-12.00
With tinsel $5.00-10.00

SANTA HEADS (Swag of Six) - Approx. 2¼"H - These are the same as the above except for size and ladder number which is #30769. All other prices and information apply.

SANTA HEADS (Swag of eight different) - Approx. 2¼"L x 1½"W - each - These Santas have a rather "square" look. They are dressed in blue, green, red and brown. Three wear fur trimmed hats and five wear hoods, but all have holly sprigs in their hair or hat. They face right, left or front. These are early pieces. (The maker is unknown, but the ladder has "printed in Germany" and #5049)

Single scrap only $1.00-2.00
Swag of eight $8.00-15.00
Full sheet of 36 $20.00-30.00
With tinsel $2.00-4.00

MINIATURE SANTAS (Swag of five different) - Approx. 1¼"L x 1"W - They all carry toys, three are dressed in red, one in blue and one in green. One in red holds a teddy bear in his left hand, another holds a tree at his right shoulder and a large toy car at his left hip. The other red Santa holds a tree by the top in his left hand and holds a long package in the left arm. The "green" Santa holds a bag on a stick over his left shoulder and a bag of fruit in his right hand. The "blue" one walks to the left, has a tree at the left shoulder and a cane in his right hand. Miniature scraps with tinsel are rare, they were usually used as riders on other items. The miniature ornaments were probably made for the small one to three foot "feather" trees. (p463c)

Single scrap only $ .50-1.00
Swag of five $3.00-5.00
With tinsel $10.00-15.00

SANTAS (Swag of three different) - Approx. 2¼"H - Santa #1 is dressed in a long blue coat with red trim. There is an undecorated tree at his left shoulder, and his left hand is raised in warning. There is a walking staff in his right hand. Santa #2 walks to his right but looks back over his shoulder. He uses a walking stick in the right hand and has a tree on the left shoulder. He, like Santa #3, wears a long red coat. Santa #3 stands to the right, has toys tied to his belt and a bag tied to his walking stick over his left shoulder.

Scrap only $5.00-10.00
With tinsel $15.00-25.00

ST. NICHOLAS HEAD - Approx. 3½"H - He is shown bearded and with long white hair. He wears a jeweled bishop's hat and collar. The cap color may be red, blue or green.

Scrap only $5.00-10.00
With tinsel $15.00-25.00

SANTA RIDING A DONKEY - The donkey in fancy harness gallops to the right with a Santa in a long coat and beehive shaped fur hat. He carries switches in his right hand, the reins in his left and has a basketful of toys on his back. (Germany, 1880s)

Scrap only $40.00-50.00
With tinsel $75.00-90.00

SANTA WINDOW DECORATION - Approx. 35"H - This sad looking Santa stands in a long fur-trimmed coat and round fur hat. His left hand holds a cane, and his arm is full of toys. His right hand holds a doll as if offering it to the viewer. A wicker basket on the ground at his feet is full of toys such as a drum, bugle, horse, baby in a buggy, etc. Scraps this size were used as decorations in store windows and counters. (Schiffer p52)

Scrap only $200.00-250.00

SANTA WINDOW DECORATION - Approx. 34½"H - This Santa is dressed in a short, green brocade, fur trimmed coat and matching pants and hat. He has a bag full of toys tied to his back and knotted across his chest. At his feet is a small girl sleeping against a footstool and holding a stocking. He is handing her a doll with his right hand. This, like the above, was probably used as a store decoration. (Schiffer p26)

$200.00-250.00

SANTA IN A WHITE FUR COAT - Approx. 7" - He walks to his right, and his coat has fur trim at the bottom, cuffs, hips, elbows and collar. His rounded cap matches the coat. The coat buckles up the front and is belted. A satchel is at the right hip, a wicker basket of fruit in his left hand.

Scrap only $30.00-40.00
With tinsel $40.00-55.00

TWO SANTAS IN A MODEL "T" TRUCK - Approx. 4½"L - This very unusual piece shows two Santas, one in a blue hooded coat and one in a red fur trimmed coat with a round hat. They ride in an old truck with the back full of toys and trees. The steering wheel is on the right hand side. This piece has a small paper bag behind it which was used for candy. A slightly larger version of it has been reproduced by Merrimack Pub. Corp. (p467)

Scrap only $25.00-35.00
With tinsel $40.00-50.00

COMICAL SANTA - Approx. 9¼" - His fat cheeked face has a comical look. He wears a green coat with a bag of toys over the right shoulder. He carries a basket of goodies in his left hand and a gingerbread house in his left arm. (p470a) $20.00-30.00

SANTA IN HOLLY - Approx. 6¾" - Santa shows from the waist up in a bunch of holly. He holds a small girl in both hands. (p462a)   Scrap only $30.00-40.00
With tinsel $45.00-55.00

SANTA WITH A PLATE OF FRUIT - Approx. 9¼" - He stands with a tree in his left hand and a plate of fruit in his right. There is a basket of toys on his back and a satchel at the right hip. The coat is red with gold embroidery. (p470b) $20.00-30.00

Angels

The angel is one of the few ornaments to represent the religious aspect of Christmas. Apart from them, there are extremely few examples of a religious nature. Angels are almost always shown as young girls or women, wearing white or pastel robes, their wings spread as though flying. Boy angels are scarce, and men angels almost unheard of in scrap Christmas ornaments. Most boy angels are portrayed as cherubs carrying flower chains, and they had widespread use on Valentine cards; while regular angel scraps were also used at Easter and other religious holidays. The use of the same scrap for different holidays was common. In fact, in my collection I have a homemade ornament which had been constructed from an old Valentine card.

Angels often carry musical instruments, candles, books or banners with mottos written on them. Only on rare occasions do they carry a cut evergreen tree, presents or anything related to the secular celebration.

Angel heads were more common than the full bodied form. Their faces were framed on either side by wings. The "Raphael" angel, shown on a cloud from the chest up with her chin resting in the left hand, was extremely popular in scraps, prints and advertising.

Angel scraps are a common theme, and large examples were sometimes used as treetops.

TWO WOMEN ANGELS - 4¾" - The left one stands slightly higher and carries a palm branch and book. The other carries an evergreen tree. Both are dressed in long flowing gowns with spread wings. (p468c)
Scrap only $5.00-10.00
With tinsel $25.00-35.00

TWO GIRL ANGELS RINGING A BELL - 7¾" - Both are dressed in long robes and stand in front of a snow and ice covered archway that holds a bell. They are pulling the rope that rings the bell. (p477)   Scrap only $10.00-20.00
With tinsel $20.00-30.00

TWO ANGELS WITH A TREE - Approx. 7"L x 3½"H - Two child-like angels dressed in drapery and standing on a cloud, hold a tall decorated tree above them. Small wings show at their bare shoulders. The tree is adorned with round ornaments and unlit candles.   Scrap only $12.00-17.00
With tinsel $25.00-35.00

TWO FLYING WOMEN ANGELS - Approx. 5" - Both are dressed in long flowing robes. The left angel is slightly higher, carries an open book, and has a ribbon belt. The right angel carries an undecorated tree in her right hand.

Both have large wings showing at the shoulder. This piece was also made in a "mirror image". (Germany, Circa 1890s, pic. Stille p127)   Scrap only $10.00-15.00
With tinsel $20.00-30.00
With mirror image on reverse $35.00-45.00

TWO LADY ANGELS - 6"H x 4½"W - The left one is brunette and slightly higher, she carries a scroll in both hands. The one on the right is blond and holds tree branches in the folds of her gown. Both wear long flowing gowns, one blue -- one white and appear to be walking to their right. Large wings frame most of their bodies. They are the swag mate to those listed below. (Germany, made by Littauer and Boysen, Berlin, 1887-1927, ladder #3313)
Scrap only $8.00-14.00
With tinsel $25.00-35.00

TWO LADY ANGELS - 6"H x 4½"W - They are the swag mate to the above. The left one is blond and holds a banner or scroll in both hands. The right young woman is brunette and holds a small tree in her left arm. One is dressed in red, the other in white. They appear to be walking to their left. All information and prices apply as mentioned above.

ANGEL WITH A BELL AND CORNUCOPIA - 7½" x 5¼" - The young girl is dressed in knee length gown with wings showing over both shoulders. She carries a hand bell in her right hand and a cornucopia in her left. She appears to be walking over a plain scroll or banner. There is a small tree at the base. This scrap was also done as a mirror image. (Germany, Circa 1890)   Scrap only $10.00-20.00
With tinsel $30.00-40.00
With mirror image on reverse $35.00-45.00

ANGEL WITH A BOOK AND CORNUCOPIA - Approx. 5" - Dressed in a long gown with a sash belt, this young woman appears to be flying in front of a large tree decorated with only a star at the top. In her left hand she holds an open book, and in her right is a cornucopia from which falls wrapped presents and holly sprigs. This piece was also made as a mirror image. (Germany, Circa 1890, pic. Stille p61)   Scrap only $10.00-20.00
With tinsel $25.00-35.00
With mirror image on reverse $30.00-40.00

ANGEL WITH A CORNUCOPIA - 8"H x 5"W - She wears a long gown with more drapery hanging from the waist. Two large wings frame most of the body. She holds a cornucopia of toys, fruit and candy in her left hand. She is heavily embossed and is the mate to the angel below. (Germany, made by Littauer & Boysen, #3006, p474)
Scrap only $15.00-20.00
With tinsel or as tree top $35.00-50.00

ANGEL WITH A HARP - 8"H x 5"W - She is similar to the above with large framing wings. She is turned slightly to her left, holds the harp or lyre in the left hand and plays with the right. She is the mate to the above piece with the same information and prices.

ANGEL WITH A HARP - 6" - This young woman stands on a cloud with wings spread. She wears a long gown, has the harp in her right hand and a flower chain over her left arm.   Scrap only $5.00-10.00
With tinsel $25.00-35.00

ANGEL WITH TREE AND CANDLE - Approx. 8"L x 6"W - The young woman is dressed in a long flowing dress with a jeweled collar and cuffs. She wears a small jeweled crown in her hair, carries a light candle in her right hand and a snow covered tree in her left. Large wings show at the back.
Scrap only $15.00-25.00
With tinsel $35.00-45.00

ANGEL WITH A CANDLE AND TREE - 8" - This woman wears a long flowing gown with a jeweled collar. Wings show at the shoulder. In her right hand, she holds a lighted candle. In her left arm, she holds a large undecorated tree with a stand. This piece was also made in a mirror image. (Germany, Circa 1890, ladder #872A)
Scrap only $15.00-20.00
With tinsel $35.00-50.00
With mirror image on reverse $40.00-60.00

ANGEL WITH A TREE BRANCH - 7"H - This young brunette woman wears a long flowing robe and holds a pine branch in her left hand. Large wings frame most of her body which stands slightly to her left. She is the swag mate to the angel below.
Scrap only $15.00-25.00
With tinsel $35.00-50.00

ANGEL WITH A SONGBOOK - 7"H - She is the mate to the angel above. This blond young woman holds an open songbook in both hands. On the book is printed "Gloria in Excelsis Deo". Large wings frame her body which stands slightly to her right. The same information and prices apply.

ANGEL WITH A BOOK AND SCROLL - 9¼" - She wears a long gown with a star studded scarf wrapped around her. She carries a book in her left hand and a scroll in her right. She has a star and crown of flowers in her hair and appears to be flying. (p476b)
Scrap only $18.00-25.00
With tinsel $35.00-50.00

ANGEL WITH A BANNER AND CROSS - Approx. 7" - This angel in a long robe appears to be flying with a large cross made of pine boughs. The cross is in her left arm, but she is only about three quarters of its size. A large banner or ribbon goes across both which says, "Ehre Sei Gott in der Hohe!" (Glory to God in the highest). This is an early piece, heavily embossed on cardboard and designed as a treetop. It would be rarer to find a piece with German writing as they were not generally exported to this country. (Germany, Circa 1880, pic. Stille p60)
Scrap only $20.00-30.00
With tinsel $40.00-55.00

ANGEL WITH A BANNER - Approx. 7" - This young girl is dressed in a robe that comes just below the knee and tied with a ribbon belt. She holds a long "rope" of pine and flowers in both hands. Beneath her feet is part of a candlelit tree and a banner that says, "Ehre Sei Gott in der Hohe!" Like the above, she, too, is an early treetop decoration and hard to find. (Germany, Circa 1880, pic. Stille p17)
Scrap only $20.00-25.00
With tinsel $40.00-50.00

ANGEL HEAD - 3" - The young girl looks off to her left with uplifted eyes. Short wings frame the lower part of her face. (p469a & p469c)
Scrap only $3.00-7.00
With tinsel $7.00-25.00

TWO ANGEL HEADS - 5½"H x 10½"W - Two girl children, one brunette and one blonde, have their heads together with wings under their chins. One looks straight, the blonde looks off to her right. Both wear small star crowns in their hair.
Scrap only $20.00-25.00
With tinsel $25.00-40.00

LARGE ANGEL HEAD WITH WINGS - Approx. 7"H x 10"W - This young girl with curly brunette hair is shown from the neck up, widespread wings join under her chin and frame most of her face. She could have been used as a treetop.
Scrap only $20.00-25.00
With tinsel $35.00-55.00

KNEELING ANGEL - 4" - This young woman kneels with hands clasped in prayer and wings spread. (p476c)
Scrap only $5.00-10.00
With tinsel $15.00-20.00

ANGEL IN A STAR MEDALLION - 3½"H x 3"W - The young girl is shown from head to hip praying inside a star shaped medallion or border. Only the border is embossed. (p480b)
Scrap only $3.00-7.00
With tinsel $15.00-20.00

ANGEL IN A CRESCENT MOON - 8¼"H x 6"W - This young girl stands inside a crescent moon and wears a long flowing robe. She has small wings, a wreath of flowers in her hair and stars fall from her left hand. (p486)
Scrap only $20.00-30.00
With tinsel $40.00-60.00

ANGEL CHILD WITH A LILY - 7"H - This brunette child with large brown eyes is shown from the hip up. She wears drapery that fastens only at her right shoulder. She holds a long stemmed lily in her left hand. Small wings show at her shoulders.
Scrap only $25.00-35.00
With tinsel $40.00-60.00

RAPHAEL ANGEL - Sizes vary greatly - The child angel is shown from the chest up on a cloud. She appears to be looking dreamily upward with her left hand under her chin and her right laying across the cloud. This was an extremely popular piece both for prints, scraps and scrap ornaments.
Scrap only (Varying sizes) $5.00-20.00
(Higher prices for larger ones)
With tinsel (Varying sizes) $10.00-40.00

ANGEL WITH A STAR - Approx. 9½" - The angel in a long flowing gown, appears to be riding on a large cloud. She holds a large six pointed star above her head with both hands. Golden rays coming from the star form the background.
Scrap only $20.00-30.00
With tinsel $40.00-60.00

ANGEL IN A FLORAL AND ICY STAR - Approx. 6" - The boy angel appears from the waist up in the center of the star, holding a blank scroll in both hands. (p472)
Scrap only $15.00-20.00
With tinsel $30.00-35.00

ANGEL IN A CRESCENT MOON - Approx. 5½"H - This sad looking girl sits facing right and the crescent moon to the left. She wears a flowing robe studded with stars. The moon and her wings have glitter trim.
Scrap only $10.00-15.00
With tinsel $20.00-30.00

ANGEL WITH AN OPEN BOOK - Approx. 4½" - The boy holds an open book in both hands and appears in a trellis covered by ice. (p475)   Scrap only $5.00-10.00
With tinsel $20.00-35.00

TWO LADY ANGELS - Approx. 8½"H - They are both shown walking to the left in long flowing gowns and large wings. The angel on the right carries roses in the fold of her gown. (p471)   Scrap only $15.00-20.00
With tinsel $35.00-50.00

PRAYING ANGEL - Approx. 7½" - A lady angel with spread wings kneels on flowers in prayer. Above her is a radiant cross with four children angel heads. (p473)Scrap only $15.00-20.00
With tinsel $30.00-40.00

TREETOP ANGEL - Approx. 14½"H - She wears a robe and stands on a cloud. She holds a banner spread between her hands which reads "Gloria in Excelsis Deo." Her wings are spread and frame the upper half of her body. This piece has an attachment for making it a treetop or an easel for standing. An excellent reproduction has been made by "Silvestre" of Chicago, Illinois. In the original the banner is an applied piece, and it is marked "Printed in Germany." (Germany, ladder #1915, p482) $40.00-50.00

Snow Angels

Snow Angels are second only to Santas in their popularity; however, they are somewhat scarcer. The difference between "snow" angels or children and regular angels should be stressed. Snow angels are always dressed in winter coats and furs with their wings showing at the back. They are also shown in wintery or snowy scenes and often carry undecorated Christmas trees, toys, packages or other Christmas related items. This gives them their direct link to the Christmas season; it also limited their use in other seasons or for other things. The snow angel may be a representation of the "Krist Kindle" or Kris Kringle form (discussed in the blown glass Santa section). Thus when shown carrying an evergreen tree or toys, the snow angel portrayed the child-like spirit of Christmas and bridged the gap between the religious and secular nature of the Christmas celebration.

Regular angels are usually dressed in long flowing gowns or drapery; however, many children were depicted as cherubs with festoons of flowers. Their use was more widespread and general, especially the cherubs since they could also be used on Valentines, greeting cards and other items throughout the year.

As mentioned before, snow angels which date from 1880-1900 are rarer and more desirable than the regular angel types.
NOTE: It is often difficult to tell the difference between a boy and girl snow angels.

SNOW ANGEL WITH A TREE - 8" - This boy is in a long fur trimmed coat and hat, face to his right and holds a cut evergreen tree in his right hand. He is a mate to the girl below. (Germany, made by Littauer and Boysen, "L&B" from 1887-1927, #2431, p478b)   Scrap only $35.00-45.00
With tinsel $40.00-50.00

SNOW ANGEL WITH A TREE AND SONGBOOK - 8" - This girl is dressed in a long fur trimmed coat and beret-type hat. She holds a songbook in both hands and cradles a tree in her right arm. She is a mate to the boy above. (Germany, made by L&B, p478a)   Scrap only $35.00-45.00
With tinsel $40.00-50.00

SNOW ANGEL BOY WITH A TREE - 2½"H & 7¾"H (but also made in other sizes) - The young boy, who is turned slightly to his right, wears a fez-like hat and is wrapped in a cloak or blanket instead of a coat. He holds a cut tree by the top in his left hand. The tree's base rests at his feet.
Scrap only $3.00-10.00
With tinsel $8.00-20.00
Larger $15.00-25.00
$25.00-35.00

SNOW ANGEL BOY WITH A TREE AND AXE - Approx. 5"H x 2½"W - This young boy, dressed in a hip length fur trimmed coat and hat, holds a cut tree across both shoulders. He has an axe in his ribbon-like belt. Ribbons also hang from his knees. He appears to be running. A wing shows at his left shoulder behind the tree. (ladder #3108)
Scrap only $20.00-25.00
With tinsel $20.00-35.00

SNOW ANGEL WITH A TREE - 6½"H x 2½"W - He is probably a boy, who wears a knee length, high-collared coat with fur trim at the cuffs. His hat resembles a toboggan hat and has a large pom-pom in front. He holds an undecorated tree by the top in his left hand. The base of the tree rests near his right foot. Small wings show at the shoulder. This is possibly a mate to the one below.
Scrap only $20.00-30.00
With Tinsel $25.00-40.00

SNOW ANGEL WITH A CANDLE AND HOLLY - 6½" x 2½" - This young girl stands wearing a long fur trimmed coat with wide sleeves. A flowing scarf wraps around her head and neck. She carries a lit candle in her right hand and holly sprigs in her left arm. She wears spats on her shoes, and small wings show at the shoulders. She is possibly a swag mate to the boy above.
Scrap only $20.00-30.00
With tinsel $25.00-40.00

SNOW ANGLE WITH CANDLE - 9" - This young girl stands facing full forward. She wears a fur trimmed coat with a ribbon belt. On her head she wears a scarf which ties under the chin. She holds a lighted candle in her right hand; her left is at the breast. Her wings frame most of her body. (Germany, made by Heymann & Schmidt, Berlin, 1878-1927)   Scrap only $35.00-45.00
With tinsel $50.00-75.00

THREE SNOW ANGELS WITH TOYS - Approx. 10" x 6" - The center angel is a young woman in a fur trimmed coat and a flowing scarf about the head and neck. She has both arms full of toys and presents which include a trumpet, ball and sheep. The angel to her right is a girl in a fur trimmed coat and hat, carrying a tree and a basket of flowers. The angel to her left appears to be a boy, carrying three hand bells. Both the boy and the center angel have wings at the shoulder.   Scrap only $40.00-50.00
With Tinsel $60.00-80.00

SNOW ANGEL WITH TOYS - Approx. 7″ - She wears a knee length coat with an up turned collar and a turban-like hat. Her left arm and hand are full of toys which include a doll, a sheep and a horn; a dropped apple is in the snow at her feet. The right hand holds a ribbon with a butterfly at the end of it. Her wings show at the back.

Scrap only $35.00-45.00
With tinsel $50.00-75.00

SNOW ANGEL WITH A BASKET OF FLOWERS - Approx. 7½″ - The young girl is turned to her right and wears a long fur trimmed coat. The scarf on her head appears to be made of snow and ice, and she wears spats on her shoes. Large wings show at the back and she carries a basket of lily-like flowers. She has glitter trim. (Germany, made by Heymann & Schmidt, "H&S" - 1876-1927, Berlin)

Scrap only $35.00-45.00
With tinsel $50.00-75.00

SNOW ANGEL WITH A BASKET OF FLOWERS - 10½″ - This young girl with short hair wears a high collar, double breasted coat and a turban-like hat. She has small wings at the shoulder and carries a basket of roses. She wears "Mary Jane" shoes and is the mate to the angel below. She has glitter trim. (Germany, made by LD&CO. #1509)

Scrap only $35.00-45.00
With tinsel $50.00-75.00

SNOW ANGEL GIRL WITH A BASKET OF FLOWERS - 10½″ - She wears a long coat with no trim but has a wide ribbon and bow tied at the waist. Her long flowing scarf covers her head, shoulders and right arm. She holds the basket of flowers in her left hand. She has small wings and appears to be walking in "Mary Janes". She is the mate to the above with all information and prices applying.

SNOW ANGEL GIRL WITH ROSES - 3½″H - She is shown from the hip up in a fur trimmed coat and bonnet that ties under her right cheek. Both hands are full of roses, as is the base of the scrap beneath her coat. Small wings show at her shoulders. She is the mate to the boy below.

Scrap only $15.00-18.00
With tinsel $20.00-30.00

SNOW ANGEL BOY WITH ROSES - 3½″H - He is the mate to the above. He too wears a fur trimmed coat and hat. He has roses in his right hand and a flower pot of roses in his left arm. The base is made of roses. The same prices apply.

SNOW ANGEL WITH HAND BELLS - Approx. 12¾″H - She wears a long caped coat and a cavalier hat with a plume. She has two hand bells in her right hand and one raised in the left. Small wings show above both shoulders. (p483)

Scrap only $45.00-55.00

Snow Children

Snow children are very similar to the Snow Angels in that they are dressed for winter, are shown in snow scenes and often carry items related to Christmas. However, they do not have wings or an angelic appearance. Many times their clothes reflect the fashions of the day, at other times they are dressed in costumes of earlier periods.

SNOW GIRL BUST - 4½″ - She wears a caped coat with a scarf over her head and pink bow at the neck. She has

white glitter trim. She is the mate to the boy below. Either of these could also be dressed in a long cotton or crepe paper coat. The price would be affected accordingly. (Germany, made by Heymann and Schmidt, H&S, Berlin, 1878-1927, ladder #1643, p481d)

Scrap only $7.00-10.00
With tinsel $20.00-30.00

SNOW BOY BUST - 4½″ - He wears a coat with fur collar and military type braid on the chest. He has no hat and is the mate to the girl above. The same information and prices apply. (p481b)

SNOW GIRL WITH FLOWERS (TYPE I) - 7″ - She wears a white coat trimmed with dark fur and has a long flowing scarf about her head and neck. She holds a bouquet of roses in her left hand. She is shown from head to hip and has glitter trim. She is the mate to the girl below. (Germany, probably by Heymann & Schmidt, p481a)

Scrap only $15.00
With tinsel $25.00-35.00

SNOW GIRL WITH FLOWERS (TYPE II) - 7″ - She wears a high collared coat with white fluffy trim and a matching hat. Her hands are in her sleeves and she carries a bouquet of roses. She is shown from head to hip, has glitter trim and is the mate to the girl above. The same information and prices apply. (p481c)

SNOW GIRL IN A WREATH OF ROSES - 10″H x 7½″W - This young girl wears a button coat with a small cape. Her hat is bonnet-like and ties with a bow at her left cheek. She appears chest high in a wreath made of roses, pine cones, pine and holly berries. She has glitter trim. (Germany, probably made by Heymann & Schmidt, p484)

Scrap only $20.00-30.00
With tinsel $50.00-60.00

SNOW CHILDREN IN THE FOREST - 9½″H x 7½″W - The two children appear in a woodland scene that forms a border all around them. It consists of flowers, ivy, holly, mistletoe and snow covered trees. The children look almost like angels. The sitting girl is wrapped in a long flowing coat and scarf. What appears to be a boy also wears a long coat and scarf and carries a cut tree. It has glitter trim. (p485)

Scrap only $35.00-45.00
With tinsel $40.00-50.00

SNOW BOY WITH A TREE - Approx. 7″ - The boy, dressed all in white, wears a hip length coat, long neck scarf and toboggan hat. He carries a snow covered tree at his left shoulder. There is a golden sun or halo behind his head. He is a mate to the girl below. They were used on "Lebkuchen". (Germany, pic Stille p84)

Scrap only $10.00-15.00
With tinsel $25.00-35.00

SNOW GIRL WITH A TREE - Approx. 7″ - Dressed like the above mentioned boy, she carries a snow covered tree in her right arm. She, too, has a golden sun or halo behind her head. All other information and prices apply.

SNOW BOY WITH PRIMROSES - Approx. 5¾″L x 2½″W - This boy with shoulder length hair wears a blue coat with fur trimmed cuffs. He has a fur trimmed cap in his left hand and primroses in his right. He wears a wide red sash, boots and "knickers". He stands in front of a small snow covered fence. He is a swag mate to the girl below.

Scrap only $10.00-15.00
With tinsel $25.00-35.00

SNOW GIRL WITH PRIMROSES - 5¾"L x 2½"W - She is dressed in a green caped coat with white fur trim. Her left hand is in a white fur muff, and her right holds a pink primrose. She wears boots, a large red hat with feathers, and stands in front of a snow covered fence. She is the mate to the boy above with the same prices applying.

Paper Doll Ornaments

"Scrap" paper dolls came into popularity during the 1870-80s and have continued down to the present day. However, in this section I will deal only with their use as tree decorations.

Paper doll ornaments, which were also known as fairies or snow fairies, were usually portrayed as babies, girls or women. Dressed in "clothes" made of crepe paper, tissue paper, spun glass, cotton batting, tarlatan or fabrics, these "fairies" reached their height of popularity from about 1870-1910. Some dolls were made in a bust form with only the head and shoulder showing out of a homemade dress. Others were depicted from head to hip and included legs and feet to be added beneath the dress. Still others were full bodied with movable arms and legs. Their clothes could come ready made or in a kit form, but most often they were homemade.

Doll ornaments were produced in varying sizes, 3", 4", 6½", 7", 9¼", 14" and 18" were some of the common sizes. But in Nerlich's 1902-3 catalogue they list one dressed in cotton batting that was some 30" tall.

Commercially produced dolls that were destined for the tree were most often dressed in crepe paper, cotton batting or spun glass skirts. They were also decorated with tinsel or "Dresden" trim to give them that special Christmas appeal, and of course, they had a string or wire loop for hanging. Homemade versions were dressed much the same as the commercial, with the additional use of tarlatan - a thin type of muslin. In homemade ornaments, the scrap pictures were often cut from advertising cards, calendars, postcards, etc. This type of scrap not only indicates they were homemade, but can also be helpful in dating them.

Whether homemade or commercial, their use by the late 1880s and 1890s was so popular that they were discussed in many ladies' magazines of the time. This one is from Peterson's Ladies National Magazine of 1888: "Fairies add greatly to the beauty of the tree; half-length figures can be cut out of colored fashion-plates in illustrated magazines. Feet must be cut out and added, attached to the back of the tarlatan skirt. Great ingenuity can be exercised in dressing these, fancy costumes being selected if desired. Tarlatan, in varied colors, is used for dressing them, elaborately trimmed with gold and silver lace and spangles."

When used as ornaments, paper dolls fulfilled several functions. They added color and the popularity of scraps to the tree. Sometimes they advertised products or businesses; other times they portrayed famous stars of the era and were collected much the same as photographs and posters are today. They also represented the toy dolls which along with other gifts were hung from the branches of early trees rather than placed under them as we do today. And they were, of course, toys in themselves to be taken off the tree and played with year after year, thus keeping the child occupied. They were also given as Twelfth Night gifts when the tree was taken down. This idea is born out by Nada Grey in her book *Holidays*. She quotes from the "Standard Designer" of 1896: "Paper dolls with jointed limbs can be bought for a few cents apiece, and may be dressed in a variety of ways: some of them even make very pretty Christmas angels when decked out with tissue paper wings and the floating robes of pale blue or pink with gilt stars for trimming." She also writes, "They continue by noting that the dolls (four to fourteen inches tall) make the tree bright but also provide acceptable gifts for little girls if outfitted with clothes that can be removed "at will" and accompanied by a few sheets of colored paper to replenish the wardrobe as needed."

It is exactly this use as a toy which has helped to make these once popular items so scarce. The dolls were often kept and used as year round toys and not saved or handed down as were the more traditional types of ornaments. Their one advantage over the popular glass ornament was that they were nearly unbreakable. However, they seemed to gather dust and dirt and were more easily damaged by dampness and mildew. So, when their bright colors faded, they were often thrown out.

The original price also helps to account for the scarcity of paper doll ornaments. At the cost of five to eighteen cents apiece, they were rather expensive for the average working class family. Those that came commercially dressed were even more expensive as evidenced by Nerlich's 1902-3 catalogue:

Dolls

Lithographed, carved head, arms and feet, fancy ornamented cotton-batting dress.

		Dozen
227/228	Assorted, 12 in., 1 doz. in pkg.	$1.20
230.	Assorted, Negroes-Boys and Girls, 1 doz. in pkg.	1.20
231.	Cat drinking coffee, dressed, 1 doz. in pkg.	1.20
346.	Long dressed baby, 1 doz. in pkg.	2.20
345/347.	Assorted, girl dolls, 16 inch size	2.20
333.	Dog smoking pipe, dressed	2.20
351.	Santa Claus with tree	2.20
352.	Assorted Dolls, 30 inch size	4.00

Although hard to find, the scrap paper doll makes a wonderful and nostalgic addition to the tree.

NOTES:

1. Any dolls listed could easily have either spun glass, pressed cotton or crepe paper clothes. The cotton is more desirable and prices will be affected accordingly.

2. Also see the section on cotton, for those dolls in which the main element of the ornament is cotton instead of a scrap. Similarly see the section on spun glass, where that is the main element of the ornament.

3. In Germany, some dolls had their "clothes" made out of edible things such as "Lebkuchen".

4. Not all of the commercially produced dolls were made in Germany. Often the scrap parts were purchased and then assembled with the dresses here in the United States.

flows from her shoulders. She is featured in Nerlich's 1902 catalogue. (R1-2) $125.00-140.00

HAPPY BABY - Approx. 4½"L (Scrap only) - This smiling baby is shown in a ruffled bonnet tied with blue bows. The scrap goes to the waist where a cotton or crepe paper dress is attached. She is the mate to the baby below. (Germany, made by Littauer & Boysen, ladder #2818, R3-4, p488) $20.00-30.00
                    With dress $75.00-85.00

CRYING BABY - Approx. 4½"L (Scrap only) - This is a mate to the one above but the bonnet has no ruffles. All other information and prices apply.

HAPPY BABY - Approx. 2½" (Scrap only) - She wears a ruffled bonnet, the ribbons of which she holds in both hands. She wears a square neck, lacy blouse. Her skirt is cotton batting and may have crepe paper trim. Below the skirt she has ribbon tied "Mary Jane" shoes and ankle socks. She is the mate to the one below. (Germany, ladder #32019, R2-3) $75.00-85.00

CRYING BABY - Approx. 2½" (Scrap only) - This one is like the one above except the collar on her dress is round. All other information and prices apply.

GIRL WITH A DOLL - 10"H x 8"W - The young girl is shown from the lower chest up in a dress with lace and ribbon. She holds a doll in her left arm. Her dress is made of cotton batting with a tinsel bow and crepe paper trim. She wears a tinsel halo or hat. (p487, R4) $80.00-100.00

GIRL WITH A KITTEN - 13"H - This girl is very similar to the one above except she holds a kitten and scrap shoes under her dress. $80.00-100.00

JOINTED DOLL - 7" & 8¾" - The young girl who is jointed at the arm and legs is also heavily embossed. She is in a crepe paper dress with "Dresden" stars, and tinsel for trim. Tinsel circles the head in a halo shape and forms the hanger. They came in at least 3 forms, one with black hair, one with brown and one blond. All the dresses and trim were slightly different. (p494 & p495a & b, R2-3) $35.00-50.00
                    Larger $50.00-75.00

LADY IN A ROUNDED SKIRT - Approx. 6" - Instead of the typical bell shaped dress, this one is round, with the scrap torso in the center. It, thus, has the appearance, that the back of the dress is "flipped-up". The dress may be made of cotton, netting tarlatan or tinsel. This type was most often homemade. (Schiffer, p67, R3) $40.00-55.00

MISS LIBERTY - Approx. 3"L (Scrap only) - Miss Liberty is shown to the waist and holds a flag. Her skirt is made of cotton or red, white and blue crepe paper. She was undoubtedly made for export to the United States. (p490, R3) $40.00-60.00

OLD MAN WITH A FEZ - Approx. 2¾"L (Scrap only) - He wears a smoking jacket, smokes a long pipe and is reading a newspaper. He is shown to the waist. His "shirt" may be made out of spun glass, crepe paper or cotton. These might have paint, glitter or "Dresden" trim added. His scrap slippers show under the shirt. He is a mate to the old woman below. (p502c, R2-3) $35.00-45.00

OLD WOMAN IN A BONNET - Approx. 2¾"L (Scrap only) - She wears a yellow shawl over both shoulders and her bonnet is tied with yellow ribbons. She holds a white cat in both hands. She is a mate to the old man above with all information and prices applying. (p502a)

PEASANT GIRL WITH A BASKET - Approx. 7" - She wears a head scarf, blouse and vest. She has a basket of wine and cheese on her right arm and flowers in her left. Her skirt may be crepe paper or spun glass. (R3)
                    $40.00-55.00

PEASANT GIRL WITH A HEART SHAPED CAKE - Approx. 8½" - She wears a scarf about her head and an embroidered, lacy blouse. She holds a large heart shaped cake in both hands. She is shown to the waist, but the ribbons around her waist hang down a crepe paper or cotton dress. Shoes show underneath. She is a mate to the boy below. (Germany, ladder #31133, R2-3) $50.00-75.00

PEASANT BOY WITH HEART SHAPED CAKE - Approx. 8½" - He wears a pillbox hat and embroidered shirt with a high collar and a vest. He carries the cake under his right arm. He is a mate to the girl above with all other information and prices applying.

PEASANT LADY WITH A BABY - Approx. 2¾"L (Scrap only) - She is shown to the hip in a peasant skirt and blouse and about her head is a printed scarf. She cradles a baby in bunting in her arms. Her "dress" may be of spun glass, crepe paper or cotton batting. She may also have scrap legs and feet. (Germany, ladder #30762, R3) $35.00-45.00

SANTA WITH A SPUN GLASS "SKIRT" (TYPE I) - Approx. 6" - He carries an undecorated tree at his left shoulder and a bag of toys over his right shoulder. He is shown to the wide belt at his waist, then has a "skirt" made of spun glass. Scrap boots show at the bottom. (Schiffer p69, R2-3)
                    $40.00-50.00

SANTA WITH A S.G. SKIRT (TYPE II) - Approx. 6" - He carries a small decorated tree with lighted candles in his left hand. In his right hand, he carries packages; and a basket of toys shows at his back. The s.g. skirt starts at his belted waist and has scrap boots below it. (Schiffer p69, R2-3)
                    $40.00-50.00

SANTA WITH A S.G. SKIRT (TYPE III) - Approx. 6" - He carries an undecorated tree at his left shoulder, and the index finger of his right hand is raised as if in warning. He is wearing a hood, and the s.g. starts at his waist. Scrap boots show beneath the skirt. (p502b, R2-3)
                    $35.00-45.00

SANTA WITH A S.G. SKIRT (TYPE IV) - Approx. 6" - He carries a tree decorated with ornaments, snow and a radiant star on his left shoulder. In his right arm and hand he carries toys which include a doll, drum and trumpet. The s.g. starts at the waist, and boots show beneath it. This is a mate to the Santa below. (Germany, ladder #31971, R2-3) $45.00-55.00

SANTA WITH A S.G. SKIRT (TYPE V) - Approx. 6" - This Santa in a fur trimmed hood, carries a snow covered tree at his left shoulder, and a satchel hangs at his left hip. He shows a toy clown with his right hand. The s.g. starts at the waist with boots beneath. He is a swag mate to the above with the same information and prices.

SANTA IN A COTTON SKIRT - Approx. 7″ - He is shown to the waist in a red fur trimmed coat and hat which also has pine sprigs in it. There is a bag over his left shoulder which he holds with both hands. The cotton skirt may have crepe paper or "Dresden" trim. $100.00-125.00

SNOW GIRL WITH A MUFF - Approx. 10″ - The scrap of a young girl is in a fur trimmed bonnet with ribbons on top and under the chin. At her waist, her scrap arms and hands are shown in a fur muff. Her caped coat is made of cotton batting, which could be plain or trimmed with tinsel, crepe paper or Dresden stars. (Schiffer p65, R2-3)
                    $100.00-125.00

SNOW GIRL WITH A DOLL - Approx. 10″-12″ - Wearing a ruffled bonnet, she is similar to the above, except she cradles a doll in her left arm. (R2-3) $100.00-125.00

SNOW GIRL - Approx. 12″ - Similar to the above two dolls, she has nothing in her arms, but "Mary Jane" shoes show under her cotton batting dress. (R2-3) $100.00-125.00

BOY IN A COTTON SNOWSUIT - Approx. 8½″ - The full length boy is "dressed" in an added coat and pants made of cotton. It has Dresden stars and tinsel trim. (p493)
                    $80.00-100.00

CAT WITH A BALL OF YARN - Approx. 18″ - She is dressed in a cotton dress with a crepe paper collar and trim. Her legs and tail show at the bottom. (p491)$160.00-180.00

LARGE SANTA DOLL - Approx. 18″ - He holds toys in one hand and a tree in the other. His body is made up of cotton. (p489) $160.00-180.00

MONKEY WITH A TAMBOURINE - Approx. 18¾″ - In this large piece, the body is made of cotton and crepe paper. (p492) $160.00-180.00

Spun Glass Ornaments

The virtually unbreakable spun glass ornament found the height of its popularity around the turn of the century, especially about 1900-1910. They were a creative combining of the already popular scrap and the new technique of "spinning" glass. Spun glass ornaments have been placed in the scrap section because their major component is the die cut, embossed chromolithograph.

Fibers of spun glass were worked into a disc shape, or other varying forms, that might range in size from two to nine inches. Then a colorful scrap, usually a Santa or an angel, would be glued to the center. The smaller ornaments were designed to twirl slowly from the tree's branches, while the larger ones might also serve as treetops.

Spun glass, as its name implies, was literally spun from hot glass rods. The ornament maker melted the end of a glass rod over his gas flame. The resulting melted glass drops were pulled out into a thin thread. Quickly, this "thread" was placed over a wheel some 15 cm. in circumference. Then working in unison, the glassworker slowly pushed the glass rods through the flame while an assistant slowly turned the wheel.

Much of the resulting glass "thread" was used in in-

dustry; but a certain amount also found use in Christmas ornaments as tails for birds or comets. Wings for angels and butterflies were also fashioned out of spun glass as were dresses for scrap dolls and the rosette or disc ornament already mentioned. Finally, the curly glass "angel hair" that spread a cloud-like haze over the tree was also made of spun glass.

For an added touch of beauty, colored glass rods were occasionally used. The resulting glass "threads" and ornament then acquired a shimmering but subtle pastel color to them.

As mentioned before, the main element of the spun glass ornament is the scrap. Therefore, prices for this type of decoration will be dictated to a certain extent by the type of scrap that is on it. Several pieces will be listed here for price guidance. Further guidance can be found in the previous lists of the scraps themselves.
NOTES:
1. SG means spun glass
2. Prices given are for ornaments in good condition. The spun glass should be full in its shape without gaps or thin spots. It should also be free of stains.
3. Pieces with scraps on both sides are slightly more desirable, as is colored SG which is rarer than the usual white tint.
4. Scraps of people with SG skirts are listed in the dolls section.
5. SG ornaments have not been reproduced.
6. Rarity - most SG ornaments fall into the 3-4 range of rarity.

SPUN GLASS ROSETTE - Approx. 2″ dia. - It has a small Santa head scrap on both sides. $20.00-30.00

SG ROSETTE - Approx. 3¼″ dia. - The glass has a pink tint. There is a cellophane flower in the center with a tinsel burst and a scrap Santa head wearing a holly crown. The reverse has a foil star. (p501c) $20.00-30.00

SG ROSETTE - Approx. 4″ dia. - Centered is a foil flower, upon which is a tinsel burst and a Santa head with a holly crown. (p501a & p503b) $20.00-30.00

SG ROSETTE - Approx. 4″ dia. - Centered on each side is a 1½″ girl angel head with wings spread around her neck. This is the most common scrap to be found on rosettes. (p498b & p503d) $20.00-30.00

SG ROSETTE WITH A COMET TAIL - Approx. 3¼″ dia. & 4″ tail - Centered on both sides is a girl angel head with wings. (p501b) $30.00-40.00

SG ROSETTE WITH A COMET TAIL - Approx. 3½″ dia. & a 4″ tail - Centered on one side is a Rapheal angel.
                    $30.00-40.00

SG ROSETTE - Approx. 5½″ in dia. - A Santa in a fur trimmed red coat with bells over his right shoulder and a bunch of holly in his left hand is on one side. An angel in a flowing green gown with hands clasped in prayer and her head raised is on the other side. $40.00-55.00

SG ROSETTE - Approx. 6″ in dia. - The scrap is of an angel in a long green gown - on one side only. $40.00-55.00

SG ROSETTE - Approx. 7½″ in dia. - This piece has a spiral wire for placing on top of the tree and string for hanging. The scrap is a large standing angel in a flowing gown with large golden wings. She holds a banner reading "EHER SEI GOTT in der HOHE" - "Glory to God in the Highest." There is a scrap on one side only.$50.00-60.00

SANTA HEAD "COMET" - Approx. 8½″L - The scrap is 2½″ long and shows a long bearded Santa in a fur trimmed hat. A long SG "comet tail" streams out from his beard and two wing-like sprays come from either side of the head area. The tail may be decorated with paint, glitter or Dresden trim. They are found with scraps on one or both sides. (p503c)   Single scrap $30.00-40.00
                   Double scrap $35.00-45.00

SANTA COMET WITH AQUA TINTED SG - Approx. 8″L - The scrap is approx. 1½″ of a short bearded Santa in a hood. The arrangement of the SG is the same, and it may be trimmed as the one listed above.
                   Single scrap $35.00-45.00
                   Double scrap $40.00-50.00

HUMMINGBIRD WITH SG WINGS - Approx. 4½″ - The scrap is of a hummingbird with the wings and tail added in spun glass. $20.00-30.00

RAPHAEL ANGEL ON A SG CLOUD - Approx. 4″ - The 2¾″ scrap shows the angel from the hip up on a cloud. One hand is under her chin, the other rests on the cloud and a small wing shows at her right shoulder. Curly SG angel hair makes up the cloud she appears to be riding on. This was a popular scrap and could be found in several sizes. (p500) $15.00-25.00

COMETS - Approx. 3″-4″ - The head is usually a gold or silver "Dresden" scrap star (also see "Dresden" ornaments) with an attached spun glass tail. $7.00-12.00

SG SEMICIRCLE WITH A "DRESDEN" SAILBOAT - Approx. 4″ in dia. - The gold sailboat is approx. 2″ and mounted along the top edge. The SG may be further embellished with small stars or "Dresden" trim. (p498a)
                   $35.00-50.00

AMERICAN ANGEL AND SG TREETOP - Approx. 8″ in dia. - This has a scalloped SG rosette in the center of which is shown an angel from the chest up. She sets on a cloud of curly angel hair, has large gold embossed wings and is surrounded by three large gold stars. Made by the National Tinsel Mfg. Co. of Wisconsin, it is still being produced today.   Old version $15.00-20.00
                   New version $5.00-10.00

SG SEMICIRCLE WITH ANGELS - Approx. 6¾″ dia. - One angel plays a harp while the other sings. The one shown is embellished with Dresden stars and "A Merry Christmas". (p499) $30.00-45.00

SANTA ON A SG COMET - Approx. 8½″L - Santa scraps are applied to a rosette with a comet tail. (p506 & p507)
                   $30.00-40.00

BLUE SG COMET - Approx. 3″ dia. & 4″ tail - The comet is a rosette with a tail, and a small angel head. It is tinted an unusual dark blue. (p530a) $35.00-45.00

Miscellaneous Scrap Themes

We now come to the miscellaneous section of scraps. This includes a variety of themes not all of which are Christmas related. Many different kinds of scraps were used as ornaments. As long as they were "cute", they would fit well into the feeling of the season. Such things as puppies and kittens with big ribbon bows, looking cuddly and irresistable remind us of their use as gifts. Adorable children, no matter how they are dressed or what they are doing, fit into the spirit of Christmas. Winter scenes of houses, animals or nature were popular as Christmas scraps, holiday cards and advertising give-aways.

Religious scraps (other than angels) and Nativity scene scraps were seldom made into ornaments, thus showing the secular nature of Christmas even in the Victorian era.

The scraps in this miscellaneous section while just as beautiful as the others listed, do not demand the same prices. This is simply because their themes are not as desirable as those related directly to Christmas. A representative sample has been listed which can give price guidance to most of the other types.

BOY AND GIRL IN AN OVAL OF FLOWERS - 3½″H - They ride double on a bicycle, the boy in a sailor suit, the girl in a caped coat and hat. The background shows snow falling, and there is a pine branch in the handlebars. Only the flower border is embossed. (p480c)Scrap only $3.00-8.00
                   With tinsel $15.00-25.00

BOY CLOWN - 3½″ - A small boy dressed in a clown suit jumps within an oval gold frame. The entire picture is embossed although it is probably a mate to the above. (p480a)
                   Scrap only $3.00-8.00
                   With tinsel $10.00-20.00

NATIVITY SCENE - 9½″ x 7″ - A large scroll at the top says "Gloria in Excelsis Deo". It shows Christ in the manger with shepherds and wise men at the sides.
                   Scrap only $8.00-12.00
                   With tinsel $20.00-30.00

OVAL SNOW SCENES - 3″ & 7″ - These show snow covered houses, mills, castles, cottages, etc. in a winter time setting. They are inside a gold or fancy oval frame.
                   Small Size - Scrap only $1.00-3.00
                   With tinsel $10.00-20.00
                   Large Size - Scrap only $2.00-5.00
                   With tinsel $15.00-25.00

SCENES OF NATURE OR ANIMALS - Sizes vary - These are most often framed inside round or oval borders. The same prices apply as for the above.

SCENES OF CHILDREN AT PLAY - Sizes vary - These too are framed in round or oval, gold or flowered borders. Children may be seen playing tag, selling toy boats, swinging, picking flowers, etc.   Scrap only $3.00-8.00
                   With tinsel $15.00-25.00

DOVE WITH AN OLIVE BRANCH - 7″W x 6½″H - This large white dove is pictured flying with the olive branch in its beak. It is an early piece. (Stille p87)
                   Scrap only $10.00-15.00
                   With tinsel $30.00-40.00

GIRL WITH A TREE - Approx. 5 " - This young blond girl is in a long dress with wide ribbon belt. She holds a small undecorated tree in her left arm; a smaller one grows at her feet. She and the next two were usually used as decoration of Christmas cakes or "Lebkuchen". She is the swag mate to the girl below. (Germany, Stille p87)

Scrap only $10.00-20.00
With tinsel $25.00-35.00

GIRL WITH A BASKET AND TREE - Approx. 5" - This young brunette girl wears a dress with a wide sash belt. She holds a wicker basket in both hands, in which is a small undecorated tree. She is a mate to the above with the same information and prices.

DECORATED TREE - Approx. 8 " - The exquisite candlelit tree is topped by a large angel and is heavily decorated. The ornaments are shown in great detail and represent decorations of the time. These include, lit candles, Santas, strings of glass beads, a horn, anchor, basket, dolls and toy animals. Beneath the tree are more toys and gifts. (Germany, Circa 1890, Stille p88)   Scrap only $15.00-25.00
With tinsel $30.00-50.00

LARGE SPRIGS OF HOLLY OR MISTLETOE - 5½ " but size will vary, with larger ones selling for more, smaller for less.   Scrap only $4.00-8.00
With tinsel $6.00-12.00

BOUQUETS OR BASKETS OF FLOWERS - 5 " but size will vary , with larger ones selling for more, smaller for less.
Scrap only $1.00-4.00
With tinsel $5.00-10.00

PATRIOTIC SCRAPS - 5 " but size will vary - These were made for export to the United States. They include flags, Miss Liberty both as a woman and a child, Washington and Lincoln, Uncle Sam and small boys dressed as Uncle Sam. Prices will vary with size. They are rare on Christmas items.
Scrap only $10.00-20.00
With tinsel $35.00-50.00
Miss Liberty with cotton skirt $40.00-60.00

NATIVITY SCENE - Approx. 3½ " - An angel and two children kneel before the manger in which baby Jesus sits. A candlelit and decorated tree stands behind the manger. (ladder #1098)   Scrap only $2.00-5.00
With tinsel $15.00-20.00

CHRIST AS AN ADULT - 7½ " H - He wears a long robe, has a halo, a walking stick in the right hand and a lamb on the left shoulder. Jesus portrayed as an adult is rarely seen as a Christmas ornament.   Scrap only $7.00-12.00
With tinsel $20.00-30.00

3-D PULL OUT NATIVITY SCENES - 5 " H x 5½ " W - The background scene is of Bethlehem. Mary, Joseph, Christ child and the Wise men are the center scene. The front scene has the stable, manger, flowers and leaves. Five angel children are on the roof, as is a banner reading "Gloria in Excelsis Deo". This opens just like 3-D Valentines.
$20.00-30.00

3-D CHRISTMAS ROOM SCENE - 4½ " x 4 " - The back scene is of a room, the center shows a Santa walking to the right carrying a cane, pouch and Christmas tree. The front

scene shows a trellis with flowers and leaves. This pulls out like 3-D Valentines. $25.00-35.00

BUST OF CHILD ON A CREPE PAPER DISC - Approx. 5 " - A bust of a Victorian girl or boy is mounted on a crepe paper disc with tinsel trim. (p497)

$20.00-30.00

SCRAPS ON A LACE ROSETTE - Approx. 4½" diameter - Scrap torsos are mounted on a rosette of lace or tarlatan. Those shown are a dressed cat and monkey which are a set, and the material may form a type of dress. The third shows an angel head with wings. (p496)   Each $30.00-40.00

New Scraps

Before passing from the subject of scraps and scrap ornaments, I feel it is appropriate to comment on some of the new scraps and scrap reproductions being produced today.

Several companies, most notable Mamelok Press of England and Paul B. Zoecke of West Germany, have manufactured scraps since the 1800s and are still carrying on their traditional business. Other companies have recently reproduced or redesigned early scraps and ornaments in light of the interest in Victorian nostalgia that has occurred over the past few years. These scrap ornaments are designed to help recreate the old fashioned Christmas of "Grandmother's tree".

Of course, these modern versions are made by offset printing and not by chromolithography; and thus, they are easily recognized from the originals. Furthermore, most new prints have been produced on thin paper with shallow embossing and have the manufacturer's name printed on the front or reverse. New scraps and reproductions are usually priced in the one to five dollar range.

Some manufacturers of new and reproduction scraps are as follows:

Paul B. Zoecke of Berlin, West Germany, was founded in 1896 as Zoecke & Mittmeyer, and thus have a rich heritage in the "scrap" industry. In the 1920s they and Mamelok Press bought out the prints, plates and machinery of the famous scrap makers Littauer & Boysen (L & B). Zoecke still uses many of the old fashioned themes and prints in its production. Their pieces are still generally sold in swags, but the paper is much thinner than in their antique originals. Their ladders are marked with the initial "PZB". Old designs still carry the mark "Printed in Germany", while newer ones have "Printed in Western Germany".

Mamelok Press Ltd. of Suffolk, England, originally began in Breslau in the early 1800s and is one of Europe's first manufacturers of chromolithographs. In the 1930s the business transferred to England in order to escape Nazi Germany. While they too, continue to print a few of the older pieces, they have modernized much of their stock to keep in fashion with the international trade. They do, however, have a series called the "Golden Series Scrap Relief" which reproduces pieces, with an antique look, taken from *A History of Printed Scraps* by New Cavendish Books. Mamelok's scraps are sold in swags and bear the ladder marking "MLP" and "Made In England".

The following companies have reproduced prints with an antique look. They are not sold in swags but as individual items or sets. Generally each piece is marked with the manufacturer's name.

The Merrimack Publishing Corp., of New York, has printed a whole array of Victorian pieces. Some are reproductions and some are new versions, but all are designed to have an antique look. Most of their prints hava a distinctive gold outline. In their product line, they carry candy containers, Santas and snow angels. Printed on heavy cardboard, they also have two series that are "replicas" of rare glass ornaments and Dresden ornaments. Their pieces are embossed and printed in Hong Kong.

Treasure House Imports of Seattle, Washington, have some nice scrap ornaments with tinsel and candy container reproductions with an antique look. Their pieces are also printed and embossed on heavy cardboard in Hong Kong.

The Old Print Factory, Inc. of New Baltimore, Michigan, are "manufacturers of quality antique paper reproductions". They do a nice job in capturing the subtle colors of the originals and they have added glitter trim, but the pieces are not embossed. Their prints are made in the United States.

Shackman's of New York, Silvestre of Chicago and Gordon Fraser of England have also produced some fine antique scrap reproductions. Shackman and Silvestre's pieces are embossed and printed in Hong Kong, while Gordon's are unembossed and printed in England.

All of these companies have produced some fine examples of the now hard to find Victorian scrap ornaments.

DRESDEN ORNAMENTS

"Dresden" embossed cardboard ornaments are some of the most beautiful, durable and clever ornaments to adorn the Christmas tree. However, because they were never as popular in the United States as they were in Germany, they also remain some of the rarest and most expensive of the Christmas ornaments.

The name "Dresden" comes from the fact that most of these pieces were produced by approximately nine companies in the Dresden-Leipzig area of Germany from about 1880 until the time of the First World War. There were, however, other areas of the country producing them, and the time frame is only an approximation. During this thirty years, there was a vast variety of shapes and sizes produced. Although many were only two to three inches in size and embossed in a metalic gold or silver, a few were considerably larger and some were realistically painted. Among dealers and collectors, there remains some confusion over exactly what is meant by the term "Dresden" ornament. The term "Dresden" is often incorrectly applied to any cardboard, die-cut or embossed paper item. More correctly, it should refer to only that type of German paper ornament that has been embossed and cut from detailed dies, and not merely constructed of cardboard. Their color is generally gold or silver. One company's intention was to make them "appear to be stamped from tin or gold plate." They bear no resemblance to the beautiful printed chromolithographs of this same period. Interestingly enough, the Germans don't apply the term "Dresden" to this type of ornament, but rather refer to them as "gold or silver cardboard ornaments."

"Dresden" ornaments were produced by stamping a $\frac{1}{32}$ inch sheet of cardboard between two dies. One was the stamping die, and the other the receiving die, which was like a negative. Each minute detailed area on the stamping die was raised, and the corresponding area on the receiving die was depressed. Thus, a double sided ornament would require four separate dies since each side is the reverse or mirror image of the other. And each three dimensional ornament would require separate dies for each applied piece. This intricate die work gave the ornament its detailed charm. After embossing and cutting, cottage laborers then gently glued and assembled the applied pieces, and painted them when necessary. The more intricate the piece would be, the more labor that would be involved, and of course, the more expensive the price would become. Cost is another reason for their scarcity in this country, they did not compete well against the cheaper glass ornament.

An advertisement from *Ehrich's Fashion Quarterly* in the winter of 1882 gives some comparative prices:

Fancy Silver & Gilt Ornaments, representing hearts, shields, globes, crosses, fishes, etc. Each ornament is formed of two pieces of embossed silver or gilt stiffened paper, firmly fixed together, so that it presents exactly the same appearance on either side. Price, per dozen. $.10. (By mail, $.05 extra.)

Same style, larger and finer. Price, per doz.$.25. (By mail, $.05 extra.)

Embossed Gold & Silver Fish seven inches long. Price, each $.05; per doz. $.50. (By mail, $.08 extra.)

Embossed Gold & Silver Dogs, four inches long. Price, each $.05; per doz. $.50.(By mail, $.08 extra.)

Embossed Gold and Silver Clocks, four and one half inches high. Price, each, $.05; per doz. $.50. (By mail, $.08 extra.)

Embossed Gold and Silver Trumpets, large size. Price, each $.05; per doz. $.50. (By mail, $.10 extra.)

Embossed Gold & Silver Crosses, five and one half inches long. Price, each $.05; per doz. $.50. (By mail, $.08 extra.)

Dressed Paper Dolls, six inches long. Price, each $.05; per doz. $.50. (By mail, $.10 extra.)

Gelatine & Gold Drums. Price, each $.05; per doz. $.50. (By mail, $.08 extra.)

Assortments of the Ornaments described above, containing some of each kind. By the dozen only. Price, per doz. $.50. (By mail $.08 extra.)

Fancy straw & Gilt Ornaments, assorted. Price, each $.05; per doz. $.50. (By mail $.08 extra.)

Larger and finer Ornaments, in embossed gilt & silver paper and gelatine; embracing stars, shells, gondolas, slippers, teapots, lamps, boots, angels, lanterns, beetles, etc. Price, each $.10; per doz.$1.00 (Assorted) (By mail, $.10 extra.)

Transparent Gelatine Lanterns. Price, each $.06; per doz. $.60. (By mail $.08 extra.)

Very Fine Embossed Gold Angels, six and one half inches long. Price, each $.08; per doz. $.80. (By mail, $.10 extra.)

Same, eight inches long. Price, each $.12; per doz. $1.20. (By mail, $.12 extra.)

One would assume, that the highly elaborate three dimensional pieces such as carriages, locomotives, passenger ships, etc. cost substantially more than twelve cents a piece. At the same time, "Fancy glass ornaments" were selling at a penny or less a piece.

Considering the average daily wages in 1882 and comparing the cost of a fancy "Dresden" to a glass ornament one can understand their scarcity. The average American family simply could not afford them. Looking through the following price guide, one can see this might be just as true today.

The "Dresden" ornament is usually found in one of three forms:

1. **Flat** - this type of ornament is designed to be

CRAYFISH - G/S, 3-D, Approx. 3¾" - It has nice detailing with eight applied legs, two claws and two antennae. (Schiffer p78, R1-2) $250.00-275.00

CRESCENT MOON - G/S, flat, Approx. 4" - The open crescent faces to the right and is embossed with small stars. A scrap angel head and tinsel may be added for decoration. (Schiffer p62, R2-3) $40.00-55.00

CROSS - G/S, flat, Approx. 3"H - It has embossed oval decoration. (Schiffer p91, R3) $40.00-50.00

CROSS - G/S, flat or double, 5½"L - (R3)Flat $45.00-60.00
Double $75.00-90.00

CROSS, MALTESE - G/S, flat or double, Approx. 3" - The cross is superimposed on a round, filigree background. It has the appearance of a military metal. (Schiffer p91, R2-3)
Flat $30.00-40.00
Double $40.00-50.00

CROWN CANDY CONTAINER - G/S, 3-D, Approx. 2¼" dia. - It has a wide band, in which the candy was stored. Eight bands bend over the top and are set with "jewels". Red paper shows through the inside of the crown, which is topped by a small cross. (Schiffer p84, R1-2)
$200.00-225.00

DOG - G/S, flat or double, Approx. 4"L - There are various breeds. (R3-4) Flat $40.00-60.00
(R2-3) Double $80.00-90.00

DOG CARRYING GLOVES AND A CANE - G/S, 3-D, 3⅛"H - The finely embossed dog is in a sitting position with the cane and glove in its mouth. (R2)$275.00-300.00

DOG - Natural, 3-D, Approx. 3⅛" - The dog is in a sitting position, with embossed collar. Same dog as above without the gloves and cane. (Snyder p139, R2) $250.00-275.00

DOG, BARKING BULLDOG - G/S, double, Approx. 3¾"W - Its front feet are straight forward, and it has an angry barking look. (p528a, R2-3) $200.00-225.00

DOG, GREYHOUND - Natural, 3-D, Approx. 3¼"W&H - This well detailed dog has a gold collar and applied tail and ears. (Schiffer p81, R1-2) $225.00-250.00

DOG, HUSKIE - Natural, 3-D, Approx. 2¾"L - The dog, possibly a huskie, is in a standing position, with its tail curled over the back. (Snyder p138, R2-3) $250.00-275.00

DOG, HUSKIE - G/S, flat, Approx. 2½"L - It stands facing the left with its tail curled over its back. The base it stands on shows grass. (Schiffer p93, R2-3) $45.00-55.00

DOG, IRISH SETTER - G/S, flat, Approx. 4"L - It appears walking to the left over a base of grass and flowers. It has a cardboard loop in its back. (Schiffer p93, R2-3)
$40.00-60.00

DOG AND DOGHOUSE - G/S, 3-D, Approx. 2"W x 1¾"H - The dog lays in front of the doghouse. They are separately made pieces attached to a base. The house has a doorway and a sloping roof. (p522, R1-2) $225.00-250.00

DONKEY - G/S, flat, Approx. 4"L - It stands facing left on a grassy base. It appears to be eating from a wicker basket and has a cardboard loop in its back for hanging. (Schiffer p94, R2-3) $40.00-60.00

DONKEY - Natural, double, Approx. 2"L - The donkey is full bodied and is in a standing position. (R2-3)
$100.00-125.00

DONKEY - G/S, Approx. 2" - It is same as below. (Stille p130, R2) $175.00-200.00

DONKEY PULLING A WAGON - G/S, 3-D, Approx. 4" - The wagon has four wheels (small in front, larger in rear) and simple rail sides. It looks like a hay wagon that carries fabric flowers, candy or straw. No driver. The donkey is full bodied and in a standing position. It has applied ears. (Stille p130, R1) $450.00-500.00

DRAGONFLY - G/S, double, Approx. 5"H - It has good detail and may have some painted metallic-like glitter on highlights. (R3) $150.00-175.00

DRINKING HORN CANDY CONTAINER - G/S, 3-D, Approx. 3¼"H - This finely detailed piece shows the drinking horn on a pedestal of stylized dolphins on a square base. The horn has three bands of ornate embossing around it. The candy bag is in the top of the horn. (Schiffer p86, R1)
$250.00-300.00

DRUM - G/S, flat, Approx. 2" - It has an embossed top and roping. (R3) $25.00-30.00

DUCK (TYPE I) - G/S or natural, 3-D, Approx. 2½"H x 3"L - It stands as though walking; there is a small bump on its erect head. The feet and feathers are applied. (p520a, R2-3) $160.00-185.00

DUCK (TYPE II) - Natural, 3-D, Approx. 3" - It stands as though walking. It has no bump on its head which is bent forward and only the feet are applied. (Schiffer p80, R2-3) $175.00-200.00

ELEPHANT WITH TRUNK DOWN - G/S, double, Approx. 2¼"L - It is full bodied with its tail up, and the trunk is in a "J" shape. It is in a walking stance. (R2-3)
$130.00-150.00

ELEPHANT WITH TRUNK UP - G/S, double, Approx. 3½"H x 3½"L - It is shown walking. The mouth shows tusks. The trunk is raised in an "S" shape. (p525a, R2)
$175.00-200.00

SMALL WALKING ELEPHANT - G/S, 3-D, Approx. 2"L x 1½"H - The trunk is down, and it wears a decorated cover on its back. (p519c, R2) $185.00-200.00

ELEPHANT - Natural, double, Approx. 1½"H x 2"L - It is greyish brown with white on its tusks. (R2-3)
$100.00-125.00

ELEPHANT HEAD CANDY CONTAINER - G/S, 3-D, Approx. 3" - This shows the head and neck which is hollow and holds the candy sack. It has large ears, tusks and a trunk which curls under the head. (Snyder p139, R2)
$325.00-350.00

ELEPHANT HEAD CANDY CONTAINER - G/S, 3-D, Approx. 3⅞" - This is very similar to the above elephant head. However, it has the addition of an embossed circus head-covering with tassels hanging by the ear. (Schiffer p81, R1-2) $325.00-350.00

ELEPHANT WITH A GAZEBO ON ITS BACK - G/S, 3-D, Approx. 3¼"L - The elephant is in a walking stance with a Victorian style gazebo or square riding box applied separately to its back. Silk curtains and silk strap around elephant's middle may be added. (Snyder, p139, R2-3) $325.00-350.00

Same elephant without gazebo (p527c) $185.00-200.00

FLAT FAN - G/S & painted, flat, 2"H x 3½"W - The fan is unfolded showing its pleats, alternate pleats are painted red. (p533d, R3) $25.00-30.00

FAN - G/S, 3-D, Approx. 5"W open - Each of its four panels have embossed details and a small scrap flower. Each panel is flat, and they are hinged at the bottom such that the fan can open and close. (Schiffer p85, R1-2)$175.00-200.00

FENCE - G/S, flat, 7¼"L x 4¼"W - The picket fence has a lithographed girl or child and lithographed flowers growing along the embossed ground. It has an embossed hanging loop. (p546, R3) $55.00-75.00

FIRE BELLOWS - G/S & red paint, 3-D, 2¾" - It has a candy container inside. (R2) $160.00-175.00

FISH - G/S, flat, 6½"L - (R4) $45.00-65.00

FISH - G/S, flat or double, 7"L - (R4) Flat $45.00-65.00
(R3-4) Double $75.00-100.00

FISH - G/S, flat, Approx. 5"L x 2"W - Its fins are painted green. The mouth is closed. It has shallow embossing. (p536a, R4) $40.00-55.00

WIDEMOUTH FISH - G/S, double, 3½" x 2½"W - The fish has a large open mouth and fins that go from head to tail on both its top and bottom. (p517a, R3-4)$100.00-125.00

FISH, BLUEGILL - G/S, double, Approx. 5⅛"L x 3"W - This large piece has one long top fin and one large and one small on the bottom. The body is larger and rounded. (p536b, R2-3) $100.00-125.00

FISH, CARP - G/S, double, Approx. 5¾L" - This large piece has one wavy fin on top and two on the bottom. (Snyder p138, #1, R2-3) $125.00-150.00

FISH, COD - G/S, double, Approx. 6"L - It has a long body with three fins on top and three on the bottom. (Schiffer p83, #5, R2-3) $150.00-175.00

FISH, FANTASY PORPOISE - Natural or G/S, 3-D, Approx. 4¼"L - Its long slender body loops and ends with a three pointed tail. The mouth is open and inside it is a candy bag. Fantasy fish like this were common Victorian decorations. (Schiffer p83, R1) $275.00-300.00

FISH, FLOUNDER - G/S, double, Approx. 3⅜"L - It has fins from head to tail, both on its top and bottom. (Snyder p138, R3) $130.00-150.00

FISH, HERRING - Natural or G/S, double, Approx. 3"L - A small fish with one small fin on top and two on the bottom. (Schiffer p83, #6, R3) $115.00-130.00

FISH, PERCH - Natural or G/S, double, Approx. 3½"L x 1½"W - It has a large and small fin on top and two small ones on bottom. (p515b, R3) $100.00-125.00

FISH, SWORDFISH - G/S, double, Approx. 6½" - It has a long dorsal fin, a split tail and a long pointed snout. (p524a, R1-2) $175.00-200.00

FLOWER - G/S, flat or double, Approx. 2¾" dia. - The opened flower shape has twelve veined leaves around the outside. Tinsel and a lithographed scrap are at the center. (R3) Flat $25.00-30.00
Double $40.00-50.00

FLY - Natural, 3-D, Approx. 3" - It has a segmented body, legs and applied wings. (Schiffer p78, R1-2)$250.00-275.00

FROG - Natural, 3-D, Approx. 2" - It is in a sitting position with its front legs spread and the rear ones folded. (Schiffer p82, R1-2) $225.00-250.00

GIRAFFE - Natural, 3-D, Approx. 2½"W x 4⅛"H - It is in a standing position, head and neck erect. (Schiffer p82, R1-2) $275.00-300.00

GOAT - Natural, double, Approx. 2" - It is shown in a standing position with a detailed shaggy coat. (Schiffer p79, R2-3) $100.00-125.00

GOAT - Natural, 3-D, Approx. 2" - The goat is in a standing position and is painted black and white with applied horns curving over the back. Same goat as in the below two carts. (Stille p130, R2-3) $175.00-200.00

GOAT PULLING A CART - Natural & G/S, 3-D, Approx. 4" - The goat is in a standing position with large curved horns coming over its back. It is larger than the wagon or driver. The wagon has two wheels, an open back and spindle-type sides. The driver is in front on the seat. The goat and driver are natural, and the wagon is G/S. (Stille p130, R1) $475.00-500.00

GOAT PULLING A WAGON - Natural & G/S, 3-D, Approx. 4" - The goat is in a standing position with large curved horns coming over its back. It is larger than the wagon or driver. The wagon has two wheels, an open back and spindle-type sides. The driver is in front on the seat. The goat and driver are natural, and the wagon is G/S. (Stille p130, R1) $500.00-525.00

GOAT, MOUNTAIN GOAT - Natural, 3-D, Approx. 5" - It appears as if it were butting. Its head is lowered with horns out and the legs charging. (Schiffer p81, R1-2) $275.00-300.00

GOAT HEAD - G/S or natural, 3-D, Approx. 2½" (horns not included) - It is shown to the neck in which is a small bag, making it a candy container. It has applied horns and ears. (Schiffer p81, R1-2) $275.00-300.00

GOLF BALL - Natural, 3-D, Approx. 1¾" dia. - This white ball is nicely detailed and opens to a candy container. (Schiffer p87, R1-2) $100.00-125.00

GRAPES - G/S, double, Approx. 3¼"L x 2¾"W - A bunch of embossed grapes with leaves. (p532c, R2)$75.00-100.00

GREEK WARRIOR - G/S, flat, 4¾"L x 2½"W - The warrior holds a shield in the left hand and is attacking with a spear in the right. He has a plumed helmet and a cloak. (p545a, R2-3) $65.00-80.00

GUITAR - G/S, flat, Approx. 3½" - (R2) $25.00-35.00

GUN, COWBOY REVOLVER - G/S, 3-D, Approx. 4½"L - There is an embossed "engraving" on it and the barrel may be a candy container. (Schiffer p85, R2)$175.00-200.00

HEART - G/S, double, Approx. 2" - Flowers are embossed in the center. (R1-2) $75.00-90.00

HEART CANDY CONTAINER (TYPE I) - G/S, 3-D, Approx. 2"L x 2"H - It has a candy bag in the top. On the front are embossed clasped hands, and on the back an anchor and cross. (R2) $140.00-160.00

HEART CANDY CONTAINER (TYPE II) - G/S, 3-D, 2½"L - This has an anchor and cross on one side and five strips or bands on the other. It has accordian-like sides and a silk bag for holding candy in the top. (p529c, R2)
                                          $140.00-160.00

HEN ON A NEST - G/S, flat, Approx. 3½" - Both the hen and nest are nicely detailed. (Schiffer p94, R3)$40.00-55.00

RACE HORSE - G/S or natural, 3-D, Approx. 3½"H x 4"L - It is standing, head erect, race horse style with applied ears. It is marked Germany in the stomach area. (p523b, R2) $275.00-310.00

HORSE HEAD - G/S or natural, 3-D, Approx. 3" - The head is shown down to the neck, which is also a candy container. It also has an applied bridle or harness. (Snyder, p139, R2) $300.00-325.00

HORSE/PONY - G/S, double, 3½" - The full bodied horse is in a trotting stance with bridle and saddle embossed.
                                          $160.00-180.00

PRANCING HORSE - G/S, double, Approx. 3½" - It appears to be prancing with its head slightly lowered and all legs bent as though in motion. It has a saddle. (p523c, R2-3)
                                          $160.00-180.00

HORSE - G/S, flat, Approx. 4½"W - It appears to be walking across a field of grass flowers. (Schiffer p94, R2-3)
                                          $50.00-65.00

HORSE WITH DANCING GIRL - G/S, 3-D, Approx. 3¾" - A girl in a ballerina outfit dances on a platform on the horse's back. The horse is in a prancing position. Both are decorated with feathered silk. (Stille p131, R1)
                                          $300.00-325.00

HORSE WITH JOCKEY - G/S, 3-D, Approx. 2½"L - The horse is in a standing position and has a bobbed tail. The applied rider wears the traditional outfit and sits high in the saddle. (Schiffer p82, R1-2) $250.00-275.00

HORSE WITH JOCKEY RIDER - Natural, 3-D, Approx. 2¾"L&H - This race horse is in a standing position with an applied jockey, saddle and harness. (Schiffer p82, R1-2)
                                          $225.00-250.00

HORSE WITH JOCKEY RIDER - Natural, 3-D, Approx. 3⅝"L - The horse is in a standing position. The jockey's right arm is raised, he is applied as are the saddle and harness. The horse appears to have a large blanket under the saddle. (Schiffer p79, R1-2) $250.00-275.00

HORSE WITH A LADY RIDER - Natural, 3-D, Approx. 2¼" - The horse stands in a prancing stance. There is an applied harness, saddle and lady who rides side-saddle. Her dress is fabric. (p527a, R1-2) $225.00-250.00

HORSE WITH RIDER, JUMPING - Natural, 3-D, Approx. 3½"L - The horse's legs are stretched almost straight and backward, and its tail is streaming back. The jockey, saddle and harness are applied. The same piece may be found jumping over a rail fence. (Schiffer p82, R1-2)
                                          $170.00-190.00
                     Jumping the fence $250.00-275.00

HORSESHOE WITH JOCKEY AND RACE HORSE - G/S, double, Approx. 2½" - Horse and rider are jumping to the right through the horseshoe. (R2-3)$200.00-225.00

HOT AIR BALLOON - G/S, 3-D, Approx. 2¼"H - It has blue cords and a pull out candy sack. (Schiffer p81, R2)
                                          $200.00-225.00

HUNTING HORN - G/S or painted, 3-D, Approx. 4"L - It has a pull out sack for candy, and the horn blows. (R2)
                                          $150.00-175.00

KANGAROO - G/S, 3-D, Approx. 3" - It is shown in the hopping position with the tail out behind. (R1-2)
                                          $250.00-275.00

KNIGHT IN A HELMET - G/S & natural, 3-D, Approx. 3"H - This highly embossed piece is of the head and upper chest. The helmet has a crest of "Feathers" down the back and a visor that lifts to reveal the natural painted face of the knight. (R1) $325.00-350.00

LADY'S BOOT AND STOCKING - G/S, 3-D, Approx. 4⅛" - This is a candy container with a high heeled boot and ruby colored buttons. A stocking shows from the top of the boot with a candy bag attached to it. (Schiffer p82, R1) $325.00-350.00

LADY'S BROOCH - G/S, double, 3"W - Lithographed flowers are inset in the center to simulate the set of the brooch. It has extra embossed decoration around the bottom. (R2) $65.00-75.00

LADY'S SHOE OR SLIPPER - G/S, 3-D, Approx. 2" - A medium height heel with a high embossed tongue has a bag for a candy container. (R3) $100.00-125.00

LADY'S SHOE OR SLIPPER - G/S, 3-D, Approx. 4" - A small low heeled shoe with a bow in front and embossed sides. (Snyder p141, R3) $200.00-225.00

LANTERN - G/S, 3-D, Approx. 3" - Its "glass" panels are made of colored cellophane. The cap lifts off for a candy container. (R1-2) $125.00-150.00

LIBERTY'S SHIELD - (American flag in shield shape) - G/S, double, 3" x 2¾" - The flag/shield is in the center with a ¼" edging of fringe and rivets. (p531a, R2)$60.00-75.00

LIBERTY'S SHIELD - G/S, double, 2" x 1¾" - It is similar to the one above. Twenty-eight stars show. (p531b, R2) $60.00-75.00

LION - G/S, flat - Only the head and mane are shown. $40.00-50.00

WALKING LION - G/S, double, 3½"L x 2½"H - It is full bodied in a walking position with a heavily embossed mane. The head is erect, and the tail hangs at the hind foot. (p535a, R2) $65.00-85.00

STALKING LION - G/S, 3-D, Approx. 4¾"L - He is in a low walking position with his tail straight back. His mouth is open, and he appears to be stalking. (Schiffer p81, R2) $190.00-225.00

LION - G/S, flat, Approx. 4"L - He walks to the left across a base of grass and flowers. It has a cardboard loop in its back for hanging. (Schiffer p93, R2-3) $45.00-60.00

LOAF OF FRENCH BREAD - G/S, 3-D, Approx. 2½" - The long oblong shape shows baker's crosscut marks. It is a candy container. (R1-2) $125.00-150.00

LOBSTER - Natural, 3-D, Approx. 3½" - This candy container has large claws that are held in front. It opens at the "waist" area. (R1) $275.00-300.00

LOCOMOTIVE OR STEAM ENGINE - G/S, 3-D, Approx. 4¾"L - This long classic style locomotive has many applied parts. The highly detailed under-carriage of wheels, gears, bars and cowcatcher are gilded. It has one smokestack with cotton smoke. This is a model of engine 999 that broke speed records in the early 1890s. (Snyder p138, R1-2) $450.00-500.00

LOCOMOTIVE, AN EARLY MODEL - G/S, 3-D, Approx. 3¼"L - This is a version of an early 19th century locomotive. It has a large smokestack, rounded steam chamber and three sets of wheels, a large one in the center and two smaller ones on either side. (Schiffer p86, R1-2) $300.00-325.00

SWAN HEAD LYRE - G/S, double, Approx. 3"H - It has swan head finals, with their necks forming the body of the lyre. (R2) $100.00-125.00

LYRE - G/S, flat or double, Approx. 2"H & 3½"H - It has a square bottomed base with four embossed strings and colored cellophane behind string area. (p532b, R3-4)
                  Flat $30.00-35.00
                  Double $50.00-60.00
                  Larger $90.00-110.00

LYRE CANDY CONTAINER - G/S, 3-D, Approx. 3"H - Dragon heads with curved necks form the side supports and finals. It has embossed strings and a pull out candy sack in the base. (R1-2) $200.00-225.00

MAN IN THE MOON - G/S, flat or double, Approx. 4½" - It is crescent-shaped. The man's face has curly hair, a beard and is frowning. Facial features are exaggerated and prominate. (Stille p120, R2-3)   Flat $80.00-100.00
                  Double $150.00-175.00

MAN IN THE SUN - G/S, double, Approx. 3¼" dia. - It is round with 24 flames coming off. The embossed face in the center shows eyes, nose, moustache and chin. (Stille p120, R2-3) $150.00-175.00

MEDALLION - G/S, flat or double, Approx. 3½" dia. - Made of three large rounded lobes, this heavily embossed piece has gelatine flower and a scrap at the center. (p543C, R3-4)   Flat $35.00-50.00
                  Double $75.00-90.00

DIAMOND MEDALLION - G/S, flat or double, Approx. 6½"W x 5¼"H - This heavily embossed piece is roughly diamond shaped and has a gelatine flower and a scrap at the center. (p543a, R3-4)   Flat $45.00-60.00
                  Double $75.00-90.00

MONKEY - G/S, flat, Approx. 4½" - It is shown facing right and climbing up a tree branch which also shows leaves and flowers. (Schiffer p80, R2) $50.00-65.00

MOOSE - Natural, double, Approx. 2¼" - The full bodied moose is in a standing position with antlers straight up. (R3) $100.00-125.00

MOOSE - G/S or natural, 3-D, Approx. 4¼" - The moose is in a standing position. There is good detailing on the mane and antlers. (Schiffer p81, R2-3) $250.00-275.00

MOUSE - G/S, 3-D - It has an unusual cord tail. $175.00-200.00

MUG WITH HANDLE - G/S, flat, Approx. 2½"H x 2"W - The mug has decorations and "A Good Child" embossed into it. (p533c, R2) $30.00-40.00

NATIVITY SCENE - G/S, flat, Approx. 6¾"L x 4¼"W - A lithographed Joseph and Mary and baby Jesus are between two elaborate columns and palm branches. They support a starry arch with a centered nativity star. (p540, R1-2) $55.00-80.00

OPERA GLASSES - Natural, 3-D, Approx. 3"W - It has two eye pieces and a focus wheel in the center that moves. The eye pieces open to hold candy. (Schiffer p81, R2) $175.00-200.00

OSTERICH - Paint & G/S, 3-D, Approx. 3"W x 4"H - The bird stands on two long slender legs. It has a small head and long curving neck. It has a cluster of applied plumage on the body. (p521a, R1-2) $250.00-275.00

OSTERICH PULLING A CART - G/S, 3-D, Approx. 6"L - The cart has two movable wheels. The body of the cart is embossed to appear like a square wicker basket and hold fabric flowers. The osterich has applied plumes, same as above. (Stille p38, R1) $475.00-500.00

OWL - Natural, 3-D, Approx. 3¾"L - Its body faces to the

left, while its head is turned to face outward. No feet or tree parts show. (Schiffer p82, R1-2) $250.00-275.00

PADLOCK - G/S, 3-D, Approx. 2¾"H - The lock is shown as closed, the bottom section is rounded and has gold "rivets". It has a keyhole in the bottom section and a gold band runs diagonally across it. (Schiffer p87, R1-2)
$225.00-250.00

PAIL - G/S, 3-D, Approx. 3"H (pail alone) - It has a brass handle, and the pail forms a candy container. It has gold embossed bands around top, middle and bottom. (Schiffer p89, R2-3) $125.00-135.00

PALM IN AN URN - G/S, flat, Approx. 3½"H x 1½"W - The palm and urn are on a large square pedestal. (p533a, R3) $25.00-35.00

PARAKEET - Natural, double, Approx. 4"L - It has colorful paint, and is probably a later piece. (R2-3)
$150.00-175.00

PROUD PEACOCK - Natural, 3-D, Approx. 4¼"H & 3¼" tail feather dia. - This is a magnificient piece with well detailed tail feathers spread in an applied circular piece. The head is proud and erect. Legs and other feathers are applied. (p526, R1) $275.00-300.00

PEANUT - Natural, 3-D, Approx. 3" & 4½" - It opens around the edge to hold candy or a small toy. Some made in Austria, and some crude versions are Japanese. (p560a, R4)   Austria $30.00-45.00
Japan $25.00-35.00

PEGASUS - G/S, flat, Approx. 4"L - A mythical horse with wings in a flying position. (R2) $60.00-75.00

PIG - Natural, 3-D, Approx. 2½" - It is in a standing position with applied ears. (Snyder p141, R1-2)$225.00-250.00

PINECONE (CORNUCOPIA) - G/S, 3-D, Approx. 4¼" - The bottom and top are rounded and covered with embossed, overlapping scallops, like a pinecone. Top lifts off for a candy container. (Stille p120, R2) $275.00-300.00

PIPE - G/S, 3-D, Approx. 6"L - It has a candy container in the pipe's bowl and applied trim. (R2) $200.00-225.00

PIPE - Natural, 3-D, Approx. 4½"L - It is the classic German pipe with a long bent stem and up-turned bowl. The bowl is also a candy container. (Schiffer p85, R1-2)
$200.00-225.00

PIPE - G/S, flat or double, Approx. 2½" - Dublin type, long bent stem.   (R3-4) Flat $20.00-25.00
(R3) Double $50.00-60.00

POSTAL HORN/HUNTING HORN - G/S, flat or double, Approx. 2½" - The horn is short and bent into a full circle. (R3)   Flat $25.00-35.00
Double $50.00-60.00

PURSE - G/S, double or 3-D, Approx. 3" - The purse is in a Victorian style with a six lobed design in the center and embossed fringe around the edge. (R2) $130.00-150.00

RUNNING RABBIT - G/S, flat, Approx. 6¼"L - It is running to the left across a base that shows grass, flowers and trees. (Schiffer p94, R3) $50.00-75.00

SITTING RABBIT - G/S, flat, Approx. 2½"W - He is sitting on his haunches, with arms out and ears raised. (p524c, R2) $30.00-40.00

RABBIT CANDY CONTAINER - Natural or G/S, 3-D, Approx. 2" - It is sitting on its haunches; embossed collar and upright ears are applied. It opens under the haunces. (p529a, R2) $175.00-200.00

RAM - G/S, 3-D, Approx. 2½" - He is in a walking position with horns curling around the side of his head. (Schiffer p79,R2) $175.00-195.00

RAM - G/S, flat, Approx. 3¾"L - It stands facing to the left on what appears to be grass and flowers. (Schiffer p94, R2-3) $50.00-60.00

RAM HEAD CANDY CONTAINER - G/S, 3-D, Approx. 2½" - It has horns that curl around the side of its face. The neck is hollow and holds the candy bag. (Schiffer p81, R1-2) $300.00-325.00

REINDEER HEAD CANDY CONTAINER - Natural, 3-D, Approx. 3" - It shows the head and neck. The head has applied antlers and inside the neck is a candy sack. (R2) $300.00-325.00

SMALL REINDEER/STAG - Natural, double, Approx. 2"L x 2"W - It is in a standing position with head raised as if calling. The antlers go back to rump. (p535b, R2-3) $100.00-125.00

REINDEER/STAG - G/S, double, Approx. 3"L - It appears in a walking stance with the head in a normal position. (Schiffer p81, R2-3) $140.00-160.00

3-D REINDEER/STAG - G/S & natural, 3-D, Approx. 3¼" - It stands with head raised and antlers back as if calling. This is a common stance for German styled reindeers or stags. (p514a, & Snyder p139, R3) $250.00-275.00

ALSO see "STAG"

FLAT ROOSTER - G/S, flat, Approx. 2" - The bird leans forward and has large tail feather plumage. (R3)
$25.00-30.00

ROOSTER - Natural, double, Approx. 3½"W x 3⅞"H - This nicely detailed bird stands with its chest out as though ready to crow. It has raised tail feathers. (Schiffer p83, R3) $125.00-150.00

3-D ROOSTER - G/S and natural, 3-D, Approx. 2¼"W x 3"H - This nicely detailed piece stands with its head slightly forward and tail feathers held high. (p520b, R2)
$250.00-275.00

ROOSTER - G/S, flat, Approx. 3" - It has detailed embossed feathers and faces to the left. It has a loop in its back for hanging. (Schiffer p94, R2-3) $35.00-50.00

ROOSTER, CHINESE - Natural, 3-D, Approx. 4½"L - It

is painted with metallic colors. It has a large comb, and its applied tail feathers make up more than half its length. It also has applied legs and feet. (p515a, R1)$250.00-275.00

ROOSTER HEAD CANDY CONTAINER - Natural, 3-D, Approx. 3" - It shows the head and large comb of the rooster down to the neck which is open and holds the candy bag. (Schiffer p81, R1) $375.00-400.00

SALAMANDER - Natural, 3-D, Approx. 4" - The body has two bends to it and the long tail is "S" shaped. The four legs show. (p514b, R1) $250.00-275.00

SANTA CLAUS - G/S, flat, Approx. 4½"H - He is dressed in a short coat with a fur cap. He carries a tree at his right shoulder and a bag of toys over his left. (Schiffer p90, R2) $75.00-100.00

SANTA CLAUS - G/S, flat, Approx. 8½" - He is dressed in a long coat and hood. He holds a tree in his right hand and a toy in the left. There is a wicker basket of toys on his back. This is a nicely detailed piece. (Schiffer p90, R2) $125.00-150.00

SANTA CLAUS (WEIHNACHTSMAN) - G/S, double, Approx. 4" - This is a German Santa with a long coat, a small hat and a small girl standing beside him. He carries a basket of toys on his back and switches in his hand. (Snyder p71, R1) $350.00-375.00

SEDAN CHAIR TYPE CARRIAGE - G/S, 3-D - Two men in small hats and skirts run with the sedan chair (a square box with a chair inside) between two poles that attach to the side of the carriage box. The carriage is also a candy container. (R1-2) $275.00-300.00

SLEIGH, ONE HORSE OPEN - Natural & G/S, Approx. 6½"L - It has a lady driver who holds a whip. It is square with the back slightly higher than the front, and the embossing is simple. Two "poles" attach on either side of the three-dimensional horse who wears a detailed harness system. (Schiffer p86, R1) $400.00-425.00

SLEIGH, ONE HORSE OPEN - G/S, 3-D, Approx. 4½"
The horse is in a running position. The sleigh is smaller than the horse and has no seat. The driver, naturally painted, stands at the rear. The sides of the sleigh, which may hold fabric flowers or candy, are fancy curved lattice work. (Stille p125, R1-2) $275.00-300.00

SLEIGH, HORSE PULLING A - G/S and natural, 3-D, Approx. 3⅞"L - The natural painted horse is in a running, prancing position. Two harness bars are attached to his side. The sleigh is G/S embossed and is a one seat, open sleigh. It looks almost like an ornate chair on runner. (R1) $275.00-300.00

SLEIGH PULLED BY 2 HORSES - G/S & natural, 3-D, Approx. 4½" - The front of the sleigh comes to a swan head whose long neck curves down to form the runners. Two horses painted white and black have feather plumes. The driver, sitting on the sleigh, is painted natural, and has a cotton and material lap robe and muffler. (Stille p124, R1) $450.00-500.00

FLAT SLIPPER - G/S, flat, Approx. 7¼"L x 2¼"W - The slipper is flat and embellished with tinsel and lithographs.

The toe area is made of net and is a candy container. (p550, R3-4) $40.00-50.00

SNOWFLAKE - G/S, flat or double, Approx. 3½" dia. - It is rounded with six large arch-like lobes, possibly held a medallion or lithographed picture in the center. (p532a, R3)
Flat $30.00-45.00
Double $50.00-65.00

SHOWFLAKE (TYPE II) - G/S, flat or double, Approx. 3¾" dia. - This heavily embossed piece has six lobes around the edge with a six pointed star in the center. (p544a, R3-4)
Flat $30.00-45.00
Double $50.00-65.00

SQUIRREL - G/S, double, Approx. 3½" - He stands on his hind legs eating a nut. His ears are erect and his large bushy tail curves up and touches his back. This piece is not well detailed. (Schiffer p79, R2) $140.00-175.00

STAG - Natural, 3-D, Approx. 2¾"L - It is in the standing position looking straight ahead. The antlers are applied. (p527b, R2) $200.00-225.00

STAR - G/S, double, Approx. 2-3" - Stars come in various sizes and shapes. (R3-4)
Flat $15.00-25.00
Double $30.00-40.00

LARGE STAR - G/S, 3-D, Approx. 5¾" dia. - This six-pointed star has a radiating leaf pattern in the center. (p534a, R1-2) $150.00-175.00

STEIN - G/S, 3-D, Approx. 3¾"H - It has embossed dragons and "open" panels which have been painted. The cone shaped lid opens, and it is a candy container inside. (Schiffer p89, R1-2) $275.00-300.00

3-D STORK (TYPE I) - Natural, 3-D, Approx. 3½"L x 4"H - It has two applied legs and embossed black and white feathers cover the body. (p521b, R2-3) $225.00-250.00

STORK - Natural, double, Approx. 3¾"H - It is painted white and black with a red bill. It shows embossed ground and grass at feet. (R2-3) $125.00-150.00

STORK - Natural, double, Approx. 4" - The bird is in a standing position with long slender legs. (R3) $125.00-150.00

STORK CANDY CONTAINER - Natural, 3-D, Approx. 4" - It has long slender legs, a beak and many applied feathers. It has a pull out candy sack that comes out of the rear of the body under the tail feathers. (R2) $250.00-275.00

3-D STORK (TYPE II) - Natural, 3-D, Approx. 3½"H - It has a small head and long applied legs. (p528b, R2) $175.00-200.00

STREETCAR/TROLLEY - G/S, 3-D, Approx. 3"L - This roofed streetcar has a front and back landing, four windows on each side and detailed embossing on the side panels. One side is marked "Registered 4446 Depose". The other side is marked "Gesetelich 4446 Geschutzt". The pictured piece has missing fringe around the roof and guard rails on the landings. (p512b, R2) $350.00-400.00

SUITCASE - G/S, double, Approx. 3" - An old fashioned type suitcase. (R3) $100.00-125.00

SUN - see MAN IN THE SUN

SWIMMING SWAN - Natural (white), double, Approx. 4″
- The swan is in a swimming position with feet showing.
(R3) $150.00-175.00

SWIMMING SWAN (TYPE II) - Natural (white), double,
Approx. 3¼″H x 2¾″W - It has an "S" shaped neck that
does not touch the body, and the feet show even though
it is in a swimming position. Good embossing on the
feathers. (p517c, R2-3) $150.00-175.00

SWAN - G/S, double, Approx. 3¼″ - Similar to the above
except the wings have a rounder shape and the "S" shaped
neck curves back and touches the body. (Schiffer p83, R3)
                                        $150.00-175.00

SWAN - G/S, double, Approx. 1½″ - This has a "S" neck
but little detail. (R3-4) $75.00-90.00

SWAN - G/S, flat, Approx. 7″L - The nicely detailed swan
is shown swimming to the left on water that also has water
lilies and reeds. There is a cardboard loop in its back for
hanging. (Schiffer p92, R2-3) $60.00-80.00

SWAN PULLING A SEASHELL BOAT - G/S & natural,
3-D, Approx. 4⅛″L - The swan with applied swept back
wings pulls an elongated half shell boat. The shell carries
a natural painted angel or cupid with a bow. (R1)
                                        $400.00-425.00

TENNIS RACKET - G/S, 3-D, Approx. 2¼″L - It is a candy box with colored cellophane behind the racket's netting.
(Snyder p71, R2) $150.00-175.00

TURTLE - Natural, 3-D, Approx. 3½″ - It has a nicely
detailed shell with a hexagonal design. It has applied legs,
tail and head showing. The underside is smooth. (p525b,
R1-2) $200.00-225.00

UMBRELLA - G/S, flat or double, Approx. 2″ - It is in an
open position with curved handle. (R3) Flat $20.00-25.00
                                        Double $30.00-45.00

URN ON A PEDESTAL - G/S, flat, Approx. 3¾″H - This
round urn with concave sides is typical of ones found in
Victorian decoration. (Schiffer p91, R3) $30.00-40.00

URN CANDY CONTAINER - G/S, 3-D, Approx. 2½″H
- It has an hour glass shape with much embossing. Handles
are applied to the sides (missing in the picture). The candy
bag is in the urn opening. (p530b, R1-2) $200.00-225.00

VASE - G/S, flat, Approx. 4″ - Vase has fine embossed
details and a tinsel spray with lithographed flowers. (R2-3)
                                        $50.00-60.00

VIOLIN - G/S, 3-D, Approx. 3¾″L - An applied bow is attached to it. (Schiffer p85, R2) $150.00-175.00

WALNUT - G/S, 3-D, Approx. 2″ - It is an embossed candy container that opens around the edges. (p560b, R3)
                                        $40.00-60.00

WHEELBARROW - G/S, 3-D, Approx. 3¼″L - Fine and
delicate embossed detail. It is a candy container. (R2)
                                        $200.00-225.00

WINE BOTTLE - G/S, 3-D, Approx. 3″ - It has an embossed grapevine and a paper label. (R2-3) $90.00-100.00

WREATH - G/S, flat or double, Approx. 3″H - It is composed of embossed holly leaves and berries. There is an embossed bow at the bottom and three tassels at the top. It
may have a scrap set into the open area. Flat $40.00-65.00
                                        Double $90.00-100.00

ZEPPELIN - G/S, 3-D, Approx. 4″L - The main body has
embossed ribbing and two stabilizing fins in the rear; it also
opens to a candy container. The zeppelin has gilded struts
that hold a gondola and flag underneath. (Snyder p138, R1)
                                        $450.00-475.00

LARGE ZEPPELIN - G/S, 3-D, Approx. 5½″ - The body
shows flat paneling, and the front has stabbling fins. The
undercarriage shows gridders and gondolas. (p512a, R1)
                                        $350.00-375.00

PAPER CANDY CONTAINERS

In the past, as is certainly still true today, candy, nuts,
fruits and "sweets", in general, played a large role as
Christmas-time gifts. They were inexpensive, decorative,
and of course, delightful to the children who rarely had such
a feast of "sweetmeats" as were available at this time of
year.

Today, most candies and fruits are placed in bowls or
"stockings hung by the chimney with care." But originally, all these tantalizing goodies were hung on the tree, itself,
hence one of its many titles -- "the sugar tree."

How this candy was placed on the tree was a problem
that produced many innovative solutions. Until the middle of the last century they were simply tied onto the branches with brightly colored string or ribbon. Soft candies,
such as marzipan and fruits were hung by small hooks or
chains which were inserted into them. Others were strung
together in chains and looped over the branches. Later,
these yule-time delights were piled into homemade containers and bags. These were generally constructed out of
materials found around the house such as scrap fabric and
netting, colorful paper, gilded egg-shells, metal and wood.

For collectors, these early homemade candy containers
are extremely difficult to find for several reasons. First of
all, most were designed to be used only once and were often
destroyed in the process of getting at the candy. Secondly, since most were made of inexpensive paper, they were
easy to replace as the yearly fashion trends dictated. There
was a prolific variety of stars, boxes and paper nets of every
description. But the simplest and most enduring of these
forms was the cone or cornucopia. All that was needed was
a sheet of paper or cardboard rolled diagonally into a cone
shape and then fastened together. Then, with the addition
of colored paper, tinsel or pictures from scraps, advertising or post cards, they had created a wonderful holder for
the sugary treasures.

Finally, we must consider as a reason for their disappearance the impact of the industrial revolution in the second half of the 19th century. The new emphasis was on
industry and commercially made items. Homemade was out
of fashion and became relegated to the poorer classes. Thus,
the old were thrown out, and a whole new line of lovely
manufactured ornaments and paper goods were welcomed
to the world of the Christmas tree.

It is to these commercially made candy containers that

I would now like to turn. With the new mechanical process for stamping, embossing and shaping cardboard, many imaginative and beautiful pieces were offered to the eagerly buying public. Some represented common everyday items with which the people were familiar. Such items as buckets, hatboxes, walnuts and suitcases fell into this category. Other items represented another way of life of which most could only dream - opera glasses, military helmets, grand pianos and crowns. In their "golden age" from about 1870-1910, hundreds and possibly thousands of variations were produced. Because of the intricate detail and charm of these commercial candy containers, they captured the imagination, and many were hung on the tree year after year, long after their sweet contents had disappeared.

But even though many were saved, these beautiful and ingenious pieces of Victorian art are seldom seen today. There are several reasons for their scarcity.

As with many other fancy products, their cost was prohibitive to some families.

Along with other "fancy German paper" products like the scraps and "Dresdens", the candy containers were hurt by the high tariffs and war embargoes of the early 20th century. And as with the others, the containers started to "die out" just as the American market really began to expand.

Many candy containers also doubled as toys and were never reused as Christmas ornaments. Indeed, some toys that hung on the trees doubled as candy containers. Early pictures show that such items as baskets, metal pails and toy teacups also held heaping mounds of sweets. By design or coincidence, many candy boxes, baskets, etc. were just the right size to be used as doll accessories. Thus after Christmas, a suitcase or hatbox that once held candy soon contained some lovely doll's traveling trousseau.

A final explanation as to why the lovely candy containers of yesteryear are so scarce can be found in the early candy containers that were discarded when their contents were consumed. Some containers, by design and others by accident, were destroyed in getting to the candy. And others, no matter how lovely, were just thrown out when they were empty. A good example of this is the familiar Animal Crackers box. Few people realize that the traditional string handle was designed for hanging on the branches of a Christmas tree, thus making it the longest produced candy/cookie container. Few of these colorful containers with their caged animals were kept after the cookies were gone. In another instance, my grandmother has a cardboard banjo that has hung on her tree since before the first World War. Her younger brother found it after Christmas in "a rich kid's" trash and brought it home, wondering why such a nice thing had been thrown out. Every year at Christmas the story was told as it was placed on the tree. After I began to collect ornaments, I discovered the secret of the banjo. It was a candy container "that the rich kid" had thrown away after its contents had been eaten.

Whatever the reasons that made them scarce, they are an important aspect in the development of Christmas ornaments, and they are a wonderful addition to anyone's collection.

NOTES:
1. Some collectors prefer to put all cardboard items into the category of "Dresden" ornaments, and some collectors may wonder why the candy containers mentioned here were not grouped with them. Indeed, there are many containers listed in that section. However, I have chosen to separate them for several reasons.

First and foremost, I believe that the term "Dresden" should apply only to those ornaments which are made of die cut, embossed cardboard and not merely any ornament that has been constructed of cardboard.

Secondly, even though many are beautifully and cleverly made, they do not bring the same price as a comparable 3-D "Dresden". Thus a separate pricing category by dealers and collectors would indicate a difference in their desirability and the necessity for a separate grouping.

Some cardboard pieces are covered with gold or silver embossed foil. Again, these do not fall into the category of a Dresden ornament in which the cardboard is embossed and then coated with gold or silver ink.

Finally, some of the candy containers were not even made in Germany, let alone in the Dresden-Lepzig area. Some containers were made in Austria, some in the United States and quite a few in Japan.

2. Only paper and cardboard containers are discussed here. Objects made out of other materials will be discussed in their relative sections. Not all candy containers were designed to hang on the tree. Those that were table or room decorations will be listed in the miscellaneous section.

3. Most candy that came in these Christmas containers were small, hard colored balls. But not all boxes were bought with candy already inside them. Many were sold empty and filled at home. The containers did not always only hold candy. Just as often, they held small presents such as porcelain, wax or celluloid dolls. Whenever possible, I have tried to note how the container opens.

4. Most finely constructed containers were European made and have a rarity rating of 1-2.

5. Candy containers were a popular item throughout the year and their themes varied greatly. This would account for many of the non-Christmas subjects. For some reason, Christmas collectors have a tendency to pay more for these items than toy and candy container collectors.

ANIMAL CRACKERS BOXES - Sizes vary - Generally only the early boxes are collected. (p564c, R2)$15.00-25.00

APPLE - Approx. 2¾" dia. - Round and colored red and yellow, it has a small stem at the top. It opens around the middle. (Schiffer p89, R2) $75.00-100.00

BANJO - Approx. 9" - It has a round body and an applied neck. The "strings" are string. It opens in the back. (p557b, R2-3) $90.00-100.00

BASKETBALL - Approx. 2" - It shows embossed ribs and lacing. It opens at the sides. (R2) $40.00-50.00

BELL - Approx. 5½"W - It has a scrap decoration although it was made in the United States during the 1930s. (R3)
$25.00-35.00

BOOK - Approx. 3"H - This is a light blue book with gold trim. It opens along the "pages" edge. (Schiffer p87, R1)
$50.00-70.00

BEER KEG - Approx. 3½" - It is made of paper mache and is hung by a cloth candy bag on the top. (R2)
$75.00-100.00

CANTEEN - Approx. 3½" dia. - This piece has "U.S. The Old Canteen" printed on the front. It is cork stopped and hung by a red, white and blue ribbon. (R2-3)$90.00-100.00

CHAMPAGNE OR WINE BOTTLE - Approx. 3" - It is made of paper mache and may have a netting covering or a paper wine label. (R2-3) $75.00-100.00

COOKING PAN WITH LID - Approx. 2½" dia. - Made to look like copper, the lid opens to hold candy inside the pan which hangs by its handle. (Schiffer p38, R2)
$100.00-125.00

CORNUCOPIAS - Approx. 4"-8" Sizes can vary - These cone-shaped pieces were both commercial and homemade products. Pieces with embossed cardboard and lithographed medallions or pictures were certainly "store bought". However, in many others the distinction is not so easily made. They could be made from decorated paper such as printed cardboard, gift wraps or wallpaper. They might also be made from embossed foil or netting. Dresden cornucopias are listed in that section. The rolled cones were almost always decorated with scraps and tinsel. (p551a & b, p552, p553, p558, p559, R3)
Embossed with Medallions $40.00-50.00
Regular cornucopias: Small or plain $30.00-45.00
Larger and elaborate $65.00-85.00

CYLINDER SHAPED CONTAINERS - Approx. 4"-5" Sizes can vary - The cardboard cylinders may be embossed or covered with paper scraps and tinsel may be added. One of the ends lifts off. (p561b & c, R2)
Embossed $100.00-125.00
Paper covered $75.00-90.00

CYLINDERS WITH EMBOSSING AND LITHOGRAPHY - Approx. 5"-5½"H - The box is heavily embossed and has "medallions" of colored lithographs. (Schiffer p97, R2)
$60.00-75.00

DRUM - Approx. 2½" dia. - It is painted white with red and blue diamonds around the side. It has two embossed gold bands around the top and bottom, and drumsticks embossed on the top. The top end with the drumsticks lifts off. (Schiffer p84, R2-3) $65.00-75.00

DRUM - Approx. 1¾" dia. - It is colored red and blue and has zig-zag cording around the side. There are no drumsticks, and the end lifts off. (Schiffer p84, R3)
$65.00-75.00

FABRIC SLIPPER - Approx. 3¾" - The cardboard slipper is covered with fabric and has Dresden trim. (p548, R2)
$100.00-125.00

FEATHER TREE IN A POT - Approx. 6"H - The small tree has spiral metal candle clips and is planted in a printed cardboard "pot" which is the candy container. This piece was not designed for hanging on the tree. (p554, Germany, R1-2) $75.00-90.00

FOIL COVERED BALL - Approx. 2" dia. - A cardboard ball is covered with foil. It separates in the center. U.S. made. (p563, R2) $2.00-8.00

FOOTBALL - Approx. 3" - It is oblong and shows seams

and stitches. It opens at the middle. (p549a, R2)
$40.00-50.00

GLOBE - 1½" & 2¾" dia. - This was a popular piece both as fun and educational, and it was made in several sizes. A paper map is glued over a round cardboard ball that opens at the "equator". (p562a & b, R3) $70.00-90.00

GRAND PIANO - Approx. 2"W - It says "Steinway" across the front. It has realistic detail added to the sides and keyboard and a floral pattern on the lid. It has three round legs. (Schiffer p84, R1) $125.00-150.00

GUITAR - Approx. 4" - It has lithographed decoration, the neck is applied and the "strings" are string. The back lifts off. (p557a, R2) $50.00-75.00

HATBOX - Approx. 2"H - It is smaller at the base than at the top. The lid is held down by a strap that goes all the way around and fastens in the front. It also has a carrying handle on the lid which is the part that lifts up. (Schiffer p84, R2) $100.00-125.00

HEART - Approx. 2" - The cardboard heart is covered with red paper and has a print of an angel. It separates at the sides. (p562c, R2) $65.00-75.00

JOCKEY HAT - Approx. 2" dia. - A rounded hat in gold and blue with a short bill. The top of the hat lifts up. (Schiffer p84, R1-2) $150.00-175.00

LADIES HIGH HEELED BOOT - Approx. 5½" - It is made of satin covered cardboard. The top is open for candy. This is a late piece. (p589a & b, R3) $20.00-30.00

MANDOLIN - Approx. 5½" - It has an egg shape with a flattened front. It has lithographed decoration. The neck is applied, and it has string "strings". (p557c, R3)
$60.00-80.00

MANDOLIN (TYPE II) - Approx. 7" - This piece is constructed out of cardboard and covered with embossed foil to simulate the more expensive Dresden pieces. Such pieces were sold commercially into the 1920's. (p555, R2-3)
$75.00-85.00

OPEN BOX - Approx. 2½" - The square box is open at the top and is covered with embossed foil. It has scrap and tinsel decorations. Such pieces were sold commercially into the 1920s. (p561a, R2-3) $40.00-50.00

OVAL CANDY BOX - Approx. 4½" - These pieces were embossed and lithographed with a wide variety of subjects. They often had a movable cardboard handle. (p556, R2)
$45.00-60.00

PARASOL - Approx. 2½" dia. - It is in the open position and has a wooden handle. Fabric and lace are part of the trim. The top lifts up to find the candy. (R2-3)$125.00-150.00

PATRIOT'S HAT - Approx. 3" - This is a three cornered hat of the kind used in the Revolutionary War. It is made of black fabric. (R1-2) $100.00-125.00

PEANUT - Approx. 2½", 3¾" & 4¼" - The outside is embossed and colored in a realistic manner. Some were European made, but some large and crude Japanese pieces were also produced. The one pictured shows the original toy inside. It separates along the side. (p560a, R3)

Small $20.00-35.00
Medium $35.00-45.00
Large Japanese $20.00-30.00

PRUSSIAN HELMET - 2¼″ - It is a turn of the century German "pickle" helmet with a spike on top. It is black with a gold embossed Imperial large and hat band on the front. (R1-2) $200.00-225.00

POTATO - Approx. 2½″ - It is a rich brown with a characteristic shape and embossed "eyes". It opens along the seam. $50.00-75.00

SANTA BOOTS - Approx. 3¼″, 4″, 5½″ & 8½″H - Made of paper mache, some have a fabric or net bag at the top for hanging. Others have a simple paper covering over the top of the boot. The smaller ones were designed for the tree and the larger ones for tabletops. (Germany, Japan & U.S. made, p565, R4-5) $10.00-20.00
With net bag $20.00-30.00
Larger $18.00-30.00

SEWING BASKET - Approx. 3″H - The round basket is designed to look like it is made of wicker or cane. The broad handle over the top actually moves. There is a candy bag inside the basket. (Schiffer p89, R2) $125.00-150.00

SUITCASE - Approx. 4″ & 2¾″ - It has applied "leather" straps and a metal latch. It opens like a suitcase. (p564a, R2-3) $40.00-50.00

SUITCASE/PURSE - Approx. 3¼″W - The covering is like a brocade material in one version and alligator hide in another. It has two non-functional straps that go around it, an applied paper "latch" and string handles. It opens down the middle. (Schiffer p89, R2-3) $125.00-150.00

TAMBOURINE (TYPE I) - 2½″ dia. - It has five brass bells around the edge. The sides are plain. One side lifts out. (p564b, R2-3) $60.00-75.00

TAMBOURINE (TYPE II) - Approx. 2″ - The edge is designed to look like wood grain. It has sets of tiny symbols. Inside is a bag to hold the candy. (Schiffer p84, R2) $65.00-80.00

TOP HAT - Approx. 2″ - It is fabric covered and holds a candy bag inside the hat. (R1-2) $100.00-125.00

TURKEY - Approx. 3½″L - It is made of paper mache. (R2) $45.00-60.00

VIOLIN - Approx. 3″ - It has a lithographed body and an applied neck. It opens in the back. (R2) $50.00-65.00

VIOLIN CASE - Approx. 3″ - It is the typical looking violin case. It is hinged on one side and opens on the other to reveal the candy. (R2) $45.00-60.00

WALL CLOCK - Approx. 3″ - It has a painted face, pendulum, weights and hands that move. (R1-2)$75.00-100.00

WALNUT - Approx. 2″ - It is realistically embossed and colored. It opens at the sides. (p560b, R2) $25.00-35.00

Reprint from an old catalog.

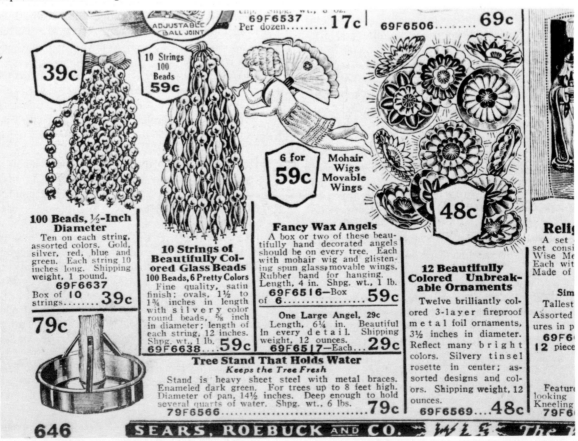

128

CHAPTER V

FABRIC ORNAMENTS

Homemade ornaments constructed from scraps of fabric, cotton, yarn, thread or string were certainly among the earliest Christmas decorations. Many were designed as candy holders, or small gifts in their own right. However, most were not considered permanent decorations to be used year after year. It was not until about the 1880s that fabric ornaments of several types were offered for sale commercially. One of the earliest of these was made of a type of stiffened velour. Such a piece, made into the shape of a butterfly, is pictured. It appears to be stamped from the material and then painted in a realistic manner. Other velour shapes included fruits and vegetables. Such early pieces were rarely exported to the United States.

Another fabric form which found little widespread use in the United States was made from crocheted material. Items such as miniature shoes, slippers, shopping baskets, birds, stars, etc. were crocheted with tight stitches from white or gold metallic thread. When finished, they were dipped into pots of hot white glue. As they cooled, the ornaments were pulled into their desired shapes and allowed to dry into a stiff form. Finishing touches might include scraps, gilding or dried flowers. Directions for making such ornaments were given in the ladies' magazines of the 1880s and 90s. They enjoyed a revival during the arts and crafts period of the 1920s and again during the late 1970s and 80s.

There are several other styles of fabric ornaments that had a lesser role or impact on the Christmas trade. From the 1930s through the 1950s some countries, notably Japan, worked with long strings of a shredded material that was closely compacted to give it a soft velvet look and feel. High quality pieces of this "chenille" were made of shredded silk, but the quality varied drastically and some cheaper versions were even made of paper. Ropes of chenille were sold for decorating the house as well as the tree. Pieces such as treetop stars and window wreathes were made by wrapping the chenille rope around cardboard forms. In later years, wire wrapped chenille. which resembled pipe cleaners, was used to make Santa figures with plaster or paper faces.

Fabric was also used in making Christmas stockings which came in several sizes. Small ones were often hung on the tree, itself, while larger versions were "hung by the chimney with care". Both Europe and America produced some beautifully lithographed and printed examples at the turn of the century. They were constructed of a sturdy linen or canvas-like material. Doubtless, they were manufactured in the same manner and by the same companies that produced the linen or fabric childrens books of the same period.

Other Victorian stockings, cornucopias and a wide range of similar decorations were made from tarlatan. This was a type of thin, stiff muslin that was used in producing both homemade and commercial ornmanents. Tarlatan often had a loose, almost net-like weave to it. Pieces made from this material were often decorated with wire tinsel and scraps.

Other stockings made of cotton, felt or wide mesh netting were made from about the 1920s onward by both American and Japanese producers. Most are large and stylized; however, some small versions appear to be real socks that were printed and modified for the Christmas trade.

Santa dolls with fabric clothing were generally made for table or house decorations. However, a few of the smaller pieces were also hung on the tree. Their bodies could be made of a type of cardboard, paper mache or "composition" that was made in both Germany and Japan. Their clothing was made from material and generally followed the scheme of a red coat and blue pants. This material clothing should not be confused with the "fluffy" covering of pressed cotton or cotton wool pieces.

A final form of fabric ornament that enjoyed more considerable popularity was the mesh net candy bags. These are generally found as a Santa with a celluloid face and small plaster arms and legs. The "body" of Santa is a net bag into which candy, nuts or small gifts could be put. The net bag Santas had many variations on the same general theme or idea. The strength of the material on these pieces has held up surprisingly well over the years. Many collectors today fill them with popcorn or cotton to fill out their form. This helps to rekindle their past charm, and one can easily imagine them hanging tantalizingly from the branch stuffed full of all the mouth watering goodies of childhood.

By far the most popular of the fabric ornaments were those made from cotton. These can be divided into three types, pressed cotton, also known as cotton batting, cotton wool and spun cotton.

Pressed cotton is smooth and found pressed together in thin layers. It was most popularly used for batting inside clothing and quilts. It is also found sprinkled with glitter and used as a "skirt" for under the tree. In another form, pressed cotton was spread over cardboard shapes to form an endless variety of homemade and commercial shapes.

Cotton wool has a natural cotton look to it. Ornaments made from it appear rough and fluffy, not at all like the flat smooth texture of pressed cotton. Cotton wool was often sold for creating snow scenes or placing on tree branches to give them a snow covered effect. Cotton wool and pressed cotton were often used interchangeably in making ornaments.

Spun cotton is easy to identify. It has a "spun" or twisted texture to it and a hardened outer "shell" which is totally unlike natural cotton.

Commercially manufactured cotton ornaments came from the cottage industry of the Sachsen and Thuringen regions. These, of course, are the same regions where many other forms of Christmas decorations were being made, most notably the glass ornament. However, they were not limited to this area. A significant cottage industry also was producing cotton pieces in Frankfurt am Main. The cotton decorations are considered to be an outgrowth of the artificial flower and "dummy" or doll trade which constructed store window and table decorations.

Cotton ornaments reached the height of their popularity around the turn of the century. A 1901 German catalog lists thirty different forms decorated with "ice glitter". They include:

"Muffs, Christmas Angels, Knecht Ruprecht, a chapel with a gold angel, white bags with gold stars, an angel's head, bottle, a chambermaid in a bright dress, little ballerinas with crepe paper dresses and gold wings, servants with jackets, a stork nest with three storks, mushrooms, a natural colored cucumber with green leaves, red double cherries, birds, butterflies and fruit."

Because the cotton pieces were unbreakable, they were often hung low on the tree and used as play things by the children. When the tree was taken down, many were given to the children as toys and not put on the tree in succeeding years. This is one reason why they are so difficult to find today. Another is the fact that they tended to gather dust and dirt during storage and from being handled. After several years of being played with, the glitter was gone, they were pushed out of shape and had a dirty grey look to them. Then one year, much to the children's sorrow, they were simply missing from the tree. By the 1920s, their popularity seemed to wane, and they disappeared as a major ornament form.

Cotton batting and cotton wool ornaments were both made in a similar manner. Figures, which were often portrayed in long hooded coats, were cut from the cotton layers and then glued over a wire or cardboard frame. Scrap faces, feet, flowers, etc. were added with "Dresden" paper wings or star shaped buttons. Occasionally crepe paper bows or trim would also be added. Next a thin film of glue was spread over the cotton, and tiny pieces of glass or mica were sprinkled on to give the piece a sparkly "ice glitter". The most popular form for pressed cotton figures were snow children, angels and Santa Claus or Father Christmas. Almost all of these pieces have a flat or pressed look to them.

There were several major variations on the types of pressed cotton and cotton wool ornaments. In one such piece, the Japanese specialized in making a cotton wool figure of Santa Claus. These came in a variety of sizes and had a round fluffy body with a plaster-like face. They were inevitably dyed red which nowadays appears as an "off" pink.

In another variation, a soft cotton body, often formed around a wire frame, was wrapped in and held together by crepe paper clothing. Such pieces often had scrap faces and the crepe paper clothes were twisted together on the ends with string or wire.

Pressed cotton was often added as a dress to a large chromolithographed scrap. The scrap usually showed the girl or woman to the waist, and the cotton skirt formed the rest of her body. In some cases scrap dolls, flowers or legs and feet were included to add to the finished product. Such pieces were not only sold as Christmas ornaments but sold year round as dolls or doll kits. Many of these ornaments are listed in the Paper Scrap Section.

In another major style of fabric ornaments, pressed cotton was glued or sewn onto cardboard forms or frames. These came in a seemingly endless variety of stars, baskets, trolleys, boats, boots, slippers, sleighs, houses and animals as well as the "gates of heaven". After fastening the cotton to the cardboard and trimming it to match the often intricate designs of its frame, scraps and tinsel were added as decoration. These pieces are usually quite large, and the cotton was usually applied to only one side. Thus the cardboard frame shows on the reverse of the ornament. Most of these pieces are homemade. They were very popular in ladies' magazines from 1880-1900, and many patterns were provided. During this same time, they were also a favorite school art project for the Christmas season. Nada Gray, in her book *Holidays*, provides patterns and pictures of many cotton pieces of this style.

Spun cotton pieces were made in a totally different process. A combination of cotton and cellulose fibers were spun together using little winding machines that twisted them inside a form. A layer of white glue gave them a thin shell for strength, smoothed the lines of the ornament and held on crushed glass glitter. These pieces such as fruits and vegetables were realistically painted. They also made birds with paper wings, mushrooms, snowmen, animals and people. Older ones were hung by a fabric covered loop.

People ornaments often had their arms, legs, head and body wound as separate pieces. When assembled, they were given scrap faces, and "clothing" made from crepe paper. Later and more deluxe models had wax, porcelain, plaster or celluloid faces provided by the toy industry. These people came in an endless variety because with each change of costume you created a new character. Additionally, these three dimensional pieces were often given cardboard or metal accessories such as skis or skates. Others might receive scrap babies, baskets of fabric flowers or crepe paper hats. Japan as well as Germany made some of these spun cotton pieces and they are often hard to tell apart.

The three dimensional spun cotton pieces were commercial products. However, those that were constructed from pressed cotton or cotton wool were both commercially and homemade. Those spun cotton pieces in the shape of people and animals top the list of popularity in cotton or fabric pieces. No matter what the form, cotton or fabric decorations add to an ornament collection a cherished link with a major style that no longer exists today.

NOTES:

1. Although some icicle forms were produced into the 1950s, most cotton pieces are "old" i.e. before 1939 so the old product-new product designation is not always necessary.
2. Plaster-like and celluloid faces are **generally** later Japanese pieces.
3. Spun cotton animals are rarer than people and generally more collectible.
4. Cotton batting and pressed cotton pieces were constructed without set forms or patterns. Therefore, each piece is more or less unique in its dress, decorations and size. Most pieces have to be lumped into a general category. Prices and desirability will vary with the condition and quality of the construction of the piece, as well as any added decorations.
5. Many pieces, such as people and animals, use a combination of spun and pressed cotton. The arms and legs may be spun with the clothing or torso made from cotton batting or pressed cotton. The forms are not always separate, and thus do not fit into nice individual categories. I have tried to place them according to which is the most obvious or the most used.
6. Also see the paper doll section for scraps dressed in cotton.

Pressed Cotton and Cotton Batting

PRESSED COTTON CHILDREN - Approx. 3"-6", Sizes can vary - These are usually portrayed as snow children in long coats with hoods. Girls often carry muffs and have crepe paper bow decorations. Babies are often shown nestled into bunting. Most have scrap faces. (Germany, p567b, OP, R2-3) $125.00-150.00

COTTON BATTING ANGELS - Approx. 3"-6", Sizes vary - These are very similar to the snow children pieces. However, gold or silver wings are attached to the back to make them angels. (Germany, p568a, OP, R2)$140.00-160.00

PRESSED COTTON OR COTTON BATTING SANTAS - Approx. 3"-6", Sizes vary - Santa or Father Christmas is usually shown in a long coat with a hood or hat. He may carry twigs or a "sprig" from a feather tree. He usually has a scrap face. The exact forms vary greatly with no two being exactly the same. (Germany, p567c, p569b, p571, p572a, OP, R2-3) $140.00-160.00

VARIATION #1: AMERICAN PRESSED COTTON SANTA - Approx. 5½" - This flat piece has widespread arms and legs and a paper face. It has ribbon decoration for the belt and cuffs. The cotton is covered with glitter decoration. (U.S., p588a, OP, R3) $15.00-25.00

VARIATION #2: COTTON BATTING SANTA WITH A WAX FACE - Approx. 5", Sizes can vary - The bearded face has a long sad appearance and is set into a hooded coat. He also has wax hands. (Germany, p570, OP, R1) $175.00-200.00

JAPANESE COTTON BATTING SANTAS - Approx. 3"-8", Sizes can vary - These pieces have a soft and fluffy body that is usually cylinder shaped. A cast plaster face, with a cotton beard, is inset into a hood. The arms and legs are wrapped tubes of cotton. The once red coat and hood now have an orange/pink look to them. (Japan, p586, p587, OP-NP, R3-4)
Small $10.00-25.00
Medium $35.00-50.00
Large $60.00-80.00

PRESSED COTTON COVERED CARDBOARD - Approx. 3"-12", Sizes vary - These were made by covering cardboard patterns with pressed cotton and applying tinsel and scraps as decorations. The cotton might be glued, but most often it was sewed onto one side of the pattern. Such Victorian pieces were almost always "homemade" products and were very popular in the Pennsylvania area. Patterns include stars, baskets, sleighs, shoes, etc. Certainly some patterns may be rarer than others, but since they are homemade, it is difficult to evaluate the individual styles. The rarity listing is for the overall type of ornament. Prices will also vary according to size (bigger does not always mean better), appeal of the shape and elaborateness of the decoration. (p591a, p591b, p592, p597, OP, R3)
Small $10.00-20.00
Medium $40.00-60.00
Large $80.00-100.00

SCRAP DOLLS WITH PRESSED COTTON SKIRTS - see "PAPER SCRAPS"

Spun Cotton

BELL - Approx. 2½" & 3½" - This is the typical bell shape with a raised area on the bottom to represent the clapper. They are often covered in crushed glass. (Germany, OP, R3) $10.00-20.00

BUCKET WITH CHAMPAGNE BOTTLES - Approx. 3½" - Three bottles rise out of disc shaped "bucket" with a wire handle for hanging. (p585b, OP, R2) $25.00-40.00

CHAMPAGNE BOTTLE - Approx. 3" - The example shown has a foil cap and is coated with crushed glass. (p585c, OP, R2) $20.00-30.00

ICICLES - Approx. 3½" & 6" - They have a long tapering shape very similar to a carrot. They have added "ridges" which help give them more of a unique shape. Some of these bear a tag marked "W. Germany" which shows they were made into the 1950s. (Germany & Japan, p584a, OP, R3)
Small $5.00-15.00
Large $10.00-20.00

SPUN COTTON ANIMALS - Approx. 2"-6", Sizes can vary - Unlike people ornaments, these are more easily recognized and described. Cotton animals, especially birds, were used throughout the year on other items such as dried flower arrangements and table decorations. I have given some prices on animals for general price guidance, individual prices may vary according to the desirability and collectibility of the type of animal. Since the pieces are individually made, even two types of the same animal will be different. Animal forms include: Dove and songbird, lion, fox, rabbit, squirrel, frog, horse, bear, reindeer, stag, pig, cat, dog and donkey. (Germany, Japan, p579, p580, p581, p582a, OP-NP [Some birds were made into the 1950s and 60s], Birds R4, others R2-3)
Birds $10.00-20.00
Squirrel $90.00-100.00
Stag $90.00-110.00
Horse $150.00-175.00
Rabbit $90.00-100.00

VARIATION: BEAR IN A SWING - This is similar to the Santa in a Swing piece. A spun cotton "teddy" bear sits in a swing with a wooden seat and a tinsel hanger. (Germany, p573, OP, R2) $175.00-200.00

SPUN COTTON FRUITS AND VEGETABLES - Approx. 2"-5", Sizes vary - These come in several styles, but many of the shapes resemble each other except for their color. Some of the earlier and more desirable pieces have fabric leaves on them. Pieces include: pears, tomatoes, turnips, bananas, cucumbers, grapes, cherries, radishes, oranges, apples, carrots, mushrooms and plums. (p582c, p582d, p583, p584)
Pears (R3-4) $10.00-20.00
Grapes (R2-3) $10.00-20.00
Cucumbers (R2) $20.00-30.00
Turnip/apple/tomato (R3-4) $20.00-30.00
Mushroom (R2) $20.00-30.00

SPUN COTTON ICE CREAM CONE - Approx. 2½" - (p585a, OP, R2) $15.00-25.00

SPUN COTTON PEOPLE - Approx. 3"-6", Sizes vary - Their bodies are assembled out of various spun parts. They can be found in a wide variety of poses and costumes. Their clothes are made of cotton, fabric or crepe paper and may have scrap or Dresden trim. The faces can be painted or applied scraps. Prices can vary widely based on condition, uniqueness of the dress and cuteness. (Germany, p567a, p569a, p574, p575, p577, p578, p594, OP, R3)
Small $150.00-175.00
Larger $180.00-220.00

VARIATION: SPUN COTTON PEOPLE WITH PORCELAIN FACES - Approx. 3"-6", Sizes vary - Small beautifully painted heads from the toy industry are mounted on spun cotton bodies. The pieces are usually dressed in crepe paper clothes. These pieces are more elaborate but also later than the scrap or painted face ornament. (Germany, Japan, p574b, p575c, p577d, OP, R2-3) $200.00-225.00

VARIATION: SPUN COTTON PEOPLE WITH PLASTER FACES - A molded plaster face, usually with a flat back, is realistically painted and applied to the spun cotton doll. Crepe paper clothes and trim are added. These pieces are usually Japanese, especially if the body underneath the paper clothes is loose and fluffy instead of spun. (Japan, p574d, p576b, p577a, p598, OP, R3) $190.00-210.00

VARIATION: SPUN COTTON PEOPLE WITH CELLULOID FACES - These are generally late pieces with the celluloid applied to the front of a round head. (OP, R3) $80.00-90.00

SPUN COTTON SANTAS - Approx. 3"-6", Sizes vary - They usually have spun arms, legs, torso and head. The face may be painted on, or it might be a scrap. They are often dressed with crepe paper and may have additional trim of tinsel, fabric, "Dresden" paper, etc. Prices will vary with constructions and elaborateness of the piece. (Germany, p572b, OP, R2-3)   Small $150.00-175.00
                                                        Larger $180.00-200.00

VARIATION #1: SPUN COTTON SANTA ON A SWING (TYPE I) - Approx. 4" - This chubby Santa with a scrap face sits in a hoop of tinsel wire. (Germany, p568b, OP R2) $175.00-200.00

VARIATION #2: SPUN COTTON SANTA ON A SWING (TYPE II) - A scrap faced Santa stands in a swing made of wood and tinsel wire. He holds onto the sides that are also decorated with small feather tree branches. He is completely dressed in crepe paper. (Germany, p508, OP, R2-3) $225.00-250.00

Fabric Candy Containers

CHENILLE BELL CANDY CONTAINER - Approx. 4" - Chenille roping is wrapped around a cardboard bell. It is often decorated with artificial holly and plaster Santa faces. The candy container opens at the bottom and has a loop for hanging on the tree. (Japan, OP, R3) $60.00-75.00

COTTON COVERED BOOT - Approx. 6½" - The boot is formed from cardboard and covered with cotton batting. A plaster faced Santa head rises out of the top of the boot and acts as a stopper. (Japan, p595, OP, R2-3)$75.00-85.00

COTTON SNOWBALL - Approx. 2" - This is made from a spun cotton ball that is flat on the bottom and holds a cardboard cylinder or box. The piece pictured is decorated with a sprig of artificial holly. (p590b, OP, R2)$60.00-75.00

COTTON SNOWMAN - Approx. 4" - This spun cotton piece has a hollow tube, for candy, coming up from the bottom. (p578b, OP, R2) $50.00-60.00

HIGH LADIES BOOT - Approx. 5½" - This high-heeled boot is shaped in cardboard and covered with satin and gold foil trim. They were made in the early 1950s. (p589, NP, R3) $20.00-30.00

NET CANDY BAGS - Approx. 6"-8" - The part that actually held the candy was made of a white, open mesh type of netting. The net might form a figure with arms and legs, or it may be attached to a cardboard bucket or cornucopia. In any case, it usually has a celluloid face of Santa or a girl on the head area. (p582b, p593, p596, OP, R3)
                                        All net body $50.00-75.00
                                        Cone body $70.00-90.00
                                        Bucket body $80.00-100.00

WAX BABY IN A SHOE - Approx. 3" - A cardboard baby shoe is covered with cotton batting. At the shoe's opening is a wax baby head with a cotton bonnet. The head lifts off to get the candy inside the shoe. (p590a & p590c, OP, R2) $125.00-150.00

Chenille

CHENILLE ROPING - Approx. 6'-180' - These long velvet-like ropes were used for tree roping as well as house decorations. There were some extreme differences in their quality. (Japan, OP, R3-4) $.50-5.00

CHENILLE SANTA WITH A PLASTER FACE - Approx. 5", Sizes vary - These pieces were Japanese made. They have the look of being made from thick pipe cleaners. The plaster-like face was cast in a small mold and painted realistically. Such pieces were used as party favors and table decorations, as well as ornaments. (Japan, p588d, p588e, OP, R4)   Small $2.00-8.00
                                                        Larger $5.00-15.00

CHENILLE SANTA WITH A PAPER FACE - Approx. 5", Sizes vary - These are very similar to the above but somewhat later in time. The plaster face has been replaced by a printed paper one. These are probably no earlier than the 1950s. (Japan, p588b, NP, R4) $2.00-10.00

CHENILLE WRAPPED STARS - Approx. 6" - In this piece, a cardboard star is wrapped with chenille roping to give it a velvet look. Such decorations often had a hole in the center for inserting a light and were used as treetop stars. (Japan, OP, R4) $1.00-6.00

Miscellaneous

CROCHETED ORNAMENTS - Approx. 3"-6", Sizes vary - These were items that were crocheted from thread or string then dipped into hot glue to make them stiff. They were produced both as a homemade ornament, according to directions in the ladies magazines of the 1880-1890s and as a commercial piece made by the German cottage industry. Shapes include baskets, shoes, slippers, snowflakes and spider webs. They were not as popular in America as in Germany, and are still not highly sought after by collectors. (Germany & homemade, p588c, OP-NP, R2)
                                           $2.00-15.00

LITHOGRAPHED STOCKINGS - These pieces were made around the turn of the century and come in sizes up to two feet long. Prices will vary with condition and quality of the design. (Schiffer p161, OP, R1-2)$250.00-275.00

PRINTED FELT STOCKINGS - These were made from about the 1920s onward. Those from the 20s and 30s are becoming collectible. (OP-NP, R3) $15.00-30.00

SMALL PRINTED SOCK - Approx. 5″ - These are a real child's sock printed with Santa and "Merry Christmas". They were from about the 1950s and were designed to hang on the tree. (NP, R3) $10.00-15.00

FABRIC BUTTERFLY - Approx. 2½″, Sizes vary - This piece appears to be made of a starched or stiffened linen. It has pastel coloring and is mounted inside a tinsel hoop. (p599, OP, R1-2) $15.00-25.00

VELOUR BUTTERFLY - Approx. 5″, Sizes can vary - The piece appears to be stamped out of a stiffened velour and then realistically painted. These early pieces had little export to the United States. (Germany, p566b, OP, R1) $40.00-50.00

TARLATAN, NET AND LACE DECORATIONS - Sizes vary greatly - Tarlatan, a type of thin and stiff muslin was used to make both homemade and commercial ornaments. The material was formed into bags, purses, cornucopias, stockings, rosettes and dresses for scrap dolls. The fabric was then decorated with ribbon, tinsel and scraps. Besides condition, price will also be affected by the type and elaborateness of the added trim. The theme of the attached scrap is also important. Some prices are given here for guidance. Also see the scrap section for dolls with fabric skirts. (p591c & p591e, OP, R2-3)Stockings $20.00-35.00
(Larger) $35.00-60.00
Rosettes $20.00-30.00
Cornucopia $25.00-35.00
Simple Shapes $20.00-30.00

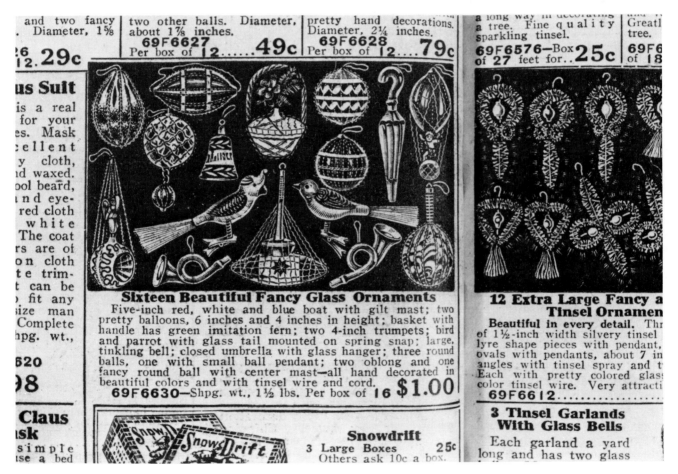

Reprint from an old catalog.

133

CHAPTER VI

METAL ORNAMENTS

This section contains several different types of ornaments made from metal. Cast tin, wire, tinsel and foil all belong to this category and will be discussed individually.

Tin and lead alloy ornaments were the first decorations to be commercially produced. They can date back to the late 1700s and were made by the toy makers in and around Nuremburg who had also specialized in metal doll furniture and dishes. They were also produced in the Freiburg and Pegau areas by producers of "casket fittings, hat decorations and technical tin ware." Another tin foundry in Diessen, established in 1796, still produces tin alloy ornaments today. In America, they found their greatest popularity from about 1870 to the turn of the century.

Tin ornaments, which were the most popular of the metal ornaments were produced in a wide variety of styles from geometric shapes and animals to three dimensional bird cages, baskets and cradles. The pieces were designed to be hung by thread behind or near candles so they would slowly twirl and reflect the light. During the last part of the 1800s, tin ornaments, especially those in a geometric or flower shape, were applied as weights on pendulum candle holders. This provided a pleasing combination of both a reflective ornament and candle holder.

Some tin decorations were cast as a single piece, while others were cast in sections and assembled into the more elaborate forms. To add to the beauty of such reflectors, many were indented with faceted shapes. When painted with bright lacquers, these indentations sparkled like gems. Phillip Snyder states that some deluxe models were indeed inset with cut glass "gems".

In a less popular form, some tin pieces were cast in just an outline shape and were then wrapped in crinkle or "leonic" wire to fill in the spaces.

A very curious type of lead ornament hung on the tree between Christmas and New Year's Eve. The figures included such "good luck" shapes as mushrooms, bells, clocks, moneybags, fish, hearts, anchors, lanterns, shells and nuts. On New Year's Eve, the ornaments were taken from the tree and melted in a casting spoon. Then in a system of divination dating back to the Middle Ages, the hot lead was dripped into a bowl of cool water. One's fortune was told by the form and imagined "pictures" of the cooled lead. By their very nature, few of these decorations survived, and they were never a popular American tradition. A selection of these ornaments can be found on page 117 of Eva Stille's book.

Tin ornaments, enjoyed a rebirth of interest following World War II. Most are made in the original slate molds and a few can still be bought today. Prices for these new pieces range from five to twenty dollars. Whether old or new, it must be remembered that tin decorations are soft and easily bent or melted if not handled with care.

Wire ornaments come in many forms and styles. The wire itself comes in a variety of forms: spiral wrapped, wavy, crinkled (leonic) and flat strips. These wires were used by the glass ornament makers to form boats, airplanes, balloons and a multitude of fancy shapes. Wire was also an important element in the "Sebnitz" ornaments where it was combined with foil, cotton, cardboard and wax to form unusual and fanciful creations.

Wire was also used by itself to form some interesting objects and designs. Using a combination of several types of wire, ornament makers from the Nuremburg regions twisted and wrapped flower baskets, houses, stars, sleighs, baby beds, etc. Unfortunately, few pieces of this style found their way to America. It is likely that they did not appeal to the larger importers. Because of their rough and, at times, crude homemade appearance, ornaments made of wire alone did not compete well against the beautiful glass, Dresden, scrap and cast tin pieces. Even today they are not widely collected. Those collectors who have examples see them as a unique and rare art form of the age of ornaments and not necessarily as an object of beauty.

Creations out of spiraled wire included metal icicles, stars, snowflakes and a hanging chandelier. However, the biggest use for wire of all types was in encasing and decorating glass ornaments.

Tinsel is a separate but closely related form of wire and foil. The process for making it dates back to the early 1600s, but it would not be until the 1870s that its use was applied to the Christmas tree. Tinsel is made from flattened strips of wire or foil, also known as lametta, which is much like our modern foil icicles. Lametta itself was used to create a cascading shower of gold or silver on the tree. When wrapped between two pieces of wire or thread and snipped short, it became tinsel. Lametta that was wrapped between string was soft and primarily used for tree and room garlands. Stiff tinsel, wrapped between wire, was used for outlining scraps or forming stars, snowflakes, hoops and rosettes that might include glass beads or larger glass ornaments. Such pieces were offered by Sears and Roebuck throughout the 1920s and 30s.

They were advertised in 1926 in this manner:

36 Glittering Tinsel Ornaments, 39¢. Pretty silver pendants, icicles and other fancy shapes. Average size about 3½ inches. Eighteen have colored glass bead. These scattered on the tree will add considerable sparkle to it. Big value assortment. Shipping weight, 8 ounces. Box of 36. . . 39¢

These were the simplest form and cost approximately one cent each. There was a set of twelve for 25¢; a set of twelve twisted and fancy shapes for 59¢; and finally, a deluxe model which held a two inch bell or reflector - six of which cost 49¢, or eight cents each. Although often shunned by collectors today, these deluxe pieces cost more than many molded glass ornaments.

Tin foil wrapped over cardboard was popular for making both homemade and commercial decorations that flashed brightly in the candlelight. An 1878 tree is shown with wide strips of perforated foil looped through the branches like roping. The "Sebnitz" ornaments were a popular form in which both tin foil and strips of perforated foil, with a web-like design, were used (See "Sebnitz Ornament"). Foil was also used for making the dresses of certain types of treetop angels -- most notably the "Nuremburg Angels". The foil was folded and pleated into long skirts and blouses with puffy sleeves as well as golden wings.

Foil was usually incorporated into other types of ornaments. But some later pieces can be found constructed entirely out of foil. Thin sheets of foil were fastened together in concentric circles, stars or rosettes to form both ornaments and foil light reflectors. Other foil was rolled, twisted and bent into more three dimensional shapes. Heavier foil was used by itself to form boot and cornucopia shaped candy containers as well as some unique treetop stars and fancy shapes.

Perhaps the most enduring use of foil is in the manufacture of icicles. These slender strips of foil were first marketed in Germany in 1878 and were known as "lametta". Sold in one gram envelopes, they came in gold, silver and a rarer purple. These early icicles had a major disadvantage of easily tarnishing. By the 1920s, Americans had marketed icicles out of lead. These did not tarnish and because of their weight draped nicely on the tree limbs. However, because of the danger of lead poisoning to small children, they were replaced in the 1960s by silvered milar, which is a type of plastic.

Besides tin, wire, tinsel and foil, there are several other metal ornament forms that found acceptance in America.

Flat strips of metal wire were also useful in the ornament industry. Some were twisted into spiraling icicles by an American manufacturer. The Germans wove similar strips of gold and silver colored metal into small baskets designed to hold nuts or candies.

During the 1870-1890s Germany also produced some lithographed tin containers in the shape of pipes, hearts, stars, globes and eggs. These opened and held candy or small gifts inside them. Other items such as small buckets or pails were not only used to hold goodies but were also given as a Christmas gift. These items along with lithographed candle holders were by-products of the toy industry which was having a great deal of success with the lithographing technique during this same time period. Unfortunately, these beautiful lithographed Christmas items did not enjoy widespread popularity in the United States.

Certain decorative pieces stamped out of sheet brass, such as angels, birds, roses and reindeer, also found limited use as Christmas decorations. They were primarily used as book covers and box decorations during the Victorian period. However when gilted and trimmed with brillant lacquered colors, they made acceptable tree ornaments and were even used as decorative counterweights on pendulum candle holders. (See *Alter Christbaumschmuck*, back cover).

Another major use of metal can be found in early lighting for the Christmas tree such as various candle holders, lanterns, reflectors, etc. These will be discussed and catalogued in the lighting section.

Germany created several other unique ornament forms out of sheet brass, iron and tin but none of these found widespread use or popularity in America.

Ornaments made from a soft tin-lead alloy were usually cast into shallow, one sided molds of slate or sand. Because of this, the backs have a rough, unfinished look from the pouring. Some molds already contained the delicate faceted shapes the reflector would show. In other pieces, these designs were stamped into the soft metal after casting. In such a case, the additional cost of a receiving die might be needed. This die would hold the ornament in shape so that the soft metal did not distort under the pressure of stamping. Still other shapes were simply stamped from flat sheets of tin. Some of the more elaborate tin ornaments were made by combining several cast pieces. These were usually bent into the desired position or shape and then soldered together. Examples of these are birdcages, baskets, boxes and stars with filigree edges. A colored lacquer glaze was then applied to the facets to give them a gem-like look.

Wire usually came to the ornament maker already prepared. Some of the widest sizes came in wrapped and twisted bands like narrow ribbon. Other wire, used for fine wrapping, was only as thick as a human hair. The most commonly used wire was the so called crinkle or "leonic" wire. This was tightly crimped or spiral wound and took on its characteristic shape after it had been slightly stretched during the wrapping process. Over the years, the continued stretching of these small kinks or bends will allow the wire to loosen. This is the cause of slipping and tangling wire in old ornaments. If allowed to continue loosening, the parts that it holds together, such as sailboat masts, are likely to come completely off the ornament.

The making of all-wire ornaments was really a matter of imagination and creativity. Heavy wire formed the frame of the piece, and then a more delicate wire was used to fill in the spaces with a type of shimmering web. Artificial flowers, scraps, cotton, glass beads or Dresden trim were often added for further decoration. Wire ornaments were produced in both a gold and silver tone. Today, both appear to be a darkly tarnished mass of black wire.

Tinsel was first manufactured in the seventeenth century and was used as braid on military uniforms. By the 1870s, the same concept was used to make tinsel ornaments and roping for the Christmas tree. Strips of silver plated or gilted wire were pulled through a series of diamond dies until they were cut as thin as hair. This wire was then rolled flat into a foil and twisted between two pieces of wire or thread. It got its "spiked" look after the tinsel was cut to the desired length. Tinsel was usually combined with glass or scraps to form ornaments and was not generally used alone except as tinsel roping.

Because they are nearly unbreakable, tarnish is the real enemy of these once bright metals. Today, dull blacks and greys have replaced the once gleaming golds and silvers that flashed and sparkled brightly amongst the dark branches of the candlelit tree. Whether tin, wire, tinsel or foil, these unique ornaments are a worthwhile addition to the colorful history of Christmas ornaments.

Tin Ornaments

STANDARD, FANCY OR GEOMETRIC SHAPES - Approx. 1½"-5", Sizes can vary - These came in a wide variety of shapes and sizes. They have been referred to as flower and "key" shapes. Individual pieces were sometimes soldered together to form larger more elaborate decorations. Price will depend on condition, coloring and uniqueness of the design. (Germany, p600d, p601, p602, p603, OP-NP, R3)

Small $15.00-25.00
Medium $25.00-35.00
Large $40.00-60.00
5 Inches $60.00-80.00

ANGEL WITH FILIGREE WINGS - (3-D) - Approx. 3"L - This piece has a nicely detailed face and hair. The wings and dress are highly detailed filigree work. The "gems" are raised not indented. (West Germany, p606a, NP)$3.00-6.00

ANCHOR - (Flat) - Approx. 2½" - This has the classic anchor shape with a curved bottom and a cross bar at the top. It is covered with faceted indents. (Germany, OP, R3) $100.00-110.00

BASKET - (Flat) - Approx. 3¼" - This shows a simple basket form with a larger loop handle. This flat piece is entirely covered by small indentations. (Germany, Schiffer p74, OP, R2) $45.00-60.00

COVERED BASKET - (3-D) - Approx. 2¼"L - This oval basket is composed of six molded parts - a base, two semicircle sides, two lids and a handle. The open work shows flowers and strawberries. The two lids or covers are hinged and actually lift. The covers are marked "Germany" but the base is stamped "Made in Western Germany". This is perhaps a retooled 1940s-50s piece. (Germany, p604a, OP-NP, R2) $70.00-100.00
Newer $15.00-25.00

FISH BASKET - (3-D) - Approx. 2"L - The basket appears to have been cast as one piece then the four sides were bent up, soldered and a handled added. The sides show fancy open weave of loops and flowers. Two fish are molded into the bottom of the basket. (Germany, p605, OP, R1-2) $40.00-55.00

ROUND BIRD CAGE - (3-D) - Approx. 1¾" - This round cage has individual bars and a base. A small cast bird can be seen on the inside. (Germany, OP-NP, R3)$35.00-45.00

SQUARE BIRD CAGE - (3-D) - Approx. 2"H x 2"W - This is made from four cast pieces with lots of bending and soldering. The sides show individual bars, one with a small door. The sloping roof has an open diamond pattern. There is a small 3-D bird inside. "Germany" is embossed on the base at the rear. (Germany, p604e, OP-NP, R1-2) $90.00-110.00

BOX - (3-D) - Approx. 1½" each side - This was cast as one piece with the sides folded and soldered. It has decorative open work that is different on all six sides and small faceted reflectors. On one side "Germany" is embossed into a band. (Germany, p604b, OP-NP, R1-2) $50.00-60.00

BUTTERFLY (TYPE I) - Approx. 2"L - The body and wings are made up of deeply embossed teardrop shapes. (Germany, p635b, OP, R2) $35.00-45.00

BUTTERFLY (TYPE II) - Approx. 2½"W - This piece is highly detailed in the body and wings. It has many small faceted indentations. The piece is flat. (Germany, p606c, OP-NP, R2 $40.00-65.00

BUTTERFLY FRAME - (Flat) - Approx. 2½" - This is the frame outline of a butterfly. The piece is then wrapped in crinkle wire to fill in the outline. (Germany, Stille p96, OP, R1-2) $30.00-45.00

CRADLE - (3-D) - Approx. 2½"L - This piece is constructed of three separate pieces. The base and sides were cast as one, then the sides were bent upward. The head and foot boards were then soldered on. The open design is composed of leaves and flowers. This could easily be doll house furniture, except for the "jeweled" reflectors along the sides. (Germany, p604d, OP, R1-2) $75.00-100.00

CROSS - Approx. 3¼", Sizes and exact pattern can vary - (Germany, p600e, OP, R2) $45.00-60.00

DOG - (Flat) - Approx. 2½" - The dog, wearing a collar, is shown walking to the right. It has one large and one small indentation. (Germany, Schiffer p71, OP, R2)$50.00-65.00

EAGLE ON A REFLECTOR - Approx. 4" - The stylized eagle is shown with raised wings. It is covered by indentations both large and small. It is perched atop a round reflector. (Germany, p600a, OP, R2) $110.00-125.00

FLYING EAGLE - (Flat) - Approx. 4½"W - It is shown in a flying position with its head turned to the left. This flat piece is covered with large and small indentations. (Germany, Schiffer p75, OP, R1-2) $110.00-125.00

FAN - Approx. 3¾" - This filigreed piece shows the fan in an open position with a long handle. The "gems" are raised instead of embossed on this flat piece. (Germany, p606b, OP, R2) $35.00-45.00

FISH ON A GRILL - (Flat) - Approx. 3" - Fish are shown laying on an open grill with a long handle. (Germany, OP, R2) $35.00-45.00

GIRAFFE - Approx. 2" - The animal is shown eating from a tall tree. Its base shows the ground. This flat piece has only one indentation. (Germany, Schiffer, p71, OP, R2) $50.00-65.00

HEART - Approx. 4" - The heart shape is deeply embossed into a faceted "bowl". The center may be decorated with fabric flowers or scraps. (Germany, p600c, OP, R2) $75.00-90.00

NATIVITY SCENE - (3-D) - Approx. 2¾"H - This is cast in several pieces that are bent and soldered together. The sides are curved in a half arch, have geometric designs and palm branches. The small figures inside are flat castings that have been painted. It is marked "Germany". (Germany, p604c, OP-NP, R1-2) $90.00-110.00

PARROT - Approx. 3½" - The parrot is portrayed sitting on a wire hoop with folded wings. He faces to the right. This piece is basically flat. (Germany, p600b, OP, R2) $50.00-75.00

STAG - (Flat) - Approx. 2" - This nicely detailed piece faces left and has a ground-like base. There is only one faceted indent in this flat piece. (Germany, Schiffer p71, OP, R2) $50.00-65.00

STAR FRAME - (Flat) - Approx. 2½" - The outline of this five pointed star is cast in tin. The piece is wrapped in crinkle wire to fill in the star's outline. (Germany, Stille p96, OP, R1-2) $30.00-40.00

SWAN - (Flat) - Approx. 2" - It is shown moving to the left in the swimming position with the head bent. This flat piece has two faceted indents. (Germany, Schiffer p71, OP, R2) $50.00-65.00

Wire

WIRE ICICLE - Approx. 5½" - This long tapering piece is made from a band of looped and folded wire. (Germany, p608a, OP-NP, R3-4) $1.00-2.00

ICICLE - Approx. 5½" - This is a simple strip of metal that has been twisted and lacquered for color. (U.S., p , OP, R4) $.10-.50

WIRE AND COTTON BED - The frame of the bed is made by heavy wire and is filled with cotton. It is then completely wrapped with crinkle wire. A half canopy, also wire wrapped, hangs over a scrap baby in the bed. (Germany, Stille p104, OP, R1) $175.00-200.00

WIRE AND COTTON FLOWER BASKET - This hanging basket has a round "pot" formed by cotton. The whole piece is covered in crinkle wire and has spiral wire rim and wire tassels. The basket holds dried and artificial flowers. (Germany, Stille p105, OP, R1) $90.00-100.00

WIRE AND COTTON ZEPPELIN - The body of this airship is filled with cotton. It is covered with crinkle wire wrapping. It has a wire propeller and a wire gondola hung underneath. (Germany, Stille p105, OP, R1) $250.00-300.00

WOVEN WIRE BASKET - Approx. 2½"-3" - Strips of flat wire are woven into baskets designed to hold candy or nuts. They come in brass and "German Silver". (Germany, p611, R4) $15.00-22.00

WIRE CHANDELIER - Approx. 6" - It is formed from a looped wire band. It has a long center shaft and six "arms" that hold wax candles. A small glass ball is attached at the base. (Germany, p608c, OP, R2-3) $15.00-22.00

WIRE SNOWFLAKE - 2¾" - This six pointed snowflake has looped and bent silver wire forming each of its arms. (Germany, p608b, OP, R3) $5.00-10.00

Tinsel

TINSEL ORNAMENTS - Sizes vary - 2"-8" - These pieces are hand wrapped and vary greatly in individual design. They can be found from simple to complex forms. Those with large glass ornaments inset in them are more desirable than most other forms. Tinsel, used in these types of ornaments, is stiffened from being wrapped with wire. Many tinsel ornaments are combined with lithographed scraps. The scrap theme can greatly enhance their value (See "Paper - Scraps"). (p465, p607, OP, R4) Small $1.00-3.00
Medium $3.00-6.00
Large $5.00-9.00
Large with glass ornaments $7.00-15.00

TINSEL ROPING - Approx. 10'-20' - This can be found in gold or silver. $2.00-5.00

Foil

FOIL ORNAMENTS - 2"-3" dia. - These ornaments were marketed during the 1920s and resemble the German foil light reflectors. They are made in concentric circles or shapes with a rosette at the center. Light reflectors will have a hole for the lightbulb. They may be trimmed with tinsel or wire. (Germany, OP, R2) $1.00-3.00

FOIL DRESSED ANGEL - "NUREMBURG ANGEL" - Approx. 6"-8", Sizes can vary - These angels were first marketed in the early 1800s and continue to be produced today. The head and arms might be made of wax, composition or procelain. The dress and wings are foil or foil stiffened with paper. They don't seem to have been imported into the United States in large quantities. Despite the fact that such pieces were usually treasured heirlooms, they are rarely found today. The price can vary greatly with age, condition and the elaborateness of the piece. The pieces pictured are circa 1890 and 1930. Their prices can help establish price guidance to many other forms. (p612 & p613)
(R1) Victorian Angel $150.00-175.00
(R3) Later Angel $40.00-50.00

ICICLES IN ORIGINAL BOXES - These are collectible if the packaging is prior to 1940. (p614) $5.00-10.00

FOIL BOOTS OR CORNUCOPIA - Approx. 6" - These were designed to be candy containers. Circa 1950. (U.S., p609, R4) $3.00-5.00

FOIL STARS - Approx. 3"-4" - The design was embossed into the foil and they were double sided. (U.S., p610, Circa 1950, R2-3) $2.00-4.00

STAMPED BRASS ORNAMENTS - Approx. 1½"-3" - These "ornaments" were originally produced as box and book cover decorations. They saw only minor use as tree ornaments; and this was with the shapes that readily lent themselves to the Christmas theme such as angels, birds, reindeer, wreathes and roses. They are deeply embossed or raised but hollow in the back. Such pieces were hung by string to allow them movement. They could be highly polished or painted gold with applied lacquer colors. Many of these have been reproduced and sold in Christmas shops and boutiques. Ironically, the new pieces sell for considerably more than the originals. These should **not** be confused with modern **flat** brass ornaments which are often engraved with names and dates. Such modern pieces have more sentimental value than any collectible value. The **old** brass pieces were both European and American made. (p606e, OP-NP, R3) Old $10.00-15.00
New $7.00-15.00

CHAPTER VII

WAX ORNAMENTS

Early wax ornaments are second only to metal in terms of their age. Considered to be more or less a permanent decoration, they were offered for sale as early as 1800 by manufacturers in the German toy industry centered in and around Nuremburg.

Wax ornaments can be divided into three major categories or styles, full bodied, flat and wax accessories. First, there are the full bodied or three dimensional pieces. These are like small toys and were made in the Nuremburg toy industry. The most popular form of this ornament, and indeed all the wax decorations, was the angel. These came in a wide variety of molded styles and were popular from 1800 until the 1930s. Some of the larger and more elaborate angels were molded in several separate pieces and assembled by local cottage workers. The most popular style for the flying wax angel was hung horizontally. It had spun glass wings and a fabric skirt. Such an angel is described in the Sears and Roebuck catalog of 1926:

FANCY WAX ANGELS - A box or two of these beautifully hand decorated angels should be on every tree. Each with mohair wig and glistening spun glass, movable wings. Rubber band for hanging. Length 4 in. shpg. wt., 1 lb.

Box of 6 . . . . . 59¢

One Large Angel . . . . . 29¢

Length 6¼ in. Beautiful in every detail.

Shipping weight, 12 ounces. Each . . . . . 29¢

The wings for angels were made from spun glass, gilted cardboard or wax which was often molded onto the figure itself. A short dress or cherbic "diaper", which was generally made of fabric and tinsel, was modestly added. Some angels might also be found carrying trumpets made of lead or tin.

Many wax angels had an inner core that was made of composition or paper mache. This stiff center was then covered with a layer of wax and painted. Ornaments constructed in this manner often develop small hairline cracks in the wax covering. Those made of solid wax do not develop such cracks and have a more translucent glow to them, but are more easily damaged by heat and dirt.

A slightly rarer form of the traditional angel is one that hangs from the head in a vertical position. These were popular treetop angels and were generally made of solid wax. They often have one hand raised in greeting or blessing and appear to be gliding effortlessly through the air.

Besides the angel, another popular wax form was the baby or "Baby Jesus" as it was referred to when used as a Christmas ornament. These pieces might range in size from one to six inches and were used as toys, in Nativity scenes, and in Victorian shadow boxes as well as Christmas decorations. The smallest versions might be placed in walnut shell "mangers" while larger versions were wrapped in cotton "swaddling clothes", or placed in small cardboard mangers. Both were popularly used for manger scenes and tree ornaments.

Other small wax figurines of people and animals were added to what are called "Sebnitz" ornaments. These pieces were made from cotton wrapped with crinkle wire and perforated metallic sheets. The wax decoration added the delicate detailing and soft texture that could not be captured in the rough wire wrapped form. Eva Stille describes several of these pieces:

"The colorfully painted wax dog sat listening in front of a Gramophone horn out of (wire and) cotton 'His Master's Voice', the fox sat under the glass grapes, the squirrel on a dog sled out of wire, the tiny eskimo lady (sat) in front of a cotton igloo. A duck and chicken modeled out of different colored wax hung in lanterns out of glittering metal spirals, and wax baby Jesus' were put in fabric containers."

Such pieces are not, strictly speaking, wax and are listed under the section -- "Sebnitz" ornaments.

A final form of the full figured, wax ornament was marketed relatively late (1930s-1950s) by an American manufacturer. These **hollow** cast figures included a Santa Claus, a girl angel, a snowman and a boot. They were cast in a brittle white wax and then painted.

The second major category of wax ornaments are those made in a relief or flat style. Although extremely few of these have survived over the years, they can be quite old. They were first produced by the makers of the "lebkuchen" forms. These molds, which date back hundreds of years, were designed for shaping cookie dough. Intricate designs, shapes and figures were hand carved into fine grained slabs of fruit wood. Cookie dough was then pressed into the form to give it shape before baking. These cookie boards, which could be from several inches to several feet in size, were unique family heirlooms passed from mother to daughter. They were commonly used for making the decorated cookies that hung on the tree. If beeswax was poured into the mold, a more or less permanent "cookie" ornament could be made. These were often painted with the same bright colors with which the original cookie was iced. But the wax had the singular disadvantage of easily being melted or distorted. This, coupled with the fact that soft wax easily gathered dirt and dust, meant they were thrown out or replaced on a regular basis. Although the form may be hundreds of years old, the wax casting itself may only be a few years old.

During the last half of the nineteenth century, these wax reliefs were widely sold on a commercial basis and were fairly popular in Europe. The castings were also sold for many other things besides Christmas decorations. An example can be found in early German Valentine gifts. In these, a flat wax figure was added to a group of artificial flowers. All of these were fastened onto a base and placed under a hand blown glass dome. Such pieces were popular in the 1860s and 70s.

Wax relief ornaments enjoyed a rebirth during Germany's arts and crafts period circa 1920, and are again being produced on a limited basis today.

Many of today's wax ornaments are still produced in

the antique molds. They are easy to distinguish from older versions which are cast in a softer beeswax or paraffin. Today's pieces are made from a hard, brittle, wax that is more melt-resistant than the early products. They are probably the only form of these perishable ornaments the collector will find.

A third major way in which wax was used can be found in decorations with wax heads, arms or legs. These cast parts, again made by the toy industry, were often incorporated into angels, dolls and Santas that were made of cotton, fabric or foil covered cardboard. Like the other wax forms, they were sold commercially during the last half of the nineteenth century, again during the German arts and crafts period and are still being produced today.

Other than decorative and figural candles, there are a couple miscellaneous wax decorations made by American manufacturers from the 1930s-50s that should be noted.

A hollow wax candy container in the shape of a choir body was marketed by Fanny Farmer Candies. Once the candy was eaten, these made lovely table decorations. In the other form, a chocolate figure, such as Santa Claus, was covered in a thick layer of wax and painted. These "Peel-Away" pieces were marketed by the W. & F. Mfg. Co., Inc. of Buffalo, NY. After freezing, the wax was easily shattered and the chocolate removed "as you would nut meat from (a) shell."

Because they were easily damaged by heat and dirt, wax ornaments did not survive well over the many years they were produced. The wax angel is without doubt the most common form, but even these pieces are not commonly found. Wax ornaments make an excellent addition to a collection, but remember to keep them wrapped in order to protect them from dirt and mildew; and while on the tree, keep them away from heat.

NOTES:
1. Prices given are for unmelted, unbroken pieces. Crisp molding is also important. Prices are lowered drastically for damaged pieces.
2. There are no known "bald" angels. Such pieces are missing their mohair wigs and should be considered damaged.
3. Prices on new wax relief castings vary from three to twenty dollars depending on size and theme.
4. Wax pieces were usually hung by a small metal loop in their back or head. However, one creative solution used a needle-like spike to pierce the branch and hold the figure on.

Wax

STANDARD WAX ANGEL - (M) - Approx. 3½", 4", 5", 5¾", 6¼", 9¾" & 14½" - These angels are shown flying in the horizontal position held by a metal loop in the back. They have movable wings made of spun glass, gilted cardboard or pressed "Dresden" cardboard. They are usually found dressed in fabric skirts and have mohair wigs. They usually have a core or inside composed of composition or paper mache. The feet are separate and the arms area bent and outstretched. (Germany, p618a, p618b, p617, OP, R3 for small, R2-3 for medium and R1-2 for largest)

Small 3-4" $40.00-60.00
Medium 5-6" $70.00-90.00
Large 7-14½" $100.00-150.00

VARIATION #1: ANGEL WITH A HORN - Sizes vary - This is the same standard angel, only a hole has been put through the hand closest to the mouth. In this hand is held a tin or lead trumpet. Add five to ten dollars to each size listed above. (p616, OP, R2-3)

VARIATION #2: ANGEL WITH GLASS EYES - Approx. 14½" - Regular glass doll eyes may be inset into the largest of the angel heads. These make a beautiful and unusual improvement over the normally painted ones. (Germany, p615, OP, R1-2) $350.00-400.00

Standing Angel

These angels appear to be standing or flying vertically. They have wax or paper wings and come in a variety of different poses which are listed separately.

SMALL BOY CHERUB - (M) - Approx. 3½" - Both legs are straight and molded together. The left arm is raised and the right is at his side. He has a molded "diaper" and Dresden wings. (Germany, p620b, OP, R2) $40.00-60.00

MEDIUM BOY CHERUB - (M) - Approx. 4¼" - In this piece, the legs are slightly bent but molded together. The left hand is raised and the right is bent in front of the body. The head is slightly tilted to his left. He wears a molded "diaper" and has Dresden wings. (Germany, p620a, OP, R2) $50.00-70.00

ANGEL WITH A FLOWER IN HER HAIR - (M) - Approx. 5" - This has slightly bent, separately molded legs. The arms are outstretched with the right the same height as the chest. She has wax wings. The drapery at the waist is well molded as is the small flower in her hair. (Germany, p622, OP, R2) $200.00-250.00

FLYING ANGEL - (M) - Approx. 5½" - Her legs are separately molded with the left bent behind the right. Her arms are outstretched and were separately molded and attached. She appears to be facing or flying to her left. She has a sash and dress made of fabric and Dresden wings. (Germany, p619, OP, R2) $200.00-250.00

LARGE FLYING ANGEL - (M) - Approx. 7" - Her legs are separately molded with the right straight and the left bent back. Both arms are raised away from the body with the left being head high. Her head is turned to her right; she has a fabric sash and skirt; mohair wig and Dresden wings. (Germany, p621, OP, R2) $250.00-275.00

SEATED ANGEL - (M) - Approx. 3" - He is seated with outstretched arms. His left hand holds a metal spear. He has molded hair and a molded diaper. Wax wings are attached to his back. He has a long needle extending from the rear by which he is fastened to the tree limb. (Germany, p623a, OP, R2) $100.00-125.00

WAX BABY OR BABY JESUS - (M) - Approx. 1", 3", 3½" & 6" - They have several different poses but are always shown laying on their back as if in a manger. The smallest versions may be found in nut shell mangers or cardboard baby buggies. Larger versions used cardboard and wooden mangers. They could also simply be laid into the tree boughs. (Germany, p623b, OP, R2)   Small $10.00-15.00
Medium $30.00-50.00
Large $50.00-75.00

VARIATION #1: JESUS IN A MANGER - These are usually medium size pieces with the manger out of thin wood or cardboard.(Germany, p624, OP, R2)$40.00-60.00

VARIATION #2: JESUS IN A WALNUT MANGER - These are the smallest of the wax pieces. The walnut shells are often decorated with more wax such as roses or fabric. (Germany, p218d, OP, R2) $35.00-45.00

WAX HEADED SANTA IN A COTTON COAT - see COTTON SECTION

WAX PEOPLE AND ANIMALS ON WIRE AND COTTON ORNAMENTS - see SEBNITZ ORNAMENTS

WAX RELIEF ORNAMENTS - (M) - Approx. 2"-12", Sizes can vary - These pieces were originally made in cookie or lebkuchen molds dating back hundreds of years. The front has the embossed and painted design, but the back is smooth. They, of course, have a certain resemblance to cookies. There are stars, hearts, pretzels and geometric shapes as well as St. Nicholas and characters dressed in clothes from the time period the molds were made. Although the molds are old, most old wax pieces will date from about 1920. Newer pieces are made from a harder melt-resistant wax and some are American made. (Germany, p626, OP-NP, R1-2)   Shapes $25.00-35.00
People $40.00-50.00
New $3.00-20.00

AMERICAN WAX ORNAMENTS - (M) - Approx. 2¼" (boot), to 2¾" (Santa) - These pieces are hollow cast in a white wax that is then painted. They have metal hanging loops in the head, except for the boot which has a wax loop at the top rear. They come in a Santa, angel, snowman, choir boy, toy soldier and boot form. (U.S., p625, NP?, R3-4) $3.00-8.00

WAX BOY OR GIRL ON A SWING - (M) - These figures are a pair and stand on a small platform or swing. They have molded clothes which include a hat. Their hands are raised and hold onto string which forms the roping of the swing. These pieces are hollow cast. (Germany, Snyder p57, OP, R1-2)   Each $100.00-125.00

BABY JESUS IN A HOLLOW WAX HEART - (M) - The wax heart has a large oval opening in which lays baby Jesus with a halo. (Germany, Stille p73, OP, R1)$75.00-100.00

WAX WALNUT - Approx. 2" - This is molded with all the detailing of its shell. (Germany, OP, R2) $25.00-35.00

WAX PEAR - Approx. 3½" - This piece is painted yellow with red blushing. It has a metal hanger in the top which would differentiate it from any other type of wax fruit. (Germany, OP, R2) $25.00-35.00

WAX, COILED CANDLE - Approx. 5" - Used to light the candles on the tree or as candles to wrap around a tree limb. It's Christmas use is indicated by the Santa scrap. (Germany, p618c, R1-2) $15.00-25.00

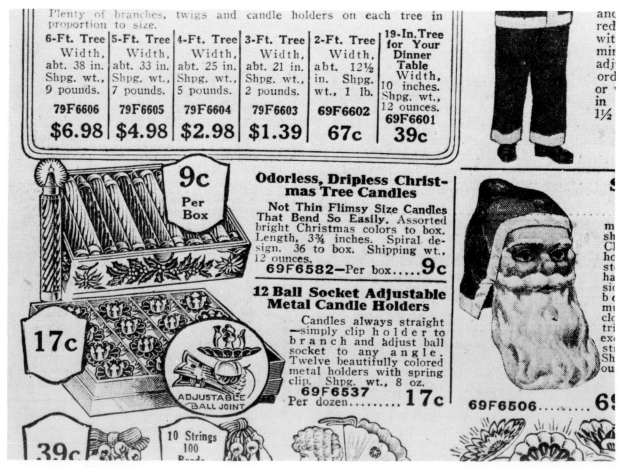

Reprint from an old catalog.

140

CHAPTER VIII

SEBNITZ ORNAMENTS

Named after the German city of Sebnitz, located near Dresden and around which their manufacture centered, these ornaments are an interesting combination of all the major ornament forms of glass, paper, fabric, metal and wax.

The Sebnitz cottage industry specialized in wrapping cotton forms in a metallic foil perforated with small holes. To this was added tiny glass tubes or beads and scrap or wax figures. The whole piece might then be mounted on foil covered cardboard and wrapped in crinkle wire.

Another type of ornament which almost exclusively uses wire and crinkle wire wrapping was made in Nuremburg. These are often mistakenly lumped under the same title of Sebnitz. (Also see Metal-Wire).

The "Sebnitz" ornaments which were made from about 1870 to 1910 are rare in this country, but are fast becoming collector items, especially the ones with wax figures. The ornaments were not made to any specified form, so most are one-of-a-kind decorations. Those listed in this section will help give guidance to most other pieces, and a rarity rating of two is given to these decorations as a general ornament form. Some pieces that have been described as being "Sebnitz" may in reality be homemade. This is true especially of those that are composed mainly of tin foil over cardboard. On page 116 of her book, Eva Stille shows two such homemade pieces. This, of course, can help explain the relative rarity of these pieces. Most of them have a crude, somewhat homemade appearance. This did not help them compete well against the more beautiful glass, "Dresden", scrap, etc., pieces. The buying public is not usually interested in purchasing items they feel they could easily make at home. In light of this, collectors might want to take a closer look at pieces of this style and evaluate their prices accordingly.

ANGEL HAIR BOAT - Approx. 4½" - This piece is formed of small glass tubes, foil discs, wire and angel hair which is stuffed into the hull of the ship. The masts, cabin and railing are made of the white glass tubes. (Germany, p627b, OP, R2) $140.00-160.00

AUTOMOBILE - Approx. 2¾"L - This is made of cardboard covered with foil and covered with crepe paper, which is additionally covered with perforated foil. It has four "Dresden" wheels, wire wrapping, glass tubes and a wax angel driver. (Germany, p629a, OP, R2) $175.00-200.00

FLOWER BOWL - Approx. 2½" - This shallow bowl with scalloped edges is made of foil covered cardboard. It has bead legs and artificial flowers. (Germany, p627a, OP, R2) $40.00-55.00

FOIL BOAT - Approx. 4½" - The hull is made of foil covered cardboard. The three masts are made of glass tubes and foil discs. It has a scrap rider. (Germany, p628b, OP, R2) $140.00-160.00

"HIS MASTER'S VOICE" - A wax dog sits in front of a Gramophone which is made of wire wrapped cotton. Both rest on a base of wire wrapped cardboard. (Germany, Stille p75, OP, R1-2) $350.00-375.00

HOUSE WITH A SCRAP JESUS - Approx. 3¼"H - The house is made of foil covered cardboard and perforated foil. It is outlined with glass tubes and beads. The spun front has dried greenery and a scarp of boy Jesus. (Germany, p627c, OP, R2) $70.00-90.00

SAILBOAT - The hull is crescent shaped and is made of cotton covered with perforated foil and wrapped with wire. The wire mast holds a small, flat, Dresden sailboat. (Germany, Snyder p80, OP, R1-2) $175.00-200.00

SLEIGH - The body of this open sleigh is made from cotton covered with perforated foil and then wire wrapped. It has long wire runners and has a wax baby driver. (Germany, Stille p75, OP, R1-2) $275.00-300.00

SOUR GRAPES FOX - A wax fox in a jacket rests against an arched grape arbor of spiraled wire. From the top hangs two glass grapes and a fabric leaf. The base is cotton and wire wrapping and holds artificial flowers. (Germany, Stille p75, OP, R1-2) $350.00-375.00

SPINNING WHEEL - Approx. 5" - It is mounted on a wire wrapped cardboard base. The frame is made of glass tubes and the wheel is Dresden. The "spindle" holds a wad of cotton. (Germany, p628c, OP, R2) $90.00-110.00

STABLE - The sloping roof and three sides are formed by cotton wrapped in perforated foil. Its sides are on a cotton covered cardboard base. The whole piece is wire wrapped and has a scrap sheep on the open part of the stable. (Germany, Stille p36, OP, R1-2) $70.00-90.00

WALL CLOCK - Approx. 4½" - The clock, itself, is made of foil covered cardboard with a scrap paper face. The pendulum and weights are formed by glass tubes and foil discs. (Germany, p628a, OP, R2) $65.00-75.00

WAX BOY ON A SWING - The swing is more of a box that is made of cotton that is wrapped in perforated foil and wire. Glass tubes connect the seat to the hanging loop. A wax baby sits on the swing. (Germany, Stille p72, OP, R2) $200.00-225.00

WAX SHEEP IN A PEN - Approx. 2¾" - A wax sheep lies on a foil covered disc and is surrounded by small glass tubes representing the fence. A set of large tubes arch overhead. (Germany, p627d, OP, R2) $150.00-175.00

WIRE BOAT - Approx. 3"L - This boat has a wire outline. The hull is made of perforated foil and is stuffed with tangl-

ed wire. It carries a scrap rider. (Germany, p629b, OP, R2)
$40.00-65.00

ZEPPELIN - In this long piece, perforated foil wraps around a cotton core and both are wrapped in crinkle wire.

A paper label on the side reads "Graf Zeppelin". The gondola hanging underneath is also wrapped cotton and holds a cast tin figure looking through a spy glass. (Germany, Stille p132, OP, R1)
$350.00-400.00

Reprint from an old catalog.

CHAPTER IX

LIGHTS AND LIGHTING
FOR THE TREE

Candles have been used for many centuries in the celebration of Christmas. In earlier times, they were used to represent the reborn sun at the winter solstice and were thought to encourage the return of warmth and light. In the Christian faith, the candle represented Christ as the light of the world.

Candles had been used on evergreen decorated Christmas pyramids for many years before they appeared on trees. The first recorded account of a lighted tree occurs in 1658 when the Countess of Orleans had a candlelit box tree in southern Germany. A description of this tree is given in the section -- "A History of the Decorated Tree." It is very likely that candles had been used for lighting trees even before this recorded use in 1658.

Over the next hundred years or so, the recorded descriptions of lighted trees increase, however they fail to describe **how** they were lighted. The exact method for attaching the lights must have been left up to the imagination of each family.

The earliest method was to simply melt the candle directly onto the limb. Some families pressed a hot needle into the bottom of the candle, and the point was pushed through a small branch. In still other instances, a length of wire was coiled around the bottom of a candle. The free end of the wire was then wrapped around the tree limb. This had the advantage of holding the candle reasonably straight and allowing slight adjustments.

Thin, flexible candles which had been used in the home and church for transferring fire to larger candles and chandeliers were also used on the tree. These were usually bought in a long coil, and because the wax was flexible, the candle itself could be wrapped around the branch. Their main disadvantage was that the thin candles burned much too quickly. In Victorian times, this same coiled candle was decorated with "scraps" and used to light the tree's candles. Enough length could be unwound to reach even the topmost tapers.

All of these early methods of putting candles on the tree had the major disadvantage of hot dripping wax staining the floor or carpet underneath the tree.

One early solution to the lighting problem did not use candles at all. Walnut or egg shells were filled with oil and a burning wick floated on top. Since these hung underneath a branch, their main disadvantage was the fact that the heat was transferred directly to the limb above. Even with this disadvantage, this proved to be one of the most enduring principles before the clip-on candle. The famous American glassblower, Baron Stiegel blew glass containers for floating wicks in the 1700s. These Christmas or "fairy" lights became more economical and thus more popular when pressed glass versions became available in the mid-eighteen hundreds.

At the turn of the eighteenth century, some German trees were lit by "hoops of fire". These were graduated hoops or rings of wood with candles attached to them. These were then laid on the tree branches. The hoops of fire were only practical on the fir known as Wiess tanne which had perfectly symmetric branches. The artificial "feather" tree was based on this type of tree.

One of the first commercial candle holders was mounted on a long rod that was designed to screw into the trunk of the tree. It too was specifically designed for the Wiess tanne tree. By the 1800s, candle holders also had a small metal disc with turned up edges to catch dripping wax. These were usually bought in a set of 12 and came in three sizes -- 22, 40 and 54 cm.

From the 1850s to 1910, the decorated tree had an unprecedented growth in popularity, and many new methods for lighting it were invented.

There were the fairy lights which were previously mentioned. Made of pressed glass, these tumbler-like pieces came in several patterns and colors. The quilted pattern is by far the most common, but they were also made in a hobnail, daisy and "thousand eye" pattern. Colors included, amber, amethyst, light and dark green, cobalt blue, ruby red, milk glass and a pastel blue milk glass. The red is the rarest of the colors. These large and heavy lights were made heavier when water, oil and a floating wick were added. They could only be suspended from the strong branches found toward the inside of the tree. This obvious disadvantage for hanging on the tree was offset by their use throughout the year at parties, in the garden and wherever festive lighting was desired. Interestingly, these same uses were advertised as a selling point for early figural lights.

Starting in the 1870s, German glassmakers also blew paper thin versions of the fairy light. Some were in the shape of an inverted beehive, some a cauldron, a flower and some were elaborately embossed with faces. Most of these were beautifully painted and served not only as light holders, but also as ornaments. The thinness of their glass helped eliminate the weight problem, but it also made it easier for them to be damaged by the flame.

A short lived experiment in lighting was tried in the 1850s when tubing for tiny gas flames, similar to the lighting fixtures of the day, were built into the tree. In 1878, one English firm unsuccessfully marketed an iron tree built for gas flames. The gas on this "Improved German Christmas Tree" circulated through the "branches" and came hissing out small holes to produce the gas flame.

In the year 1867, the "socket and pin" holder was patented. This was another early attempt to fasten the candle holder to the tree limb using a tack or small nail. This was pushed through the branch to hold the candle in place. This method had several disadvantages. The thin branches on the tips of the tree were difficult to pierce and they did not hold the candle firmly. This allowed the candle to wobble and tilt dangerously. This was a rather short lived idea, for a far safer method was also developed that year.

On Christmas Eve 1867, Charles Kirchhof of Newark, New Jersey, patented the pendulum weighted candle holder. This piece had a candle holder and wax pan at the top. A long thin wire with a bent hook, for hanging, hung from the drip pan. A painted clay ball at the bottom served as a weight. Also known as a counterweighted candle holder, this bottom weight helped ensure that the candle remained upright on the branch. These holders were ideal on upsweeping tree branches; but again their weight kept them from being used on the ends of small limbs. For evergreens with flimsy branches like hemlock, cedar and some spruces, they were impossible to use. The Germans took this basic idea of the counterweight and improved it. Within a few years, the painted clay balls were replaced by molded lead weights in the form of pine cones, angels, birds and stars. Tin reflector ornaments were also used as the pendulum weight. These did double duty as both counterweight and ornament.

By 1878 German ornament makers were selling **double** counterweighted holders. In this model, the candle socket was attached to an inverted "V" shaped wire with weights on the two ends. This balanced itself upright, like a tight rope walker, on the tree limb.

An unusual and rare variation of the pendulum principle used a drip pan as the counterweight. The candle was held in place by a spring clip. The bottom of the candle extending out of the clip formed the "hook" for holding it on the limb. An adjustable wire connected it to the large drip pan which was suspended three or four inches below the candle. The pendulum weighted holder would continue to be improved into the early twentieth century with such improvements as a spring operated holder for the candle. But it, too, was replaced by the most popular of all candle holders -- the clip-on.

In 1879, Frederick Arzt of New York, patented the spring operated, clip-on candle holder. It eliminated the weight problem and could be placed almost anywhere on the tree branch. It was a great success and remained a best seller until the 1920's when candles were finally replaced by lights.

As with other major inventions, there were many variations of the clip-on candle holder. The earliest versions clipped upright onto the tree limb. The part that held the candle in place was actually part of the wire spring. They had no wax pan, but rather caught the drips and funneled them onto the branch. Some had geometric patterns stamped into them while others had beautiful lithographs. Children, angels, birds -- both common and exotic butterflies, Santa Claus, a Christmas tree and a child on a hobby horse, were all turned into beautiful lithographed candle clips.

The familiar clip-on that attached to the side of the branch contained a drip pan and came in a wide range of styles that were stamped out of tin and painted with brilliant lacquers. There were geometric shapes, fish, lyres, praying hands, pine cones, birds, etc.

Probably the most beautiful and elaborate of the clip-on candle holders were those with blown glass globes or candle shades. The hand blown globes were fitted onto the clip by a row of metal flanges that held it firmly in place. The shades, themselves, ranged from simple free blown globes or ovals, to molded flowers, fruits and even faces. The molds used to make "fairy lamps" and candle shades were often used interchangably. The shades not only provided a certain amount of safety, but they also gave a warm subtle glow to the candlelight. The candle holder with shades seemed to enjoy its greatest popularity from about 1900 to 1920. They did not however, compete successfully with the growing popularity of the electric lights.

In the 1860s oil lamps for the tree were devised. These were egg shaped globes of ribbed glass. A long needle was melted into one end, and the other had a small opening with a wick. When filled with oil, these glass balloons or "Chinese lanterns" would burn from one to three hours. As with other light holders that used needles to hold them in place, there was a certain amount of difficulty in keeping them upright. However, they were for sale as late as 1882 when Ehrich's Fashion Quarterly described them:

> "Combination candle and bracket cones will burn for three hours without dripping or danger of fire. Price per dozen 45 cents."

At the same time regular candle holders sold for four cents a dozen, and a dozen pendulum weighted holders cost twenty-one cents.

In 1887, John Barth of Louisville, Kentucky, patented a much safer oil lamp. Barth's lamp had a light weight glass cylinder about two and a half inches long that hooked over the tree limb; it also had a small glass globe to protect the flame. His invention was featured in *Scientific American Magazine* and, a few were sold, but examples are quite rare today.

Lanterns were another early form of lighting the Christmas tree. Early versions were small squares with decorative "windows" cut out of brass or metal. Inserts of "gelatine" colored glass, or cellophane were placed inside and added color to the tree when the candlelight shone through. By the late 1870s, the panels were made of colored isinglass. The lanterns came in varying sizes with four to eight glass panels. At the turn of the century, folding lanterns with colored celluloid panels were offered for sale. Listed in the Sears and Roebuck Catalogue of 1907, they had the advantage of folding flat for storage. However, the celluloid was easily damaged and dangerously flammable.

Around the turn of the century, another interesting candle novelty was developed -- the candle chime. A "fly wheel" was fastened on a wire above a clip-on candle holder. The wheel was turned by the heat of the candle, and tiny attached balls struck a small bell or chime as they rotated past it. A tree decorated with these provided not only light, but sound and movement as well.

From about 1900-1920, there were many experiments with attaching candles to the tree branches. Several types reverted to the older idea of wrapping the end of the holder around the branch. Still others used the soft tin to form a clasp that fastens onto the branch. But by 1910, candle holders were already being replaced by the greatest advance in tree lighting -- the electric light bulb.

In 1882, while most of the different types of the candle holders and lights were still being developed, an event occurred which rendered them obsolete even before they were invented. In that year, Edward H. Johnson, a vice-president in Edison's newly founded electric company, set up the first electrically lighted Christmas tree. A full description of this event can be found in the section titled "A History of the Decorated Christmas Tree." At the time, Johnson's tree was only a novelty and did not receive widespread publicity.

Since electric wire had to be run to the house and each light had to be individually wired, an electric lighted tree was an expense that the average family could not even consider. Still by the 1890s, electrified trees had become the rage among the wealthy. In 1895, President Cleveland had the first electrically lighted tree in the White House.

It has been estimated that lighting on these early trees cost a dollar a light bulb. This included the electrician, the wiring, the sockets and the bulb. These early miniature bulbs were produced on a limited commission type basis.

By 1901, General Electric, who had bought out the Edison Company, marketed miniature lights for the Christmas tree. They were advertised in the *Ladies Home Journal* and *Scientific American* magazines for the Christmas season:

Miniature incandescent lamps are perfectly adapted to Christmas tree lighting. The element of danger ever present with candles is entirely removed, as well as the inconvenience of grease, smoke and dirt. The lamps are all lighted at once by the turning of a switch, will burn as long as desired without attention, and can be readily extinguished. Miniature lamps can be placed in locations where candles could not be used and much greater freedom is thus allowed in Christmas tree decorations with electric lamps. Lamps of various sizes can be adapted for different sizes of trees, and the most charming effects are produced by the use of lamps of different colors.

However, it was not until 1903 that strings or light **sets** were marketed by the EverReady Co. Even these were still quite expensive, a set of twenty cost twelve dollars. By 1907 Sears and Roebuck advertised a string of lights for $4.67. But still this was very much out of the price range of the average family.

These early lights were pear-shaped with a sharp "exhaust tip" at the top. This was where the air was drawn out of the bulb to create the necessary vacuum inside. In later years, a way was found to exhaust the air out of the bottom of the bulb and thus allow the screw-in base to cover the exhaust tip.

In 1909, the Kremenetzky Electric Co. of Vienna, Austria marketed the first figural lights. These clear glass bulbs were hand blown, with exhaust tips and beautifully painted. They duplicated some popular glass ornaments as well as created new designs of their own. The shapes included Santa and St. Nicholas, a dog, canaries and songbirds, clown, a snowman, flowers and fruits such as peaches, pears and apples. General Electric quickly responded in 1910 and marketed their own American made figural lights in the shape of fruits and nuts. Later pieces would include birds, a chick, a monkey, Santa and Uncle Sam, himself.

While all these developments in electric lighting were going on, it had little or no impact on the average family. Many people had never seen or even heard of electric Christmas lights, let alone have them on their tree. For the vast majority of Americans and Europeans, lighting the tree with candles was still the tradition.

Although the warm golden glow of a candlelit tree could not be rivaled, they certainly had some major drawbacks. The ever present danger of fire was the foremost problem, and there were far too many Christmas time disasters caused by candles on trees. Contrary to popular belief, however, these fires were not the main reason for the disappearance of the candlelit tree. We must remember that prior to the 1920s, people were used to dealing with fire in all facets of their life. Cooking, heating and lighting were all done with an open flame. People were conscious of the problems and were used to working with it on a daily basis. We also need to see the tree fires in perspective. Terrible as they were, they amounted to only a small fraction of the house fires caused by other reasons. Furthermore, a freshly cut pine kept in a cool parlor does not burn up instantaneously in a ball of fire. Dry trees were not much of a problem until well into the twentieth century. This is when mass cutting of trees began in August,

and they were set up shortly after Thanksgiving in well heated homes.

The real reason for the disappearance of candles on the Christmas tree is the same reason that took away candles and oil lamps for lighting the home. It is the same reason that we as humans progress to most new things -- **convenience**. If safety were the main reason, there would not be a three hundred year old history of candlelit trees.

By the 1920s, the use of electricity was sufficiently widespread and the cost of Christmas light bulbs was low enough that there was a major switch to electric lights. People were attracted to them for several reasons. First, they had the glamour of being new and modern. Furthermore, the inconvenience of dripping wax and replacing candles was gone. The electric lights could be switched on and left relatively unattended for hours. They also added a new dimension of colored light. The modern convenience of the electric light was the real reason for the disappearance of candlelit trees, not the safety factor.

Two major changes took place in the light industry during the second decade of the twentieth century. Carbon filaments were replaced by cooler, longer lasting tungsten, and World War I cut off the imports of European figural lights. In response to wartime shortages, Louis Szel of the Five Seas Trading Co. set out to find a new source of figural bulbs in Japan. Within a year, Tokyo was the center for a new light bulb industry that had remarkable similarities to the European cottage industry.

Home workshops produced the hand blown lamps, often times relying heavily on child labor. The lamps were transported by their makers to larger "collectors" and warehouses where they were displayed, sold and shipped to American importers. The early Japanese bulbs were hand blown from clear glass into metal molds. The first examples were usually crude copies of the European lamps. However, the early Japanese lights had a major problem with flaking and peeling paint. This problem can readily be seen in the examples found today. About 1925, in an attempt to improve the looks of the lights and help stop the cracking and peeling paint, lamp makers began to use milk glass. The milk glass not only held the paint better, but it also gave the light a translucent beauty of its own, even if the paint was missing. Indeed, some pieces were only sparsely painted, allowing the white glass to be the major color.

The bulbs were packaged and shipped in boxes of twenty-five, fifty or one hundred each. Americans sold most of these lights as individual pieces. However, a few, like nursery rhyme characters, were assembled into light sets by American companies. It would not be until the 1950s that complete sets were produced in Japan.

There are probably as many different molded lights as there are figural ornaments. In fact, many lights were copied directly from popular European ornaments. Still others were imaginative creations in their own right. Fruits, flowers, birds and Santas were, as always, popular subjects. But other popular themes were nursery rhyme, fairy tale and popular comic strip characters of the 1920s and 30s. Like the ornaments, **figural** lights are the most collectible form of lighting.

Japan dominated the figural light business from the 1920s until World War II when for obvious reasons it ceased. There was another early production after the war and into the mid 1950s. However, the American desire for figural lights seemed to have passed, and the lights were replaced by a new craze -- the bubble light.

In 1936, Carl Otis, an accountant for Montgomery

Ward, invented the bubble light. In this novel light, a small 15 volt lamp was set inside a plastic base that varied in design from globes, to discs, to rocket ships. Mounted atop this base was a long clear glass tube that held a colored liquid. This liquid contained the chemical methaline chloride, which would send up a stream of small bubbles when heated by the lamp.

NOMA bought the rights to Otis' invention and began marketing them in 1946. The Paramount Company also experimented with bubble lights and produced one with an oil base. The tiny effervescent bubbles moved in a constant, delicate stream through the heavy liquid. By the 1950s bubble lights were the rage on American trees, and the figural lights dimmed from the scene. But bubble lights too, were replaced as American tastes in lighted trees changed rapidly over the next twenty-five years.

First there was the rotating color wheel. This system was used primarily with aluminum trees and consisted of a flood light mounted behind a rotating wheel. The wheel contained cellophane panels of red, blue, green, white and gold that covered the tree and its immediate background with color. This style was followed by a desire to have a tree full of flashing lights. This, of course, ushered in the age of the midget or "twinkle" lights. These miniature one inch lamps were produced in Germany, Switzerland, Japan, Italy and Holland. The Italian product being the most perferred. Early miniature lamps were wired in a series circuit, and this had the old disadvantage of one burned out bulb blacking out the entire string. In various modified forms, the miniature lights with their tiny star-like effect remain the most popular form of lighting today.

Thus far, this discussion has centered around the individual lamps themselves. That is, those pieces that are vacuum sealed with the lighting filaments inside them. However, another major form of lighting, especially in figural lights, used the idea of a lamp cover. In these, a small, plain lamp was the light source for a more elaborate outer cover. The previously discussed "bubble" lights fall into this category. The advantage of using light covers was twofold. First, the designs could be more elaborate or even constructed out of several pieces. Secondly, the light bulb could be replaced, at least in theory, thus allowing the cover to be used for many years.

Some early American made, "Mazda" figural lights experimented with this cover method. A thin, tubular light was inserted into the base of a fancy blown glass cover. Examples of these include Uncle Sam, Santa, a bird and a monkey. Unfortunately, these lamps were fastened onto the cover and are not replaceable.

From about 1915-1925, some light producers experimented with using lamp covers made of an early form of plastic known as celluloid. Making nicely detailed toys, animals and even Christmas ornaments out of this easily formable material had been popular for several years. Most often, the light cover was a toy that was already being produced. This was then modified by placing a 3.5 volt bulb into it at some convenient point. The thin and colorful plastic allowed the light to shine through with a gentle glow. The major drawback with celluloid as a lamp cover was its flammability. The fact that they were run off a dry cell battery and used only 3.5 volts helped to control the heat, but it was all too easy for a hot bulb to set its beautiful celluloid cover on fire.

A slightly more successful use of lamp shades was started by NOMA in 1929. Marketed as the "Dresden Fancy Lamp Outfit", the glass covers were made in Germany and were sold both as sets and individual pieces. The unique feature of the lights was the readily replaceable bulb made possible by a 1927 invention of Bernhardt Haupt for a double socket. A small Christmas light was screwed into one end of the double socket, and the other was fitted into the light string. There was a wide disc between the two sockets which screwed into an opening in the figural light cover. In theory, these beautiful lights could be used repeatedly not only for Christmas but "for all occassions", without the fear of them burning out. There were however, several serious drawbacks. First, the covers were much larger than normal lights and were quite bulky. The pieces that were designed to stand up on a branch, i.e. that had a base on the bottom, were too heavy to be held in place. Secondly, the paint did not adhere well to the glass, and there was a serious problem with cracking and chipping. The fact that the metal disc in the light socket and the receiving socket in the lamp cover were of two different metals caused them to corrode. This corrosion caused the parts to hold together. And since excessive twisting or pressure shattered the thin glass of the cover, the bulb became irreplaceable. Finally, timing was also an enemy of the Dresden lamp. They were marketed at an expensive $5.50 a set just as the Great Depression commenced.

Another beautiful lamp cover was produced by the Matchless Corp. of Maryland. Their "Wonder Star" was made of cut glass in the form of small pointed crystals. These were arranged around a button-like center in a single or double rowed sun burst. When lit by the small bulb in the back, the light radiated and bounced through the crystals in a lovely display. These were produced from about 1925-1945 and were sold in several different sizes and base sizes.

In the late 1930s Japan produced the "Kristal Star" light covers which were marketed by Reliance. These were metal, five pointed stars with glass or plastic tips. The metal was painted and covered with glitter. The lamp attached in the back.

Another common lamp cover was produced by NOMA in 1952. Called "Fancy Figures", the shades were made out of a hard molded plastic. Shapes included Santa, a snowman, an angel, a bird, a dog, etc. The heat from the light, especially C-7½ versions, caused the plastic to crack and distort. These shades are commonly found in poor condition.

There are many other styles and forms of lights experimented with throughout the century. However, the most common has remained the cone or flame shape which was designed to simulate a candle flame. As with the collectors of glass ornaments, molded figural lights are the most sought after by collectors.

Whether the lights glowed with the warmth of a flame or twinkled merrily with the miracle of electricity, the lighted tree reflects the star decked heavens and represents not only Christ as the "Light of the World", but also a yuletime custom that goes back to the dim beginnings of time.

NOTES:
1. Abbreviations used in the light section:
   MG - Milk Glass   CG - Clear Glass
   C6 - A small base size (not midget) found in old series sets of lights. They were common before 1950 and are usually 14 or 15 volts.
   C7½ - A large base size commonly found after the 1950s. These were used in parallel sets and took a full 120 volts.
   Standard - The base is the large size used in standard

household sockets.

BT - The metal screw base is in the top of the light.

BB - The base is in the bottom of the lamp.

Approx. 2½" - This is the approximate size, to the nearest quarter inch, of the light **not** measuring the base.

Ornament - This means that an ornament exactly like the light can be found.

2. Lights dating before the 1950s have a base made out of brass. Those after 1950 usually are made of a silver colored aluminum.

3. An external exhaust tip on a bulb usually indicated it was produced prior to 1920. Milk glass became the major type of glass in lights about 1925.

4. The insulator in the bottom of the base can help determine age. White porcelain between the anode, center "button" and the cathode or outside thread base, indicates a European piece prior to 1915. A type of fiber board was used by early Japanese lamp makers. A shiny, black plastic insulation is from a later period.

5. Lamp filiments were originally made of carbon but changed to a longer lasting tungsten in the 1920s. Those should not be mixed on the same string. The carbon will burn much dimmer than the tungsten. Because of differences in electrical resistance, the older carbon bulbs will burn out quickly if mixed with the tungsten.

6. Prices given are for lamps in good condition. This means the paint is in good shape, there are no breaks or cracks in the glass, and the base is not loose or missing. Whether or not a light works is up to the individual collector. Most agree however that to get the best price, the light should still work.

7. A 14-15 volt light can be safely checked to see if it works by using a small 9 volt battery. Put one pole of the battery on the center "button" at the base and touch the outside of the base against the other pole.

8. Voltage, country of origin and the manufacturer's name or mark can often be found embossed into the metal base.

PRE-ELECTRIC LIGHTING

Clip-On Candle Holders

GENERIC CLIP-ON CANDLE HOLDERS - Approx. 1½"-2" - These were invented in 1879 by an American named Frederick Artz. A simple spring between two stamped, tin pieces clamps the holder onto the tree limb. These came in various styles: plain, a fish, praying hands, a lyre, etc. They were popular into the 1920s and are quite common even today. (American & European made, p630, R4-5)

Each $1.00-3.00

"BALL AND SOCKET" CANDLE HOLDERS - Approx. 1¾"-2½" - Between the spring clip-on and the drip pan there is a ball and socket joint. This allows the pan and the candle to be moved or adjusted after it has been fastened onto the tree. Since the candle could always be positioned upright, this was a much safer improvement over early clip-ons. Later pieces had a spring holder for the candle as well. They are still being marketed in limited quantities. (Germany, p632a, p632b, & p632c, Circa 1920, R2-3)

Each $2.00-4.00

LITHOGRAPHED CANDLE HOLDERS - Approx. 1½"-2", Sizes can vary - These pieces are often stamped

out of tin to match the picture that is placed on them. The candle fits inside the spring clip of these early pieces, and there is no drip pan. Opposite sides are usually the same. (Germany, p631, Circa 1890, R2)

Embossed Bird large & small (Stille p68, R1-2)	$60.00-75.00
Embossed Butterfly (Stille p39, R1-2)	$70.00-80.00
Embossed Child on Rocking Horse (Stille p68, R1-2)	$70.00-80.00
Embossed Christmas Tree (Stille p68, R1-2)	$50.00-60.00
Embossed Girl (Stille p68, R1-2)	$70.00-80.00
Embossed Geometric Patterns (p633a, d, e, g, R2-3)	$5.00-10.00
Embossed Parrot (p631a, R1-2)	$50.00-60.00
Embossed Santa (Stille p68, R1-2)	$70.00-80.00
Lithographed only, Approx. 1¼"-2"	
Various small angels (p631d, e, f, R2)	$40.00-50.00
Large angel with wings (p631b, R2)	$70.00-90.00
Deer in a Woodland (p631c, R2)	$40.00-50.00

Pendulum Weighted Candle Holders

STANDARD PENDULUM CANDLE HOLDERS - Approx. 5½", but sizes can vary - They have a metal holder for the candle and small drip pan. There is a colored clay ball at the end of a wire rod. (U.S., p634b, Circa 1870-1890, R3)

$10.00-20.00

KIRCHHOF PENDULUM WEIGHTED CANDLE HOLDER - Approx. 5¼" - There is a small drip pan and a clay ball weight at the end of a long bent wire. "Kirchhof, Pat. Dec.24 67" is stamped into the bottom of the drip pan. (U.S., p634a, R2)

$15.00-25.00

DOUBLE WEIGHTED PENDULUM CANDLE HOLDER - Approx. 4-5½", but sizes can vary - Two wires come out in an inverted "V" shape from the candle holder. At the ends are clay balls or cast lead figures. The holder balances on the tree limb between the two wires. (Germany, p638, Circa 1890, R1-2)

Clay balls	$20.00-25.00
Roses	$30.00-40.00
Cherubs	$50.00-60.00
Stars	$30.00-40.00

DRIP PAN WEIGHTED CANDLE HOLDER - Approx. 5½" - A large drip pan attached to an extendable wire forms the pendulum weight. (p632d, Circa 1870, R1) $30.00-40.00

CANDLE HOLDER WITH STAMPED BRASS WEIGHTS - Approx. 5-6", sizes can vary - A candle holder with or without a drip pan has a piece stamped from brass attached to the bottom. A small piece of lead may be added for extra weight. (Stille back cover, Circa 1890, R1-2)

Angels	$50.00-75.00
Birds	$50.00-75.00
Flowers	$50.00-75.00

OUTDOOR PENDULUM CANDLE HOLDER - Approx.

11" - The drip pan is more like a small heavy cup. A star forms the pendulum weight. This holds a large candle and was designed for large or outdoor trees. (Germany, p637, R1-2) $40.00-50.00

PENDULUM CANDLE HOLDER WITH CAST TIN REFLECTOR - Approx. 6", but sizes can vary - The cast tin reflector were ornaments by themselves but they were sometimes added as the "weight" for a pendulum candle holder. Common shapes were discs, stars and butterflies. (Germany, p635, p636, Circa 1890, R2-3)

Round $40.00-60.00
Stars $40.00-60.00
Butterflies $50.00-75.00

PENDULUM CANDLE HOLDER WITH SHAPED WEIGHT - Approx. 5¾" - The drip pan is bigger than American versions. At the end of the metal wire is a pine cone, star or other shapes of weight cast from lead. It may be cast directly onto the wire or hung on it by a loop. Later versions have a spring clip to hold the candle. (Germany, p634c & d, Circa 1900 and 1980 pine cone reproduction, R2-3)

Pine Cone $15.00-25.00
Six or Seven Pointed Star $25.00-30.00
Rose $25.00-30.00

Fairy Lights

MOLDED FAIRY LIGHTS - Approx. 4" - These thick tumbler-like pieces are made of pressed or molded glass. They come in many colors which include: cobalt blue, amber, dark green, amethyst, ruby, milk glass and a light blue milk glass. Patterns include: hobnail, diamond or quilted, daisy and "thousand eye". These were popular for festive lighting throughout the year. (U.S., p639, Circa 1850, R3)

Quilted $15.00-25.00
Other Patterns $20.00-30.00
Ruby $40.00-50.00

ORNAMENT "FAIRY" LIGHTS - Approx. 3", but sizes can vary - These were blown or molded out of paper thin glass. This helped to eliminate the weight problem with the pressed glass "tumblers". These could either hold a small candle or a floating wick. When decorated with faces, they also served as ornaments in their own right. They were hung from a wire loop or could be clipped onto the branch. They are hollow and have a large opening in the top. (Germany, Circa 1870-1900, R2-3)

Beehive (p633b) $40.00-50.00
Smiling Boy Head (p640b) $325.00-350.00
Large Cauldron (p191d) $25.00-35.00
Face (p640a) $325.00-350.00
Rose (p109) $60.00-75.00

Lanterns

Lanterns are constructed of a metal frame and colored "isin" glass panels. Both the small and large versions were used on the tree as well as for mantel and room decorations. The candle was placed into a socket in the bottom of the lantern. Lanterns had two disadvantages; first, they were heavy and required being placed on the interior of the tree. Secondly, as they hung from their handle, they transferred the heat of the flame directly onto the tree branch above. The colored glass panels of red, green, blue and gold indicate their use for Christmas as opposed to other miniature lanterns that might be used year around. (Approx. 2½"-5" not measuring the handle, Circa 1890, R3)

Large four sided, Approx. 4¾", (p647a) $40.00-60.00
Small four sided, Approx. 2½", (p645a) $30.00-40.00
Small six sided, Approx. 3½", (p645b) $40.00-50.00
Small squares, Approx. 3" $50.00-70.00
"V" shaped, Approx. 4½", (p644) $40.00-55.00

"FOLD UP" LANTERNS - Approx. 3"H & 4"H with a 5½" fold dia. - These were popular from the turn of the century into the 1920s. They have a brass frame work and twelve panels of colored celluloid. Folded, it looks like a six armed star. The celluloid panels are rarely found in good condition. They did not hold up well in the folding, and the heat from the candle tended to warp them. Caution should be used with these lanterns since the celluloid panels are flammable. (Germany, p647b, 648a, Circa 1900-1920, R3) $25.00-35.00

SANTA HEAD LANTERN - Approx. 3"-5½" (5" pictured) - The head is made of paper mache covered with plaster. The eyes and mouth are "open" and backed with thin paper that shows eyes and teeth. The candle inside the head shines out the top and through the eyes and mouth. (Germany, p646, R1-2) $250.00-300.00

Miscellaneous

BARTH OIL LAMP - Approx. 3" - Patented by John Barth these lamps had a glass cylinder for holding oil and a small globular shade around the wick. A hook on the side fastened over the tree limb. (U.S., Snyder p105, Circa 1887, R1) $100.00-125.00

CANDLE HOLDERS WITH GLASS SHADES - Approx. 3", but sizes can vary - A glass shade either free-blown or molded is attached to a metal clip-on candle holder. The holder has a set of six flanges that hold the shade from either the inside or outside. The decorated shade not only provided protection, but it gave off a beautiful warm glow. (Germany, Circa 1920, R2) Types of shades:

Arched Panels (Stille p71) $50.00-70.00
Cat Head (Schiffer p146) $300.00-350.00
Cherries (p633c) $60.00-80.00
Ribbed Cylinder (p640c) $35.00-50.00
Free Blown Oval (p641a) $40.00-50.00
Oval Rose (p640d) $65.00-80.00
Slender Rose (p642) $65.00-80.00
Tulip (Schiffer p146) $65.00-80.00

"CHINESE" OR "BALLOON" OIL LAMPS - These egg shaped glass pieces have embossed ribbing. They were filled with oil which burned at a wick in the top. The bottom had a long needle for pushing through the tree branch. (Germany, Stille p66, Circa 1860, R1) $100.00-125.00

CLIP-ON CANDLE HOLDER WITH GLASS ORNAMENT WEIGHTS - Approx. 4", but sizes can vary - In this style, a blown glass ornament is attached to a clip-on candle holder by means of a spiral spring. The ornament provided a type of counterweight, and any kind could be used although fruits and flowers were the most popular. The price of this style will depend upon the ornament itself. (Germany, R2)

Apple (p643b) $45.00-55.00
Indian on a Cone (p331a) $250.00-275.00
Pear (p643a) $40.00-50.00
Rose (p643c) $30.00-40.00

COILED CHRISTMAS CANDLE - Approx. 5″ - This is a coil of a thin pliable candle. Sections could be cut off and wrapped around the branch of the tree. By unwinding a long length, it was also used to light candles on the tree. The Santa scrap indicates its specific Christmas use. (p618c, R1-2)　　　$15.00-25.00

TACK OR NAIL CANDLE HOLDERS - Approx. 1-2″ - The bottom of the drip pan has a small tack or nail. These were pushed through the branch to hold the candle upright. They are early and dangerous. (p632f, Circa 1867, R2)　　　$1.50-3.00

ELECTRIC LIGHTS

Animals

SITTING BEAR - (MG/C6/BT) - Approx. 2¾″ - He sits on his haunches with the front paws at the chest area. He looks off to his right. (Japan, p665h, Circa 1950, R2)　　　$40.00-50.00

SITTING TEDDY BEAR - (MG/C6/BT) - Approx. 2¾″ - The bear is shown sitting with all four paws pointed outward. There is a bow at the neck. This could also be a cat. (Japan, p667b, 670a, R2)　　　$30.00-40.00

WAVING BEAR - (MG/C7/BB) - Approx. 2¾″ - The standing bear shows molded fur. The right hand is at the cheek as though waving, the left hand is at the stomach. (Japan, p669f, Circa 1940, R1-2)　　　$40.00-50.00

Birds

BIRD IN A BIRD HOUSE - (MG/C6/BT) - Approx. 1½″ - The house with a sloping roof has a hole near the top with a small bird in it. (Japan, p664f, Circa 1935-1950, R2)　　　$30.00-40.00

CHICK - (CG/C6/BB) - Approx. 1½″ - It stands with its small wings folded. Ornament. (p657d, R2) $40.00-50.00

CHICK IN AN EGG - (CG/C6/BT) - Approx. 2¼″ - The head and shoulders are shown breaking out of an egg. (Japan, p657c, Circa, R1-2)　　　$35.00-45.00

COMMON SONGBIRDS - (MG & CG/C6/BT) - Approx. 3¼″ - The birds are shown lengthwise with folded wings. The base is in the back. (Japan, p666g & p666h, Circa 1920-1955, R5)　　　$8.00-12.00

DRESSED DUCK - (MG/C6/BT) - Approx. 2¼″ - He wears a shirt and pants. His head is turned slightly to the right, and his arms are crossed. (Japan, p666c, Circa 1950, R2)　　　$35.00-45.00

EXHAUST TIP BIRDS - (CG/C6/BB) - 3″-4″, Sizes can vary - They are usually beautifully painted and come in several styles. The exhaust tip is in the beak. (Europe, p654c, p654d, p656c, p656d & p664d, R2-3) $40.00-60.00

OWL IN A VEST AND TOP HAT - (MG/C6/BT) - Approx. 2¼″ - It stands with wings folded. Ornament. (Japan, p671d, R2)　　　$30.00-40.00

PARROTS AND PARAKEETS - (MG/C6/BT) - Approx.

2″-3″ - These are usually shown with a crest, and the base is in the head area. (Japan, p666f, Circa 1950, R3-4)　　　$12.00-17.00

FULL FEATHERED PEACOCK - (MG/C6/BT) - Approx. 1¾″ & 2¼″ dia. - The full feathers form a disc behind the embossed bird. Double sided. (Japan, p664g & p664h, Circa 1950, R2-3)　　　$30.00-40.00

PEACOCK WITH WEDGE SHAPED TAIL FEATHERS - (MG/C6/BT) - Approx. 2¼″ - The bird is large and well defined. The spread tail does not go all around the bird but forms a wedge shape. (Japan, p673f, R2)　　　$50.00-60.00

PELICAN - (MG/C6/BT) - Approx. 2¼″ - The long bill is tucked to the chest in this undetailed piece. (Japan, p665g, Circa 1950, R1-2)　　　$50.00-60.00

ROOSTER IN A TUB - (MG/C6/BT) - Approx. 2¼″ - The rooster with a comb and folded wings, sits on a round base that looks like a tub. (Japan, p674a, R2) $60.00-80.00

ROOSTER PLAYING GOLF - (MG/C6/BT) - Approx. 2¾″ - He appears hunchbacked. He wears shorts and carries a golf club. (Japan, p666b, Circa 1950, R2-3) $30.00-40.00

ROUND BIRD - (MG/C6/BT) - Approx. 2″ - This piece appears to be made of two balls, one for the body with embossed wings and one for the head with an open back. It has also been called a chick. (Japan, p666e, Circa 1950, R2-3)　　　$20.00-30.00

ROUND BIRD CAGE - (MG/C6/BT) - Approx. 2″ - (Japan, Circa 1935-1955, R3)　　　$15.00-25.00

"MAZDA" CANARY - (CG/C6/BB) - Approx. 4″L - The bird is mounted on an extra long pike. The light is made by a glass tube inside the bird. (U.S., p655h, Circa 1920, R1-2)　　　$75.00-90.00

Cats

"BECKONING" CAT - (CG/C6/BT) - Approx. 2½″ - The cat sits on its hind legs with one paw raised to the ear. (Japan, Circa 1925, R3)　　　$25.00-35.00

BEGGING CAT - (MG/C6/BT) - Approx. 2½″ - The cat sits on its haunches with the front paws raised to the ribbon around its neck. It has large eyes. (Japan, p668d, R3)　　　$25.00-35.00

CAT IN AN EVENING GOWN - (MG/C6/BT) - Approx. 3″ - This sitting cat is shown in a long dress. (Japan, p668f, Circa 1950, R2)　　　$60.00-75.00

CAT IN A SUIT WITH GLASSES - (CG/C6/BB) - Approx. 2¼″ - He wears a coat, vest, tie and glasses. His paws are in the pockets. (p654h, R2)　　　$50.00-65.00

CAT WITH A BALL - (MG/C6/BT) - Approx. 2¼″ - The cat stands on its hind feet and holds the ball in its front paws. (Japan, p668a, R2)　　　$30.00-40.00

CAT WITH A MANDOLIN (FIDDLE) - (MG & CG/C6 & C7/BT) - Approx. 2½″, 3¼″ & 3½″ - The cat sits on it haun-

ANDY GUMP - (CG & MG/C6) - Approx. 2¾" - He does not have a lower jaw. He wears a vest and tie, and has a large mustache. (Japan, Circa 1935 [CG], R2-3)$40.00-50.00
(Japan, Circa 1955 [MG], R2-3) $35.00-45.00

BETTY BOOP - (CG & MG/C6 - C7 MG only) - Approx. 2¼" - She wears a short strapless dress. Short hair curls around her face. (Japan, Circa 1930, '35 & '55, R2-3)
MG $50.00-60.00
CG $55.00-65.00

DICK TRACY - (CG & MG/C6) - Approx. 2½" - He wears a hat and has a large square jaw. (Japan, Circa 1935 & '55, R2-3)
Milk Glass $40.00-50.00
Clear Glass $50.00-60.00

KAYO - (MG/C6) - Approx. 2¼" - He appears to be squatting. He wears a round hat and his arms are folded. This piece is sometimes called "Peewee". (Japan, Circa 1935, R2-3)
$35.00-45.00

LITTLE ORPHAN ANNIE - (CG & MG/C6) - Approx. 2½" - She has short curly hair, a dress and her hands are together at the chest. (Japan, Circa 1935-55, R3
CG $45.00-55.00
MG $35.00-45.00

MOON MULLINS - (MG/C6) - Approx. 2½" - He wears a round hat, his hands are in his pockets and his head is turned to the right. (Japan, Circa 1955, R2-3)
$35.00-45.00

SANDY - (MG/C6) - Approx. 2¼" - This is Orphan Annie's dog. He sits on his haunches facing left. He is almost always painted a tan/orange. Kaufman states that the earlier version is 12 volt instead of the normal 15. (Japan, and "Franco", Circa 1955 & 1930 respectively, R2-3)
Later $40.00-50.00
Earlier $ 50.00-60.00

SMITTY - (MG/C6) - Approx. 2½" - He wears a suit with a flat golf-like hat. His hands are at the hips. (Japan, Circa 1955, R2-3)
$25.00-35.00

Crosses

CROSS ON A DISC - (MG/C6/BT) - Approx. 2" - A cross and flower design are embossed into the disc. (Japan, p671e, R3-4)
$15.00-25.00

CROSS WITH A STAR IN THE CENTER - (MG/C6/BT) - Approx. 2" - A flat, "square" cross with an embossed star at the center. (Japan, Circa 1950, R3)
$15.00-25.00

LARGE CROSS - (CG/C7½/BT) - Approx. 3" - It has a flat square look. (Japan, Circa 1925, R2)
$20.00-30.00

TUBULAR CROSS - (CG/C6/BT) - Approx. 3" - The cross is made up of rounded glass and tubes. (Japan, Circa 1925, R2-3)
$15.00-25.00

Flowers

FLOWER IN A SEASHELL - (MG/C6/BT) - Approx. 2¼" - The ten petaled flower is open and shows three stamens. (Japan, p674d, R2)
$50.00-65.00

LARGE OPEN ROSE - (MG/C6/BT) - Approx. 2" - It is nicely molded. (Japan, p681i, Circa 1950, R3$10.00-20.00

SMALL COMMON FLOWERS - (CG & MG/C6/BT) - Approx. 1½", but sizes can vary - These come in shapes such as roses, rose buds, clover blossoms and tulips. (Japan, p681a, b, c, d, e & f, Circa 1920-1950, R5) $5.00-10.00

"WATT" ROSE - (CG/C6/BT) - Approx. 1½" - This is a rounded piece with good molding and pastel colors ornament. "Watt" is marked on the base insulator. (U.S., p655a, Circa 1920, R2-3) $35.00-45.00

Fruits and Vegetables

APPLE - (MG/C7½/BT) - Approx. 2½" - It is oval shaped, and embossed leaves show at the top. (Japan, p681h, R2)
$15.00-25.00

BANANA - (CG/C6/BT) - Approx. 3" - A slightly curved banana. (Japan, Circa 1925, R2) $20.00-30.00

BANANA WITH A FACE - (MG/C6/BT) - Approx. 2¼" - This is a curved banana with eyes and an open mouth embossed into it. (Japan, p674h, Circa 1950, R2)
$50.00-75.00

EAR OF CORN - (MG/C6/BT) - Approx. 4" - Individual kernels show between two large leaves. (Japan, p681j, R2-3)
$25.00-35.00

SMALL EAR OF CORN - (CG/C6/BT) - Approx. 2¼" - The early piece shows individual kernels and leaves at the top. (Europe, p657b, Circa 1904, R1-2) $60.00-75.00

LARGE FRUIT BASKET - (MG/C6/BT) - Approx. 2¾" - The round woven basket shows various fruits. Ornament. (Japan, p681g, R3) $20.00-30.00

JACK-O'-LANTERN - (CG & MG/C6/BT) - Approx. 1½" - It has a ribbed body, with rounded eyes, a triangle nose and a wide smile. (p653c, R2) $40.00-55.00

MILK GLASS JACK-O'-LANTERN - (MG/C6/BT) - Approx. 2" - This has a round shape with embossed ribs. The eyes and nose are triangular. Leaves show at the top. (Japan, p671c, Circa 1950, R2-3) $25.00-35.00

SMALL BUNCH OF GRAPES - (MG/C6/BT) - Approx. 2" - The grapes are small round bumps. Leaves show at the top. (Japan, Circa 1950, R4) $6.00-12.00

MUSHROOM - (MG/C6/BB) - Approx. 2" - This is a mushroom with a thick stalk. (p654b, R2-3) $25.00-35.00

ORANGE - (CG/C6/BB) - Approx. 1¾" - (Japan, p659f, Circa 1925, R2-3) $20.00-30.00

"WATT" ORANGE - (CG/C6/BT) - Approx. 1½" - It has dimpled skin. "Watt" is marked on the base insulator. (U.S., p655b, Circa 1930, R2-3) $30.00-40.00

PEACH - (CG/C6/BT) - Approx. 2" - (p659g, Circa 1920, R2-3) $15.00-25.00

EXHAUST TIP PEACH - (CG/C6/BT) - Approx. 1¾″ - (Europe, p659e, Circa 1915, R2) $30.00-40.00

LARGE PEAR - (CG/C6/BT) - Approx. 2¼″ - (p659h, Circa 1920, R3) $10.00-20.00

SMALL PEAR - (CG & MG/C6/BT) - Approx. 1½″ - (Japan, Circa 1920-1939, R4) $6.00-12.00

PINEAPPLE - (MG/C6/BT) - Approx. 2″ - It has a raised diamond pattern and leaves at the bottom. (Japan, p671f, Circa 1950, R2) $50.00-60.00

PLUM - (CG/C6/BT) - Approx. 1¾″ - Small with a crease down the center. (p659c, Circa 1920, R2) $15.00-25.00

RASPBERRY - (CG/C6/BT) - Approx. 1½″ - It has an exhaust tip, a bumpy pattern and leaves at the top. (p655c, R2) $20.00-30.00

ROUND BERRY - (CG/C6/BT) - Approx. 1¼″ - It has an exhaust tip. It has a round shape with a bumpy pattern. (p655d, R2) $15.00-20.00

LONG SQUASH - (CG/C6/BT) - Approx. 2¾″ - This long piece has a slight figure eight shape with embossed ribs. (p657a, R2) $40.00-50.00

STRAWBERRY - (CG/C6/BT) - Approx. 1½″ - It has a strawberry shape with a dimpled pattern. (Japan, p659b, Circa 1920, R3-4) $7.00-15.00

WALNUT - (CG/C6/BT) - Approx. 1¾″ - (p659d, Circa 1920, R2-3) $20.00-35.00

EXHAUST TIP WALNUT - (CG/C6/BT) - Approx. 1½″ - (Europe, p659a, Circa 1915, R2) $30.00-40.00

Houses

BUILDING ON A ROCK - "Alcatraz" - (MG/C6/BT) - Approx. 1½″ - This building sits on a high rock and has been referred to as the famous prison on the rock -- Alcatraz. (Japan, p674b, Circa 1950, R2) $45.00-55.00

COTTAGE IN A HILLSIDE - (MG/C6/BT) - Approx. 2¼″ - The small cottage is built into the hillside. (Japan, p678b, Circa 1950, R2) $25.00-35.00

LOG CABIN - (MG/C6/BT) - Approx. 2″ - Built of thick "logs", all four sides are the same, and the roof is snow covered. (Japan, p678a, Circa 1950s, R3) $20.00-30.00

SNOW COVERED COTTAGE - (MG/C6 & C7½/BT) - Approx. 2″ & 2¾″ - The roof of this six sided house is snow covered. (Japan, p678f, p678g, R4-5) $6.00-12.00

SMALL SQUARE HOUSE - (CG/C6/BT) - Approx. 1¾″ - It has embossed doors and windows. (Japan, p678d, Circa 1925, R3-4) $10.00-20.00

Lanterns

BALLOON SHAPED "GIFU" LANTERNS - (MG & CG/C6, C7½ & standard base/BT) - Approx. 1¾″, 2¼″, 3″ & 4½″ - This is molded after Japanese paper lanterns.

(Japan, p680a, p680b, p680c, Circa 1925-1950, R5) $6.00-12.00
Standard Base $10.00-20.00

CARRIAGE LANTERN WITH EXHAUST TIP - (CG/C6/BB) - Approx. 2¼″ - This is a four sided lantern with a sloping top. The exhaust tip forms the final of the lantern. (p657g, R1-2) $40.00-50.00

CYLINDER SHAPED "ODAWARA" LANTERN - (MG/C6/BT) - Approx. 3″ - (Japan, p680k, R4) $6.00-12.00

MINIATURE LANTERNS - (CG/C6/BT) - Approx. 1¾″ - The exact styles vary. (Japan, p680f, p680g & p680h, Circa 1925, R4) $4.00-6.00

ROUND JAPANESE LANTERN - (MG/C6/BT) - Approx. 1¾″ & 2″ - These have a ball or oval shape. (Japan, p680d & p680e, Circa 1950, R4) $3.00-10.00

SNOW COVERED LANTERN - (MG/C6/BT) - Approx. 2″ - It has a rounded pile of snow on top and lantern panes on the bottom. (Japan, p678c, R4-5) $5.00-10.00

Light Shades

PLASTIC LIGHT SHADES - Approx. 2″ - These cup shaped pieces were designed to fit over C6 base lamps. They were made of hard colored plastic and had different character decals on them. They can be found separately or as a set. They were American made and produced circa 1936. Mickey Mouse Shades $10.00-15.00;
Box set $150.00-175.00
Christmas Scenes Each $4.00-8.00
Flash Gordon Shades Each $4.00-8.00
Katzenjammer Kids Shades Each $4.00-8.00
Plain Plastic (No decals) Shades $.50-1.00
Popeye Shades Each $4.00-8.00
Silly Symphonies (Disney) Each $8.00-10.00
Boxed Set $100.00-110.00

"WHIRL-GLO" PAPER LIGHT SHADES - These came in a boxed set of five or ten shades. A paper cone with a needle sat on top of the light bulb. The top of the shade was metal and had vanes. The heat from the light turned the shade which was printed with colorful pictures. (U.S. - Sail-Me Co., p648c, Circa 1936, R3-4)
Shades Each $2.00-3.00

People and Characters

"PUTTI" ANGEL HEAD - (CG/C6/BB) - Approx. 2¼″ - This little girl head has short curly hair. Small wings show under her chin. Ornament. (Europe, p660b, R1-2)
$175.00-200.00

STANDING ANGEL - (CG/C6/BB) - Approx. 2½″ - The angel stands in a long robe. Wings show at the back and sides. She also wears a sash. (Japan, p654g, Circa 1925, R2-3) $25.00-35.00

AUSTRIAN MAN WITH PIPE - (CG & MG/C6/BT) - Approx. 2¾″ - He wears shorts with suspenders and a coat and tie. He has a cap and a pipe in the left hand. (Japan, p677b, Circa 1925-1950, R2) Clear Glass $30.00-40.00
Milk Glass $20.00-30.00

were designed as early window displays. The early pieces, which are the most collectible, have spring-wound clockwork in them. The usual movement is a nodding head. Key-wound Victorian pieces, which are usually three feet or under, are the most desirable. Price depends on size, age, complexity of the movement and condition.

$2,000.00-3,000.00

EARLY SANTA AND SLEIGH - Approx. 10" - The Santa is dressed in red and blue felt, has a plaster face with a fur beard and sits on the sleigh. The sleigh is wood and made of split twigs. It is pulled by a plaster reindeer with lead antlers. Such pieces originally held candy or small gifts and were used as table decorations. (Germany, p692, OP, R2)

$250.00-300.00

GLASS SANTA CANDY CONTAINER - Approx. 5¾" - This piece has a molded plastic head that screws off. He is portrayed as fat and jolly with his hands at his side. (p702, OP, R3-4)

$20.00-30.00

LARGE SANTA HEAD - Approx. 18" - This large head made of paper mache and plaster shows a smiling American style Santa. These were used as both store and home decorations. (p684)

$40.00-65.00

MECHANICAL SANTA - Approx. 5½" - Made by Chein. This tin windup toy walks and is lithographed. (p70)

$70.00-90.00

SANTA AND HONEYCOMB WAGON - Approx. 8"L & 8"H - This early table decoration shows Santa riding a wagon which is made of honeycombed tissue paper. It carries a honeycomb tree which has scrap candles and gifts. The wagon is pulled by two scrap mules with angel riders. (Germany, p714, OP, R1)

$15.00-25.00

SANTA HEAD LANTERN - 6" - The milk glass head is double faced. The base holds the switch and battery. Made by Amico. (Japan, p703b, OP, R3)

$25.00-35.00

SANTA LANTERN - Approx. 6½" - The shade is a hollow, full-figured Santa. The metal base holds batteries and a switch. It was made by Amico. (Japan, p703a, OP-NP, R3)

$25.00-35.00

SANTA LIGHT LANTERN - Approx. 6" - This child's lantern features a miniature Santa light bulb in it. Made by Hilco. (Hong Kong, p703c, NP, R3)

$20.00-30.00

SANTA CANDY MOLDS - Sizes vary - These were used for producing chocolate Santa candies during the Christmas season. The ages on these also vary greatly but some determination can be made from the style of dress. Double-sided pieces are generally more desirable than single-sided pieces. (p718 to p721, OP-NP, R3)

Each $35.00-55.00

SANTA MECHANICAL BANK - Approx. 6½" - Santa with a basket on his back, stands beside a chimney. When operated, his raised hand drops a coin into a slot in the chimney. (p701, OP, R2-3)

$150.00-200.00

SANTA ON A LARGE WOODEN SLEIGH - Approx. 12" - Santa is dressed in red and blue felt. He has a real fur beard and sits in a large sleigh made of wood and twigs. Such pieces originally held gifts or candy and were used

as centerpiece or mantel decoration. (Germany, p691, OP, R2)

$250.00-350.00

SANTA "SQUEEK" TOY - Approx. 6½" - This early piece has a carved face, a real fur beard and a round ball body that holds the squeeker. When the head is pushed down he "squeeks". (p689, OP, R1-2)

$375.00-400.00

WINDUP SANTA AND SLEIGH - Approx. 12½" - This mechanical toy made by Strauss circa 1923, shows Santa in a sleigh pulled by two reindeer. The whole piece is lithographed. (p693)

$600.00-750.00

CARDBOARD SLEIGH - Approx. 12" - The glitter covered cardboard sleigh is pulled by two celluloid reindeer & has a celluloid Santa. (Japan, p695, OP, R3-4)$45.00-65.00

Santa Dolls

These pieces vary greatly in style, shape, composition and price. They are popular pieces for doll and toy collectors as well as those who collect "Christmas". Since these dolls cannot be lumped or priced together in a general category, only individual pieces are described, pictured and priced.

LARGE CELLULOID SANTA AND SLEIGH - Approx. 12" - Santa, the sleigh, and the two reindeer are all molded separately and assembled. (Japan, p697, OP, R2-3)

$50.00-65.00

LARGE, STRAW STUFFED, SANTA DOLL - Approx. 25", but sizes vary - His fabric body is stuffed with straw which can be felt and heard when squeezed. His coat and pants are usually made of red satin. His face is a type of painted canvas. (p685)

$175.00-200.00

POST WAR PLASTER SANTA - Approx. 8" - He is dressed in a long felt coat with white "fur" trim. He holds a plastic tree which is a later addition. (Germany, p688, NP)

$50.00-75.00

RUBBER "SQUEAK TOY" SANTA IN SLEIGH - Approx. 6" - Santa leans back in a sleigh full of toys that is labeled "Xmas Express". The soft rubber toy squeeks when squeezed. (p698, NP)

$5.00-10.00

SMALL CELLULOID SANTAS IN SLEIGHS - Approx. 4" - These came in several varieties and are molded as one piece. They were produced in both Germany and Japan. (p698, OP, R3)

$30.00-40.00

SMALL SANTA WITH A LARGE BAG - Approx. 4½" - The Santa is paper mache and plaster. The clothes are red and blue felt, and the beard is rabbit fur. The large gift bag has been added. (Germany, p687, OP, R3)$100.00-125.00

WESTERN GERMAN PLASTER SANTA - Approx. 9" - Made of plaster, he wears a felt coat and hood. He holds a small artificial tree and is marked on the bottom, "Made in Western Germany". (Germany, p686, NP)$75.00-100.00

WINDUP SANTA ON A SLEIGH - Approx. 7½" - The metal sleigh is flat with three wheels underneath and a bell on the back. The reindeer and Santa are celluloid. When wound, the sleigh moves in a circle and the bell rings. (Japan, p696, OP, R3)

$40.00-55.00

WINDUP SANTA ON A TRICYCLE - Approx. 3" - The tricycle is metal and has a small bell on the back. Santa is celluloid. (Japan, NP, R3-4) $25.00-35.00

"BELSNICKLES" - PAPER MACHE SANTAS - Approx. 5"-12" - The exact sizes and forms of these pieces vary greatly as do their colors. They were made in Germany between 1870 and World War I. They are hollow cast, in two molds and covered with a thin layer of plaster. Only a very few were used as candy containers, most were simply designed as table or mantel decorations. Some of the smallest could also have hung on the tree. Most are shown standing on a small rounded base with their hands in their sleeves and holding a sprig of inserted greenery in the right arm. "Belsnickle" is a German variation on Santa Claus. He came with St. Nicholas and handed out goodies and switches. Colors as well as shape variations are collectible. Some of the more common colors are: red, blue, yellow/gold and white/silver grey. Rarer colors include: purple/lavender, pink, a couple shades of green, brown and black. Although Belsnickles are not uncommon, prices are high and vary widely depending on condition, molding and style, color, size, etc. The prices listed are for the more standard forms. (Germany, p704 to p711, OP, R3) $550.00-800.00

"ECKHARDT" MUSICAL TREE STAND - 14" dia. - The stand is round and usually silver looking. It is key wound and plays two tunes including "Silent Night". It also rotates the tree. Markings include: "1901 and DRCM". (Germany, OP, R1-2) $275.00-300.00

STAMPED CARDBOARD TABLE DECORATIONS - These pieces were produced during the 1930s in Germany. They were cut, stamped and embossed in a manner that was reminiscent of both the lithographed scraps and the "Dresden" ornaments. The pieces were painted and came with an easel back for standing on the table or mantel. Other holiday decorations such as Halloween were also made in the same manner. (Germany, p716 & p717, OP, R3)
Santa in a sleigh, Approx. 9" $30.00-40.00
Santa with a bell, Approx. 10" $30.00-40.00
Pine tree, Approx. 12" $20.00-30.00

THE NIGHT BEFORE CHRISTMAS STORY BOOKS - There are many versions of Clement Moore's 1822 poem originally titled - "A Visit from St. Nicholas". The most collected are those from the publishers Raphael Tuck and Sons and McLoughin Bros. The age and condition play a large role in the price.   1910 & After $10.00-25.00
1880-1910 $25.00-50.00
Earlier Examples $40.00 & Up

"UNDER THE TREE" CHRISTMAS FENCES - These usually come in sections about one foot long and six inches high. They were designed to put a miniature fence around the tree or village scenes. The exact design can vary greatly but they usually include two to four gate sections. Fences can be found in metal, wood and a rare "feather tree" fence. Wood was also a popular form for making homemade versions. Although they are sold as a set, I have priced the fences by section. This is because the exact number of pieces in a set can vary. Gate sections are worth slightly more than straight fence sections. (p712)
Wood $10.00-15.00
Metal $25.00-30.00
"Feather" $50.00-60.00

ARTIFICIAL TREES - Other than the "feather" trees which were previously discussed, several other types of artificial trees werer produced from the 1930s to 1950s. At first glance they often resemble the feather tree but closer examination will show they are made of: Green cellophane circa 1935, crepe paper circa 1940 or Visca which is like shredded rayon, circa 1950.   Cellophane $20.00-35.00
Crepe paper $30.00-40.00
Green & white Visca, 3½'-5' $30.00-45.00
6'-7' $50.00-80.00

Reprint from an old catalog.

COLOR PLATES   Animals

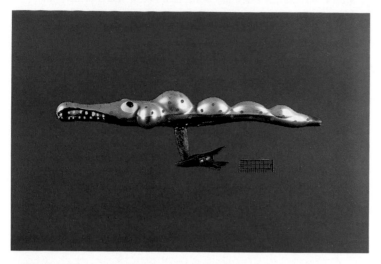

1. Free-blown Czech Alligator.

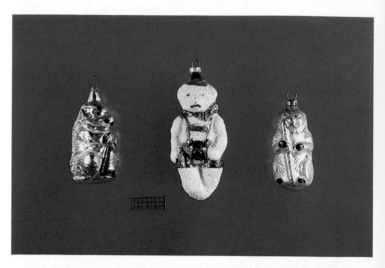

2a, b & c. Bear with a Club. Bear in Leather Shorts and Suspenders. Bear Carrying a Stick.

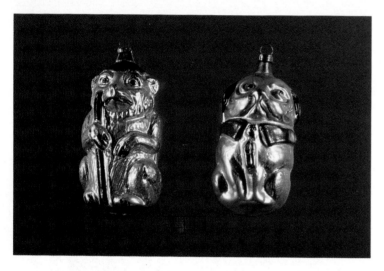

3a & b. Bear Carrying a Stick - large size. Dog in a Collar and Necktie.

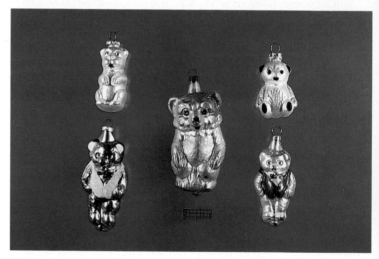

4a, b, c, d & e. Begging Terrier. Sitting "Teddy" Bear. Standing Bear. Bear in a Vest and Bow Tie - large. Bear in a Vest and Bow Tie - small.

5a, b & c. Bear Holding a Heart. Rabbit in an Egg. Bear in a Clown Suit - large.

6a & b. Bear with Chenille Arms and Legs. Bear with a Muff.

7a, b, & c. Bear with a Bow - Large. Bear with Annealed Legs. Bear in a Clown Suit - small.

8a & b. Bear in a Cap. Embossed Moth.

9a, b & c. Bird and Gnome on a Tree Trunk. Birdbath with Water. Birdbath.

10. Victorian Bird Cage, pedestal type with a Dresden Bird.

11a & b. Rooster on a Chicken Coop - large. Bird House - large.

12a, b, c & d. Dove with a Letter. Bird Cage, square. Songbird - bird indent. Bird House with Doves.

13a, b & c. Chenille Bird on a Nest (Early). Bird on a Nest - standard form. New version of a Bird on a Nest.

14. Early Unsilvered Bird on a Nest.

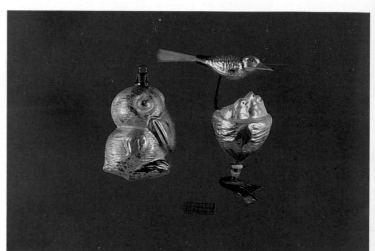

15a & b. Pelican. Baby Birds in a Nest with Mother Bird - the nest has molded leaves.

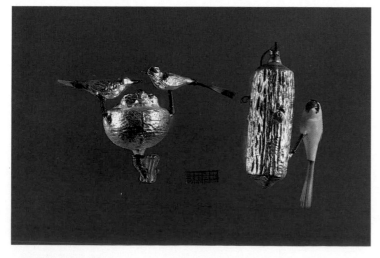

16a & b. Baby Birds in a Nest with Mother and Father. Woodpecker on a Tree Trunk.

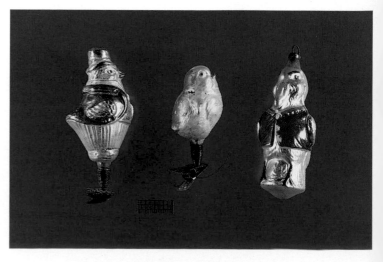

17a, b & c. Cock Robin. Chick. Duck in a Vest.

18a & b. Duck in an Egg. Hen on a Basket.

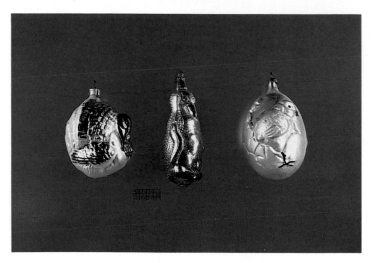

19a, b & c. Turkey. Penguin - Type I. Chick on an Egg.

20a & b. Eagle and Liberty Shield - egg shaped. Bird on a Disc.

21a, b, c & d. Cockateel - small. Milk Glass Stork. Cockateel - larger.
Stork - standard form.

22a, b & c. Two Storks on a Clip-on. Stork with a Baby. Osterich.

23a, b, c & d. Clip-on Owl - Type I - small. Songbirds - Two Birds on a
Clip-on - medium size. Songbird - Bird with a Topknot. Soaring Dove.

24a & b. Tropical Bird with a long bill. Duck, Mallard.

25. Duck in a Bonnet - "Baby Huey".

26. American Eagle with Liberty Shield on its Chest - top view.

28a, b, c, d & e. Eagle on Top of a Ball. Molded Duck. "Germany" Swan - "Germany" is embossed on the chest. Rooster embossed on an Oval. Songbird - Bird with a Berry in its Mouth.

27. American Eagle with Liberty Shield on its Chest - bottom view.

29a, b & c. Free-blown Flamingo with Annealed Legs - large. Free-blown Stork. Free-blown Flamingo with Annealed Legs.

30a, b & c. Bird on Three Pine Cones - embossed. Owl on a Leaf. Turkey - Type II.

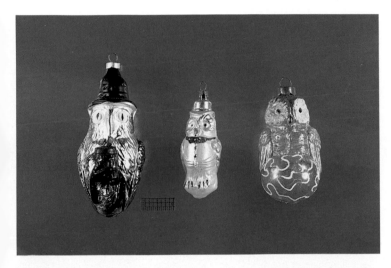

31a, b & c. Owl with a Top Hat and Beer Stein. Owl with a Top Hat and Vest. Owl on a Ball.

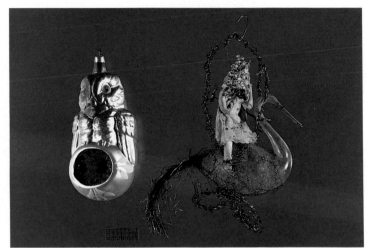

32a & b. Owl on an Indented Ball. Swan with Spun Cotton Rider.

33. Three variations on the standard form Owl.

34a, b & c. Variations on the standard form Owl. Clip-on Owl - Type I - large.

35a & b. Cat Head. Owl Head - Type I.

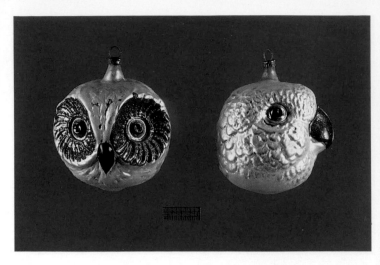

36a & b. Owl Head - Type II. Parrot Head.

37a, b, c & d. Parrot with the Hanger in the Top Knot. Various sizes of Parrots.

39. Peacock Baby Rattle - front view.

38a, b, c, d & e. Standard form Peacocks. Peacock with a Fanned Out Tail. Peacock with a Trailing Tail. Two Peacocks on a Clip-on.

40. *Peacock Baby Rattle - back view.*

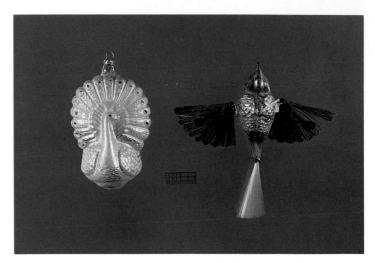

41a, b. *Molded Peacock. Swan with Spun Glass Wings and Tail.*

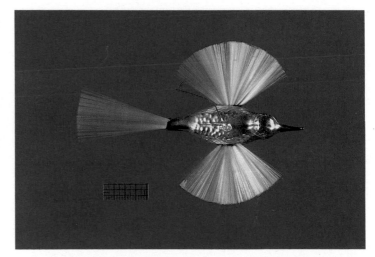

42. *Songbird with SG Wings - also called a Hummingbird.*

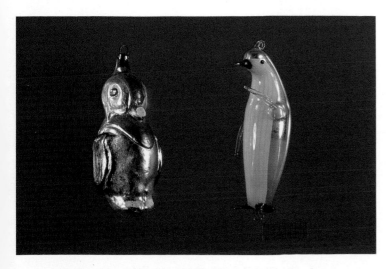

43a & b. *Penguin - Type II. Free-blown Penguin - large.*

44a & b. *An unusual Songbird. Flying Free-blown Swan.*

169

45. A collection of the Common Songbirds.

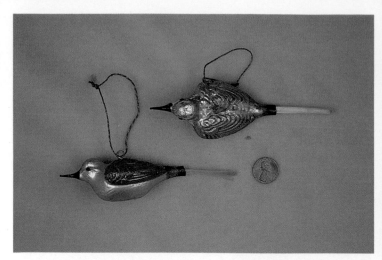

46. A top and side view of a Standard Form Songbird.

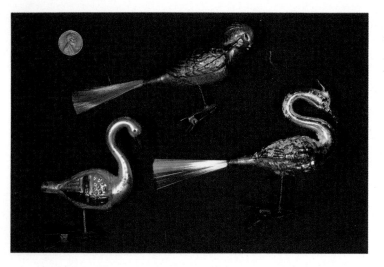

47a, b & c. Parrot - standard form. Swan with a molded body. Flamingo.

48a, b, c, d & e. A standard form Swan - medium. Swan with a molded body. FB Swan in a tinsel hoop. FB Swan with tinsel wings. FB Swan with indents - small.

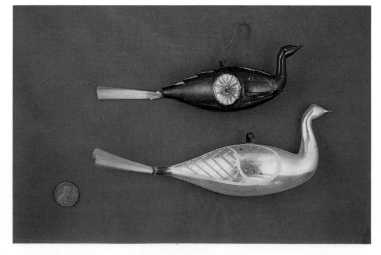

49a & b. FB Swan with indents. Standard form Swan - medium size.

50. FB Swan with Scrap Riders.

51. Two sizes of Swan Boats.

52. Swan Boat with Scrap Sails.

53. FB Swan Sleigh with a Cotton Rider.

54, 55 & 56. A Three Faced Ornament - an Owl, a Cat, and a Bulldog.   *55.*

56.

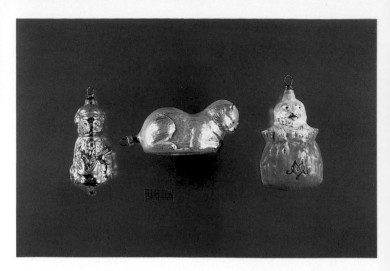

57a, b & c. Student Cat with a Mandolin. Crounched Cat Playing with a Ball. Cat in a Bag.

58a, b & c. Roly-Poly Cat. Cat in a Stocking. Two Kittens in a Basket - large, Czech.

59a, b & c. Cat in a Shoe. Sleeping Cat in a Shoe - Type I. Cat in a "Window" - same face on opposite side.

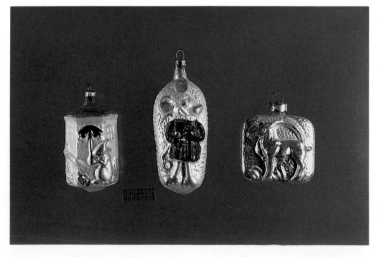

60a, b & c. Embossed Rabbit with an Umbrella - on a six sided house. Embossed "Church" Mouse. Antelope Embossed onto a Square.

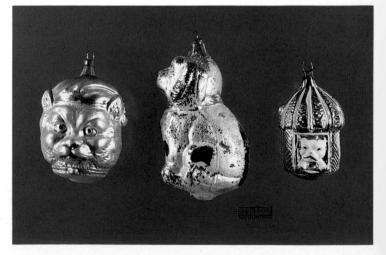

61a, b & c. Cat in a Night Cap. Sitting Spaniel - large. Dog in a Dog House.

62a, b, c & d. Free-blown and Annealed Milk Glass Cat, circa 1920. Free-blown and Annealed Milk Glass Whippets, circa 1920. Milk Glass Swan.

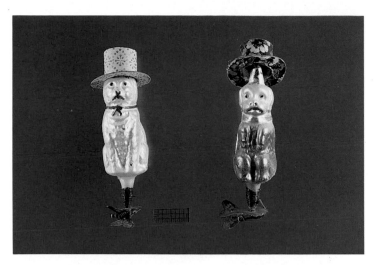

63. Cat and Dog with Cardboard Hats.

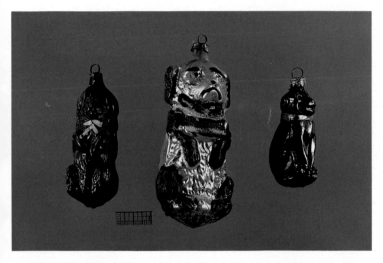

64a, b & c. Begging Spaniel. Begging Dog with a Basket - large. Smiling Dog.

65a & b. Begging Dog - Type I - this mold was used to make the Dog in a Ball. Begging Dog in a Ball.

66a, b & c. Dog Blowing a Horn. Sitting Spaniel - medium. Sitting Spaniel - small.

67. Bulldog Head.

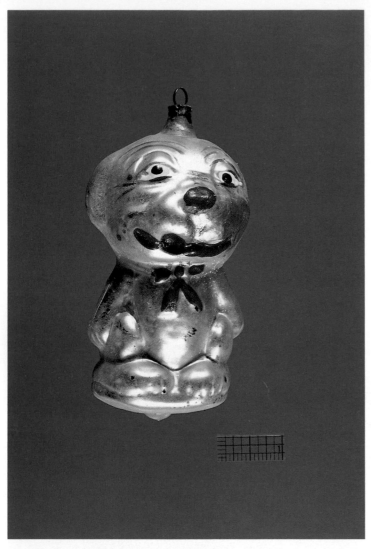

68. Cigar Smoking Dog (cigar missing).

69a, b & c. Scotty Dog - this is a thin looking piece. Bulldog Head - large. Standing Dog.

70a & b. Elf on a Stump - embossed. Begging Dog - Type II.

71a & b. Free-blown and Annealed Milk Glass Greyhound, circa 1920. Free-blown and Annealed Milk Glass Stag, circa 1920.

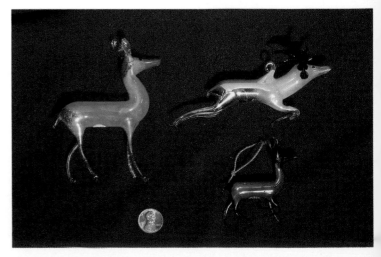

72a, b & c. Leaping Deer, circa 1920. Blue Glass Deer. Free-blown and Annealed Doe.

73a, b & c. Standing Deer. Leaping Deer. Leaping Deer - small.

74a & b. Walking Elephant with a Fringed Blanket. Scotty Dog - Large.

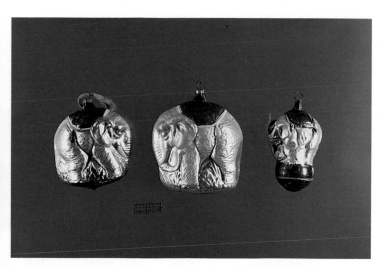

75a, b & c. Walking Elephant - small and large. Elephant Standing on a Ball.

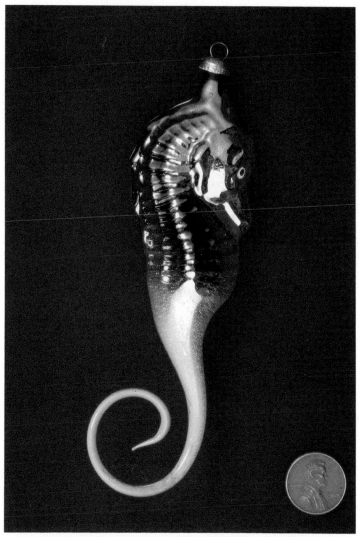

77. Sea Horse - molded and free-blown.

76a & b. "Goldilocks" Mermaid. Early Wire Wrapped Porpoise - unsilvered.

78a, b, c & d. Two large standard form Fish. Clam Shell. Lobster.

79a & b. Variation on a standard form Fish - large. Fish with a long Dorsal Fin.

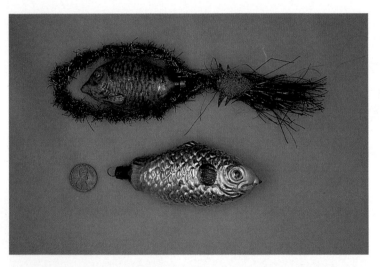

80. Two standard Fish - the small one is mounted in tinsel.

81a, b, c, d & e. Standard Fish that look like Goldfish. Fish with a Curved Body.

82a, b & c. Fat standard form Fish. Fish with a "Dresden" Tail - paper fins are missing. Japanese Fish.

83. Fish with Embossed "Waves".

84a, b, c & d. Variations on the standard form Fish. Early Wire Wrapped Fish.

85a & b. Standard Fish - large. Shark - Japanese.

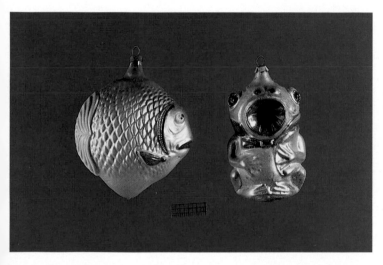

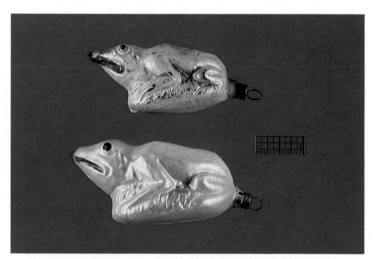

86a & b. Fat, Flat Angel Fish - large size. Singing Frog.

87. Small and large Hopping Frogs.

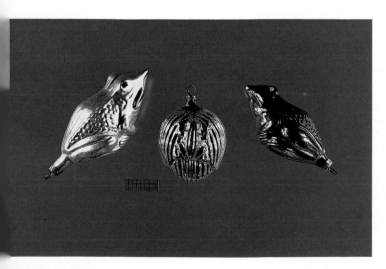

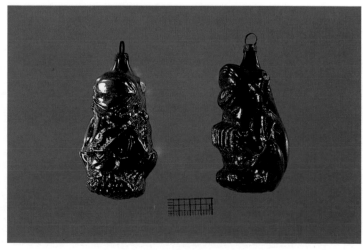

88a, b & c. Small and large Frog. Frog on a Leaf - sometimes called a Tulip.

89a & b. Frog Playing a Violin. Frog Playing a Concertina.

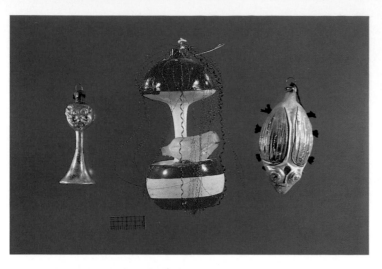

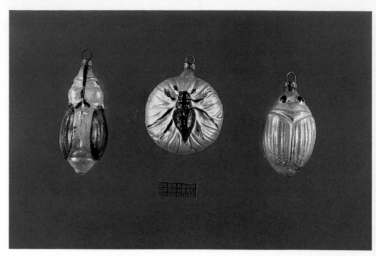

90a, b & c. Cat and Dog Headed Horn - one face on each side. Frog Under a Mushroom. Beetle with Paper Legs.

91a, b & c. Beetle - Type II. Bee on a Flower - it has mistakenly been called a Spider in a Web. Beetle - Type I.

92. Spider in a Web - Types I & II.

93. Three sizes of Moths with beautiful spun glass wings - they have been mistakenly called Butterflies.

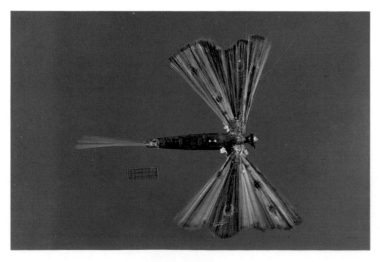

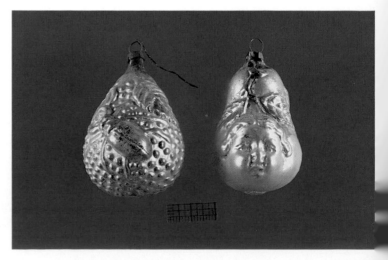

94. Dragonfly.

95a & b. Beetle on a Pear. Girl's Head in a Pear.

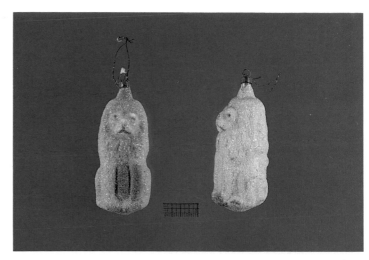

96a, b & c. Roaring Lion Head. Leopard Head - also mistakenly called a Fox Head. Lion Head.

97. Front and side views of a Sitting Lion.

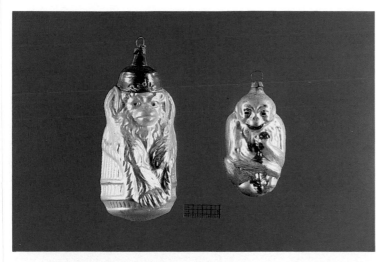

98a & b. "Radio" Monkey - large. Monkey with a Vine.

99a, b & c. "Radio" Monkey - small. Monkey with a Fur Ruffle. Squatting Monkey.

100. Monkey in a Clown Suit.

110a, b, c, d, e, f & g. Rosebud - small. Various "Open Roses" - a very common piece. "Rosette" - rose shape made of paper thin glass - early and unsilvered.

109a, b & c. Rose Goblet - hollow. Hollow Rose - early clip-on. Artichoke - hollow - clip-on.

111a, b, c & d. Two sizes of Tulips - "D" has stamens. Two sizes of Rosebuds covered with crushed glass. "C" has fabric leaves.

112a & b. Hollow Trumpet Flower - an early mold blown version. Tulip.

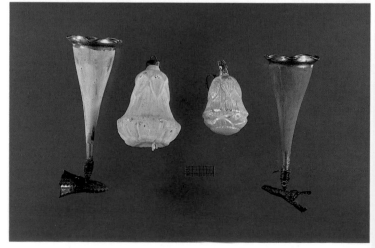

113a, b, c & d. Free-blown Trumpet Flowers - hollow. Lotus with Stamens. Lotus Flower.

114a, b & c. Molded Trumpet Flower. Angel in a Basket of Flowers. "Pillow" Flower.

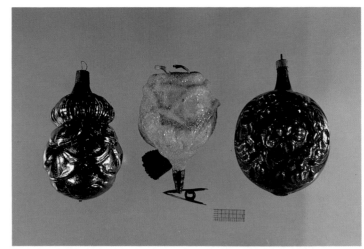

115a, b & c. Rose with a Hip of Leaves. Open Rose with Stamens. An Embossed Rose.

116a, b & c. Daisy. Rose on a Leaf. "Narrow Limb" Tree.

117a, b & c. Basket of Grapes and Pears. Basket of Grapes. Round Basket of Fruit - Type I.

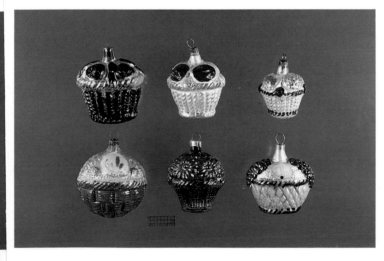

118a, b, c, d, e & f. Three sizes of Rose Basket - Type I. "D" Round Basket of Fruit - Type II. Daisy Basket. Basket of Apples and Grapes.

119a, b & c. Basket of Roses - Type III. Fruit Basket - heaped high with goodies. Basket with Fabric Flowers - small.

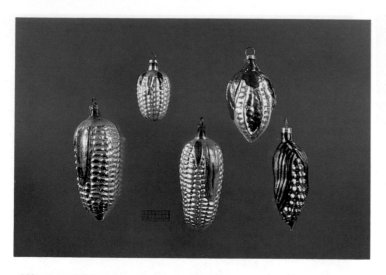

129a, b, c, d & e. "A", "C" & "D" Three sizes of Corn with Leaves - small through medium. Corn with Large Leaves - crude. "E" Corn inside Leaves.

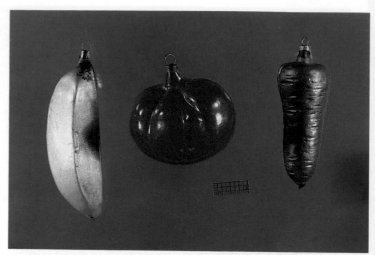

130a, b & c. Banana - Type II. Tomato - unsilvered. Carrot - Type I - silvered.

131a, b & c. Free-blown Radish. Squash. Carrot - Type II.

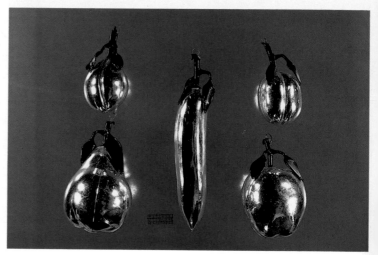

132a, b, c, d & e. All are "Artistic Period" fruit from Germany, circa 1920. All are silvered, some have "blushing". Plum. Peach. Banana. Pear. Apple.

133a, b & c. More "Artistic Period" Fruit. Tomato. Crabapple. Strawberry.

134a & b. Large, crushed glass covered Peach. Peach with large Leaves.

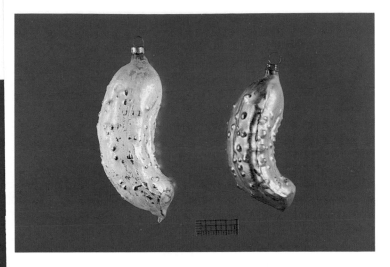

135. Two sizes of the Gherkin Pickle.

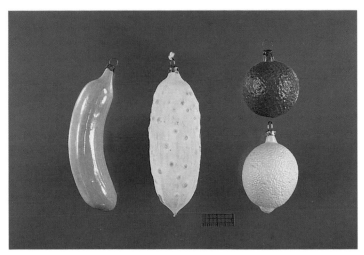

136a, b, c & d. Banana - Type I - large. "Heinz" Pickle - unsilvered. Small Unsilvered Orange. Small Unsilvered Lemon.

137a & b. Pineapple. Potato.

138. Large Silvered Strawberry.

139a, b, c, d & e. "Ribbed" Pear. Free-blown Pear covered with Crushed Glass. Unusual, Unsilvered, Half a Pear. "D" & "E" Small and large mold blown Pears.

140a, b & c. Clip-on Strawberry with Fabric Leaf - early and unsilvered. Large Free-blown Pear - unsilvered. Large Unsilvered Lemon - unusual color.

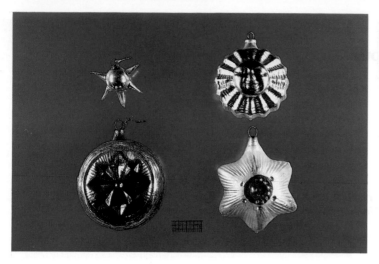

151a, b, c & d. Spiked Star. Sun and Moon on a Disc - moon face on the opposite side. Large Star Embossed on a Disc. Large Molded Star.

152. Three Wire and Glass Stars.

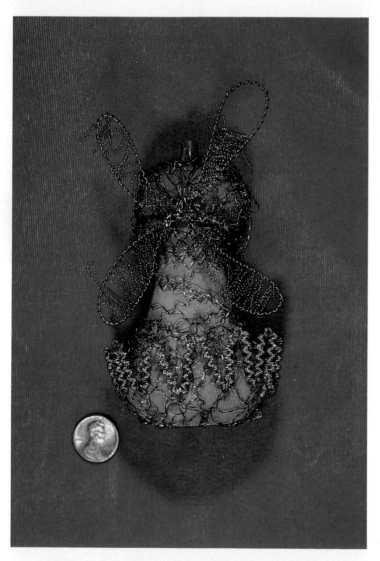

154a, b & c. Two sizes of the Standard Cottage. "Tree" House - Type I.

153. Early Wire Wrapped Windmill - unsilvered - Type I.

155a, b & c. Gingerbread House. Castle Tower. Town Hall Building - large.

156a, b & c. Standard Cottage. "Tree" House - Type II. House with a Turkey - large, German version.

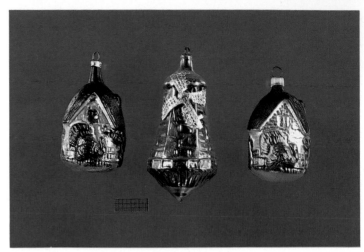

157a, b & c. House with a Turkey - medium German piece - note the smooth panels between the gables. Windmill - Type II. House with a Turkey - Austrian version - note the brickwork in the gable.

158a & b. Free-blown, Wire Wrapped Barrel. Windmill - Type I - early and unsilvered.

160a & b. Lighthouse. Windmill with Embossed Arms.

159a & b. Windmill - Type I. Free-blown Windmill - Type II.

191

161a, b & c. Round, Snow Covered House - large size. Windmill on a Disc. Church on an Egg.

162a, b, c & d. German Church. Czech Church. Large Church - German. Victorian House.

163a & b. Church on a Disc. House with a Turkey - small German version.

164. Houses with Pine Roping - medium and large sizes.

165a, b & c. House with Pine Roping - small. Tall House - unsilvered with clear windows. Square House.

166a, b & c. Town Hall Building - small. Chalet. Large Stucco House.

167. "Merry Xmas" Baby Rattle.

168. Barrel Baby Rattle - or a Gavel - wire wrapped, unsilvered.

169. Three Bottles with Paper Labels.

170a, b & c. Free-blown Bottle with a Wire Handle. Molded Coffee Pot with a Rose. It has annealed spout and handle. Free-blown Flask with Scrap, Wire and Fabric Decoration.

171a, b & c. Reverse Carrousel - the horses move in the opposite direction. Carrousel. Small Carrousel.

172a & b. Lighthouse. Carrousel with a Round Top.

173. Cornucopia of Toys.

174a & b. Early Free-blown Gramophone. Early, Unsilvered and Unusual Basket of Flowers.

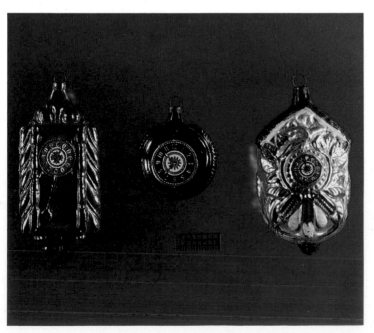

175a, b & c. Clocks with Paper Dials. Wall Clock. Pocket Watch. Cuckoo Clock - large size.

176a, b & c. Pocket Watch with an Embossed Face. Cuckoo Clock with a Paper Face - small version. Telephone.

177a, b & c. "Flower" Clock. Street Lamp. Bottle - missing the paper label.

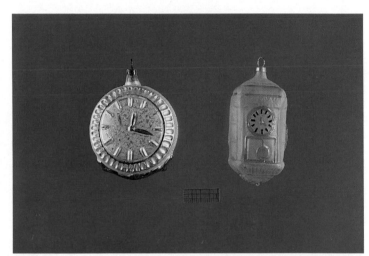

179a & b. Clock and Sundial - sundial on the back. Rectangular Clock.

178. "Egg Indent" Clock.

180a & b. Football. Box Radio.

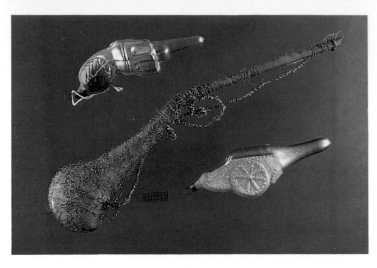

181a, b & c. Revolver. Free-blown, wire wrapped Rifle. Cannon.

182a, b & c. Quilted Pillow - Type I. Dice. Quilted Pillow - Type II.

183a & b. Wine Glass - free-blown, unsilvered and wire wrapped. Champagne Glass - free-blown, unsilvered and wire wrapped.

184. Two Free Blown Banquet Lamps. "B" has a replaced fabric shade.

185. Gas Lamp Chandelier - Type I.

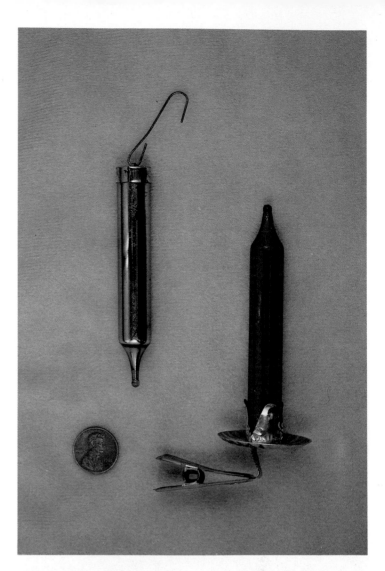

186. Free-blown Candles - Type I - two ways of attaching them to the tree.

187a, b & c. Large Table Lamp. Large Banquet Lamp with Molded, Milk Glass Shade. Knit Stocking with a Ball.

188a, b & c. Candle Chandelier - free-blown and annealed. Free-blown Banquet Lamp with Molded Shade. Hanging Oil Lamp with a Metal Hanging Bracket.

197

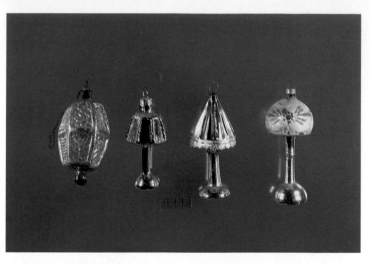

189a, b, c & d. *Paneled Lantern. Variations on the Table Lamp.*

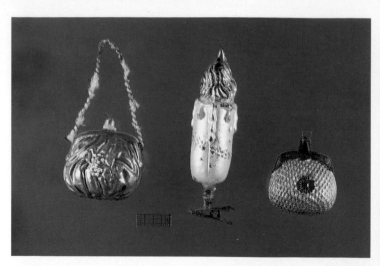

190a, b & c. *Wrinkled Purse. Clip-on, Molded Candle. Purse with an Embossed Flower.*

191a, b, c & d. *Purse with Embossed Leaves. Skein of Yarn - small. Purse with Embossed Roses. Free-blown, Hollow Cauldron.*

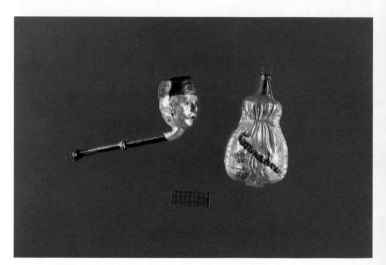

192a & b. *Man's Head Pipe - Type I. "Pompadour" Bag.*

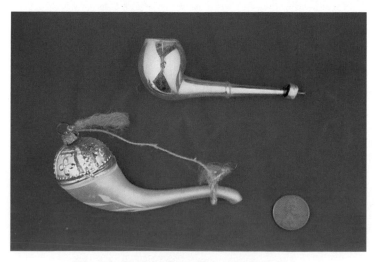

193a & b. *Straight Stem Pipe. "Dublin" Pipe.*

194. *Two versions of the "Dublin" Pipe.*

198

195a & b. German Pipe. German Pipe with Smoke.

196. Three variations of the Straight Stem Pipe.

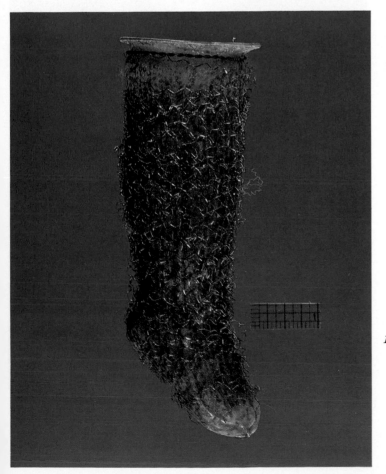

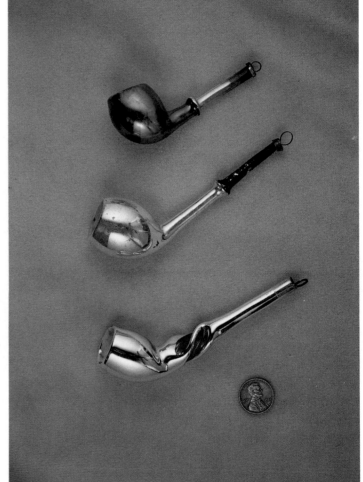

197. Hollow Stocking - unsilvered and wire wrapped.

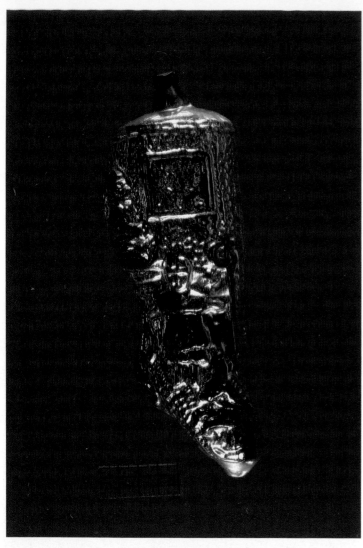

198. Christmas Stocking.

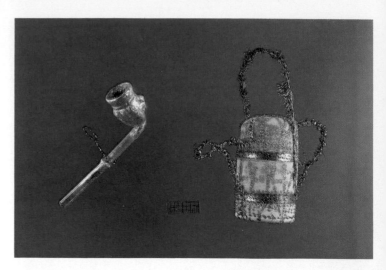

199a & b. Man's Head Pipe - Type II. Free-blown and wire wrapped Watering Can - early.

200a & b. Standard Shoe - large. Double Strapped Shoe.

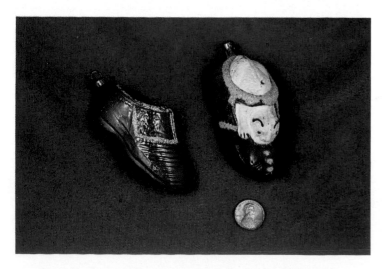

201a & b. Cat in a Shoe - unsilvered. Shoe with a Ribbed Toe.

202a, b, c & d. Cat Sleeping in a Shoe - Type II. Standard Shoes - medium and small. Scrap Baby Face in a Baby Shoe.

203. Pair of Skis.

204a, b & c. Free-blown Urn or Sugar Pot. Free-blown Coffeepot. Free-blown Teapot.

205. Three various, closed Umbrellas - "B" and "C" are Victorian.

206. Open Umbrella.

201

207. Kugel Grapes in an Oval Cluster.

208. Kugel Grapes in a Cluster - This unusual piece is unsilvered and blown in colored glass.

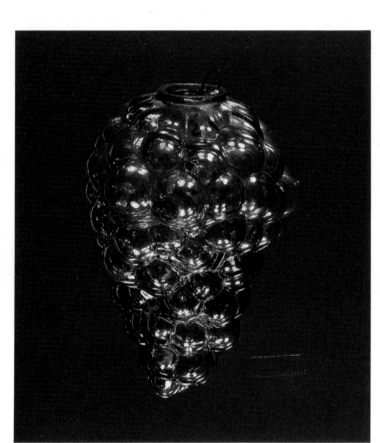

209. Kugel Grapes in a Cluster.

210. Kugel - An egg or pear shape depending on the end the cap is in.

211. Various sizes and colors of Kugel Balls.

212a & b. "Schecken" Kugel - The interior is decorated with paint and wax. Early Kugel with Pike - rare ruby red.

213. Four forms of free-blown Mushrooms.

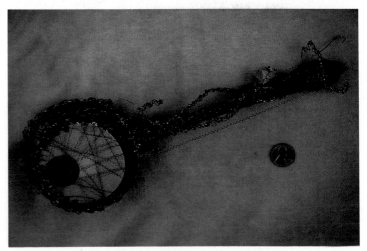

214. Banjo - free-blown and unsilvered.

215. Kugel - Ribbed Ball.

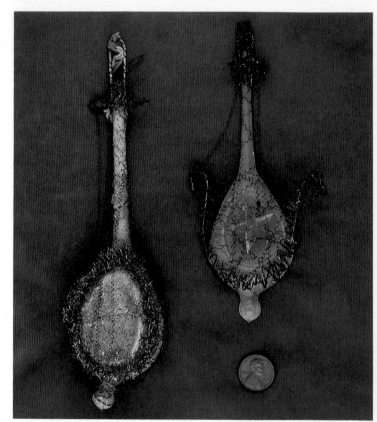

216. Two Free-blown Mandolins - both unsilvered and early.

217a, b & c. Hunting Horns that have molded parts. "C" Free-blown Hunting Horn.

218a, b, c, d & e. "A" & "B" Real Nuts that have been silvered and gilded to hang on the tree. "D" Small Glass Walnut.. Half Walnut Shell decorated with fabric and a tiny wax Baby Jesus. Real Walnut Purse - a Victorian homemade decoration.

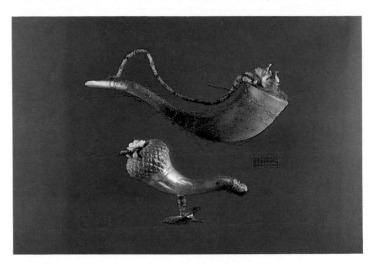

219a, b, c & d. Large and early, free-blown Musical Instruments. All are wire wrapped and unsilvered. Banjo. "B" & "D" Mandolins. Clarinet.

220a & b. Hollow Hunting Horn. Clip-on Hunting Horn.

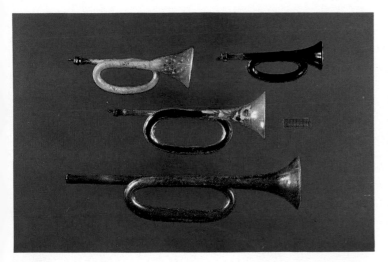

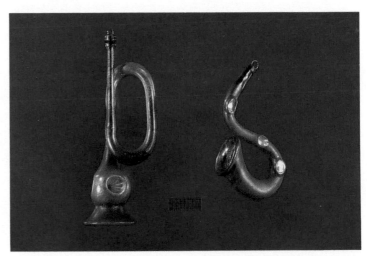

221. Four variations of Trumpets - "A" has a molded bell, and "D" is very large.

222a & b. Trumpet with Indents. Saxophone.

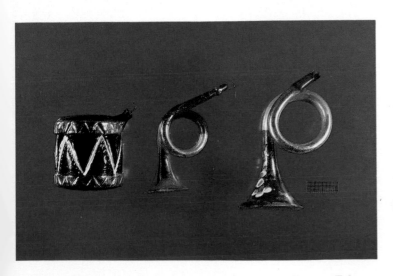

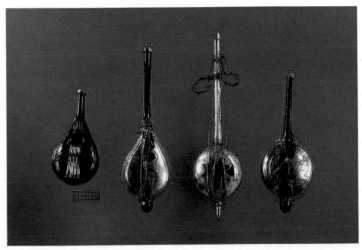

223a, b & c. Drum. Two sizes of free-blown French Horn or Tuba.

224a, b, c & d. Mandolins. "D" Molded Banjo.

205

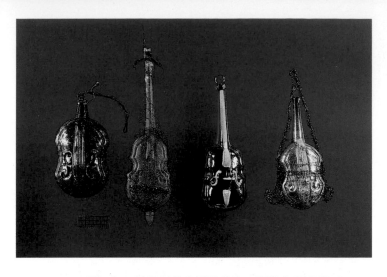

225a, b, c & d. "A" & "B" Cellos. "C" & "D" Violins.

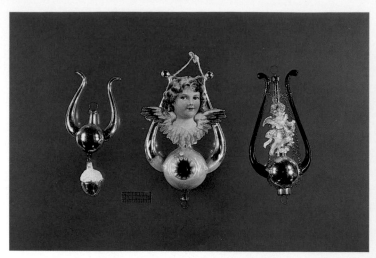

226. Lyres - free-blown and annealed.

227a, b, c, d, e & f. Bell with an Embossed Church. Bell with Flowers. Bell with Geometric Designs. Bell with a Crown - Type II. Hand Bell - Type I. Bell with a Crown - Type I.

228a, b & c. Bell with a Crown - Type I. Common Bell with Scrap Decoration. Bell with an Embossed Eagle.

229a, b & c. Acorn Chain. Two sizes of Acorns.

230a, b, c, d, e & f. Miniature and Small Acorns. "C" & "E" Acorns on an Oak Leaf - two sizes. "D" Standard Acorn - large. "E" Paneled Acorn.

People

231a, b & c. Cherub on a Ball. Standing Angel Treetop. Standing Angel - Type II.

232a & b. Beautiful New Angel Bust - no "Old" examples are known. "Raphael" Angel on a Cloud - a new production.

233a, b & c. Mother and Child Angel. "Raphael" Angel. Kneeling Angel - Type I.

234a, b & c. "Raphael" Angel - still another style. Boy Cherub. Angel on a Harp.

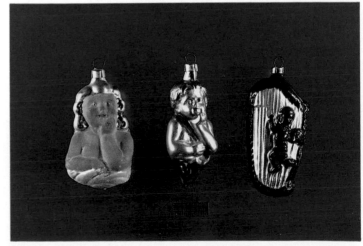

235a, b, c, d & e. Seated Angel on a Heart. "Raphael" Angel on an Egg. Baby Jesus on a Leaf. Double Faced Angel Head. Flying Angel on a Disc.

236. A newer Mary Pickford without legs - also called an angelic girl.

237a & b. Angel Blowing a Horn. Standing Angel with Folded Wings.

238a & b. Angel on a Cloud of Angel Hair. Dutch Boy - Type I.

239a, b & c. "Raphael" Angel on a Disc. "Putti" Angel Heads - small, Type I and large, Type II.

240a & b. Angel Head Embossed on a Disc. "Putti" Angel Head - medium.

241a, b & c. Snow Angel with a Basket of Flowers. Angel in a Hoop Skirt. Standing Angel - Type I.

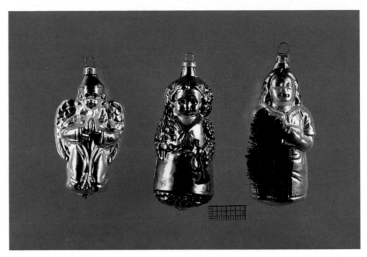

242a, b & c. Kneeling Angel with Molded Wings. Angel with a Tree and Horn. Angel with a Fabric Tree.

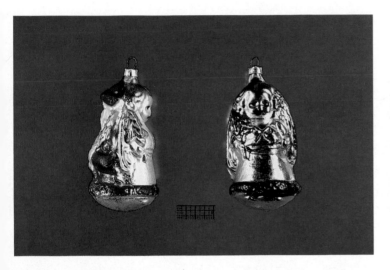

243. Double Ornament - Angel and Santa - the Santa is a standard form. Two views of the piece.

244a, b & c. "Goldilocks". Kneeling Angel - Type II. Baby with a Bottle.

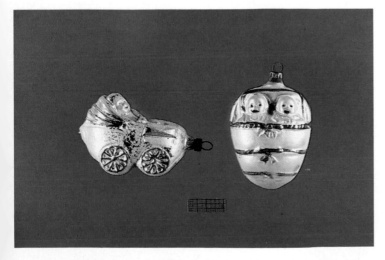

245a & b. Baby in a Buggy - large size. Twins in Bunting.

246a, b & c. Scrap Faced Baby. Baby in a Bathtub. Baby in Bunting with a Scrap Face.

209

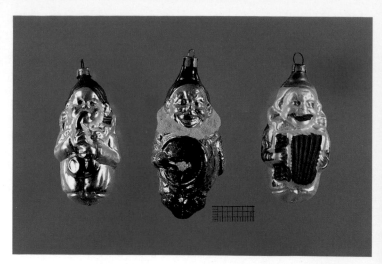

247a & b. "Joey" Clown Head - large. "Joey" Clown Head with a Spun Glass Collar.

248a, b & c. "Joey" Clown with a Saxophone. "Joey" Clown with a Drum. "Joey" Clown with an Accordian.

249a, b & c. Boy Clown. Variation on the standard form. Clown Torso - Type I.

250a, b, & c. Roly-Poly Clown. Comic Keystone Cop. Fat Man Playing a Concertina.

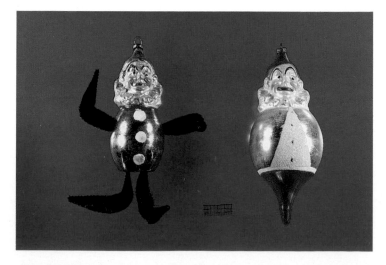

251a & b. "Joey" Clown with Chenille Arms and Legs. "Joey" Clown with a Stylized Body.

252a, b, c & d. Boy Clown on a Ball. Front and back views of the standard form Clown. "D" Standard Form Clown.

253a & b. "Judy" Bell, doublefaced - Judy is half of the famous "Punch and Judy" Clowns. "Hans" Clown Head on a Spike.

254a, b & c. Clown Playing a Concertina - a variation in the standard clown. "500,000" Clown - large. Clown in a Boot.

255. Boy Clown on an Indent.

256. Clown Head, Doublefaced - the opposite side is the same.

257. *Front view of Punch and Judy Show - Type I.*

258. *Back view of Punch and Judy Show - Type I.*

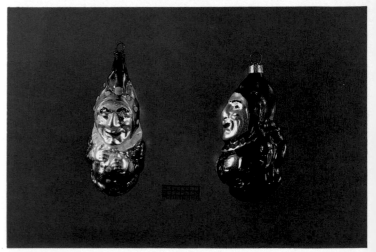

259a, b & c. *Punch and Judy Show - Type I. Punch and Judy Show - Type III. Punch and Judy Show - Type II.*

260a & b. *Front and side view of the "Punch" Clown. "B" is newer than "A".*

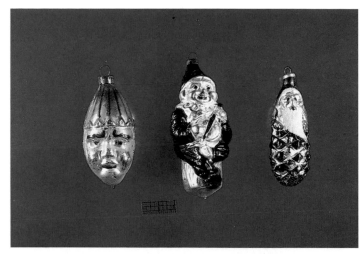

261a & b. Doublefaced "Judy" on a Body. Clown Head Indent - embossed onto a free blown shape.

262a, b & c. "Judy" Clown Head - single sided. Clown on a Stump Playing a Banjo - large size. Santa or Dwarf in a Pine Cone.

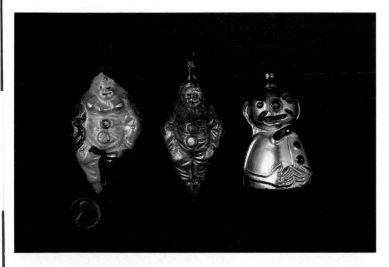

263a, b & c. Two sizes of the "Diamond" Clown - so named because of its shape. Comic Figure.

264a & b. Clown in a Drum. The Fisherman - embossed.

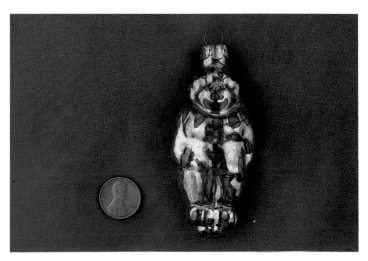

265a, b & c. Clown on a Log Playing a Banjo - a 1950s piece. "Snowman" Clown - so called because of the shape of the three stacked balls. Large Headed Clown - Type II.

266. American made Clown - the silvering is on the outside of this unusual piece.

275a, b & c. "Kate Greenaway" Girl - large. Long Haired Boy. Angel with a Lithographed Face - large and unsilvered.

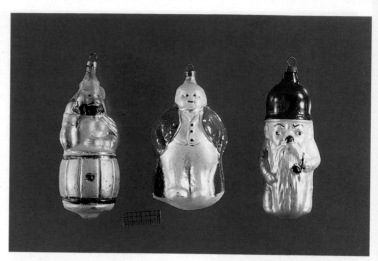

276a, b & c. "Ali Babba" in a Barrel. The Ringmaster. Gnome in a Large Hat.

277a & b. Balding Clown Head - this is very similar to the Bust of John Bull and may have been a political jab at the British. Comic Man with an Umbrella - large.

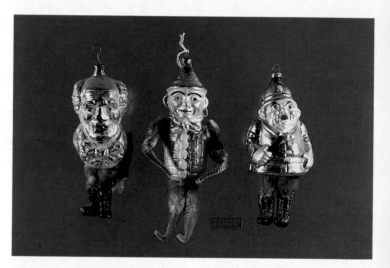

278a, b & c. Bust of John Bull with chenille arms and legs - the hands and boots are wax. Eddy Cantor with chenille arms and legs. Comic Keystone Cop with chenille legs.

279a, b & c. Two sizes of a Comic Man with an Umbrella. Winston Churchill.

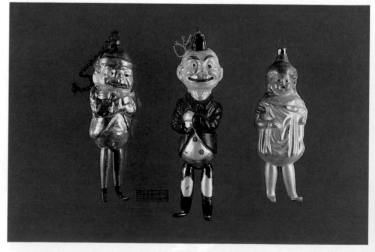

280a, b & c. Palmer Cox Brownie. Happy Hooligan - Type II. Mary Pickford with Annealed Legs.

281a, b & c. Squatting Black Boy. Pinocchio. Smitty - Type II.

282a, b & c. Unsilvered Chinaman's Head. "Devil" Head. "Devil" Head with a Neck - Type I.

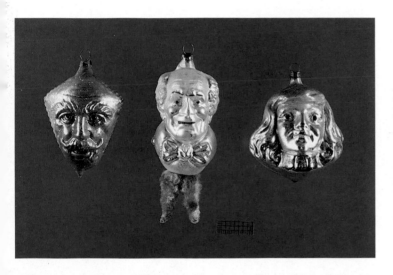

283a, b & c. "Einstein" Face on a Kite Shape. Bust of John Bull with Chenille Legs. Buster Brown Head.

284a, b & c. Little Black Sambo. Moon Mullins - Type II. Amelia Earhart, also called the Explorer - small.

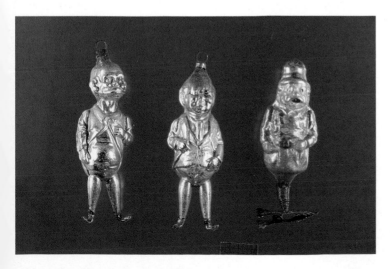

285a, b & c. Happy Hooligan - Type I. Foxy Grandpa. Keystone Cop.

286. Two sizes of "Little Miss Muffet".

287a, b, c & d. *Boy or Child in a Snowsuit. Miss Liberty. Miss Liberty in a Flag. Boy in a Flower Basket - small.*

288. *Smitty - Type I.*

289a, b & c. *"Kate Greenaway" Girl - small. Girl in a Fur Coat. "Bismarck" - a 1920s German Leader.*

290a, b & c. *Chubby Boy in a Toboggan Cap - large. Pig in a Tuxedo. Kayo.*

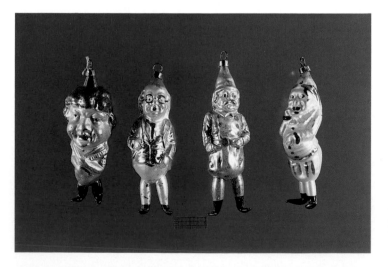

291a, b, c & d. *Large Headed Girl with Annealed Legs - "ZaZu". Foxy Grandpa with Annealed Legs. Keystone Cop with Annealed Legs. "Punch" Clown with Annealed Legs.*

292a, b & c. *Angel with a Lithographed Face - small. Scrap Girl with a Blown Glass Skirt. Santa with a Scrap Face.*

293a & b. "Hansel" or School Boy. Girl Holding a Teddy Bear.

294a & b. "Gretel". Dutch Boy - Type II - 1950s Production.

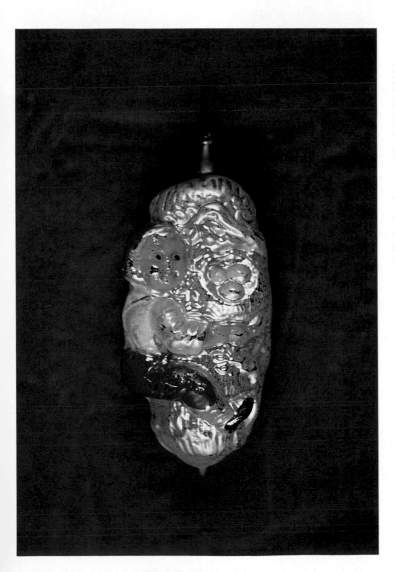

295. Egg Stealing Boy.

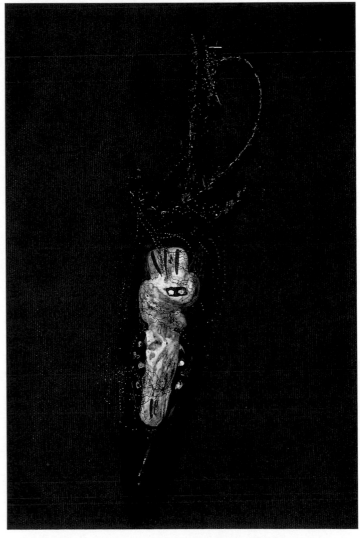

296. Uncle Sam in a Boot - unsilvered and wire wrapped.

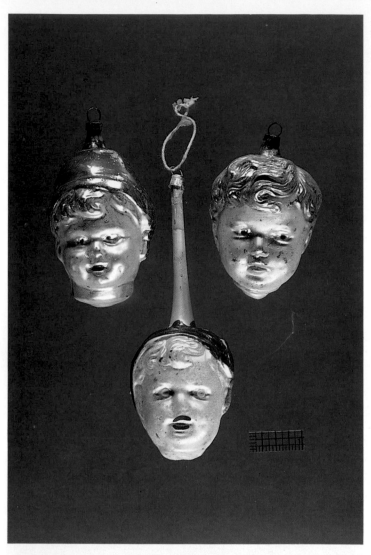

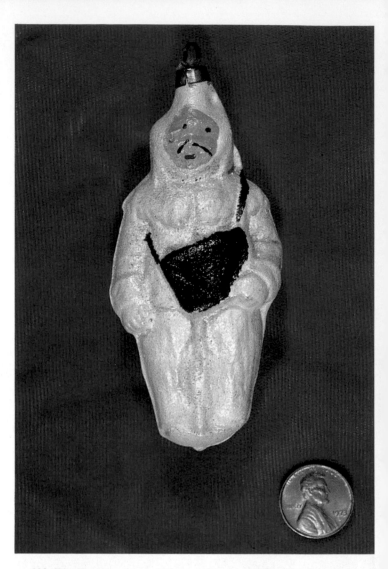

297a, b & c. Boy in a Nightcap with a Neck. Boy in a Nightcap Baby Rattle. Boy's Head - Type II.

298. The Explorer - a variation on the Amelia Earhart Ornament - larger size.

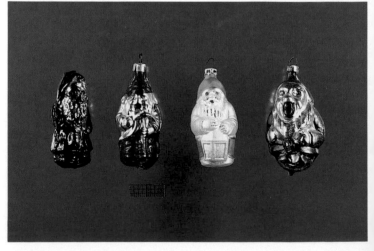

299a, b & c. Elf on a Stump - embossed. Gnome Playing a Concertina. Elf Atop a Mushroom.

300a, b, c & d. Dwarf with a Money Bag. Dwarf with a Pick. Dwarf with a Lantern - a post war piece only. Singing Dwarf.

301. Set of Double Glo's Snow White and the Seven Dwarves - American made.

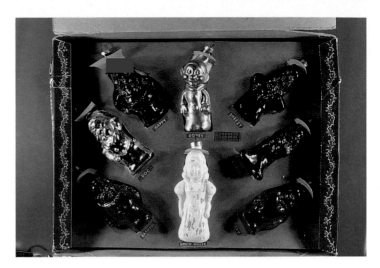

302. Double Glo's Snow White and the Seven Dwarves.

303a, b & c. Mushroom Man with a Pipe and Walking Stick. Mushroom Man with a Money Bag. Mushroom Girl with a Pipe.

304. Front and side views of the Mushroom Man.

305a, b & c. Mushroom Girl - Type II. Elf Under a Mushroom (embossed). Mushroom Girl - Type I.

306a, b & c. Three Faced Baby Indent - one cries, one smiles, one is "normal". Red Riding Hood and Wolf - embossed. Elf Head.

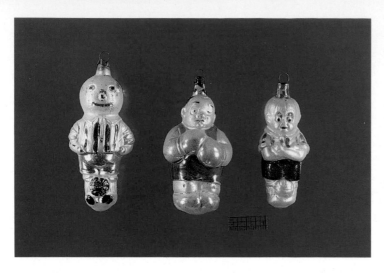

307a, b & c. Soccer Ball Man. The "Boxer". Soccer Boy.

308a & b. The Roly-Poly Boxer. Clown Clip-on.

309a, b & c. Clown Playing a Bass Fiddle. Girl Bell. Baby in Bunting with a Pacifier.

310a, b & c. The Chimney Sweep. Baby Girl Carrying a Tree - large size. "Fluffy".

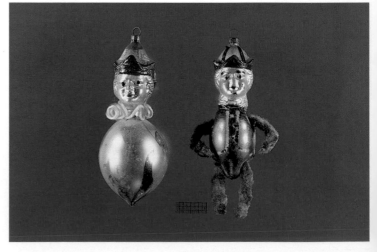

311a, b & c. "Prince" Head on a Ball. Boy's Head with a Crown - "The Prince". Hans Clown Head on an Indent.

312a & b. "The Prince" on a stylized body with a spun glass collar. "The Prince" with chenille arms and legs.

313a & b. Dutch Girl's Head - medium. Boy's Head - Type I.

314a, b & c. Girls' Faces in an Egg - the rear face is slightly different. "The Conductor" Head. Girl's Head - Type II.

315a, b & c. Flapper Girl's Head. Two Sizes of Goldilocks' Head.

316a & b. Gnome in a Triangle Window - 1950s version. Goldilocks' Head.

317a, b & c. Boy's Clown Head (found under Clowns). Boy's Head in a Toboggan Hat. Smitty Head.

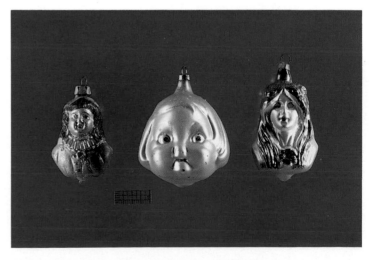

318a, b & c. Indian Princess Bust. Dolly Dingle Head. Bust of an Art Nouveau Lady.

319a, b & c. *Italian Angel Head with Large Wings. Girl's Head - Type III. Baby Jesus Head - small.*

320a & b. *Boy in a Nightcap. Baby Jesus Head - large.*

321a, b & c. *Girl's Head - Type I. Baby Girl's Head - Type I. Girl's Head Wearing a Dust Cap.*

322. *Three views of the "Three Faced Boy Head - one shows a smiling boy, one an angry boy and one a silly boy.*

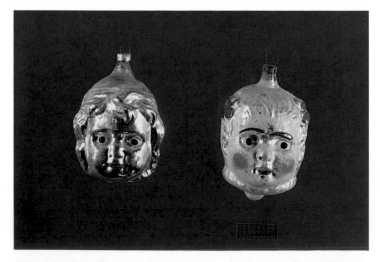

323a & b. *Girl's Head in a Toboggan Cap. Baby Girl's Head - Type II.*

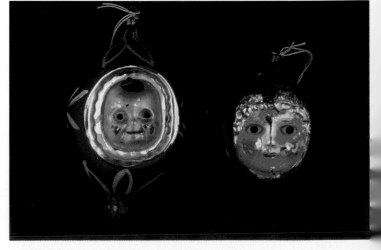

324a & b. *"Campbell Soup Kids" indent - the head on the reverse is different. Both have glass eyes. Little Red Riding Hood Head.*

224

325. Comic Baby Boy's Head (listed under Men & Boys).

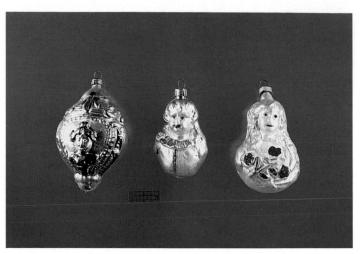

326a, b & c. Victorian Lady on an Urn. Bust of a Victorian Girl. Bust of a Lady with Flowers.

327a, b & c. Barney Google Head. Joan of Arc Head. Charlie Chaplin Head.

328a, b & c. Crude Head (found under Men and Boys) - possibly a Chinaman. Priest's Head - large. Ringmaster's Head.

329a, b, c, d & e. Round Man in the Moon - double faced. "Thor" Face - it is missing a spun glass beard. Al Jolson Head in Black Face. Small Chinaman's Head. Double Faced Boy's Head. Sometimes called a Negro or Aunt Jemima's Head.

330a, b & c. Indian Head in a Headdress - Type I. Grim faced Indian with a Headdress - Type I. Indian in a Bust Form.

331a & b. Indian Head on a Pine Cone - large. Indian in a Canoe.

332a, b & c. Indian Standing and Smoking a Pipe - West German. Indian in a Headdress - Type II - West German. Indian Head - West German.

333a & b. Standing Madonna and Child - 1950s - Type II. Madonna and Child.

334a, b & c. Joseph, Mary and Child Nativity Set - West German. Joseph. Child in the Manger. Virgin Mary.

335. Grim faced Indian with a Headdress - Type II.

336. Baby Jesus Embossed on an Egg.

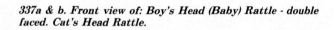

337a & b. Front view of: Boy's Head (Baby) Rattle - double faced. Cat's Head Rattle.

338a & b. Back view of 337.

339a & b. Standing Madonna and Child - early - Type I. Bust of Madonna and Child.

340a, b, c & d. Chubby Boy in a Toboggan Hat - small. Peasant Woman with a Spoon. Sailor with a Pilot's Wheel. Chubby Boy Riding a Toy Car.

341a, b & c. Snow Girl with a Rose. Girl's Head on a Heart. Angelic Girl.

342a, b & c. Woman Playing a Guitar. Man Playing an Accordian. Man Playing a Saxophone.

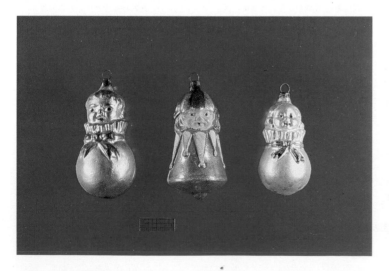

343a, b & c. Boy in a Bag - small. Girl Jester - small (under Clowns). Girl in a Bag - small.

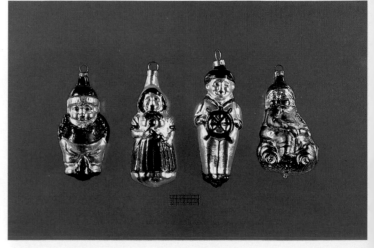

344a & b. Boy in a Bag - large version. Girl Jester - large version.

345a, b & c. Girl in a "LM" Sack. Girl in a Bag. Little Miss Muffet.

346a, b & c. Mrs. Santa Claus. Girl's Torso with a Present. Peasant Lady.

347a & b. Grotesque Uncle Sam. "Joey" Clown Headed Snake.

348. The Hat that goes with the Grotesque Uncle Sam.

349. Snowman in a Ball.

350a, b, c & d. Japanese Santa with his hands in his sleeves. Santa in a Glass Triangle. Santa on an Egg Shape. Miniature Gnome - unsilvered.

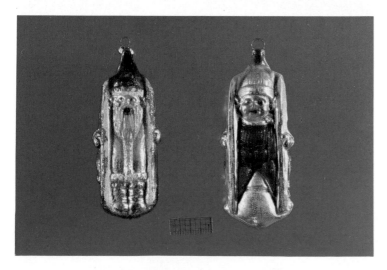

351a & b. Santa in a Sled. Boy in a Sled.

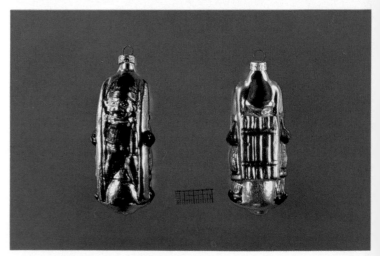

352. Front and back view of a Boy in a Sled.

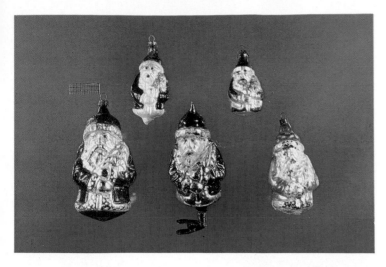

353. *Various forms and sizes of the Standard Form Santa.*

354a, b, c, d & e. *Various Clip-on Santas. "A" & "D" Santas with their arms in their sleeves. "B" & "E" Standard Form Santas. "C" Santa with a Basket.*

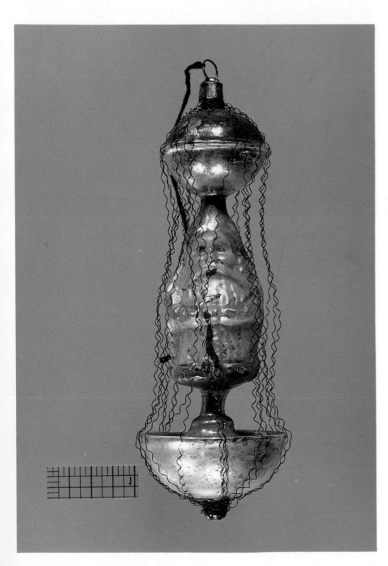

355. *Santa in a Balloon - early.*

356. *Santa in a Tinsel Wreath - large.*

357a & b. Father Christmas with a Bag and Tree. Santa with chenille legs.

358. Double Santa on a Ball. Reverse Satna is same as the front.

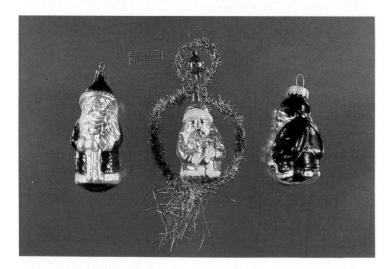

359a, b & c. A Standard Form of Santa. Standard Form Santa in a Tinsel Wreath. Santa with a Large Bag.

360. Three forms of Santas with their hands in their sleeves.

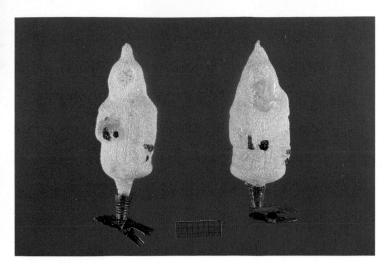

361a & b. *Two Scrap Faced Santas with Missing Faces - note the flattened area on the face used for attaching the lithograph. Santa Wears a Fur Trimmed Hat and Coat. "B" Father Christmas is Wearing a Hooded Cape.*

362a, b & c. *Father Christmas Holding a Small Bag - Type II - probably not German. Square Santa with a Tree and Bag - probably not German. Santa with a Bag and Toys (under Santas With Feet).*

363a & b. *Santa with a Tree and Drum. Roly-Poly Santa with a Heart.*

364a, b & c. *Variation of a Santa with his arms in his sleeves. Stern-Faced Father Christmas. Father Christmas Holding a Small Bag - Type I - large size.*

365a, b & c. *Stooped-Over Father Christmas. Japanese Santa with a Tree - molded after the European piece. This is remarkably well made. Frowning Santa with a Basket.*

366a & b. *"American" Santa with a Tree. American Santa - possibly made by Corning Glass.*

367a, b & c. Two sizes of Santas with chenille legs. Jolly Santa in a Tassel Cap - Type I.

368a, b & c. Father Christmas Head with Glass Eyes. Santa with Annealed Legs. Santa Head with Glass Eyes.

369a & b. Roly-Poly Santa. Mushroom with a Face.

370a, b, c & d. Clip-on Father Christmas Head with glass eyes - eyes missing. Small and large versions of the Standard Father Christmas Head. Jolly Santa Head in a Tassel Cap - Type I.

371a & b. Santa Head with a Leaf Cap. Santa in a Fur Cap on a Pike.

372a, b, c, d, e & f. Czech Santa Head. Standard Father Christmas Head - medium sized. Father Christmas Head - Variation #1. Jolly Santa in a Tassel Cap - Type II. Weihnachtsman Head - "E" is German and "F" is Czech.

373a, b & c. Santa Head with a Cap. Santa on an Oval. Small Santa Head on a Pine Cone.

374a & b. Santa Indent. Father Christmas on an Oak Leaf - American.

375a, b & c. Santa on a "Leaf" - the back is the same. Father Christmas on a Pine Cone. Father Christmas on an Egg Shape.

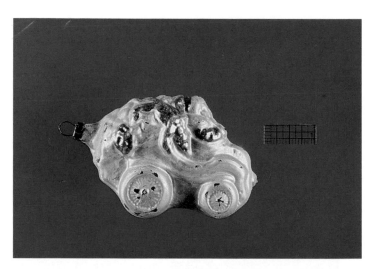

376. Santa in an Automobile.

377a, b & c. The Parachutist. Santa in a Coach. Santa in a Parachute.

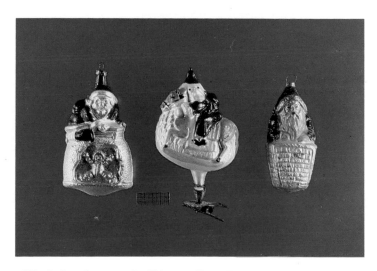

378a, b & c. Santa at the Chimney. Santa Riding a Horse. Santa in a Basket - Type II.

411. Three sizes and styles of the "Double Balloon".

412a & b. Double Balloon. Balloon with an attached tinsel "basket" and scrap angel rider.

413. Single Balloon - large and mold blown.

414a & b. Automobile - Type I. Variation: A Police Car.

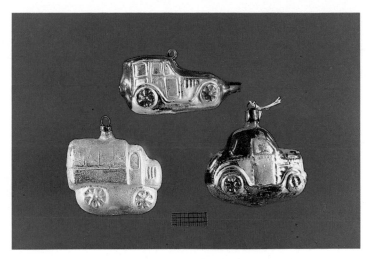

415a & b. Automobile - Type II. Touring Car - Type I.

416a, b & c. Touring Car - Type II. Truck. Comic Car.

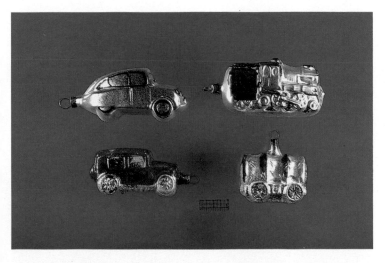

417a, b, c & d. VW Car - post war production. Locomotive.
Automobile - Type II. Covered Wagon.

418. Two sizes of the "Square Car".

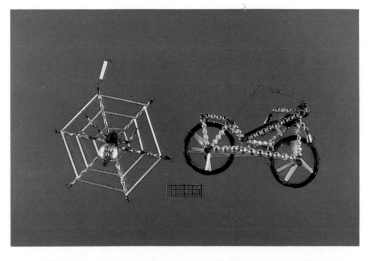

419a & b. Balloon with a Flower Basket. Indented Balloon.

420a & b. Czech Beaded Spider Web. Czech Beaded Bicycle.

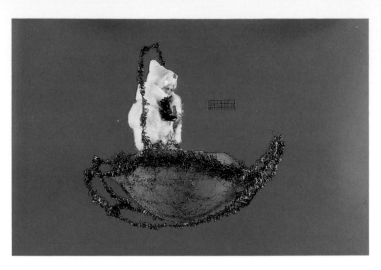

421. Sleigh with a Cotton Batting Rider.

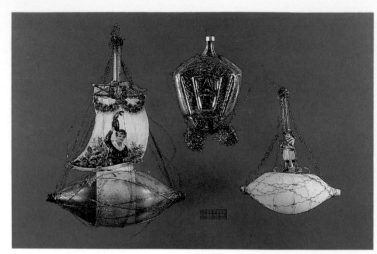

422a, b & c. Two versions of a Sailboat - "A" is a patriotic boat. Cinderella's Carriage - wire wrapped.

423. "Crown" Sailboat.

424. Free-blown Steamship - wire wrapped.

425. A collection of Free-blown Sail Boats - small to large.

244

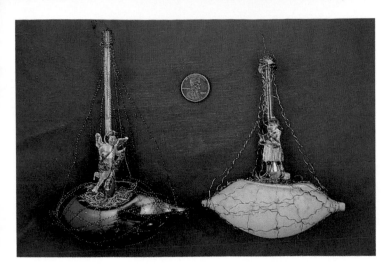

426. Medium sized Sailboats.

427a & b. Sailboat with "Dresden" sails. Sailboat with paper sails.

428a & b. Passenger Ship. Austrian Passenger Ship (new).

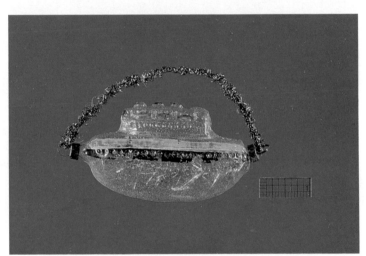

429. "Bremen" Steamship.

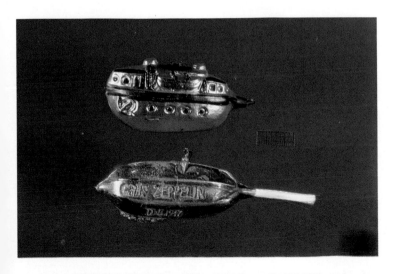

430a & b. Passenger Ship. Graf Zeppelin DL127.

431a, b & c. Graf Zeppelin DL127. Free-blown Graf Zeppelin with an American flag. "Los Angeles" Zeppelin.

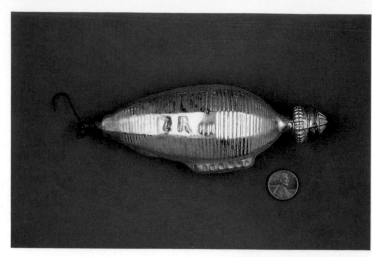

432. Large "ZR111" Zeppelin.

433a, b & c. Free-blown Zeppelin with Santa rider. Santa in a Large Gondola. Balloon Riding Santa.

434a, b, c & d. Free-blown, Patriotic Zeppelin. Simple Airplane shape. Zeppelin - Type II. Small free-blown Dirigible.

Miscellaneous Glass Ornaments

435. A collection of various sizes and styles of Pine Cones. "A & C" are American made.

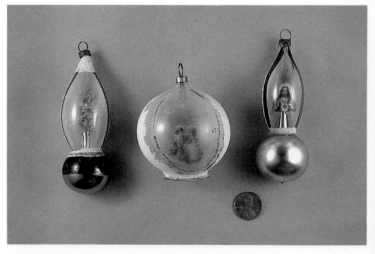

436. Three Scrap and Glass Ornaments. The Scraps are enclosed in the ornament and seen through clear glass windows.

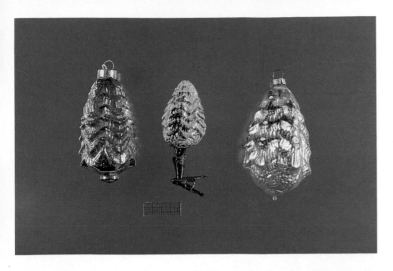

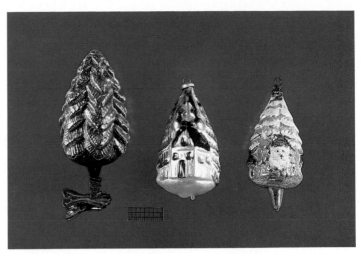

437a, b, & c. American Tree - possibly made by Corning Glass. Small standard form Tree. "Decorated" Tree - painted dots represent ornaments.

438a, b & c. Large standard form Tree. House under a Tree - embossed. Santa Face under a Pine Tree.

439. Ball with Painted House - look through clear glass window and see scrap children playing inside.

440. Free-blown Tree.

441. Milk Glass Egg - decorated with scraps and "Dresden" paper.

442. Part of complete set of Miniature Ornaments. The box was marked "Made in Germany, Russian Zone".

443a & b. Hollow Blown Tree - filled with dyed sawdust. Oyster Shell with a Pearl.

444. Crown - large size.

445a, b, c & d. Crown on an Egg. Small Crown. Free-blown Toy Top. Free-blown "Ice Cream Cone".

446. Glass Balls with Miniature Ornaments inside.

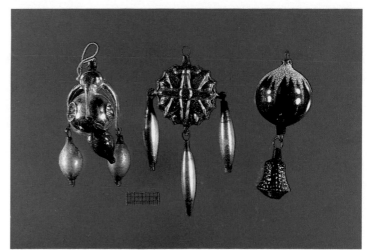

447. Ornaments with extended "Arms" or hanging pieces.

448. A selection of Fancy German Shapes, all mold made.

449. Various sizes and shapes of Reflective and Indented Ornaments.

450a, b, c, d, e, f, g, h, i & j. A collection of American fancy molded ornaments, all pre-war. Fruit Basket. Guitar. Rose with a Hip of Leaves. Lantern. Large and small Japanese Lanterns. Three styles of Bells. Candle.

451a, b, c, d, e, f, g & h. A collection of American Figural Ornaments, all circa 1935-40. Santa Claus. Bunch of Grapes embossed on a Heart. Father Christmas on an Oak Leaf. Pine or Christmas Tree. Large Bunch of Grapes - Type II. Small Bunch of Grapes - Type I. Two sizes of Pine Cones.

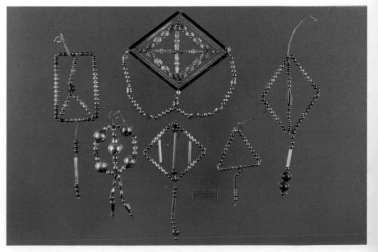

452. A collection of fancy, American Shapes. All of these are mold made and circa 1935-1940. "I & K" are "Odawara" type Japanese Lanterns.

453a, b, c & d. Four Unusual Ornaments. Glass Peach covered with a "fuzzy" fabric or flocking. "B, C & D" are three dimensional pieces made of cardboard & covered with crushed glass. They are: a butterfly, acorn & apple.

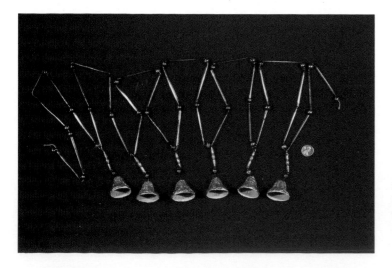

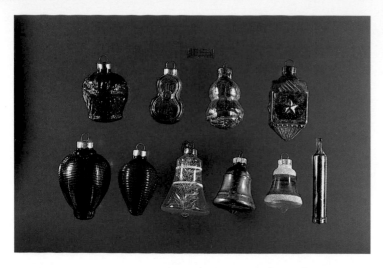

454. Chain made of glass tubes and cardboard bells, probably Japanese.

455. A collection of various Czech Beaded Ornaments in geometric shapes.

456. Japanese Beaded Ornaments.

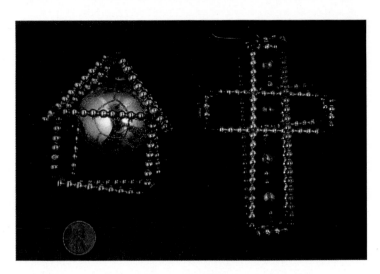

457a & b. Japanese Beaded House. Japanese Beaded Cross.

Paper (Scrap) Ornaments

458. Santa with Tree and Toys (4) - Type IV.

459. Santa with Tree (1) - Type I.

460. Santa with Tree and Toys (3) - Type III.

461. Advertising Santa with Tree and Toys.

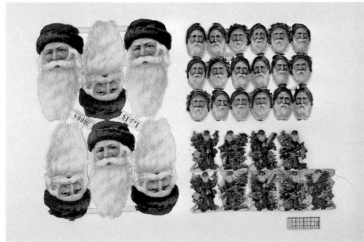

462a & b. Santa in Holly. Santa Head.

463a, b & c. Santa Heads Type III - made by Littauer and Boysen. Small Father Christmas Heads. Miniature Santas.

464. Santa in Wicker Basket.

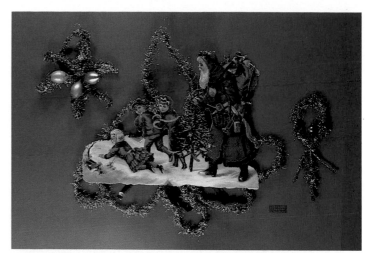

465. Santa and Children (Type II) - two tinsel ornaments with glass beads.

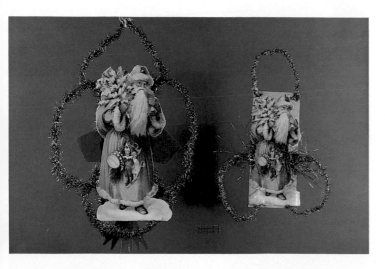

466. Two sizes of Santas with Tree and Toys (Type II).

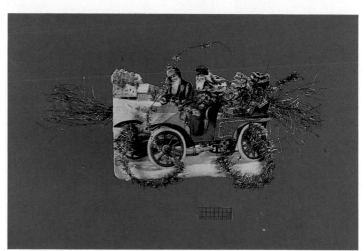

467. Two Santas in a Model "T" Truck.

468a, b & c. Two small Santa Scraps. Two Women Angels.

469a, b & c. Two Angel Heads - small. Santa Head - Type I.

470a & b. Comical Santa. Santa with a Plate of Fruit.

471. Two Lady Angels.

472. Angel in a Floral and Icy Star.

473. Praying Angel.

474. Angel with a Cornucopia - Treetop.

475. Angel with an Open Book.

255

476a, b & c. *Christmas Angel Postcard, circa 1900. Angel with a Book and Scroll. Kneeling Angel.*

477. *Two Girl Angels Ringing a Bell.*

478a & b. *Snow Angel with a Tree and Songbook. Snow Angel with a Tree.*

479. *Two homemade scrap ornaments, both circa 1910. "A" is made from a postcard. "B" is made from a Valentine Card.*

480a, b & c. Boy Clown (found under Miscellaneous Scrap themes). Angel in a Star Medallion. Boy and Girl in an Oval of Flowers (found under the Miscellaneous Scrap themes).

481a, b, c & d. A group of Four Snow Children. Snow Girl with Flowers (Type I) Snow Boy Bust. Snow Girl with Flowers (Type II) Snow Girl Bust.

482. Treetop Angel.

483. Snow Angel with Hand Bells.

484. Snow Girl in a Wreath of Roses.

485. Snow Children in the Forest.

486. Angel in a Crescent Moon.

487. Girl with a Doll and Cotton Skirt (Paper Doll Ornaments).

488. Happy Baby (Paper Doll Ornaments).

489. Large Santa Doll.

490. Miss Liberty (Paper Doll Ornaments).

491. Cat with a Ball of Yarn (Paper Doll Ornaments).

492. Monkey with a Tambourine (Paper Doll Ornaments).

493. Boy in a Cotton Snowsuit.

494. Jointed Doll.

495. Jointed Dolls in crepe paper dresses and tinsel trim.

496. Scraps on a Lace Rosette (under Miscellaneous Scraps).

261

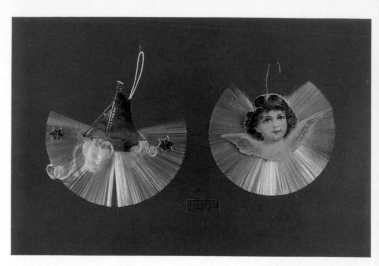

497. *Bust of Child on crepe paper disc (under Miscellaneous Scraps).*

498a & b. *Spun Glass Semi-Circle with a "Dresden" Sailboat. Spun Glass Rosette with Large Angel Head.*

499. *SG Semi-Circle with Angels.*

500. *Raphael Angel on a SG Cloud.*

501a, b & c. *SG Rosette with a Foil Flower. SG Rosette with a Comet Tail with Angel Head Scrap. SG Rosette with a Pink Tint.*

502a, b, & c. *Old Woman in a Bonnet with a SG Skirt (under Paper Doll Ornaments). Santa with a SG Skirt (Type III). Old Man with a Fez with a SG Skirt (under Paper Doll Ornaments).*

503a, b, c & d. *Blue SG Comet. SG Rosette. Santa Head Comet. SG Rosette with Angel Head.*

504. *A comparison of Old and New Scraps. Group A - Antique version made by "FWKB". Group B - Larger new version by Paul B. Zoecke. Group C - New Zoecke reprint using the old plates.*

505a, b & c. *Antique Angels. Modern version printed by Mamelok Press of England.*

506. *Santa on a SG Comet.*

507. Santa on a SG Comet.

508. Spun Cotton and Crepe Paper Santa on a Swing - Type II.

509. Golden Series Scrap Relief by Mamelok Press of England. These are specifically designed to have an antique look.

Dresden Ornaments and Paper Candy Containers

510. Dresden Airplane (3-D).

511a & b. Dresden Steamship (3-D). Paddle Wheel Dresden Boat (3-D).

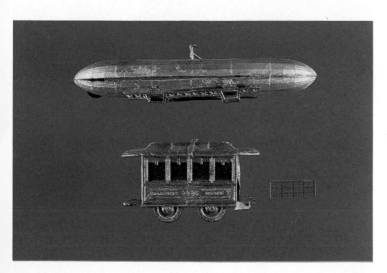

512a & b. Large Zeppelin (3-D). Street Car or Trolley marked "Registered 4446 Depose" (3-D).

513. Chariot with a Horse and Cherub Rider (3-D).

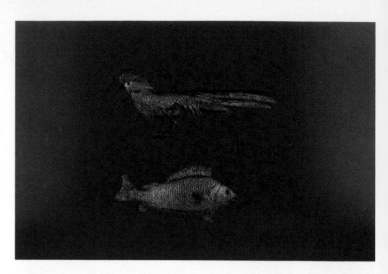

514a & b. *Reindeer/Stag - head raised as if calling (3-D). Salamander (3-D).*

515a & b. *"Chinese" Rooster (3-D). A "Dresden" Perch - the fish are so accurately molded that they can be identified as to what kind they are (double).*

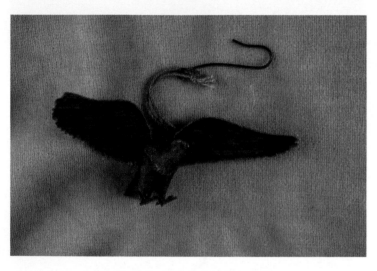

516. *Eagle in a Flying Position (3-D).*

517a, b & c. *Large Mouthed Fish (double). Clam Shell (double). Swimming Swan - Type II (double).*

518a & b. *Sailboat (flat) Standard Camel (double).*

519a, b, c & d. *Examples of two cherubic riders that were often added to Dresden ornaments (3-D). Small Walking Elephant (3-D). Walking 3-D Camel.*

520a & b. 3-D Duck - Type I. 3-D "Dresden" Rooster.

521a & b. Osterich (3-D). 3-D Stork - Type I

532

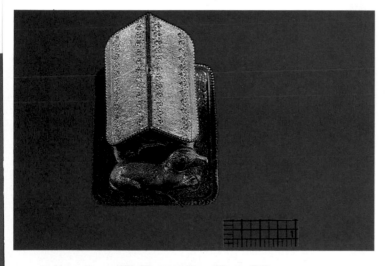

522. Dog and Dog House (3-D).

523a, b & c. Holstein Cow (3-D). Race Horse (3-D). Prancing Horse (double).

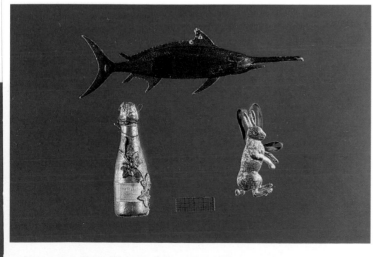

524a, b & c. Swordfish (double). "Carte Blanche" Champagne Bottle (3-D). Sitting Rabbit - deeply embossed, but one sided.

525a, b & c. Elephant with its Trunk Up (double). Turtle (3-D). Arched Back Cat (double).

536a & b. Generic Fish (flat). "Bluegill" (double).

537a, b, c & d. Small Angel applied to a cardboard disc. Three versions of a "Dresden" Comet.

538. Treetop Angel - large size.

539. Birdcage - large size (flat).

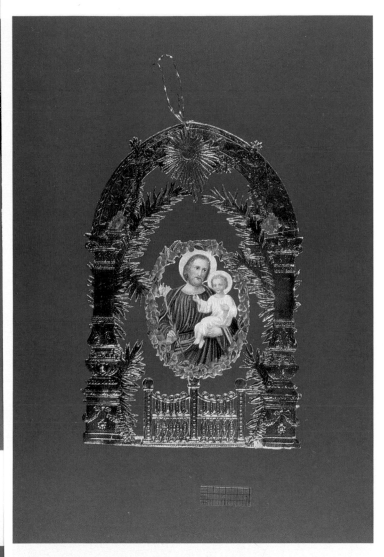

540. Nativity Scene (flat).

541. Angel with a Crepe Paper Skirt (flat).

542. Flat Coach Pulled by a Horse.

543a, b, & c. Large Diamond Shaped Medallion (flat). Flower with Tinsel and Scrap (flat). Medallion with a "gelatine" Flower and Scrap (flat).

553. Commercially made Paper Cornucopias with Applied Lithograph.

554. Feather Tree in a Pot Candy Container.

555. Mandolin Candy Container - Type II. Pieces of this type are cardboard covered with gold foil. They are NOT Dresden ornaments. They can be homemade or commercial.

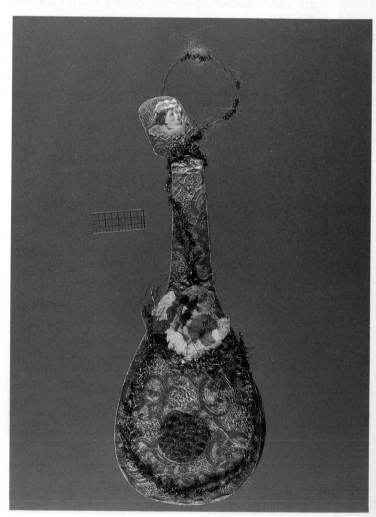

556. Oval Candy Box.

557a, b & c. Guitar Candy Container. "Rich Kid's" Banjo Candy Container. Mandolin Candy Container - Type I.

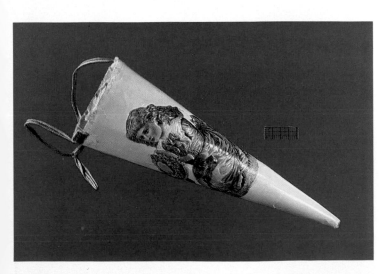

558. Commercially made Cornucopia with Applied Lithograph.

559. A selection of three elaborate Cornucopias - commercially made.

560a & b. Opened Peanut Candy Container. Medium sized and marked "Made in Austria". Open Walnut Candy Containers.

561a, b & c. Open box Candy Container. Two cylinder shaped Candy Containers.

562a, b & c. Two sizes of Globe Candy Containers. Heart Candy Container with an Angel Print.

563. Foil Covered Bell - an American made candy container.

564a, b & c. Suitcase Candy Container - pieces like this often ended up as doll accessories. Tambourine Candy Container - Type I. Early "Animal Crackers" Box - probably the longest running candy box designed to hang on the tree.

565a & b. "A" Two Santa Boot Candy Containers. Marked "Made in Germany" and has a fabric bag. "B" Probably Japanese.

Fabric Ornaments

566a & b. Early German, Velour Butterfly. Early German Paper and Tinsel Flower, circa 1870.

567a, b & c. Spun Cotton Girl with Pressed Cotton Clothes. Pressed Cotton Girl with Doll. Pressed Cotton Santa.

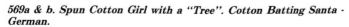

568a & b. Pressed Cotton Angel. Spun Cotton Santa in a Swing - Type I.

569a & b. Spun Cotton Girl with a "Tree". Cotton Batting Santa - German.

570. Cotton Batting Santa with a Wax Face.

571. Two Cotton Batting Santas.

572a & b. Cotton Batting Santa. Spun Cotton Santa.

573. Spun Cotton Bear on a Swing.

574a, b, c & d. A collection of Spun Cotton People. Clothing includes cotton batting and crepe paper. Clown with a Carrot Nose. Ice Skater with Metal or Dresden Skates and a Porcelain Head. Military Man. Lady with Birds - she has a plaster face.

575a, b, c & d. A collection of Spun Cotton People - most are dressed in crepe paper. Man with a Top Hat, Vest and Coat. Peasant Lady. Jester with a Porcelain Face. Snow Girl with a Muff and Scrap Face.

576a & b. Two Japanese Spun Cotton Ladies. Damaged Face was painted. Plaster Face.

577a, b, c & d. A collection of four Spun Cotton Girls. Girl with Crepe Paper Dress and Plaster Face. Girl with Crepe Paper Dress and Scrap Face. Snow Girl with Cotton Clothes and Scrap Face. Girl Jester with Porcelain Face.

578a, b & c. Spun Cotton Boy. Spun Cotton Snowman - also a candy container. Spun Cotton Girl.

579a, b, c & d. Spun Cotton Animals and a Man. Squirrel with Nut. Man with Stick. Reindeer with Rider. Horse and Saddle.

279

580a, b, c & d. Spun Cotton Animals. Horse. Fox. Donkey with Bags. Cat.

581a, b, c & d. Spun Cotton Animals. Sheep. Frog. Dog. Lion.

582a, b, c & d. Spun Cotton Dove with Paper Wings - Japanese. Santa with Celluloid Face - net bag candy container. Two Spun Cotton Pears.

583a & b. Spun Cotton Fruit. Grapes. Pears with Wire Wrapping and Fabric Leaves.

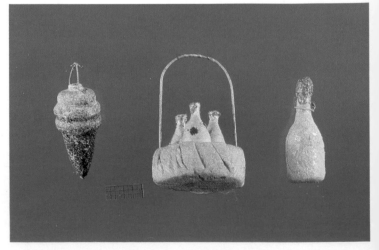

584a, b, c & d. Spun Cotton Fruit. Carrot or Icicle. Tomato. Turnip. Pear.

585a & b. Spun Cotton Ice Cream Cone. Spun Cotton Bucket with Champagne Bottles. Blue Champagne Bottle.

586. Various sizes of Japanese Cotton Batting Santas.

587. Variouse sizes of Japanese Cotton Batting Santas.

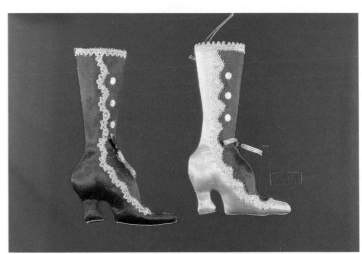

588a, b, c, d & e. An American Press Cotton Santa. Chenille Santa with a Paper Face - Japanese. Stiffened Crocheted Slipper - German. Chenille Santas with a Plaster Face - Japanese.

589. Two High Ladies Boot Candy Containers - they are made of cardboard and covered with satin. Circa 1950.

590a, b & c. Cotton Candy Containers. Wax Baby in a Shoe. Snowball.

591a, b, c, d & e. Pressed Cotton Covering a Cardboard Frame - boats with scrap children. These were probably homemade. Tarlatan Stocking. Scrap Angel with a Cotton Dress. Santa on a Net Stocking.

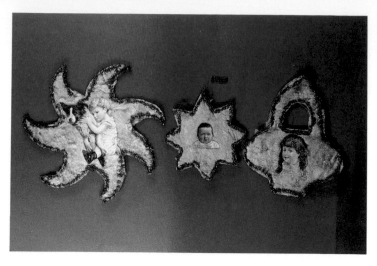

592. Three Victorian Ornaments made with pressed cotton covering a cardboard frame. They are homemade.

593. Net Bag Candy Container - A girl with a celluloid face.

594. Spun Cotton Lady.

595a & b. Boot Candy Containers with Plaster Santa Heads - both Japanese. Foil Covered. Fabric Covered.

597. A Victorian "Gates of Heaven" - cotton covering a cardboard frame.

596. Santa, Net Candy Containers. The bottom is a cardboard cone.

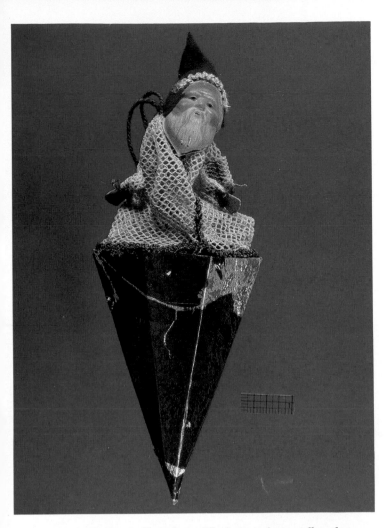

599. Fabric Butterfly in a Tinsel Hoop.

598a & b. Two Japanese Spun Cotton Pieces. Chinaman with Crepe Paper Clothes and Plaster Face. Man with Crepe Paper Clothes and Plaster Face.

283

Metal Ornaments

600a, b, c, d & e. A collection of Tin-Lead Alloy Ornaments designed as light reflectors. Eagle on a Reflector. Parrot. Heart. Fancy Geometric Shape. Cross.

601. Three Fancy Geometric Shapes.

602. Four Fancy Geometric Shapes.

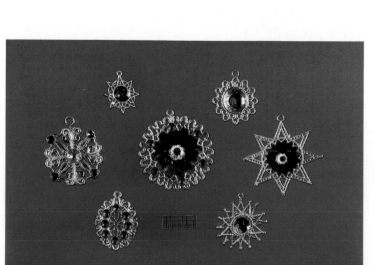

603. Seven Fancy Geometric Shapes - "C&F" are unusual in that they are double sided.

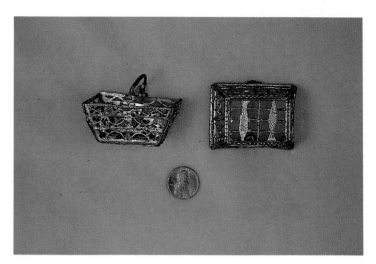

604a, b, c, d & e. Covered Basket. Box. Nativity Scene. Cradle. Square Bird Cage. All are three dimensional.

605. Fish Basket - side and bottom view.

606a, b, c, d & e. Angel with Filigree Wings - West German. Fan. Butterfly - Type II. Star Made of Rolled Foil. Stamped Brass Bird.

607. A collection of Tinsel Ornaments with added glass pieces.

608a, b & c. Wire Icicle. Wire Snowflake. Wire Chandelier with Wax Candles.

609a, b & c. Foil Candy Containers - American, circa 1950. Cornucopias. Boot.

285

610. Foil Stars - American, circa 1950.

611. Woven Wire Baskets of Brass and German Silver. "B" is marked Germany.

612. "Nuremburg" Angel dressed in foil, circa 1890.

613. "Nuremburg" Angel dressed in foil, circa 1930.

614. Early package of Lametta or icicles.

Wax and Sebnitz Ornaments

615. Large 14½″ Wax Angel with Glass Eyes.

616. Angel with a Horn.

617. Large 14 inch, standard form Wax Angel.

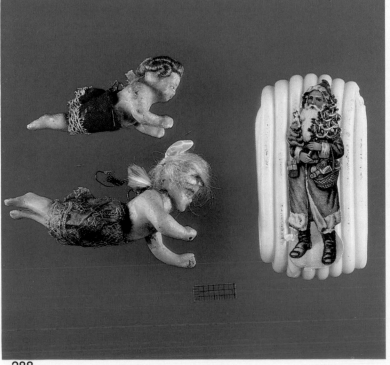

619. Flying Angel with Dresden Wings - she is made entirely of wax, and her missing arms show how many angels were put together in pieces.

618a, b & c. Small and medium standard form Wax Angels. Coiled Wax Candle - used for lighting the candles on the tree.

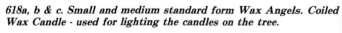

620a & b. Two "Standing Angels". Small Boy Cherub. Medium Boy Cherub.

621. Large Flying Angel with a Mohair Wig.

622. Angel with a Flower in her Hair - she has wax wings.

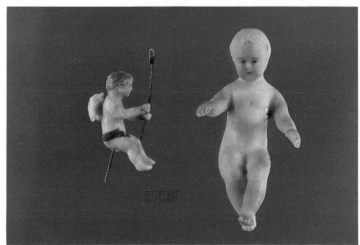

623a & b. Seated Angel with a Spike for holding it on the Tree. Large Wax Baby Jesus.

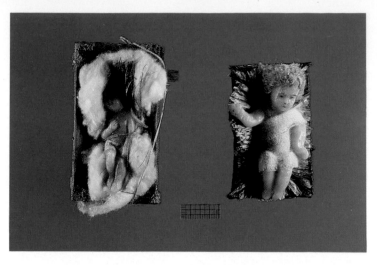

624. Two Forms of Wax Baby Jesus in a Manger.

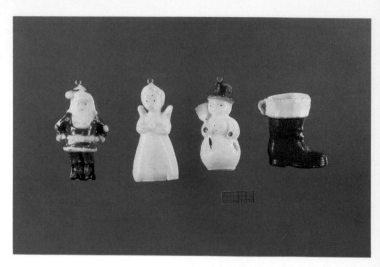

625. American Wax Ornaments, circa 1950.

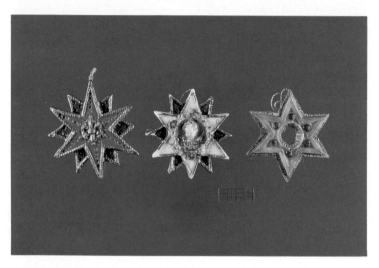

626. Three Wax Relief Ornaments - originally made in cookie molds. These pieces are new, but made in antique molds.

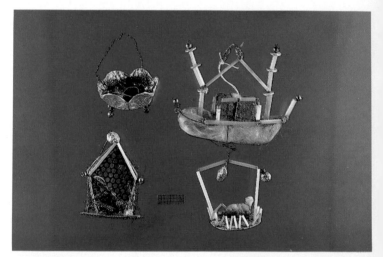

627a, b, c & d. Four Sebnitz Ornaments. Flower bowl. Angel Hair Boat. House with a Scrap Jesus. Wax Sheep in a Pen.

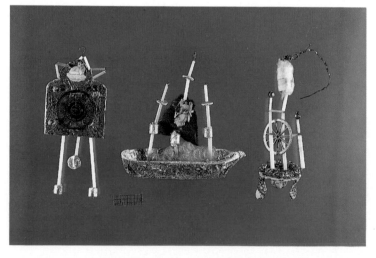

628a, b & c. Three Sebnitz Ornaments. Wall Clock. Foil Boat. Spinning Wheel.

629a & b. Two Sebnitz Ornaments. Automobile. Wire Boat.

Lights and Lighting for the Tree

630. Common, Clip-on Candle Holders.

631. Lithographed Candle Holders, circa 1890.

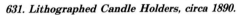

632a, b, c, d, e & f. Three forms of the Ball and Socket Candle Holder, circa 1920. Drip Pan Weighted Candle Holder. Unusual Clip-on Style. Early Style Holder with a Nail for pushing through the Tree Limb.

633a, b, c, d, e, f & g. Early Holders Embossed with Geometric Designs, circa 1890. Beehive Fairy Light - paper thin, circa 1880. Candle Holder with a Glass Shade - cherries are embossed into the sides. "F" Innovative Clamp on Candle Holder, circa 1920.

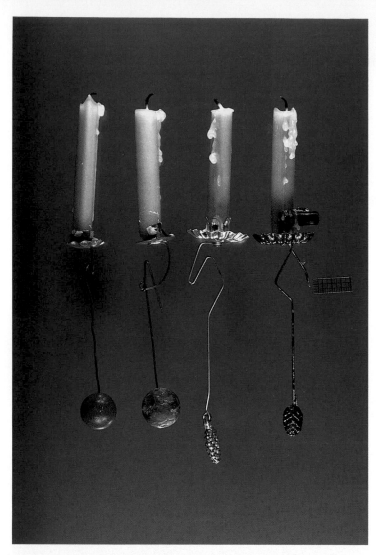

634a, b, c & d. Four Pendulum Weighted Candle Holders. Kirchhof Holder - marked "Kirchhof, Pat. Dec.24,67". Standard Holder with a Clay Ball Weight - American. Later versions with Cast Lead Pine Cones as counterweights - German.

635a & b. Two Pendulum Candle Holders with Cast Tin Reflectors. Flower & Butterfly.

636. Three Holders with Tin Reflectors - geometric patterns.

637. Pendulum Candle Holder designed for outdoor use.

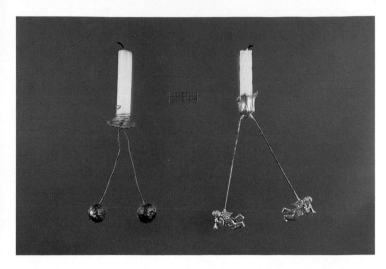

638a & b. Two Double Weighted Pendulum Holders. Clay Balls. Cast Lead Cherubs.

639a, b, c & d. Molded Fairy Lights of Thick Glass. Quilted or Diamond Pattern. "B" Daisy Pattern.

640a, b, c & d. Ornament Fairy Light - face. Ornament Fairy Light - Smiling Boy Head. Clip-on with a Glass Shade - ribbed cylinder. Clip-on with a Glass Shade - oval rose.

641a & b. Clip-on Candle Holder with an Oval Shade. Free-blown, Wire Wrapped Vase - unsilvered.

642. Clip-on Candle Holder with a Slender Rose Shade - molded.

643a, b & c. Clip-on Candle Holders with Glass Ornament Weights. Pear. Apple. Rose.

644. "V" Shaped Christmas Lantern.

645a & b. Small Four Sided Lantern. Small Six Sided Lantern.

646. Santa Head Lantern - made of paper and plaster.

647a & b. Large Four Sided Christmas Lantern with a Smoke Bell. "Fold Up" Lantern - folded.

648a, b & c. "Fold Up" Lantern - opened. Dresden Light Cover - Bunch of Grapes. "Whirl-Glo" paper light shade.

649. Early celluloid lights with the wooden battery connection.

650. Celluloid Lights.

651. *Various Bubble Light Styles in the C-6 Base.*

652. *Various Bubble Light Styles in the C-7 Base.*

653a, b, c, d, e, f, g & h. *Early Clear Glass Lights. Japanese Sitting Cat with a Bow. Sitting, Smiling Dog. Jack-O'-Lantern. "Joey" Clown Head. Monkey Holding a Vine. Monkey Holding a Vine. Old King Cole. Exhaust Tip Snowman with Stick.*

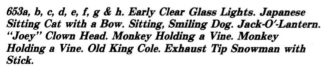

654a, b, c, d, e, f, g & h. *Early Clear Glass Lights. Milk glass Seashell. Mushroom. Two Exhaust Tip European Birds. Mazda Monkey. Kewpie Doll with No Clothes. Standing Angel. Cat in a Suit with Glasses.*

655a, b, c, d, e, f, g & h. Early Clear Glass Lights. "Watt" Rose. "Watt" Orange. Exhaust Tip Raspberry. Round Berry. The Horn Blower. Exhaust Tip Santa with His Hands in His Sleeves. Exhaust Tip Clown. Mazda Canary.

656a, b, c, d, e, f, g & h. Sitting Lion. European Sitting Cat. Two European Exhaust Tip Birds. Exhaust Tip "Joey" Clown Head. Indian Chief. Dwarf with a Shovel. "Judy" Clown Head or Drama Face - double.

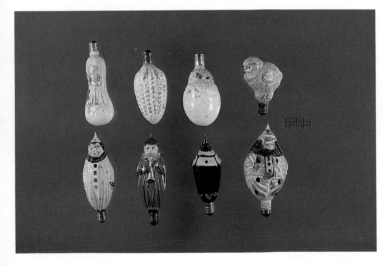

657a, b, c, d, e, f, g & h. Early Clear Glass Lights. Long Squash. Small Ear of Corn. Chick in an Egg. Chick. Exhaust Tip Clown. Exhaust Tip Horn Blower. Carriage Lantern with an Exhaust Tip. Exhaust Tip Fat Clown.

658a, b, c, d, e, f, g, h & i. Early Clear Glass Santas. Santa with Hands in His Sleeves. Exhaust Tip St. Nicholas - Type II. Large Mazda Santa. Green Coated Santa with Exhaust Tip also St. Patrick. Exhaust Tip St. Nicholas - Type I - fat. Exhaust Tip St. Nicholas - Type I - slender. St. Nicholas without Exhaust Tip. Santa with Hands in His Sleeves. St. Nicholas in Robes.

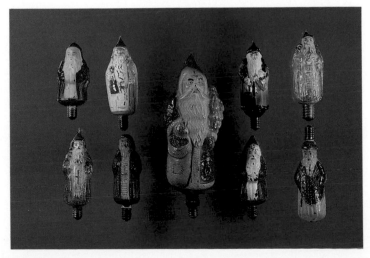

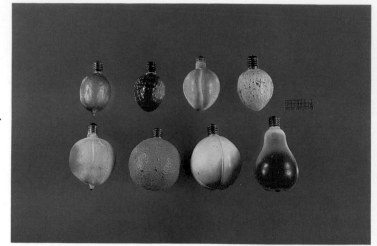

659a, b, c, d, e, f, g & h. Early Clear Glass Fruit. Exhaust Tip Walnut. Strawberry. Plum. Walnut. Exhaust Tip Peach. Orange. Peach. Pear.

660a, b & c. Early Clear Glass Character Lights - all European. Dwarf with a Shovel. Putti Angel Head. Girl with a Trumpet.

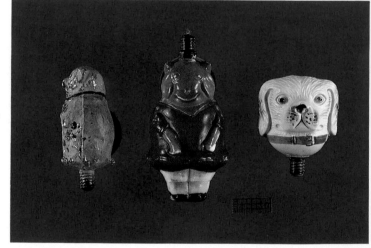

661a, b & c. Sitting Dog with an Exhaust Tip Tail. Hippo Girl. Celluloid Spaniel Dog Head.

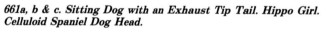

662. A collection of miniature lights both clear and milk glass. The last three are examples of C-7½ base American lamps that were never marketed.

298

663a, b, c, d, e & f. Miniature Lights. Indian Chief. Dog in a Round Basket. "Dismal Desmond" Dog Head. Drum. Snow Covered House. American Rabbit.

664a, b, c, d, e, f, g & h. Tadpole. Large Head Pig in a Suit. Rabbit Playing a Banjo. European Exhaust Tip Bird. Bulldog Sitting on a Ball. Bird in a Bird House. Two Sizes of Full Feathered Peacocks.

665a, b, c, d, e, f, g & h. A collection of Japanese Milk Glass Lights. Puffed Up Cat. Sitting Cat with a Tag. Frowning Dog in a Basket. Tall Hound Dog. Pig Playing a Drum. Guppy Fish. Pelican. Sitting Bear.

666a, b, c, d, e, f, g & h. Milk Glass Frog. Rooster Playing Golf. Dress Duck. Mother and Pup Dogs. Round Bird. Milk Glass Parrot. Milk Glass Common Songbirds.

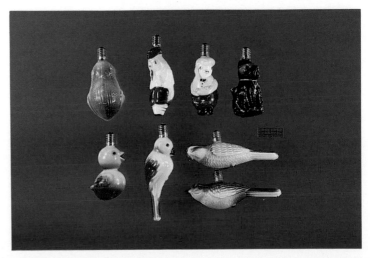

667a, b, c, d, e, f, g & h. Japanese Milk Glass Animals. Elephant Sitting on a Ball. Sitting Teddy Bear. Dog in a Polo Outfit. Dog in a Clown Outfit. Lion with a Tennis Racket. Lion in a Suit with a Pipe. Bulldog in a Vest. Horse Head in a Horseshoe.

668a, b, c, d, e, f, g & h. Japanese Milk Glass Cats. Cat with a Ball. Two Cats in a Basket. Sitting Cat with a Tag. Bagging Cat. Tall, Goofy Cat. Cat in an Evening Gown. Cat with a Mandolin (fiddle). Double Side Cat.

669a, b, c, d, e, f, g & h. Japanese Milk Glass Lights. Mother Goose Riding a Goose. Children in a Shoe. Bozo Clown. Egg Shaped Frog. Pig Playing a Tuba. Waving Bear. Squirrel. Three Sided Light - a bunny, a chick and mother goose or a duck in a bonnet.

670a, b, c, d, e, f, g & h. Sitting Teddy Bear. Pig in a Dress. Dragon on a Lantern. Common Fish. Elephant with Trunk Down. Pointed Head Dog. Wolf Head or Rin Tin Tin. Indians on a Square.

671a, b, c, d, e, f, g & h. *Roly-Poly Boy. Snowman Skier. Milk Glass Jack-O'-Lantern. Owl in a Vest and Top Hat. Cross on a Disc. Pineapple. Celluloid Santa in a Cardboard Disc. Hippo with Raised Arms.*

672a, b, c, d, e, f, g, h, i & j. *Pluto. Pinocchio. Jiminy Cricket. "Fiddler" Pig. Snowman with an Umbrella. Milk Glass St. Nicholas. Double Face Girl's Head. Milk Glass Bulldog on a Ball. Double Faced Humpty Dumpty Egg. Elephant with its Trunk Up.*

673a, b, c, d, e, f, g & h. *Olympic Torch. Puppy on a Ball. Sitting Rabbit. Small Girl in a Snowsuit. Large Spotted Clown. Peacock with Wedge Shaped Tail Feathers. Doc Head. Choir Girl.*

674a, b, c, d, e, f, g & h. *Rooster in a Tub. Building on a Rock - "Alcatraz". Angel Fish. Flower in a Seashell. The Aviator. Marching Drummer. Canadian Mountie. Banana with a Face.*

675a & b. Large Hump-backed Santa. Large Snowman with a Stick.

676a, b, c, d, e, f, g & h. Santa in a Chimney. Santa Face in a Pine Cone. Small Standing Santa with a Boy. Three Faced Santa. Small Standing Santa with a Bag. Small Standing Santa with a Bag. Common Santa. Large Santa with a Bag.

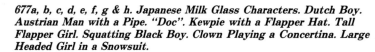

677a, b, c, d, e, f, g & h. Japanese Milk Glass Characters. Dutch Boy. Austrian Man with a Pipe. "Doc". Kewpie with a Flapper Hat. Tall Flapper Girl. Squatting Black Boy. Clown Playing a Concertina. Large Headed Girl in a Snowsuit.

678a, b, c, d, e, f, g, h, i & j. Log Cabin. Cottage in a Hillside. Snow Covered Lantern. Small Square House. Heavy Tin Light Reflector. Snow Covered Cottage - large. Snow Covered Cottage - small. "Matchless" Star. "Kristal" Star. German foil light reflector.

679a, b, c, d, e & f. Transportation Lights. Oceanliner. Zeppelin or Dirigible with the American Flag. World War I Tank. Square Car. Miniature Car. Square Car.

680a, b, c, d, e, f, g, h, i, j & k. Three Sizes of Japanese "Gifu" Lanterns. Two Sizes of Round Japanese Lanterns. Miniature Lanterns. Santa Face in a Bell - Type II. Santa Face in a Bell - Type I. Cylinder Shaped "Odawara" Lantern.

681a, b, c, d, e, f, g, h, i & j. Top Row: Small Common Flowers. Bottom Row: Large Fruit Basket. Apple. Large Open Rose. Ear of Corn.

682. New Issue of Figural Lights. They are clear glass and have no base marking. Packaging states "Color Art Decorated Bulbs - Indoor Set. Universal Lights."

303

683. *New Issue of Figural Lights - Milk Glass. These are made in Taiwan and marketed by Avon for the Henry Ford Museum. The base is marked "HFM".*

Miscellaneous Christmas Ornaments

684. *Large Santa Head - made of paper mache.*

685. *Large Straw Stuffed Santa Doll.*

686. Santa Doll - Western German Plaster Santa.

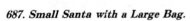
687. Small Santa with a Large Bag.

688. Post War Plaster Santa.

305

689. Santa Squeak Toy.

690. Santa Doll.

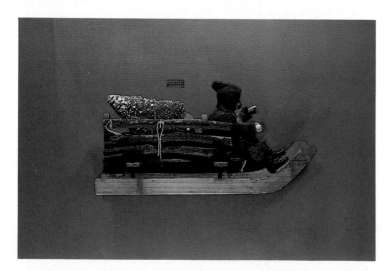

691. Santa on a Large Wooden Sleigh. Sleigh used to contain candy.

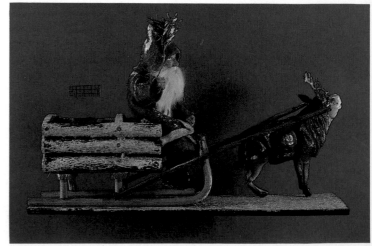

692. Early Santa and Sleigh with Plaster Reindeer.

693. *Windup Santa and Sleigh by Strauss.*

694. *Cast Iron Santa and Sleigh.*

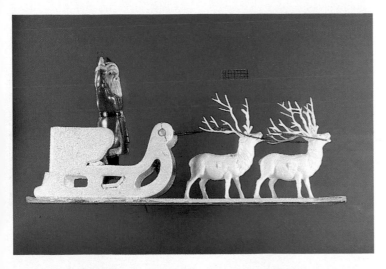

695. *Celluloid Santa and Reindeer in Cardboard Sleigh.*

696. *Windup Santa on a Sleigh.*

697. *Large Celluloid Santa and Sleigh.*

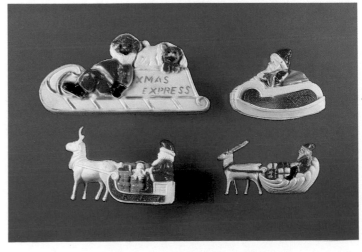

698. *Small Celluloid Santas in Sleighs.*

699. Celluloid Santas.

700. Mechanical Santa made by Chein.

701. Santa Mechanical Bank.

702. Glass Santa Candy Container.

703a, b & c. *Santa Lantern. Santa Head Lantern. Santa Light Lantern.*

705.

706.

704-711. *"Belsnickles" - Paper Mache and Plaster Santas. Some were designed to hold candy. Others were simply table or mantle decorations.*

707.

708.

709.

710.

711.

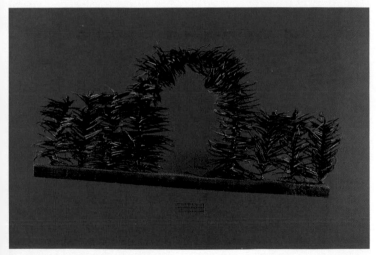

712. "Under the Tree" Christmas Fence. This is an unusual fence in that it is made of wire and dyed goose feathers, like "feather tree".

713a, b & c. "Heubach" Candy Containers. Boy on Box. Two Children on a Sled. Boy on a Snowball.

714. Santa and Honeycomb Wagon.

715. Bubble Light Tree.

716-717. Stamped Cardboard Table Decorations.

718. Santa Ice Cream Mold.

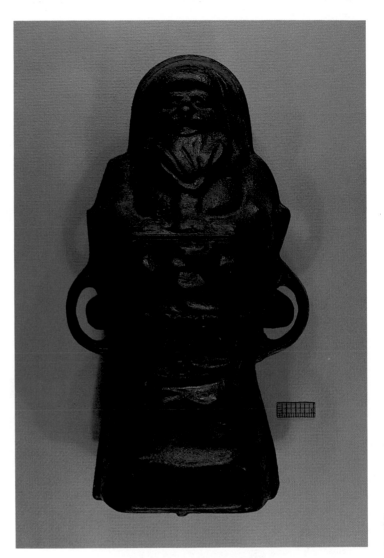

719-721. Santa Candy Molds.

720.

721.

AFTERWORD

Several Christmas trees have come and gone since I first put pen to paper and wrote the "Foreword" to this book. It is considerably larger, and I believe, better than I had first envisioned. The time and effort consumed by such a project is enormous yet worthwhile and satisfying.

In looking over my unused notes and pictures, I realize that there is still much to be written and yet discovered in this fascinating field of antique Christmas ornaments and decorations. Perhaps with the efforts of other collectors this may only be the beginning of this catalog. As I stated in the foreword, this has been a book by collectors for collectors. I am deeply indebted to those people who, in the true spirit of Christmas have generously shared their knowledge and their collections.

SELECT BIBLIOGRAPHY

Christbaumschmuck - Eva Stille, Hans Carl Nurnberg, 1979

Christmas All Through The House - John B. Brimer, Funk & Wagnals, 1968

Christmas Lighting and Decorating - Theodore A. Saros, D. van Nostrand Comp., Inc., 1954

Christmas Ornaments - A Festive Study - Margaret Schiffer, Schiffer Pub., Co., 1984

Chromos - A Guide to Paper Collectables - Francine Kirsch, A.S. Barnes & Co., 1981

Holidays - Victorian Women Celebrate In Pennsylvania - Nada Gray, Pennsylvania State University Press, 1983

The Christmas Tree - Daniel J. Foley, Chilton Co., 1960

The Christmas Tree Book - Phillip V. Snyder, Viking Press, 1976

The Glass Christmas Ornament: Old and New - Maggie Rogers and Judith Hawkins, Timber Press, 1977 & 1983

The History and Catalog of Electric Christmas Light Bulbs - J.G. Kaufman and J. Ehernberger, Christmas Antiques, Inc., 1978

The Santa Claus Book - E. Willis Jones, Walker & Co., 1976

The Trees of Christmas - Edna Metcalfe, Abingdon Press, 1969

Auction Catalogues of:

Bob and Sally Connelly
Robert Regni
Knight Antiques

Newsletters

"Spirit of Christmas" - Steve Kelsay, Editor
"Golden Glow" - Jerry Ehernberger, Editor

Selected articles by Harry Wilson Stuart appearing in *Spinning Wheel* magazine.

PERSONAL INVENTORY

At the suggestion of some collectors, I have included space to inventory your own collection. By using the picture numbering system and the ornament description, collectors can keep track of their personal ornaments. This same system can be used for insurance purposes, retailing for dealers and trading with other collectors thru the mail.

Picture Number	Ornament Description	Date Bought	Amount Paid
_____	_____	_____	_____
_____	_____	_____	_____
_____	_____	_____	_____
_____	_____	_____	_____
_____	_____	_____	_____
_____	_____	_____	_____
_____	_____	_____	_____
_____	_____	_____	_____
_____	_____	_____	_____
_____	_____	_____	_____
_____	_____	_____	_____
_____	_____	_____	_____
_____	_____	_____	_____
_____	_____	_____	_____
_____	_____	_____	_____
_____	_____	_____	_____
_____	_____	_____	_____
_____	_____	_____	_____
_____	_____	_____	_____
_____	_____	_____	_____
_____	_____	_____	_____
_____	_____	_____	_____
_____	_____	_____	_____
_____	_____	_____	_____
_____	_____	_____	_____
_____	_____	_____	_____

Picture Number	Ornament Description	Date Bought	Amount Paid
_____	_____	_____	_____
_____	_____	_____	_____
_____	_____	_____	_____
_____	_____	_____	_____
_____	_____	_____	_____
_____	_____	_____	_____
_____	_____	_____	_____
_____	_____	_____	_____
_____	_____	_____	_____
_____	_____	_____	_____
_____	_____	_____	_____
_____	_____	_____	_____
_____	_____	_____	_____
_____	_____	_____	_____
_____	_____	_____	_____
_____	_____	_____	_____
_____	_____	_____	_____
_____	_____	_____	_____
_____	_____	_____	_____
_____	_____	_____	_____
_____	_____	_____	_____
_____	_____	_____	_____
_____	_____	_____	_____
_____	_____	_____	_____
_____	_____	_____	_____
_____	_____	_____	_____
_____	_____	_____	_____
_____	_____	_____	_____
_____	_____	_____	_____
_____	_____	_____	_____
_____	_____	_____	_____

Picture Number	Ornament Description	Date Bought	Amount Paid
_____	_____	_____	_____
_____	_____	_____	_____
_____	_____	_____	_____
_____	_____	_____	_____
_____	_____	_____	_____
_____	_____	_____	_____
_____	_____	_____	_____
_____	_____	_____	_____
_____	_____	_____	_____
_____	_____	_____	_____
_____	_____	_____	_____
_____	_____	_____	_____
_____	_____	_____	_____
_____	_____	_____	_____
_____	_____	_____	_____
_____	_____	_____	_____
_____	_____	_____	_____
_____	_____	_____	_____
_____	_____	_____	_____
_____	_____	_____	_____
_____	_____	_____	_____
_____	_____	_____	_____
_____	_____	_____	_____
_____	_____	_____	_____
_____	_____	_____	_____
_____	_____	_____	_____
_____	_____	_____	_____
_____	_____	_____	_____
_____	_____	_____	_____
_____	_____	_____	_____
_____	_____	_____	_____

The Dear Old Tree

BY LUELLA WILSON SMITH

There's a
dear old tree,
an evergreen
tree,
And it blossoms
once a year.
'Tis loaded
with fruit from
top to root,
And it brings to
all good cheer.

For its blossoms
bright are small
candles white
And it's fruit is
dolls and toys.
And they all are
free for both
you and me
If we're good little
girls & boys.

Schroeder's Antiques Price Guide

Schroeder's Antiques Price Guide has climbed its way to the top in a field already supplied with several well-established publications! The word is out, *Schroeder's Price Guide* is the best buy at any price. Over 500 categories are covered, with more than 50,000 listings. But it's not volume alone that makes Schroeder's the unique guide it is recognized to be. From ABC Plates to Zsolnay, if it merits the interest of today's collector, you'll find it in Schroeder's. Each subject is represented with histories and background information. In addition, hundreds of sharp original photos are used each year to illustrate not only the rare and the unusual, but the everyday "fun-type" collectibles as well -- not postage stamp pictures, but large close-up shots that show important details clearly.

Each edition is completely re-typeset from all new sources. We have not and will not simply change prices in each new edition. All new copy and all new illustrations make Schroeder's THE price guide on antiques and collectibles.

The writing and researching team behind this giant is proportionately large. It is backed by a staff of more than seventy of Collector Books' finest authors, as well as a board of advisors made up of well-known antique authorities and the country's top dealers, all specialists in their fields. Accuracy is their primary aim. Prices are gathered over the entire year previous to publication from ads and personal contacts. Then each category is thoroughly checked to spot inconsistencies, listings that may not be entirely reflective of actual market dealings, and lines too vague to be of merit.

Only the best of the lot remains for publication. You'll find *Schroeder's Antiques Price Guide* the one to buy for factual information and quality.

No dealer, collector or investor can afford not to own this book. It is available from your favorite bookseller or antiques dealer at the low price of $12.95. If you are unable to find this price guide in your area, it's available from Collector Books, P. O. Box 3009, Paducah, KY 42001 at $12.95 plus $2.00 for postage and handling.

8½ x 11, 608 Pages $12.95